Principles
of
Investigation

Principles
of
Investigation

John P. Kenney
California State University
Long Beach, California

Harry W. More, Jr.
San Jose State University
San Jose, California

Criminal Justice Series

West Publishing Company
St. Paul • New York • Los Angeles • San Francisco

CONTRIBUTING AUTHORS

George Felkenes — Chapter Two
Denny F. Pace — Chapter Three
M. A. Leon — Chapter Four
Pamela Mayhall — Chapter Four
Chris J. Flammang — Chapter Five
George Rosbrook — Chapter Six
Douglas Lazo — Chapter Seven
John L. Ragle — Chapter Eight
Harold Van Alstyne — Chapter Nine
Philip G. Averill — Chapter Ten
Erik Beckman — Chapter Eleven
Judith Hails — Chapter Thirteen

The publisher wishes to acknowledge the editorial
contribution of Pamela Lee Espeland
in preparing this book for production.

COPYRIGHT © 1979 By WEST PUBLISHING CO.
50 West Kellogg Boulevard
P.O. Box 3526
St. Paul, Minnesota 55165

Printed in the United States of America

Library of Congress Cataloging in Publication Data

Main entry under title:
Principles of investigation.

(Criminal justice series)
Includes bibliographies and index.

1. Criminal investigation. 2. Criminal procedure. I. Kenney, John Paul, 1920-
II. More, Harry W. III. Series.

HV8073.P715   364.12   79-11280

ISBN 0-8299-0284-8

Preface

This book is designed to serve as an introductory text for college and university students majoring in the administration of criminal justice and as a resource in the training of police recruits. In addition, the police investigator may well find that it is comprehensive enough to serve as a ready reference guide.

In looking over the text, readers will quickly recognize that we have departed from the approach taken by other books dealing with the subject of criminal investigation. *Principles of Investigation* naturally deals with the techniques of investigation, but it also approaches the topic from a conceptual viewpoint in order to bring the ethical and legal obligations of the investigator into proper perspective. The contributing authors, all experts in their fields, have emphasized the need for meticulous adherence to rules of law and ethical practices as investigations proceed from the initial actions taken when a crime is discovered through the steps leading to criminal prosecution in a court of law.

We wish to express our deep appreciation of the scholarly endeavors and unstinting cooperation of the contributing authors. We are also indebted to Dr. Jack Whitehouse and Wayne Schapper for their research and editing efforts. The tender, loving support and understanding of our wives, Dorothy and Virginia, merits our love and care forever.

John P. Kenney
Harry W. More, Jr.

Contents

SIX

Processing the Crime Scene   **161**

SEVEN

Recording the Crime Scene   **189**

ELEVEN

The Victim and the Witness: Sources of Information   313

TWELVE

The Quality of Investigations: A Matter of Management   343

Principles
of
Investigation

ONE

Criminal Investigation: A Process and A Partnership

Chapter Objectives

After reading this chapter, the student should be able to:

☑ Identify the differences between the myth of the detective and the realities of investigative work.

☑ Summarize the historical origins of the investigator in the United States.

☑ Explain how the entire police department is involved in the investigative process.

☑ Define the investigative process.

☑ Explain how the roles of patrol officer and investigator are integrated and complementary.

☑ Describe how the role of the patrol officer is changing using a series of suggested models.

☑ Describe initiatives that management can take in enhancing the investigative function of patrol.

The Detective:
Unraveling the Myth

Everyone knows what a detective is: someone who wears a trench coat and carries a magnifying glass; someone who's always in the right place at the right time to discover the perfect clue; someone who never fails to solve one tough case before beginning another. Usually, the detective works alone, the better to be available in the middle of the night to track down leads or take mysterious phone calls; occasionally, he has a faithful sidekick who handles the menial details and makes endless pots of coffee. The detective is the real hero of the police profession, and his role symbolizes the heights of status and achievement. Right?

Wrong. Although we've all grown up with the likes of Nancy Drew and the Hardy Boys, James Bond and Sam Spade, Kojak and Columbo and Inspector Erskine, these fictional characters—and they are, after all, only fictional characters—serve to distort reality rather than represent it. The media and the detective novel have glamorized the criminal investigator's function while ignoring the facts. Crimes are solved *not* because the detective is luckier and smarter than everyone else on the force, from the captain all the way down to the rookie, but because *every* individual in a contemporary police department actively and skillfully contributes to the investigative process. Patrol officers and investigators alike must be willing to work together for the common goal of crime solving, and police management is responsible for making sure that the activities of patrol officers and investigators are integrated and complementary.

While it's commonly assumed that the detective—and the detective alone—is the only member of a police department who investigates and solves crimes, the truth is that there are few aspects of police work in general that do *not* affect the outcome of criminal investigations. No one will argue that criminal investigation is and should be viewed as a highly professional and specialized undertaking, but it's time to dispel the myth that the detective is the only individual in the police department who possesses the skills and qualifications needed to solve crimes.

Typical Detective Duties

The investigator's work varies from agency to agency depending upon the operation's size and location. In small agencies, the investigator, of necessity, is a generalist and performs all types of investigative tasks.

In urban police departments specialization of investigative functions takes place as detectives concentrate on specific functions such as burglary, robbery, homicide, narcotics, intelligence or general crime.

No matter what type of offense occurs, an official response must be made. In the instance of a major offense, the department will become involved in various aspects of the case: The crime scene must be searched, and evidence collected and processed. Witnesses are interviewed and suspects interrogated. The Prosecuting Attorney must be consulted as the investigative function evolves and above all—numerous reports must be written.

The bane of all investigators is the preparation of the initial or follow-up report. While time consuming, it is also an essential ingredient of the investigation process. Accurate and comprehensive reports become the vehicle for effective investigation leading eventually to successful prosecution.

For the sake of clarification, a typical case can be described as follows: Detective Joe Smith works for a large urban police department where he has specialized in the investigation of residential burglaries for several years. In investigating cases relating to this common offense, Detective Smith will perform a wide variety of tasks. His initial reaction to a preliminary report prepared by a patrol officer is to conduct a crime scene search. If appropriate, a detailed search is made for latent fingerprints as well as footprints, tire tracks, pry marks or other physical traces left by the perpetrator(s). If necessary the crime scene is photographed.

Victims are questioned and witnesses are contacted for additional information. Statements are taken and "all points bulletins" are sent out for the apprehension of suspects. Hopefully, stolen property will also be recovered. In many instances investigative leads require further investigation and coordination with private, federal, state, or other local law enforcement agencies.

Above all, the detective seems to become "married" to the police records division. Index files, MO files, and field interrogation cards are searched in an effort to obtain further leads to help identify the suspect(s).

Supplemental reports are completed and cases are presented to the Prosecuting Attorney. Warrants of arrest and/or search warrants are obtained and (providing all factors fall into place) arrests are made and property is recovered.

With the arrest accomplished, it would seem that Detective Smith's work would be finished, but in most instances, it has just begun. Reports must be written, physical evidence identified and the suspects must be linked to the actual crime. Interrogations are conducted in order to obtain admissions or confessions and all investigative leads must be pursued.

As the case comes to trial, Detective Smith works with a Prosecuting Attorney and the case is prepared for prosecution. If all phases have been successfully accomplished, the defendant is found guilty. After a final report is filed, stolen property may be returned to the victim, and the detective, in most instances, will consult with a probation officer regarding a possible sentence report to be presented to the judge.

The following is a fictitious example of specialized duties performed by another investigator: Jane Jones works as a detective in a large metropolitan police agency where she performs specific responsibilities and duties as a court liaison officer. Jane is responsible for preparing misdemeanor cases for trial. She analyses cases, notifies victims, witnesses and officers of pending trial dates and discusses each case with a Prosecuting Attorney in order to reach a decision as to whether the case should be continued or subjected to plea bargaining.

A key responsibility of Detective Jones is to follow the "Readiness and Motion Court Calendars" and record information that affects her cases so she can then take the proper actions. Defense attorneys can appear in court and request a change of plea, ask for continuances or request a change in the type of trial (from court to a jury). Such changes have a direct bearing on each misdemeanor case so she must notify all parties involved.

All of the above described activities insure the proper preparation of a case—Jane's coordination of these activities is essential to the successful prosecution of each.

A Brief History of the Detective in America

No one knows precisely who the first detective was, or when the position of criminal investigator became an official one. The structure and organization of the American police system as a whole can, of course, be traced directly to the police services of England and Wales. They were the prototypes of the police departments which were established in major American cities during the mid-nineteenth century as a response to the crime problems of vice, disorderly conduct, drunkenness, and brawling. As the cities grew, so did the incidence and complexity of crime, and police forces were organized and reorganized in the response to the increasing incidence of disorders and riots. Traditionally, as police forces grew in size, scant attention was paid to the specific functions of various members of the forces; thus, the investigative role as such was slow to develop and be recognized.

Early police forces aimed at reaction rather than prevention; law enforcement officers most often simply responded to direct requests for help.[1] The crime victim would contact a watchman and apply to a local justice for a warrant; a constable would then either arrest the suspect or assist the victim in making the arrest.[2] Economic crimes, particularly those involving counterfeiting, resulted in rewards being offered for the apprehension of the offenders. Crime victims either posted their own rewards, or pressured local agencies to post them. This technique soon encompassed other types of crime as well, and became an integral part of the investigative process. The recovery of property became the central focus of the police function and, as a result, police officers cultivated underworld contacts in order to accomplish this task.[3]

The reward system became so popular that police officers often were more concerned with recovering property and reaping rewards than they were with actually apprehending criminals. Even after the creation of organized police departments, detectives continued to function on a fee basis. This system proved very lucrative; one New York detective, over a brief period of time, collected sufficient rewards to double his salary.[4] It also opened the door to several problems:

> To be effective, detectives needed wide knowledge of professional criminals who alone could provide them with the stolen property they sought to recover. Compounding with the thief was the easiest way to recover property. The detective gave the thief either money or immunity in return for the stolen goods, and the rightful owner received his property less whatever he had agreed upon as a reward with the detective. Some victims found it cheaper to advertise in the newspaper and deal directly with the thieves, thus eliminating the detective as a middleman.[5]

Exactly when the first detective was appointed is not known. Investigation became a specific governmental function in 1836, however, when Congress authorized the Post Office Department to hire agents to investigate postal matters. Ten years later, in 1846, it became a specific police function when Francis Tukey of the Boston Police Department appointed three detectives to that city's force; in 1857, twenty policemen were assigned to detective positions in New York City; in 1860, Chicago established its first detective unit; and in 1865, Massachusetts formed a state investigative agency.

Meanwhile, private investigators were enjoying a great deal of success and fame. In fact, the early history of government or police investigators has often been confused with or overshadowed by that of private investigators. The most famous of these was Allen Pinkerton, who in 1850 established a general detective agency in the midwestern United States. (He had been appointed as Chicago's first detective in 1849.) His agency addressed itself to the investigation of all types of criminal offenses, and was so successful that it soon extended its influence and scope throughout the country. Pinkerton agents—or "Pinks," as they were called—investigated train robberies and provided protection for President Abraham Lincoln, in addition to performing other duties. Pinkerton and his agents worked for a flat fee plus expenses, which helped to eliminate the reward system common among both private and police investigators up until that time.

Table 1-1

Significant Events Related
To The Investigative Process

Date	Event
1836	Congress authorized the Post Office Department to hire agents to investigate postal matters.
1849	Allen Pinkerton was appointed as Chicago's first detective. This was the first effort to separate the investigative function from patrol.
1850	Creation of the Pinkerton Detective Agency occurred. As a private investigative agency, emphasis was placed on offering services to railroad properties and other business enterprises.
1851	Detectives appointed in Boston by Marshal Francis Turkey. This appointment represented the first such efforts in New England.
1851	Weekly line-up established in Boston by Francis Turkey. Suspected offenders were inspected by the entire police department.
1857	New York created 20 detective positions.
1858	New York City police created a photographic rogues' gallery.
1860	Chicago established its first detective unit as a result of the increased demand for the performance of investigative functions.
1865	The U.S. Secret Service was organized to suppress counterfeiting. Through the years, the Secret Service loaned investigators to other federal agencies.
1865	Massachusetts formed a state investigative agency.
1871	The U.S. Attorney General received $50,000 for the detection and prosecution of crimes.
1878	Boston instituted the investigation of deaths by a medical examiner. This effort represented the first application of pathological investigations of violent crimes.
1879	Alphonse Bertillon began to develop a method for measuring the body for identification and then coupled this with fullface and profile photographs.
1892	Francis Galton published a book entitled FINGERPRINTS. He developed the foundations of a fingerprint classification system that replaced the Bertillon system.
1893	Hans Gross wrote a treatise on CRIMINAL INVESTIGATION. This work became a landmark text emphasizing the importance of reconstructing the crime scene for investigative purposes.
1897	The National Bureau of Criminal Identification was established by the International Association of Chiefs of Police (IACP) and was located in Chicago.
1901	Dr. Karl Landsteiner discovered blood grouping. This, in turn, became a key factor in identification.
1905	U.S. Attorney General Charles Bonaparte established the Bureau of Investigation in the U.S. Department of Justice.
1910	Albert S. Osborn wrote a text entitled QUESTIONED DOCUMENTS. This pioneering work led to the acceptance of the scientific examination of documents in courts.
1915	Dr. Leone Lattes developed a procedure for determining the blood group of a dried bloodstain.
1923	Colonel Calvin Goddard utilized the comparison microscope for ballistics. This process provided a means for comparing a cartridge or bullet found at the scene of a crime to the suspect's firearms, based upon unique markings.
1923	August Vollmer established the first forensic laboratory (it was located in the Los Angeles Police Department), thus instituting the application of science and technology to crime fighting.
1924	J. Edgar Hoover became the director of the Bureau of Investigation. Appointment of investigators was no longer made by political appointment, therefore professionalism was instituted.
1924	The National Bureau of Criminal Identification became a division of the Bureau of Investigation, U.S. Department of Justice. This was a land mark decision because it placed the Bureau in a focal position and added to its prestige. As a central clearinghouse for criminal statistics, local agencies became increasingly reliant on this agency.
1930	The Federal Bureau of Narcotics was established in the Treasury Department.
1932	The Bureau of Investigation established another forensic laboratory. Its creation, at the national level, heightened the importance of processing physical evidence.
1934	Calvin Goddard became the director of the Scientific Crime Detection Laboratory at Northwestern University, formed as a response to the St. Valentine's Day Massacre. It fostered the ever-increasing significance of the crime laboratory.
1934	Investigative forces of the U.S. Justice Department were authorized to carry weapons, serve subpoenas and make arrests.
1935	The Bureau of Investigation was renamed the Federal Bureau of Investigation (FBI).
1935	The FBI established the National Police Academy. Its initial course was attended by twenty-three local police officers. Since its inception, the Academy's acceptance by the law enforcement community has placed it in a preeminent position.
1942	The Office of Security was established in the U.S. State Department. This office provided protection against subversive activities and espionage. A major task was to conduct background investigations on applicants.
1952	The Inspection Service of the Internal Revenue Service (IRS) was created. Its primary function was to maintain internal security. Initial investigative efforts centered on bribery attempts and embezzlement.
1952	In the state of California, the Commission on Peace Officers Standards and training was organized. Among other accomplishments, special classes for investigators were created.
1963	The Illinois State Legislature passed a bill establishing the Illinois Crime Investigating Commission. Its entire efforts were directed toward eliminating organized crime.
1965	The FBI started to develop the National Crime Information Center (NCIC). This information system collects data on wanted persons, stolen vehicles and stolen property. Many police departments had terminals to give them immediate access to the data-base.

Allan Pinkerton added to his fame during the Civil War by working for the Union Army's "Secret Service." He had a special flair for publicity and gained a great deal of notoriety as an operative. Some historians give credit to Pinkerton as the first Chief of the U.S. Secret Service, but such is not the case. The first Chief was William P. Wood who assumed office on July 5, 1865 after being sworn in by Secretary of the Treasury, Hugh McCulloch.[6]

The effectiveness of "Pinks" was best illustrated by their handling of train robberies. Local marshals and sheriffs were unable to cope with this crime. As our nation turned westward, trains became choice targets of opportunity for criminals as vast sums of money were transported over great distances. Without the benefit of effective law enforcement communications and coordination, the outlaws operated with relative immunity.

Pinkerton's operatives proceeded to place extraordinary emphasis on a detailed investigation of each robbery. All leads were investigated thoroughly. Operatives engaged in an extensive manhunt until all perpetrators were identified. This successful end-result was sometimes accomplished because "wanted notices" were issued and widely distributed offering a reward for information leading to the arrest and conviction of offenders. This operative system proved to be the key to the effective investigative process developed by Pinkerton's national detective agency.

The popularity of the criminal as a folk hero occurred during this unique era. Historian Samuel Walker points out that between 1874 and 1885, Pinkerton published more than eighteen books on criminal activity—each describing the special techniques utilized by the criminal in accomplishing a crime. Pinkerton's influence on law enforcement was unprecedented because he worked so successfully in these seemingly opposite directions—glorifying the criminal on the one hand while effectively leading his men in their capture, on the other. Pinkerton's sons were also uniquely influential. As members of the International Association of Chiefs of Police (IACP) they gave numerous lectures describing the exploits of criminals![7]

Gustavus H. Thiel was another famous private investigator. He was president and founder of the Thiel Detective Service Company, and received some of his early training as secretary of the Secret Service under Allen Pinkerton during the Civil War. Thiel participated personally in the arrest of many notorious criminals; for example, in 1889,

> . . . a train on the Iron Mountain Road had been held up in Arkansas, the conductor killed and several of the other trainmen shot. It was known that "Ol" Truman, a notorious border ruffian, with six companions, were guilty of the crime. Thiel assembled a band of western deputy sheriffs and took up the trail. The gang was overtaken in a clump of woods in Indian Territory. A pitched battle ensued with the desperadoes entrenched behind boulders. In the fight Thiel received a bullet wound in one knee. Elmer, one of the pursuing party, finally executed a flank movement and shot Truman. His companions finally surrendered or were killed. Four of them met their death at the end of a cattleman's noose.[8]

Slowly but surely, the role of the detective became a prestigious one. The "real" police mission was soon perceived as the detection and apprehension of suspects. And the mystique of the detective grew; in 1900, Inspector John D. Shea of the Chicago Police Department described the detective as a strong, determined individual:

> In personal appearance a detective does not differ from the ordinary individual. Sometimes he is young, sometimes old. Perhaps he is large or small, but whatever his appearance is, he must be possessed of good, sound, common sense. A collegiate education is by no means essential—just a general knowledge of persons and things. He must be able to judge human nature at a glance, be quick of perception and quick to act; he must form an opinion instantly, and act firmly and resolutely on that opinion, and must not waver, or be half-hearted in actions; he must pay strict attention to the minutest details, as often it is from these the missing link of great cases are found. Self-reliance and confidence are absolutely necessary. He must feel that he is competent to penetrate the unknown surroundings of crime.[9]

Meanwhile, criminal investigation was becoming more and more of a science. Francis Galton's book, *Fingerprints*, published in 1892, and Hans Gross' treatise, *Criminal Investigation*, published in 1893, became classics. In 1901, Dr. Karl Landsteiner discovered blood grouping and in 1915 Dr. Leon Lattes developed a procedure for determining the blood group of dried bloodstains. In 1923, Colonel Calvin Goddard utilized the comparison microscope for ballistics (later, in 1934, he became the director of the Scientific Crime Detection Laboratory at Northwestern University). In 1923, August Vollmer established the first forensic laboratory in the country in the Los Angeles Police Department; this was followed in 1932 by the FBI's establishment of a national forensic laboratory.

J. Edgar Hoover's influence on law enforcement in the United States is legendary. He transformed an inept "Bureau of Investigation" into what became an acclaimed (worldwide) investigative agency, the "Federal Bureau of Investigation". Hoover institutionalized the crime fighting model of law enforcement. The FBI became the nation's response to what was perceived as a serious crime problem.

A significant event in the growth and development of the FBI was the "Lindberg Kidnapping" in 1932. The abduction of the one and one-half year old son of the famous aviator, Charles Lindberg, received a great deal of publicity because of Lindberg's international fame. With little hesitation, Congress passed the "Lindberg Law," making kidnapping a federal crime. As a federal crime, it came under the FBI's jurisdiction.

The FBI, as a result of new jurisdictional responsibilities, proved to be the nemesis of such glamorized crooks as John Dillinger, Pretty Boy Floyd, Baby Face Nelson and Ma Barker. The FBI, under the direction of J. Edgar Hoover, capitalized on the crime-wave scare caused by people like Dillinger and became the dominating influence on law enforcement in the United States. Its reputation and prestige were greatly enhanced by opening a national crime laboratory, developing the Uniform Crime Report System, creating the National Academy to train local police officers and offering other services to state and local law enforcement agencies. Success thus begot success and the FBI's influence was expanded.

The reputation of the FBI has been slightly tarnished in recent years due to the practice of some questionable investigative techniques fostered by Hoover prior to his death. None-the-less, the FBI has definitely dominated the growth and development of the law enforcement field since 1934.

Today's criminal investigator has come a long way from the first police and private detectives, with their undefined roles and lack of adequate facilities. He is a professional in every sense of the word—intelligent, educated, with a wealth of scientific and technical resources at his disposal. Nevertheless, the key to effective criminal investigation and crime solving lies not with the detective alone, but with total agency response. All resources within a department must be ready and willing to contribute to conclusive investigations. This will be obvious from the following description of the phases involved in the investigative process.

The Investigative Process: A Definition

Criminal cases are investigated for the purposes of (a) making a critical search for truth and information, and (b) gathering facts and data in order to bring cases to satisfactory conclusions. The investigative process itself is an essential element of the criminal justice system, since it comprises the vital link between mere suspicion that a crime has been committed and the formal accusation of the person or persons suspected of having committed the offense (or some other resolution). It provides the means by which judicial evidence is prepared, and evidence, of course, is what eventually determines the guilt or innocence of a suspect.

Basically, a criminal investigation encompasses everything the police do from the time when they first become aware that a crime has been committed until all investigative efforts have come to an end, whether or not a prosecution results. It's crucial to the success of these efforts that the integrity of the investigation be maintained throughout the process, since this often determines the outcome of subsequent proceedings against the accused.[10]

The integrity of a case is maintained in a number of ways. First and foremost, the investigator(s) must keep accurate and complete notes on all actions taken. Secondly, the processing of evidence from the time it is picked up at the scene of a crime until it is presented in court by the prosecutor and preserved for appellate court decisions must show at all steps who has custody and where it is maintained. It is important that all police personnel including the investigator(s), the records clerks, property clerks, evidence technicians, and criminalists be absolutely honest in the gathering, processing and custody of the evidence, in the preparation of reports, and in testifying in court.

More than anything else, though, the criminal investigative process is a reasoning process. After the investigator is confronted with a given amount of information and number of facts, he must be able to put them together to reach a logical conclusion. He must determine the *corpus delecti* of a crime or an offense (literally, "the body of the crime," or the substantive and factual information which indicates that a crime has been committed) and then decide what should be done about it.

Two specific types of reasoning are used during this process: deductive and inductive. Deductive reasoning requires that the investigator deduce, or decide, that what seems to have happened actually took place because the course of events and collection of facts indicate only one possible conclusion. Inductive reasoning is much less specific; during this process, the investigator may only be able to infer that a corpus delecti exists, and that what he thinks happened probably did happen. Both types of reasoning are essential elements of the investigative process.

The deductive reasoning process is exemplified by a suicide case. The victim shoots herself with a "38" calibre revolver. It is found encased in her right hand. Powder burns are in evidence on her chest. A suicide note is found indicating that the victim has determined to take her own life by means of the revolver. There is no evidence indicating a reasonable possibility of murder.

The inductive reasoning process is illustrated by a suicide case in which the victim appears to have taken an overdose of the drug valium. The victim is found dead in his apartment and a half empty vial containing the prescription drug is found in the victim's bedroom. There is no evidence of a struggle nor any other evidence of foul play. The victim has no history of drug abuse. The investigator may thus infer that the case is one of suicide but cannot be certain until an autopsy has been performed.

The process of investigation consists of two distinct phases: the *preliminary*, or initial, investigation, and the *follow-up* investigation.

The preliminary investigation covers the activities and responsibilities of the officers who (a) initially respond to a *complaint* from a victim, or (b) observe that a crime *has been* committed, or (c) observe that a crime *is being* committed. It covers the time period beginning with the officers' instructions to proceed to the scene, or their observations that a crime has been or is being committed, and continues until on-scene activities have ended. The investigation may be postponed for whatever reason, or the responsibility for the investigation may be transferred to another unit or detail.

The follow-up investigation encompasses all police activities which take place after the preliminary investigation has been completed and prior to adjudication in court, or until the investigation is ended for whatever reason without adjudication. This may begin when the responsibility for an investigation is transferred from the officers who conducted the preliminary investigation to the officers of another unit or detail, or when officers of another unit or detail resume the investigative effort after a period of inactivity, or when the initial investigation officers resume their investigative efforts following a period of inactivity—e.g., in subsequent tours of duty. This phase may last for only a few hours, or a few days, or may extend over months or even years in very complex or major cases.

The Preliminary Investigation

The officer or officers conducting the Preliminary Investigation (usually field patrol personnel) must keep several goals in mind. These include:

- finding out precisely what happened (this requires the officers to be observant even when initially responding to a call and departing from the patrol vehicle at the scene);

- locating witnesses and discovering other sources of evidence to help determine what happened;

- figuring out what further investigative steps they themselves will need to take, and what steps will need to be taken by other officers, technicians, and investigators;

- attempting to understand the motivation of the victims and/or witnesses in reporting the crime, and evaluating the accuracy of their statements (this occasionally includes deciding whether or not some other officer or investigator might be more successful in this endeavor); and

- recording the three major types of information collected during the preliminary investigation:
    1. what has been done;
    2. what has been learned; and
    3. what remains to be done.[11]

This initial phase of the investigative process may include a multitude of activities, depending on the type and nature of the case, the qualifications and capabilities of the officers responding to the call, and the resources immediately available, such as identification kits and cameras. It will also at least partially be shaped by relevant departmental policies and procedures.

The following activities are usually considered basic to an effective and thorough preliminary investigation:

- First, of course, the investigating officers should determine whether an offense has actually been committed and, if it has, what its precise nature and circumstances are.

- Second, the officers should accurately and completely record whatever information they obtain during the preliminary investigation, on official report forms when possible.

Other duties and responsibilities focus on the victim and/or witnesses, the suspect(s), and the scene itself.

Concerning the victim of and/or witnesses to the crime, the investigating officers should:

- immediately render assistance to any injured persons;
- interview the complainant and any witnesses, taking care to determine what information is actually *known* by those people and making sure to obtain complete identifications of all parties; and
- obtain statements from victims and witnesses if such statements can be legally obtained (in writing, when circumstances permit).

Concerning the suspect(s), the investigating officers should:

- determine their identity and effect an arrest if possible at the scene, or by immediate pursuit;
- interrogate them; and
- obtain statements from them, if they can be legally obtained (in writing, when circumstances permit).

And, finally, with regard to the crime scene itself, the officers should:

- protect it to ensure that evidence is not lost or tampered with; and
- arrange for the collection of evidence at a later time if it cannot be collected immediately.

After these steps have been completed, the officers should furnish other field units, through the communication center, with descriptions of the scene, victims, and suspects. If the suspects have left the scene, the officer should also supply other units with any relevant information concerning their appearance, the method and direction of flight, the descriptions of vehicles used.

Whether or not a case is solved often depends on how thorough and complete the preliminary investigation is. More specifically, *the single most important factor* which determines the outcome of a case is the information the victim supplies to the responding officers. If information that uniquely identifies the suspect is not given at the time when the crime is first reported and described, chances are that the suspect will never be identified.[12] This, of course, implies that the officer must know what kinds of questions to ask in order to get the proper information needed to proceed in the investigation; what types of questions should be asked, and how they should be determined, will be discussed later in this chapter.

The Patrol Officer's Role in the Preliminary Investigation.

Uniformed patrol field officers are usually responsible for conducting preliminary investigations of criminal offenses. They are the ones who are most often dispatched to investigate an offense, or who observe that an offense has been committed or is being committed during the normal course of their patrol duties. (Exceptions include "victimless" crimes, such as gambling, vice, and narcotics, and offenses such as fraud or forgeries.) In most cases, patrol officers initiate and complete as many of the activities listed previously as are relevant to the incident at hand. Circumstances usually dictate which activities are required and/or feasible.

As soon as the preliminary investigation has been completed, the officers should organize the information they have gathered prior to completing their field reports. The actual preparation of these reports may be done by hand in the field; they may also be dictated over the telephone or into a tape recorder, or typed later at the station.

In some instances, the presence of uniformed officers may actually prevent or inhibit a proper preliminary investigation from being made. If and when this seems to be the case, the preliminary investigation should be conducted by other police personnel. These might include special details or units, or technicians trained in determining certain types of evidence and dealing with certain types of witnesses. The uniformed patrol officers should contact these personnel as soon as possible, describing the particular cases to them and furnishing them with any other details they may need. Cases in which this transfer of responsibilities might be desirable include major offenses such as arson, train wrecking, and homicide, and specific other offenses such as "victimless" crimes, forgeries, and child molestations, which are normally investigated by specially trained personnel. The proper report form facilitates transfer from the patrol officer to the specialist investigator.

Although uniformed officers may be qualified to undertake most investigations there are some offenses for which specialized investigative techniques are required. Most police officers are not well trained to investigate such cases as arsons, narcotics sale and use, child molestations, involved homicides, safe burglaries and forgeries. The uniformed officers' role in such cases is one of preserving the scene until a specialty investigator may initiate the preliminary investigation.

The Follow-Up Investigation

The follow-up investigation is basically an extension of the preliminary investigation. The time frame during which a preliminary investigation is normally conducted simply doesn't allow for all details to be taken care of, especially in complex cases. Even in so-called "open and shut" cases, during which an arrest is made, property is recovered, and all relevant information and evidence is obtained during the preliminary investigation, there are still tasks which remain to be performed and actions which need to be taken. Thus, the follow-up investigation is conducted in order to complete what the preliminary investigation began and may be performed by either the officer who performs the preliminary investigation or another investigator.

The follow-up investigation has several purposes; these include:

- finding out additional information in order to make it possible to arrest suspect(s) not arrested at the scene or during the preliminary investigation;

- recovering stolen property for use as evidence and/or to return to the owner; and

- preparing the case for prosecution and adjudication (or, in those cases which may not be prosecuted or adjudicated, bringing them to a satisfactory close).

The persons responsible for conducting the follow-up investigation usually perform the following basic activities or tasks:

- identifying and apprehending suspects;

- interrogating suspects, and taking statements when necessary and legal;

- determining whether the suspects may have committed other crimes in addition to the one being investigated;

- arranging for the analysis and evaluation of evidence;

- recovering stolen property and either retaining it for use as evidence or returning it to the victim;

- interviewing (or re-interviewing) victims and witnesses, taking statements if necessary;

- completely and carefully recording all information obtained;

- preparing the case for prosecution and adjudication, or other disposition where appropriate;

- filing the complaint with the prosecutor, and

- serving subpoenas, where required.

The assignment of personnel to the follow-up investigative process varies from department to department, depending on the number of personnel available, departmental policies, procedures, and the capabilities of specific persons. While the uniformed police officer usually performs the preliminary investigation, he can also be responsible for all or part of the follow-up; there are three general situations in which the uniformed police officer is assigned this task:

• in smaller departments of thirty persons or less, in which specialization is limited and most persons perform a variety of duties. If a department of this size does have a detective, he will probably be restricted to follow-up work only in the more complex cases and to those investigations involving forgery, fraud, and "victimless" crimes.

• in departments which have adopted the Vollmer-Berkeley, California-organizational model; so-called because it was widely publicized by August Vollmer, Chief of Police in Berkeley from 1905 to 1932. Under this model, uniformed field officers are responsible for both preliminary and follow-up investigations of all cases except for those specifically referred to the detective division. The detectives assist the field officers by performing tasks which the officers can't easily do during regular tours of duty. For example, if an officer is restricted to certain beat areas, detectives will conduct the investigations which involve widely separated locations or other jurisdictions. The detectives also aid the officers in apprehending and/or interrogating suspects and in researching and correlating related cases.

• Some departments have adopted the team policing model, which generally calls for the assignment of follow-up investigations to the uniformed field officers. More complex cases are referred to detective specialists for follow-up, as are those which require investigation in widely separated locations and other jurisdictions. In other applications of this model, field officers may be limited to preliminary investigations alone.[13]

In larger departments, and those which have adopted neither of the three above models, responsibilities for follow-up investigation are usually assigned to a combination of uniformed field officers, identification technicians, specialist detectives, generalist investigators, and criminalists. Some departments have identification technicians available on a round-the-clock basis, and they participate in both preliminary and follow-up procedures; others furnish them for follow-up purposes alone. Generalist investigators, who can be either detectives or officers designated as investigators, may assist the uniformed officers in some preliminary investigations or, in more complex cases, actually perform the preliminary investigations themselves. They also perform follow-up investigations in all but the most complex cases which require specialists. Most commonly, however, cases are referred for follow-up to a detective division or bureau, which is organized into specialty details, and specialists perform the follow-up function. Thus, the follow-up investigation may require the skills and abilities of many different types of personnel, depending on the circumstances and policies of a particular department.*

The Patrol Officer and the Detective: Partners in Crime-Solving

As should be obvious from the preceding discussion, both phases of the investigative process can involve all members of a police department and require that they work together in order to bring a case to a successful close. Sometimes, patrol officers are called on to carry out an entire investigation; at other times, they are assisted by detectives or other specialists; at still other times, the detectives or specialists rely on the patrol officers for assistance. Thus, the patrol and detective roles cannot be seen as separate and distinct, but rather as complementary.

As uniformed field officers are given more and more responsibility for conducting investigations—which is occurring in many police departments across the country—detectives are being relieved of much of the responsibility for the preliminary investigation and can devote a greater amount of their time and effort to lengthy and involved follow-up work. Both detectives and field officers, however, share equal responsibility for making sure that all of the evidence and information needed to complete an investigation is gathered efficiently and competently. This may mean that the patrol officers get even more involved in the investigative process itself; again, both uniformed officers and detectives, although they may perform very separate functions, must be willing to cooperate with one another if an investigation is going to be successful.

Detectives are usually responsible for preparing felony cases for presentation in court; this doesn't mean, however, that patrol officers who may be

---

*Note—It is important that an investigation be complete and thorough from a technical standpoint. It is also important that it reflects adherence to all legal requirements with special attention to the rights of an accused suspect. Too often cases are not prosecuted or are lost in court because officers have failed to follow legally prescribed procedures.

The United States Supreme Court has rendered a number of decisions which are designed to protect the rights of suspects. These include admonitions from the investigator that the suspect must be apprised of his right to remain silent by not answering interrogation questions and his right to confer with an attorney before an interrogation may proceed. Also an investigator is directed not to use undue force in the making of an arrest.

The processing of evidence requires that the chain of custody be such that it cannot be contaminated. This means that from the time that evidence is collected at the scene of a crime, presented in court and held for an appellate court decision, the investigator and all other persons charged with the processing and custody of the evidence must be able to testify that there could not possibly be any tampering with it from an outside source.

Chapters which follow cover the subject in detail.

involved in the investigation are relieved of the responsibility for making sure that all aspects of their investigative efforts are thoroughly and completely reported, and that the evidence they obtain is properly processed. In many cases, both detectives and patrol officers may be called on to testify in court; every person who has participated in an investigation in any way must be prepared to present his findings clearly and thoroughly.

In task or strike force operations, where patrol officers and detectives work as a team, all are considered equally responsible for every facet of the investigative process. In this type of arrangement, each member is expected to cooperate with the others; no single person bears the responsibility for the entire investigation, and all must be willing to share what they know. The detective who cracks a case on his own is rare indeed; the combined efforts of all members of a department are what generally make the difference between a solved case and an unsolved one.

The Patrol Officer and the Investigative Function: A Matrix of Roles*

Since patrol officers are being given—and are taking—more and more responsibility for conducting investigations, both preliminary and follow-up, it should prove helpful to examine the many possible roles they can take *via* the matrix which follows in Table 1-2. Again, precisely what a patrol officer's duties will be may vary according to circumstances and departmental policies and regulations; it can probably be assumed, however, that he will fall somewhere within the five models suggested.

No one of the five is proposed as *the* model to follow or adopt, since an officer's responsibilities will never be as clear-cut as any model, no matter how elaborate or detailed, can represent. What the matrix does is to suggest a sequence of models, with each successive one illustrating an enhanced view of the patrol officer's role in the investigative process. Within each model can be found the following:

- an outline of the patrol responsibility;
- a description of the process by which patrol assists in referring cases for continued investigation;
- some consequences of the particular model regarding the investigative process; and
- suggested management policies for facilitating and implementing the model.

---

*Excerpts from Donald F. Cawley, *et al.*, *Managing Criminal Investigations: A Manual* (University Research Corporation, Washington, D.C., 1976), page 20-34. This manual was prepared pursuant to Contract J-LEAA-022-76 with the Law Enforcement Assistance Administration, National Institute of Law Enforcement and Criminal Justice. (Materials used with permission of the National Institute for Law Enforcement.)

Table 1.2 Matrix of Model Roles of Patrol Officers in Conducting Criminal Investigations*

(Each Model Builds Upon and Includes Activities Outlined in Preceding Model)

Models	Patrol Responsibility	Case Referral Procedure	Consequences	Management Policies
A. Typical	• Prepare and complete basic report form.	• Refer all cases, including preliminary investigations, to detectives.	• Redundancy • Insufficient data collected • Low level of productivity • Low morale in patrol.	
B. Better Information Collection	• Conduct a complete initial investigation and fill out revised initial investigation report for selected categories of crime.	• Refer the reports of the initial investigations for selected categories of crime to detectives for follow-up investigation. (In these types of cases, detectives do not conduct preliminary investigations.)	• Elimination of redundancy • More complete data collected. • Productivity increased. • Improved case load for detectives. • Better morale.	• Define crime categories to be investigated by patrol. • Define exceptions. • Design new initial investigation form. • Train patrol and detectives in use of new forms. • Train supervisors.
C. Patrol Recommendation	• Conduct initial investigation and complete detailed investigation report. • Decide whether to call for forensic or evidence specialists. • Recommend closing or continuing case based on presence or absence of solvability factors.	• Supervisor reviews patrol recommendation. • Case screening criteria are used to close cases when initial investigation reveals lack of solvability factors. OR • Case screening criteria are used to refer cases for follow up Investigation by detectives.	• Recommendation and screening, after initial investigation by patrol, focuses resources only on probably solvable cases. • Increases productivity. • Promotes Interdependancy between detectives and patrol.	• Establish policy and procedures for case screening. • Establish policy and procedures detailing the role of patrol and follow-up role detectives. • Provide additional training for patrol and supervisors.
D. Limited Investigative Role of Patrol	• Investigate crimes in selected categories beyond initial investigation phase. • Patrol continues and completes investigation of certain categories of crime which do not require the service of detective specialists.	• Crime cases in selected categories are not referred. • Other cases are referred to detectives for follow-up investigation.	• Reduces detective workload. • Permits detective to increase specialty or to adopt new roles.	• Establish policy and procedures delineating investigative roles of patrol in selected categories of criminal investigation and of detectives in other categories of crime. • Provide additional training for patrol.

*Donald F. Cawley, *et al. Managing Criminal Investigations: A Manual* (University Research Corporation, Washington, D.C., 1976.)

Table 1.2 Matrix of Model Roles of Patrol Officers in Conducting Criminal Investigations (Continued)

(Each Model Builds Upon and Includes Activities Outlined in Preceding Model)

Models	Patrol Responsibility	Case Referral Procedure	Consequences	Management Policies
E. Enhanced Investigative Role of Patrol	• Investigate crimes in increased number of categories. • Closure can occur on scene after initial investigation.	• Refer only those cases which require high level of skill or which are of an exceptional nature.	• Maximal use of detectives by assigning them to follow up only those cases with high probability of solution and/or those which require specialized skills. • Maximal use of patrol resourcces in all investigtions. • Improved relationships between public and police. • New roles and opportunities available for detectives.	• Establish policies detailing the differing authority and relationships between patrol and detectives. • Adopt case screening system which incorporates early, on-scene, case-closure criteria.

Model A: The Typical Approach

This model describes what the patrol officer's responsibilities have normally been during the investigative process, and still are in some departments. Basically, the patrol officer collects information for the detective and transcribes this information onto a relatively simple crime report form. He questions the victim and witnesses and writes down the answers according to the dictates of the form; he then hands the form over for supervisory review and subsequent transmittal to the investigative unit.

How successful this type of investigation will be depends almost entirely on how well the officer fills out the form. If the information recorded there is in any way inadequate or incomplete, the case may have to be discontinued, or the detective may have to go through the entire information collecting process again. In any case, the initial effort is wasted. This model poses problems in that the form actually conditions and affects the way in which the investigation will proceed. Not only may the form itself be unsatisfactory, but any errors or gaps in it can result in the detective having to retrace the patrol officer's footsteps—which is often difficult, if not impossible. Thus, productivity may decline, and morale problems may surface within the department as a whole. When the patrol officer's role is reduced to that of "report taker," the emphasis is not on effective investigative techniques, but on paperwork, and neither the skills nor the abilities of the patrol officer are used to their best advantage.

Model B: Better Information Collection

In this model, the patrol officer is truly responsible for conducting the preliminary investigation and collecting relevant and meaningful facts which can be utilized by follow-up personnel. Here, also, a report form is used, but rather than being vague or insufficient, it is carefully designed to incorporate prescribed and structured questions which virtually guarantee that all available, appropriate information is gathered and documented for subsequent use.

This model begins to solve the common problem of how management should limit the role of the patrol officer during the investigation while at the same time ensuring that the preliminary phase is carried out in a thorough and complete manner. Previous definitions and theories about the preliminary investigation process have suggested that the investigation "terminates after [the patrol officer] has completed all that he *can* possibly accomplish."[14] This assumption is inadequate because it doesn't define what an officer *should* accomplish. A carefully thought-out and designed report form can clarify these goals; structured questions, derived from the prior identification of solvability factors (that is, those types of information which will actually be useful in solving a case) can help an officer to know what's expected of him.

Not all cases can be solved by investigation. Therefore there is a need to concentrate investigative efforts on those cases where there is a reasonable hope for success. Probability of success can be determined by identification of the quality and quantity evidence available at the time of the preliminary investigation or at later stages of the investigation. Such evidence is referred to as the solvability factors available. Key solvability factors developed by the Rochester, N.Y. Police Department are as follows:

- Was there a witness to the crime?
- Can a suspect be named?
- Can a suspect be located?
- Can a suspect be described?
- Can a suspect be identified?
- Can a suspect vehicle be identified?
- Is the stolen property traceable?
- Is there a significant *modus operandi* present?
- Is there significant physical evidence present?
- Has an evidence technician been called? Is the technician's report positive?
- Is there a significant reason to believe that the crime may be solved by a reasonable amount of investigative effort.
- Was there a definite limited opportunity for anyone except the suspect to commit the crime?

Solvability factors are important enough to merit some discussion here. The experience of police managers, in addition to recent studies, have identified those solvability factors—those information elements which are considered most important to the successful resolution of a case—which can effectively be used in devoping an expanded role for the patrol officer in the investigative process. Solvability factors have been shown to have such a direct relationship to case solutions that several police agencies have applied them when developing management strategies for the improvement of the criminal investigation process.

Once an agency has determined the solvability factors relevant to its situation and function within the community (these factors may vary from department to department), the patrol officer can use them when conducting the preliminary investigation to ensure that that phase of the investigative process will be carried out as efficiently as possible. Basically, he can use these factors to determine the following:

- whether the reported case is founded or unfounded (this will often determine whether an investigation should be continued or terminated);

- whether to make an arrest;

- whether the reported case should be continued and/or referred to other personnel within the department (sometimes, this will be advisable even when solvability factors *aren't* present; this decision often depends on the discretion of the officer at the scene); and/or

- whether the case should be closed without further investigation.

When an officer is required to direct his attention only to those areas of inquiry which are the most promising—in other words, those which tend to result in the successful resolution of cases—his role is effectively limited and the preliminary investigation is carried out in as thorough a way as possible. And, after the preliminary investigation has been concluded, when the patrol officer yields the case to the investigator for follow-up, he can be assured of having filed a report containing clear and detailed information. The investigators won't have to repeat any steps taken previously, and the case can proceed smoothly.

Figure 1-1 is an example of an effective report form. Basically, it leads the officer through the preliminary investigation *via* a series of steps, and requires that he fill it in with the type of information needed for efficient follow-up. Six copies of the report are prepared, and the final copy is given to the victim; on the reverse of the victim's copy is found the letter seen in Figure 1-2. By requesting that the victim get involved in the investigation by furnishing the police with additional information as it becomes available, the letter also aids in the follow-up process. (Both forms are used with the permission of Thomas F. Hastings, Chief of Police, Rochester, New York.)

Figure 1-1 BASIC INVESTIGATIVE REPORT FORM

(left vertical margin: rochester police department crime investigation report — PAGE 1 OF)

1. OFFENSE OR CHARGE (INCLUDE DEGREE & LAW SECTION NO.)	2. CLASSIFICATION OF OFFENSE (SUPERVISORY REVIEW)	3. CR #

4. TIME OF OCCURRENCE M___ D___ Y___ T___	5. WHEN REPORTED DISPATCHED TO M D Y T	6. LOCATION OF OFFENSE (HOUSE NO. STREET NAME)

7. VICTIMS NAME (LAST, FIRST, MIDDLE) OR FIRM NAME IF BUSINESS	8. VICTIMS ADDRESS (HOUSE NUMBER, STREET NAME)	9. RESIDENCE PHONE DAY NIGHT

10. VICTIMS PLACE OF EMPLOY, OR SCHOOL NAME	11. BUSINESS PHONE DAY NIGHT	12. VICTIM'S SEX / RACE / AGE	13. REPORTING PERSONS SIGNATURE DATE

14. WAS THERE A WITNESS TO THE CRIME? IF NO PLACE AN X IN BOX A——— A.

15. INDICATE WITH PROPER CODE IN BOXES PROVIDED, PERSON'S RELATIONSHIP TO INVESTIGATION. W-1 WITNESS #1; NI: NOT INTERVIEWED #2, R REPORTING PERSON. PK: PERSON WITH KNOWLEDGE (INCLUDING REPORTING PERSON'S NAME IF DIFFERENT FROM VICTIM'S). IF CITIZEN INFORMATION FORM R.P.D. 1148 IS LEFT WITH ANY OF THESE PERSON'S INDICATE BY CIRCLING PERSONS DESIGNATED

ADDRESS CHECKED	APT.#	PERSON INTERVIEWED	AGE	HOME ADDRESS	APT#	TEL	RES. BUS.

16. CAN A SUSPECT BE NAMED? IF NO PLACE AN X IN BOX B——— B.

SUSPECT #1 NAME (INCLUDE ANY A-K-A- INFO)	SUSPECT #2 (INCLUDE ANY A-K-A INFO)

17. CAN SUSPECT BE LOCATED? IF NO PLACE AN X IN BOX C——— C.

SUSPECT #1 CAN BE LOCATED AT	SUSPECT #2 CAN BE LOCATED AT

18. CAN SUSPECT BE DESCRIBED? IF NO PLACE AN X IN BOX D——— D.

SUSPECT #1 DESCRIPTION   SUSPECT #2 DESCRIPTION

DESCRIBE EACH SUSPECT USING AGE, SEX, RACE, HEIGHT, WEIGHT, ANY IDENTIFYING SCARS, MARKS & CLOTHING DESCRIPTION

ARRESTED ☐YES ☐NO   ARRESTED ☐YES ☐NO

19. CAN SUSPECT BE IDENTIFIED? IF NO PLACE AN X IN BOX E——— E.

USING APPROPRIATE CODES IN THE BOXES PROVIDED, INDICATE WHO CAN IDENTIFY SUSPECT.   20. TIME SUSPECT INFORMATION BROADCAST 20.

21. REGISTRATION INFORMATION	STATE	YEAR	MAKE	MODEL & TYPE	COLOR TOP/BOTTOM	IDENTIFYING CHARACTERISTICS

22. CAN SUSPECT VEHICLE BE IDENTIFIED? IF NO PLACE AN X IN BOX F——— F.

23. TIME SUSPECT VEHICLE INFORMATION BROADCAST. PLACE TIME IN BOX 23 —— 23.

24. IS STOLEN PROPERTY TRACEABLE? IF NO PLACE AN X IN BOX G——— G.

25. DESCRIBE PROPERTY STOLEN / DAMAGED	26. REMOVED FROM	27. PROPERTY IDENTIFICATION INFORMATION	28. PROP. VALUE

29. NATURE OF INJURY	30. TYPE OF INSTRUMENT, WEAPON OR FORCE USED	TOTAL VALUE

31. WHERE HOSPITALIZED	32. ATTENDING PHYSICIAN	33. PRONOUNCING PHYSICIAN/WHERE	34. DATE TIME PRONOUNCED	35. NAME OF MEDICAL EXAMINER

36. IS THERE A SIGNIFICANT M.O. PRESENT? IF YES, DESCRIBE IN NARRATIVE   IF NO PLACE AN X IN BOX H——— H.

37. IS THERE SIGNIFICANT PHYSICAL EVIDENCE PRESENT? IF YES, DESCRIBE IN NARRATIVE. IF NO PLACE AN X IN BOX I——— I.

38. HAS EVIDENCE TECH WORK BEEN PERFORMED? (By:_____) REQUESTED? IF NO PLACE AN X IN BOX J——— J.
TECH WORK PERFORMED / REQUESTED: ☐PHOTO ☐FINGERPRINT ☐COMPOSITE ☐OTHER _____

39. IS THERE REASON TO BELIEVE THAT THE PRELIMINARY INVESTIGATION CANNOT BE COMPLETED AT THIS TIME? IF NO PLACE AN X IN BOX K——— K.

40. CAN CRIME BE SOLVED WITH A REASONABLE AMOUNT OF INVESTIGATIVE EFFORT?   IF NO PLACE AN X IN BOX L——— L.

41. WAS THERE A DEFINITE LIMITED OPPORTUNITY FOR ANYONE EXCEPT THE SUSPECT TO COMMIT THE CRIME? IF NO PLACE AN X IN BOX M——— M.

42. POINT OF CRIME	43. PREMISE DESCRIPTION	44. PROP. INV. #

45. NARRATIVE SUMMARIZE DETAILS OF CRIME INCLUDING PROGRESSION OF EVENTS, NAMES OF OTHER OFFICERS OR UNITS ASSISTING. FOR ANY ADDITIONAL INFORMATION WHICH IS AN EXTENSION OF ANY OF THE ABOVE BLOCKS, INDICATE BLOCK NUMBER AT LEFT.

BLOCK NO.   ASSIST   ASSIST   ASSIST   ASSIST

46. IS ONE OF THE SOLVABILITY FACTORS PRESENT IN THIS REPORT? ☐NO. OFFICE ☐YES, FIELD ☐YES, CLOSED	47. REPORTING OFFICER(S)	ASSIGNED BEAT NO.	51.

48. FIELD SUPERVISORY DECISION ☐OFFICE ☐FIELD ☐CLOSED	REVIEWER	50. CLOSED BY ☐ARREST ☐WARRANT ADVISED

49. IF FIELD, INVESTIGATOR SHOULD FOLLOW-UP SOLVABILITY FACTORS   ☐NO ARREST ☐UNFOUNDED   ☐NO PROSECUTION ☐JUVENILE DIVERSION

Figure 1-2 LETTER TO VICTIMS

**N
E
W**

**L
E
A
D
S**

Police Department	**Civic Center Plaza** **Rochester, New York 14614**

This is a copy of the Police Department's investigation of the incident you reported. Further investigation may be undertaken dependent upon a review of the information it contains, and the analysis of similar incidents which have occurred in Rochester.

You can assist us in our investigation by promptly reporting:

— new information you discover or remember

— added property missing

— property recoverd

— other information, such as serial number or complete descriptions of stolen property.

To report additional information, call 428-7155

**V
I
C
T
I
M
S**

As a crime victim you are entitled to the services of the Victim Assistance Program of the Rochester Police Department. To obtain information about the status of your case and other available services, call 428-6630 or 428-6631 or come into the Victim Service Center on the Plaza level of the City Public Safety Building.

Para obtener información sobre el progreso de su caso y sobre los servicios disponibles por el programa, llame al 428-6630 ópase por la oficina en el nivel "Plaza" del Public Safety Building.

Services include:

1) court procedure information

2) property return assistance

3) aid in filing for New York State Crime Victims Compensation

4) transportation to court

5) referral to financial, legal and counseling services.

**W
A
R
R
A
N
T
S**

If the officer investigating the complaint advised you to obtain a warrant for the suspect's arrest, you may do so by appearing at the City Court Complaint Office, Room 123, Plaza level of the City Public Safety Building between 9 A.M. and 5 P.M., Monday through Friday or 9 A.M. to 12 A.M. on Saturday. Bring this copy of the crime report with you.

Sincerely,

Thomas F. Hastings
Chief of Police

This type of report form incorporates many of the elements found in the legendary mnemonic, PRELIMINARY:

- **P:** Proceed to the scene promptly and safely.
- **R:** Render assistance to the injured.
- **E:** Effect the arrest of the suspect.
- **L:** Locate and identify witnesses.
- **I:** Interview the complainant and the witnesses.
- **M:** Maintain the crime scene and protect the evidence.
- **I:** Interrogate the suspect.
- **N:** Note conditions, events, and remarks.
- **A:** Arrange for the collection of evidence, or collect it at the time.
- **R:** Report the incident fully and accurately.
- **Y:** Yield the responsibility for the investigation to the follow-up investigator.

The questions prescribe a directed search for predetermined solvability factors, and the patrol officer assumes an active rather than passive "report-taking" role in the investigative process by collecting information which may lead directly to the apprehension of a suspect. And, by requiring the type of information which will prove useful later on during the investigation, the form acknowledges that the roles of the detective and the patrol officer are interdependent and inseparable.

Managerial responsibilities under this model include defining the types of crimes which patrol should be responsible for investigating, in addition to defining the exceptions to these types. Some cases are better handled by specialists, and management should recognize which ones are and which can be reasonably left to patrol officers. Management should also be prepared to design an initial investigation form which incorporates the objectives of this model; that is, the questions should be directed and structured in such a way as to result in the officer's virtually not being able to avoid gathering information that will prove helpful during follow-up. Of course, both patrol officers and detectives will have to be trained in the use of this form in order for it to realize its full potential; supervisors may have to be trained as well. The results will be well worth the initial time and effort spent on the training process.

Model C: Patrol Recommendation

Model C takes Model B one step further. Practiced use of a structured report form, like the one shown in Figure 1-1, when prefaced with inservice training and supported by improved communications between patrol officers and detectives, can equip the patrol officer to take on additional responsibilities and authority. Model C suggests that patrol officers also be permitted to recommend that a case be closed immediately or continued through follow-up, basing his recommendations on the findings of the initial investigation which he has conducted.

This heightened responsibility can't be given or expected all at once, however; the management decision of whether or not to give it should be founded on how much training and experience a particular officer has had in performing investigative functions, and how much skill, knowledge, and ability he possesses in predicting the outcomes of certain types of cases. Some cases will have little, if any, probability of a successful solution, while others will have a high probability; being able to recognize the signs and make educated recommendations are skills which come with practice. If an officer has experience in this area and has demonstrated a measure of expertise, there's no reason why he shouldn't be allowed to make recommendations when appropriate and feasible.

Almost all patrol officers who have had a certain degree of experience in the field know that some cases will never be solved. In most departments, an informal process operates that, in effect, closes cases like these; they're simply placed on the bottom of the detectives' caseload, or filed in an active—but suspended—file. Model C suggests that this process, which is already being enacted informally, be formalized. If a trained, capable officer who has followed departmental policies and procedures in conducting a preliminary investigation is permitted to officially recommend that the case in question be closed, the process can be carried out efficiently rather than by default.

It's expected under this model that the patrol officer will have received training in technical investigative procedures so that, if he decides to call for specialists (such as evidence technicians), his decision will be based on the judgment that their services will increase the chances that the case will be solved. Since most agencies have only a limited number of technical personnel, they must be used as efficiently as possible; a trained officer skilled in making appropriate recommendations can help to ensure that technicians won't be called upon unnecessarily.

In this model, then, two factors form the basis for deciding whether or not a case will be assigned for continued investigation or follow-up: the report form, and the patrol officer's recommendation. Other cases may require an evidence technician's report, in addition to supervisory discretion; all of the above determinants should be directly related to the solvability factors established earlier by management. In short, this model helps to eliminate wasted or inefficient investigative effort on the part of agency personnel. It also presupposes the existence of formal administrative controls which focus limited agency resources on those cases which seem most likely to be solved.

Before this model can be put into effect, both patrol officers and their supervisors will need to be trained. How they are trained should depend on the understanding each already possesses of the concept of solvability that has been adopted by the agency as a whole. This will further increase productivity and stress the interdependency of the patrol and detective functions.

Management will also need to clarify policies regarding the recommending and decision-making roles of patrol officers and detectives alike. The establishment of a departmental policy regarding case-screening criterial which has to do with identification of cases which need further investigation and those for which further investigation will not be worthwhile (See Chapter 12), will lessen the possibility of misunderstandings and reduce the need for detectives to repeat complicated investigative actions taken earlier by patrol officers.

Model D: Limited Investigative Role of Patrol

Model D logically extends the role described in Model C, with one refinement: the patrol officer is not only allowed to make recommendations, but is also trained and authorized to make decisions regarding whether or not the investigation of certain cases should be continued beyond the preliminary phase. In all previous models, the investigative role of patrol comes to a close when the preliminary investigative report forms are turned over to the supervisor; in this model, however, the patrol officer has the actual authority to continue and complete the investigations of certain crimes. This authority, of course, is shaped by clearly established departmental policies.

This model recognizes that some types of crimes do not require the assistance or skills of specialists. Not all cases need to be referred for follow-up; to do so is to waste the resources of the department as a whole. When this model is implemented, the detective workload is reduced, and the specialists' skills and abilities are used to their greatest advantage—where they're most needed. In addition, when patrol officers are allowed to conduct and complete investigations under certain conditions, their skills, talents, and abilities improve; thus, the police manager is able to make more educated decisions when career advancement opportunities open up.

In this model, management policy-making focuses on specifying those cases which should be handled by detectives and those which can be handled at the patrol level. Again, both patrol officers and detectives are made conscious of the need to work together.

Model E: Enhanced Investigative Role of Patrol

Model E outlines the most effective utilization of the patrol officer's skills and abilities during the preliminary investigation process. In this model, the patrol officer not only completes a detailed report, but also has the authority to complete the entire investigation and to close the case on scene in those instances in which it seems advisable to do so. Of course, he can also refer other cases for follow-up. Those which require the skills of specialists—such as homicide, rape, and fraud—are referred to detectives, as usual; management is responsible for determining which crime categories the patrol officer is authorized to investigate and make decisions on.

The officer at the scene is required to conduct a prompt and effective investigation of those crimes which local policy has determined can and should be handled at that time. He conducts a comprehensive investigation and makes appropriate use of technical and scientific examinations; he is trained ahead of time in their application. The additional authority and responsibility suggested by this model—where the patrol officer can decide to close a case on scene, or as early as possible—enhances the patrol function and allows for its fullest and most efficient use. Of course, a case-screening system needs to be established ahead of time and understood throughout the department.

This model also requires patrol officers to work very closely with the complainant. During the investigation, both preliminary and follow-up, the patrol officers should maintain regular contact with the complainant in person or by telephone. When this is done complainants tend to react in a positive and supportive manner, and the investigation proceeds even more smoothly.[15]

The Matrix of Roles: A New Definition of the Investigative Role of the Patrol Officer

The definition of the enhanced role of the patrol officer set forth by the matrix overcomes some of the limitations implicit in other descriptions and theories about the investigative role of patrol. It states clearly that the preliminary investigation has a definite and significant goal: to get the facts that will enable the officer to make reasoned decisions about whether or not the investigation is worth continuing. It also states the manner in which that goal is to be realized: by the educated "hunt" for solvability factors that local policy has determined can significantly affect the outcome of criminal cases. In light of this matrix and its models, then, police management has a definite task: to organize the resources of their departments in such a way that the patrol officer receives guidance, support, and direction in conducting the all-important search for solvability factors during the preliminary investigation.

It's necessary to keep in mind, however, precisely what the definition *does* and *does not* state about the role of the patrol officer in the investigative process:

- It *does not* state that patrol officers will be responsible for conducting and completing entire investigations for all types of crimes. It *does* state that patrol officers will be expected to follow agency policies and

- It *does not* state that patrol officers will act entirely on their own when making decisions or determinations about a specific case. It *does* state that they will be able to make certain determinations based on local police policies and procedures. This, of course, includes procedures regarding the supervisory review of decisions or determinations made by the officer in the field.

- It *does not* state that the structure of the agency as a whole or of the individual patrol or detective units must be reorganized, or that police personnel must be deployed in a different way. It *does* state that each employee should be able to make the best use of his skills and abilities.

- It *does not* state that the patrol officer cannot perform services within the investigatory process which aren't included in the definition. It *does*, however, set forth the essential investigative elements of the preliminary investigation process.

As was stated earlier, none of the five models is meant to be considered *the* model that's best for every agency; no such perfect model exists. Similarly, the matrix does not propose to encompass all the possible roles that patrol officers can take during the investigative process; these, too, will vary according to circumstances and departmental regulations and policies. These roles merely represent the ones that are most commonly seen at the present time. It seems obvious, then, that whatever new roles are assigned in the future will not only affect the outcome of criminal investigations, but will also influence the management of the entire investigative process. There is still much room for needed change.

Summary

The role of the criminal investigator—also known as the detective—has long been shrouded in myth and mystery. It's often been seen as a sort of heroic function, and the detective has been viewed as the person who's solely responsible for finding out all of the facts that lead to the successful resolution of a case. The investigative role is not nearly as clear-cut as that misconception indicates, however; instead of being a one-person function, it's most often the combined responsibility of patrol officers and specialists who work together for the duration of the investigation.

A brief look at the history of the criminal investigative role sheds some light on how this misconception came to be. Private investigators, as opposed to governmental or police investigators, sometimes did work alone, and did achieve heroic reputations; in addition, the investigative role often wasn't as clearly defined as it should have been. Today, criminal investigation is both a complex art and a science which calls upon the skills of all types of police personnel and requires them to cooperate and share information; in many instances, the investigative role is one that's carefully defined, and each participant in an investigation is expected to take on certain responsibilities and perform certain duties.

The investigative process itself consists of two distinct phases: the preliminary investigation, and the follow-up investigation. The follow-up is usually intended to complete what the initial phase began; thus, it's of primary importance that each step in the preliminary phase may be completed in a competent and thorough manner. In many agencies, the uniformed patrol officer—who sees a crime being committed, or comes across evidence that a crime has been committed, or is called to the scene of a crime—is responsible for carrying out the initial phase of the investigative process. He must be able to find out certain types of information, based on predetermined solvability factors, that will lead to the successful resolution of a case. This requires specific skills that come with practice and training; management should help this process along not only by furnishing officers with appropriate training, but also by making sure that officers are knowledgeable about using report forms that aid them in the fact-finding process.

Patrol officers are playing increasingly more responsible roles in the investigative process as a whole. They are usually the ones who conduct preliminary investigations, and the information they gather at those times can virtually make or break a case. Precisely how much responsibility they are allowed to take is usually determined by departmental policies and procedures; sometimes, officers will merely gather certain types of information during the preliminary phase and pass it on to their supervisors; at other times, they will be expected to make decisions and determinations regarding the final outcome of a case in question. The detective often relies on the patrol officer for help, and the patrol officer turns to the detective for his expertise; the two can accomplish a great deal more by working together than they can by working alone.

The matrix found in Table 1-2 illustrates the different roles that patrol officers might take during the investigative process. Traditionally, officers have merely filed their reports, and detectives have been expected to complete the follow-up phase based on this information; often, however, this caused many problems because the nature of the report itself dictated the outcome of an investigation, and there was always room for error. More recently, patrol officers have been given greater responsibility during investigations, and this has resulted in increased efficiency, more foreseeable results, and more skilled and competent personnel in general. The goals of police management have also changed; today's effective manager is concerned with seeing that the abilities of all personnel are used to their fullest capacity, and this often means giving patrol officers more say during the investigative process.

In short, it's obvious that the roles of patrol officers and detectives can no longer be viewed as completely separate and distinct. True, each has certain areas of specialization, but each is necessary to the other if investigations are going to be successfully resolved. In the final analysis, however, the greatest weight seems to rest not on the detective but on the patrol officer; how a case is concluded often depends on how effectively he initially documents the events of a crime. No detective, regardless of how brilliant he may be, can solve a crime which has been inefficiently or incorrectly reported.

Questions and Topics for Discussion

1. What was your impression of the detective's role prior to reading this chapter? How has that initial impression changed?

2. Think for a moment about the history of the criminal investigator in this country. How has that history affected the current role of the criminal investigator? How has that role changed, and what has caused it to change? Be sure to consider influential scientific and educational developments.

3. Was the reward system a good one? Why or why not?

4. Why is criminal investigation both an art and a science?

5. Why should the criminal investigation process be considered a *reasoning* process? Name and discuss the two types of reasoning used during an investigation.

6. What are the differences between the preliminary investigation and the follow-up investigation? What are the important steps involved in each?

7. What is the single most important factor which can be seen as determining the outcome of a case? Why is it so important? How can this factor be affected by the patrol officer?

8. Discuss the patrol officer's role in the preliminary investigation.

9. Why should the detective and the patrol officers be considered "partners?" What could happen to the outcome of a criminal investigation if the two refused to cooperate with one another?

10. Discuss the typical approach to defining the patrol officer's role in the investigative process. What are the dangers inherent in this definition?

11. Discuss the other roles suggested by models B through E of the matrix found in Table 1-2. How does each succeeding model enhance the previous one? Mention the important elements of each.

12. Define solvability factors and discuss their importance to the investigative process.

13. Why is the report form important to the criminal investigation as a whole? What are some of the factors which management should consider when compiling such a form?

14. Predict the kinds of investigative responsibilities that patrol officers might be taking in the future.

Footnotes and References

1. Christian P. Potholm and Richard E. Morgan, *Focus on Police: Police in American Society* (Halsted Publishers, 1976), p. 37.

2. Roger Lane, *Policing the City: Boston, 1822-1885* (Cambridge: Harvard University Press, 1967), p. 33.

3. Paul B. Weston and Kenneth Wells, *Criminal Investigation: Basic Perspectives*, 2nd Edition (Prentice-Hall, Englewood Cliffs, New Jersey, 1974), p. 10.

4. James F. Richardson, *The New York Police: Colonial Times to 1901* (Kennikat Press, Port Washington, N.Y., 1970), p. 33.

5. *Ibid.*, p. 111.

6. Andrew Tulley, *Treasury Agent* (Simon and Schuster, 1958), p. 19.

7. Samuel Walker, *Critical History of Police Reform* (Lexington, 1977), p. 23.

8. Donald C. Dilworth, *The Blue and the Brass: American Policing, 1980-1910* (I.A.C.P., Gaithersburg, Md., 1976), p. 26.

9. *Ibid.*, p. 52.

10. John P. Kenney, *Police Administration*, 3rd Rev. Printing (Charles C. Thomas, Publisher, Springfield, Ill., 1975), p. 187.

11. Peter Bloch and Donald Weidman, *Managing Criminal Investigations* (The Urban Institute, Washington, D.C., 1975), p. 1.

12. Peter W. Greenwood and Joan R. Petersilia, *The Criminal Investigation Process, Volume I: Summary and Policy Implications* (The Rand Corporation, R-1776-DOJ, October 1975), p. vii and Chapter 3.

13. Kenney 1975, pp. 7d to 11d.

14. Bloch and Weidman, 1975, p. 24.

15. *Ibid.*, page 31.

Annotated Bibliography

Carte, Gene E. and Elaine H., *Police Reform in the United States*, Berkeley: University of California Press, 1975. Illustrates how professionalism has become the standard for contemporary police reform; analyzes the career and ideas of August Vollmer.

Hahn, Harlan, editor, *Police in Urban Society*, Beverly Hills: Sage Publications, 1970. Twenty social scientists address some of the basic questions concerning the police and society. Includes a review of the growth of police problems.

Hormachea, Carroll, *Sourcebook in Criminalistics*, Reston, Virginia: Reston Publishing Company, 1974. A compilation of material concerning the gathering, study, interpretation, and evaluation of criminal evidence *via* conventional and modern technological methods.

Huston, Luther A., *The Department of Justice*, New York: Frederick A. Praeger, Publisher, 1967. A brief historical sketch of the Department of Justice.

Parker, Alfred E., *The Berkeley Police Story*, Springfield, Illinois: Charles C. Thomas, Publisher, 1972. A definitive story of the Berkeley police department; describes many of its "firsts" in the areas of police procedures and equipment, and discusses the scientific methods utilized by that department in the apprehension of criminals.

Potholm, Christian P. and Richard E. Morgan, *Focus on Police: Police in American Society*, New York: Schenkman Publishing Company, Inc., 1976. An anthology focusing on the current crises and conflicts of day-to-day police work. Includes a brief history of law enforcement.

Richardson, James F., *Urban Police in the United States*, Port Washington, New York: Kennikat Press, 1974. Examines the police officer both as an individual and as part of a community institution.

Saferstein, Richard, *Criminalistics: An Introduction to Forensic Science*, Englewood Cliffs, New Jersey: Prentice-Hall, Inc., 1977. A basic overview of forensic science. Reviews techniques and practices; includes documented case studies and examples, along with a short history of the development of forensic science.

TWO

Legal Aspects of the Criminal Investigation

Chapter Objectives

After reading this chapter, the student should be able to:

☑ Explain how constitutional law and the laws of criminal procedure and evidence influence a criminal investigation.

☑ Explain why evidence is important in a criminal prosecution and explain an investigator's role in such a prosecution.

☑ List the types of evidence an investigator encounters.

☑ Explain the importance of evidentiary rules.

☑ Define "admissibility" and explain its importance.

☑ Define "quantum of evidence" and list the various levels of evidence needed in different stages of criminal prosecution.

☑ Describe an investigator's relationships with both suspects and witnesses.

☑ Describe the factors necessary for a legal arrest.

☑ Explain why cooperative relationships are necessary within the criminal justice system.

☑ Describe the qualities a good investigator has.

The Investigator's Role: A Delicate Balance

The criminal investigator plays a crucial part in the administration of criminal justice. Whether or not a prosecution is successful often depends on how thorough an investigator is when collecting facts and information. Thoroughness isn't the only criterion, however; the investigator must also walk a fine line between what's legal and what isn't, both when developing and seizing evidence and when preparing it for use during a prosecution.

Many legal limitations and guidelines exist which help an investigator to know precisely what he can and can't do during an investigation. The competent investigator, then, will have a working knowlege of these limitations and guidelines. For example, the law defines what types of evidence are admissible and what types aren't, in addition to stating how evidence can and can't be presented. A lack of familiarity with these definitions—or an unwillingness to go along with them—can lead to unneccessary complications and cause problems later on.

The investigator must also realize the boundaries of his role. Basically, the investigator is a gatherer of facts; he is *never* judge, jury, prosecutor, and/or accuser, and should never presume to be. He is responsible for providing the legal evidence necessary to prove or disprove some element of a case; his opinions or personal feelings must not be permitted to come into play.

As was emphasized in Chapter One, the investigator isn't a loner, and a successful investigation isn't the result of only one person's efforts. Instead, many different people and agencies—federal, state, and local—are often involved in an investigation, and they must be willing to work together. The investigator should be aware of and understand the rights and responsibilities of others involved in a case and see to it that information is passed on to appropriate persons and offices.

Thus, the investigator's role is a fact-finding one defined by a number of legal considerations. He should know the law, know the limitations of his role, and always be conscious of the delicate balance between what the law requires and what the law allows.

Evidence: The Tools of the Prosecution

A criminal trial is a formal hearing which seeks to determine whether or not a defendant has in fact committed the crime of which he has been accused. No trial can proceed without the known existence of evidence, or something which proves or tends to prove the state's allegations, or claims of the defendant's guilt. Since the criminal investigator is often the one who's responsible for collecting and organizing evidence, he must be aware of both what it is and how it can be gathered and used. And, since evidence is the key to a successful prosecution, the investigator must be willing to devote careful, time-consuming effort to it.

There are many different types of evidence; these will be discussed below. In addition, there are many different types of evidentiary rules which serve as guidelines for the criminal investigator all the way from the beginnings of an investigation to the conclusion of the trial. Collecting, preserving, and presenting evidence are steps which involve many legal complexities and intricacies of which the investigator must be fully aware. Since one of the overriding concerns of the criminal justice system is to protect citizens' individual rights—including those of the defendant—it's crucial that all steps are taken in ways that are both legally and technically sound.

The Corpus Delicti

The *corpus delicti*—literally, "the body of the crime" or "the elements of the crime"—has to be proved to exist before the criminal justice system can be set in motion. Not even a defendant's admission or confession is enough to establish the fact of a corpus delicti; independent evidence that proves that a crime has been committed must also be present. (This evidentiary rule indicates the courts' distrust of voluntary confessions and protects both the legal system and private individuals from the dangers of false confessions.)

Admissibility: The Bottom Line

It's often been said that the purpose of a trial, criminal or otherwise, is to find out the truth of the matter. While much evidence may in fact be *true*, however, it may not be considered *admissible* . In other words, all evidence is virtually useless unless it can be admitted into the court proceedings for consideration by the trier of fact.

Whether or not an item of evidence will be judged admissible depends on many factors. First of all, it must have been *legally obtained*, with proper regard for the constitutional rights of the defendant. Any evidence that isn't legally obtained won't be admitted. For example, if an officer takes a bag of heroin from a person without there having been *probable cause*—or reasonable grounds—to search the person and seize the drug, the heroin won't be admitted as evidence because the seizure was illegal.

An item of evidence must also be judged *material, relevant, important* and *competent* before it can be considered admissible.

Materiality

The terms *relevant* and *material* are often used interchangeably, but used precisely there is a difference. *Materiality* refers to whether the evidence offered relates to a legal question that is at issue in the case. In deciding whether a piece of evidence is material, the question is "Does the evidence relate to a point of law necessary to a decision in the case?" For example, in a trial on a charge of negligent homicide, evidence of the defendant's intent would be immaterial since intent is not one of the elements necessary to prove the case. It makes no difference—it is *immaterial*—whether the defendant intended to commit the homicide or not. Evidence tending to prove that the defendant was careless would, on the other hand be material.

Relevancy

Assuming that a piece of evidence is material, the next question to ask is whether the evidence is *relevant*. The test of relevancy is whether the evidence does indeed tend to prove the proposition that it is offered to prove. If it does not, it is irrelevant. For example, evidence showing that the defendant was careless on a previous occasion would be material to the case in the above example since it speaks to the question of his negligence. It would not, however, be relevant since evidence of negligence on a prior occasion does not tend to prove that the defendant was negligent at the time the homicide was committed.

Importance

Even though evidence is relevant, it may still be excluded. A judge has the discretion to exclude evidence if it is not of sufficient importance. Evidence may take an undue amount of time to present. It may create a side issue that will distract the jury. A judge must balance factors such as these against the *importance* of a piece of evidence to decide whether it should be admitted.

Competency

Even though a piece of evidence is material and relevant, it may still be excluded because it may be *incompetent*. Simply put, evidence is competent if it does not violate one of many exclusionary rules. Exclusionary rules are designed to either insure the reliability or truthfulness of evidence or preserve social interests that the courts consider of overriding importance. For example, the hearsay rule and the best evidence rules are designed to insure truthfulness. The rule against an individual testifying against his spouse is an example of an exlusionary rule designed to protect a social interest.

Again, any evidence which is collected illegally, or without proper regard for the rights of the defendant, is inadmissible. Even if the person mentioned earlier were caught red-handed with heroin in his possession, this very relevant fact wouldn't be admitted for consideration if the substance was seized illegally. If, in this instance, the entire case was based on the need to prove the person guilty of possessing the drug, the prosecution's chances of success would be very slim indeed.

A criminal investigator will find it helpful to keep one question in mind during the entire investigative process: Will a particular item of evidence help to establish the specific proposition of a case at which it's directed? If it does—and if it's been collected in a legally acceptable way—then it will normally be considered relevant and admissible. The judge is the one who makes the final decision, however.

Evidence which may be inadmissible when attempting to prove one point of a case may very well be admissible when trying to prove another. For example, if a defendant is being tried for committing a specific crime, the prosecutor won't be allowed to prove that he also committed a *different* crime unless that proof can help to establish a motive or intent for committing the crime in question.

The circumstances of a particular case will also determine what types of evidence will be considered and what types won't. For example, in homicide cases the victim's character is usually considered *immaterial*. If the defendant claims that he killed the victim in self-defense, however, he may be permitted to discuss the victim's character in an attempt to throw some light on the situation.

Evidence: A Catalogue of Types

Direct and Indirect Evidence

Most evidence falls within one of two categories: *direct*, or *indirect*. (Indirect evidence is also called *circumstantial* evidence.) Direct evidence is a fact which proves the issue at hand without being open to inferences. For example, in a murder case, if a witness testifies that he saw the defendant shoot the victim, the testimony is direct evidence. If the witness testifies that he heard a shot and then saw the defendant leaving the scene with a gun in his hand, the testimony is indirect evidence that the defendant committed the murder. The inference is that the defendant did the shooting.

While circumstantial evidence doesn't directly prove the accuracy of a certain fact, it does give rise to a *logical inference* that the fact exists or is true. The admissibility of this type of evidence is based on the recognition that human beings tend to draw conclusions from certain sets or series of conditions which are obviously related or connected in some way. For example, if a crime has been committed, and if an investigator finds a shoe impression at the scene, and if the impression fits that of a shoe owned by a suspect, then it can be logically inferred that the suspect was at the scene.

In criminal cases, which are complex, intricate fact situations often require the trier of fact to draw conclusions. Indirect or circumstantial evidence plays an important role.

Testimonial Evidence

Testimonial evidence is evidence which is given orally or by a witness. It's offered in an attempt to persuade the trier of fact that a specific proposition at which the testimony is directed is either true or false.

Documentary Evidence

In contrast to testimonial evidence, documentary evidence is never oral but rather written or permanently recorded in some other way. Documentary evidence can include anything from handwritten materials to typewritten, printed, photographed, and photostatted items, among others. Even a piece of wood with initials carved into it would be considered as documentary evidence, as would a photograph of it.

Real Evidence

Real evidence, also called *physical* evidence, consists of those objects or things which are related to a case and which can be perceived and recognized by the senses.

The criminal investigator most often becomes involved with real evidence at the scene of a crime. In addition to recording and taking notes of the physical appearance of the scene, he is also responsible for looking for and picking up articles and traces of articles believed to have been left at the scene by the person or persons who committed the crime. Of course, the investigator also searches for anything which may have been used to commit the offense.

Real evidence can include photographs and sketches of the crime scene; in some cases, the jury is taken directly to the scene and permitted to view it in person. Other common types of real evidence include weapons, tools, bullets, cartridge casings, powder burns, markings, and bullet holes. Some types of circumstantial, or indirect, evidence which tends to connect a defendant to a crime may also be considered as real evidence, such as fingerprints, footprints, clothing, tire marks, bloodstains, wood particles, glass, metals, dust, dirt, body fluids, hair, skin, and the like.

In order to be admissible, real evidence must be accompanied by testimonial evidence. Material or physical objects don't in and of themselves prove anything; their relevancy must be established by a witness. A witness must show that the evidence is connected to the crime.

Before an item of real evidence can be admitted for consideration during a trial, a *foundation*—also called a *predicate*—for admitting it must be laid.

Basically, a foundation gives credibility to an item of real evidence and establishes its connection to the case. As a minimum, a foundation must set forth the following:

- that the evidence is in some way connected with the crime;
- that the evidence is in some way connected with the defendant;
- that the evidence offered is the same as that to which the testimony refers; and
- that the evidence is in the same or substantially the same condition as it was when it was first discovered. If it isn't, any changes which have occurred or been made must be satisfactorily explained to the trier of fact.

According to the above criteria, then, the fact that a piece of evidence is real doesn't necessarily mean that it will also be admissible. For example, if a person has been murdered, physical objects which could have been used to commit the murder and which were found in the defendant's possession shortly after the crime was committed are usually accepted as evidence. Instruments which could have been used to commit a *different* type of crime are *not* admitted, however. In other words, if a person was stabbed to death and the defendant was found possessing both a knife *and* a gun, the knife would be admissible as real evidence while the gun wouldn't be. The fact that a specific type of weapon was found on a defendant isn't considered relevant or admissible unless that type of weapon was used to commit the crime.

Photographs

Photographs are frequently used as evidence during criminal trials. Although they are usually considered to be secondary rather than primary evidence, when correctly used they can be a powerful tool in the investigator's—and prosecutor's—hands.

Basically, a photograph is admissible if it correctly portrays the scene or object under legal scrutiny; the testimony of a witness is necessary to prove that it does. Again, a foundation must be laid before this type of evidence can be admitted; testimonial evidence on the part of a witness can accomplish this. The witness can either be the person who actually took the photograph, or someone who can vouch for its accuracy.

There is no specific legal requirement or stipulation as to when a photograph can or should be taken, just as long as it correctly portrays the object or scene and is considered relevant to the case.

Photographs of crime victims are commonly admitted as evidence; when they're very gruesome, however, or when their only real value is to emotionally sway the jury, they are usually *not* admitted. They are excluded because they are *prejudicial*. Posed photographs, which are usually intended to show how a crime was committed or what a crime scene looked like, are sometimes used in the absence of photographs taken at the time; they are usually *not* admissible, however, unless they can be shown to be identical to the way things really were.

The criminal investigator must keep in mind that the mere existence of a photograph doesn't constitute evidence; it must be verified by a witness, and it must be relevant.

Films or Movies

Motion pictures, with or without sound recordings made at the same time, are usually considered to be accurate portrayals of actual occurrences. During a trial, they are treated much as photographs are; in other words, the testimony of a witness is necessary before they will be considered admissible, and care must be exercised both during the filming itself and when presenting the film as evidence. The courts are especially cautious about this sort of thing, since films may give juries false or biased impressions of what really happened.

Sound Recordings

Sound recordings, usually in the form of tape recordings, are common types of real evidence. They are also among the most controversial types of evidence known, and three legal issues are often raised around them.

The first concerns the technical process by which the recording was made; the second concerns the conversation which was recorded; and the third has to do with the legality of the process as a whole. In other words, *how* something was recorded, *who* and *what* were recorded, and *whether* a recording was a legally proper step to take are all matters of great concern to the investigator and the courts alike.

The first issue—how the recording was made—involves the technical process used to make the recording and the people and instruments which played parts in that process. Before a recording can even be considered to be admissible, it must first be established that the equipment used was capable of recording the conversation under question. How far away the equipment was from the scene of the conversation, and how capable it was of faithfully and accurately recording the voices (are the voices recognizable on the tape, or aren't they?) are questions which are frequently raised to challenge the admissibility of a recording. The competence of the operator, or the person who made the recording, may also be disputed. (Can he or she vouch for the completeness and authenticity of the recording by testifying that it hasn't been spliced or otherwise tampered with?) An experienced operator will usually place some type of identifying marks on the tape itself; otherwise, he may not be able to answer questions like this one to the court's satisfaction, and a seemingly crucial recording will not be admitted as evidence.

The second issue—which concerns who was recorded and what was said during the recorded conversation—requires that the speakers be identifiable. This is easy enough when one of the voices is that of a police officer or some other witness for the prosecution, or when the operator can testify to the time and place of the conversation. In instances in which the operator is *not* familiar with the voices on the tape, the testimony of witnesses familiar with the participants in the conversation may have to be introduced. Regardless of how carefully a recording is made and how positive identification of the voices may be, though, it still may be declared inadmissible. For example, the defense may object to the introduction of a recording as evidence if it can prove that certain parts of the conversation in question are irrelevant to the case.

The third issue—which concerns the legality of the recording—is the most touchy of the three, and the most difficult to define or establish criteria for. The newly emerging standards of the search and seizure mandates of the Fourth Amendment make it difficult for an investigator to know precisely when and under what circumstances a recording will be considered legal and admissible. The right to privacy means that a warrant is necessary before a conversation can be "seized," or recorded, and such a warrant will usually be issued only if reasonable cause exists to believe that an incriminating conversation will take place between specific persons within a specific time period. At the federal level, for example, a warrant of this nature won't be issued until the United States Attorney General approves it, and a Federal District Judge will then have to decide when the warrant should be issued. Obviously, this requires the investigator to wade through a lot of red tape; even when a recording is obtained with the utmost caution and under strictly legal circumstances, however, it still may not be admitted as evidence, depending on the discretion of the court.

When one party to a conversation agrees to cooperate with the police and allow the conversation to be recorded, the recording can be made without the investigator having to first obtain a warrant, according to most states and federal law. The reasonable right to privacy doesn't apply to situations where one party to the conversation consents to the recording.

Before either recording a conversation or assigning an operator to do it, then, the investigator must carefully check the statutes of his own state, and federal statutes where applicable; they do differ, and a mistake in this area can have grave consequences.

Maps, Charts, Diagrams, and Models

Occasionally, a criminal investigator is required—or finds it helpful—to prepare maps, models, or the like in connection with an investigation. These are admissible only when properly authenticated, either by the person who made them or by a witness who can prove that he or she had knowledge of their authenticity.

Witnesses often use diagrams or models to convey their perceptions of an event; these can be made either inside or outside of a court. Often, they can serve to clarify testimony and highlight specific points.

Because these kinds of tools are often very useful to an understanding of the evidence related to a case, they are routinely admitted, at the discretion of the court.

Experiments

Experiments may also be used during a criminal investigation or in court to prove a specific point. The question most often raised when proposing that an experiment be conducted is: Will it actually aid the trier of fact in making a decision, or will it be so time-consuming as to be virtually worthless and a nuisance besides?

The investigator who wishes to use an experiment must make absolutely certain that close similarities exist between the relevant fact he is trying to prove and the experiment itself. Where little or no similarity can be established, neither the evidence of an out-of-court experiment nor the use of an in-court one will be admissible. The judge has a great deal of discretion in deciding the admissibility of such experiments.

Corroborative Evidence

To corroborate means to strengthen, add weight or credibility to, or confirm. Thus, corroborative evidence is that which supplements some other type of evidence while at the same time strengthening it.

While the testimony of a single witness is generally sufficient to convict or acquit the defendant in most criminal cases, there are some crimes or situations which require more than one testimony. These include, among others, the crimes of perjury, treason, and solicitation. In these instances, the investigator must furnish additional evidence that tends to support the testimony given by the original witness.

There is a major qualification to this standard, however. Called the *accomplice corroboration rule*, it's an important one for the investigator to be aware of when seeking testimony. An *accomplice* is a person who works with another to commit a crime, and can be tried as a co-defendant for that crime; frequently, the testimony of an accomplice is sought to aid the prosecution in convicting a defendant. Generally, the accomplice corroboration rule states that the uncorroborated testimony of an accomplice is insufficient to convict a defendant; this testimony must also be supplemented by other evidence that tends to connect the defendant with the crime.

If the testimony of an accomplice is used to effect the arrest of a suspect—or as a basis for legally detaining him following a preliminary hearing—the investigator must be sure that probable cause exists to make that arrest, or problems may result. Frequently, state laws prohibit this type of arrest unless corroborative testimony from someone other than one accomplice is also obtained. In other words, the testimony of one accomplice is never sufficient to corroborate that of another.

In establishing the fact that a crime has been committed, a defendant's confession alone is not enough. Again, corroborative evidence—in particular, a *corpus delicti*—must exist before the defendant can be proved guilty.

While there are many sources of corroborative evidence, circumstantial evidence is the most common. It doesn't make any difference, though, whether corroborative evidence is circumstantial or direct; it must simply connect the defendant with the crime.

The Quantum of Evidence: A Measure of Importance

How much evidence is required at different stages in a criminal case depends on the case itself. There are several legal concepts which affect the amount of evidence required in criminal cases, however; these include *proof beyond a reasonable doubt, clear and convincing evidence, a preponderance of evidence, prima facie evidence, probable cause,* and *reasonable suspicion.* Each of these will be discussed in detail below. The relative significance of each is illustrated by the chart found in Figure 2-1.

Proof Beyond a Reasonable Doubt

In most criminal cases, the prosecution must prove a defendant guilty by presenting evidence which establishes his guilt beyond a reasonable doubt. This, of course, puts the *burden of proof* on the state; it must produce enough evidence to convince the trier of fact that, within a degree of moral certainty, the defendant is guilty. This does *not* mean, however, that the evidence must prove the defendant absolutely guilty, or guilty beyond any question at all; if this were the case, it would be nearly impossible to convict anyone of anything.

Reasonable doubt simply means that, even after hearing all of the evidence and having had time to consider and compare it, the trier of fact is still *not* convinced, or morally certain, that the defendant is guilty. Thus, the evidence presented must be sufficient to take the trier of fact *beyond* this frame of mind—beyond a reasonable doubt, in other words—before a guilty verdict can be reached. The defendant never has to prove his or her own *innocence* beyond a reasonable doubt, of course; the *presumption of innocence* states that a person is innocent until proved guilty. He is only required to furnish evidence which contradicts that presented by the prosecutor and raises a reasonable doubt in the mind of the trier of fact.

The reasonable doubt doctrine, then, is closely tied to the presumption of innocence. The prosecutor must overcome this presumption of innocence by assuming the burden of proof and gathering enough evidence to establish the defendant's guilt. The criminal investigator plays an important role in this process, since he is the one who's responsible for collecting and developing the types of evidence that will be convincing in a court.

Figure 2-1.
Quantum of Evidence

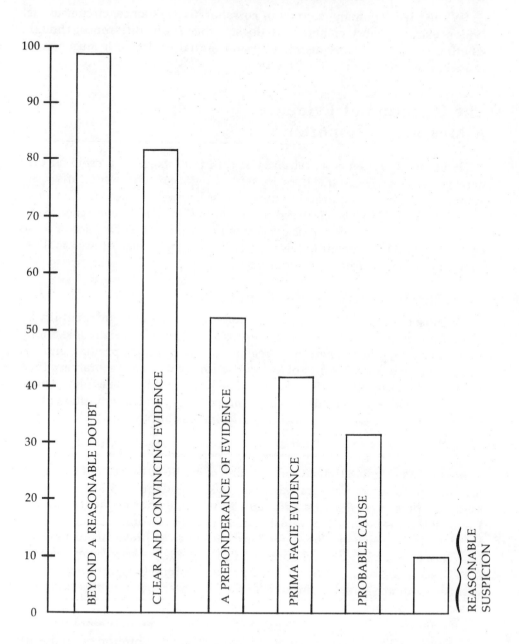

Whether the outcome of a trial is decided by a jury or a single judge, the investigator must be acutely aware of the total impact that the evidence he collects will have on his audience. True, the prosecutor will try to be as persuasive as possible when presenting his arguments, but the real determinant of the outcome of a criminal case will always be the quality and quantity of evidence gathered by the investigator.

Clear and Convincing Evidence and A Preponderance of Evidence

Since these two concepts are closely related, it will be helpful to view them together.

In order for a trier of fact to be convinced of something—for example, a certain fact of a crime under consideration—he must be made to feel that the existence of that fact is more probable than not. In other words, if it were possible to weigh the evidence in a case on a scale, at least fifty-one percent of it—a *preponderance*—would have to be convincing.

In some jurisdictions, substantially more certainty may be required than a mere preponderance of evidence; to put it in another way, *clear and convincing evidence*—or evidence that's about eighty percent convincing—would be necessary. Basically, the existence of clear and convincing evidence will produce in the mind of the trier of fact a firm or strong belief that what the prosecution is trying to prove is in fact true. (Both a preponderance of evidence and clear and convincing evidence are less than the quantity of evidence required for proof beyond a reasonable doubt, however, as is clear from Figure 2-1.)

Prima Facie Evidence

Prima face evidence—literally, "first appearance" or "first impression" evidence—is sufficient to raise a presumption of fact (that is, one fact that can be inferred from the proved existence of another) or establish some fact in question if it hasn't already been *rebutted*, or refuted. In other words, an item of this kind of evidence may stand on its own merits without explanation if it isn't contradicted. For example, an account book which on face value indicates that certain goods were sold illegally may be considered prima facie evidence, provided that the sale can be proved to have taken place and evidence isn't introduced to prove otherwise.

Reasonable Suspicion

The reasonable suspicion concept is of special importance to the police officer. As a general rule, an officer has the right and duty when carrying out his police responsibilities to maintain the peace, prevent crime, apprehend criminals, and make reasonable investigations of all suspicious activities, even though these activities may not seem to justify an arrest or thorough search. For example, the courts have consistently held that there's nothing unreasonable about an officer stopping a person and questioning him, or seeking out interviews with possible suspects or witnesses, or calling on people in their homes when there seem to be good reasons for doing so. The officer's responsibilities are limited by people's rights as guaranteed by the Constitution, however; an officer may not demand that a suspect open his door or force his way into a suspect's home (without a warrant, that is).

Evidentiary Rules:
A Help or a Hindrance?

Evidentiary rules have been developed over the centuries for two major reasons: first, to protect the individual (who is, of course, presumed innocent until proved guilty) and, second, to ensure that the trier of fact—either the jury or judge—will only be presented with those kinds of evidence which are both reliable and trustworthy. Not only is the individual protected, then, but the court is, too; it doesn't have to spend valuable time, effort, and resources in considering evidence which doesn't really have anything to do with the case at hand. Thus, the effective criminal investigator always keeps in mind the procedural and constitutionally mandated rules which affect his role.

The law enforcement officer who is assigned to investigate a criminal case for the first time in his career may well be confused about what evidence really *is*. The definition of evidence is very broad—basically, evidence can include anything that may help to convince a trier of fact of the guilt or innocence of the accused—but the officer must be careful not to be fooled by the generosity of this definition. *Evidence is not proof;* the violation of some evidentiary rule can mean that a perfectly obvious piece of evidence, or a particularly incriminating one, can't be used.

The investigator must also exercise caution in another sense. As was pointed out earlier, he is never judge, jury, prosecutor, and/or defense, but merely a gatherer of facts. This may mean that he spends the greater part of his time seeking out evidence to prove only one seemingly minor fact of a criminal case. The investigator who gets carried away and imagines himself as some sort of supersleuth may miss the point of an investigation entirely. An apparently inconsequential or unimportant piece of evidence can turn a case around; the investigator must never let himself forget this.

Although it's an often-heard complaint that the evidentiary rules work *only* on behalf of the defendant and often stand in the way of the legal process, the opposite is in fact true. The rules have been established primarily because of the existence of the jury system. Since the jury is frequently responsible for deciding the innocence or guilt of a defendant, the facts presented to it must be sifted so that only those which have a direct and genuine bearing on the issue will be presented. Otherwise, the jury may receive a distorted or inaccurate picture of what really occurred and reach conclusions that can't be legally justified—and the entire investigative effort, from its beginnings through the trial itself, will have been in vain.

Suspects and Witnesses: The Human Factors

Except in cases where the corpus delicti is literally a body, a large amount of the evidence collected by the investigator will consist of things, such as objects collected from the crime scene, tools or weapons used to commit the crime, photographs of the scene, recordings, and so on. Every crime has its perpetrator, however, and every trial its witnesses; thus, the investigator must know how to work with people, too.

There are laws which determine how a suspect should be identified and, if necessary, arrested. How a witness should be treated isn't defined by law as much as it is by other considerations, however. Most prosecutions depend on testimonial evidence; what a witness says and how he says it can often make the difference between a solved case and unsolved one.

Identifying the Perpetrator

The criminal investigator often spends a great deal of time and effort in simply making sure that the defendant can be identified in court as the perpetrator of the crime under investigation. Most often, the investigator must seek the testimony of witnesses for identification purposes.

There are many legal rules which are helpful during this stage of the criminal justice process. For example, it isn't necessary to make a *positive* identification of the perpetrator; courts routinely accept the testimony of witnesses that a defendant *resembles* the perpetrator. Sometimes, when a witness testifies that he *isn't* absolutely sure that the defendant is the perpetrator, but *is* certain to the best of his knowledge, this is suffcient to sustain an identification. It isn't always necessary that the witness see the perpetrator's face, either; he may later identify the defendant's voice as that of the perpetrator, or compare the defendant's walk, size, and/or general appearance with those of the perpetrator, or point out unique characteristics or marks (such as tattoos, scars, and the like).

How a witness identifies a defendant is usually considered immaterial; it's generally sufficient if he points to the defendant as the perpetrator, or nods his head when asked if the defendant was at the crime scene.

Extrajudicial Identification. *Extrajudicial identification* is an identification which takes place out of court, and is admissible only to corroborate an identification of the defendant made in court. This type of identification may, for example, be made at the crime scene. If the defendant is *not* also identified in court as the perpetrator, however, this kind of extrajudicial identification must be corroborated by other evidence. A witness may also identify a defendant as the perpetrator by viewing photographs or picking the defendant out of a line-up or show-up.

The Line Up. There are basic rules which govern the line-up, and the criminal investigator must be very familiar with them. Although there's nothing unconstitutional about compelling a person to appear in a line-up, certain safeguards against unfairness during that procedure have been mandated by the Supreme Court.

For example, the defendant has the *right to counsel*, or the right to have his attorney present, during a *post-indictment line-up* (that is, one that takes place *after* the defendant has been formally charged with some crime). This right protects the defendant from procedures which might prove unfair or unduly suggestive.

A suspect does *not* have the right to counsel prior to an indictment or some other formal charge, however. Similarly, a defendant's photograph may be shown to a witness without the defendant's attorney being present; this can occur even *after* he or she has been indicted or charged.

Arresting the Suspect

The criminal ivestigator may be called upon to arrest a suspect at some point during the investigative process, especially if the suspect wasn't arrested at the crime scene. He must be very careful when taking this step, since an illegal arrest can result in the courts excluding important evidence from the trial.

Basically, an arrest is defined as the taking of a person into custody in order that he may be held to answer for the commission of a crime. An arrest should never be made unless *probable cause* exists to make it, however.

Probable Cause. Probable cause is defined as the showing that *reasonable grounds* exist to make an arrest. It requires more than the presence of mere suspicion or rumors, but it does *not* require the same quantity or quality of evidence needed to prove guilt during a trial.

The information which serves as the basis for probable cause must be current. For example, it may be supplied by an informant if that informant is known to the officer and if the officer believes that he is trustworthy and reliable. An officer may never arrest a suspect while acting in "good faith" that probable cause exists—especially if it turns out later that the arrest was made illegally. An officer can never arrest a person on suspicion alone and then interrogate him to gain enough evidence to justify the arrest, nor can the police arrest a group of people and then interrogate them all at the station-house to determine who should be charged with the crime in question.

The facts and circumstances of each case must be examined before the officer can decide whether probable cause exists to arrest a suspect. The following factors are usually considered useful when making this decision:

- the suspect flees upon seeing the police;
- the suspect acts in a furtive way upon seeing the police;
- the suspect refuses to answer a few preliminary questions, or gives evasive answers;
- the suspect makes a voluntary admission of guilt;
- the suspect is found in a place where it's generally known that vice activities occur;
- the suspect is found in an area where several crimes have recently been committed;
- the suspect associates with others whom the police have the authority to arrest;
- the police receive information from a reliable informant which seems to connect the suspect with a crime;
- the police receive information from a police broadcast which seems to connect the suspect with the crime;
- the suspect fits the description of a person who's committed a crime;
- the suspect is driving what officers reasonably believe to be a stolen vehicle;
- the suspect is driving a vehicle which fits the description of one used in a recent crime;
- the suspect is seen carrying the "fruits" of a recent crime—he is wearing stolen jewelry, for example.

In short, then, probable cause to arrest exists when the facts and circumstances known to the officer are sufficient in themselves to warrant *a person of reasonable caution* to believe that an offense has been or is being committed. It isn't necessary that the arrested person be found guilty later, nor is it necessary that he be found carrying incriminating materials.

The Use of Force. Sometimes, a person who's being arrested will accompany the officer quietly; at other times, however, it may be necessary for the officer to use force to effect the arrest.

How much force should be used in these circumstances is more or less left to the officer's discretion, but he must be very careful not to subject an arrested person to greater restraint than is *necessary and proper*. If a person who's being arrested either flees or forcibly resists arrest, for example, the officer may use whatever means are necessary and proper to restrain him.

An officer may ask private citizens to aid him in making an arrest, and it's generally considered a crime if they refuse.

Warrants. Generally, it doesn't make much difference whether or not an officer has a warrant to make an arrest if probable cause exists; a warrant helps, though, since it gives the officer the benefit of a judicial decision that probable cause exists.

Arrest statutues usually state that either a private person or a police officer may arrest someone without a warrant under the following circumstances:

- if a crime is being committed or attempted in his presence;
- if an individual has in fact committed a felony though not in the officer's presence;
- if a felony in fact has been committed and there's probable cause to believe that the suspect has committed it.

An officer's arrest power is, of course, much broader than that of the private citizen because the officer can make a felony arrest based on probable cause, but the private citizen is restricted to making an arrest on probable cause where in fact a felony has been committed.

Each state has various technical rules which govern when and how warrants can be issued. The basic guideline for these rules is found in the Fourth Amendment to the United States Constitution:

> The right of the people to be secure in their persons, houses, papers, and effects, against unreasonable searches and seizures, shall not be violated, and no Warrants shall issue, but upon probable cause, supported by Oath or affirmation, and particularly describing the place to be searched, and the persons or things to be seized.

In other words, the issuance of a warrant must be based on probable cause. A warrant is usually issued after a *complaint* has been made, or an *affidavit* has been written in support of the warrant; this complaint or affidavit must support the existence of probable cause that an offense has been committed and that the suspect is the one who committed it.

A warrant must be signed by designated judicial officers. It must contain the name of the defendant or, if his name is unknown, any name or description which can identify him with reasonable certainty. As a general rule, there is no automatic expiration date for an arrest warrant, nor does the suspect have the constitutional right to be arrested promptly. The arresting officer must give a copy of the complaint and the warrant to the arrested person as soon as possible; a lawful arrest doesn't become an unlawful arrest, however, if the suspect isn't given his copies at the time of the arrest.

Witnesses

The criminal investigator must be willing to devote a great deal of time and attention to witnesses or potential witnesses. From eighty to ninety percent of all court evidence is testimonial; in other words, witnesses are the keys to most successful prosecutions.

The investigator must never forget that the witness is a human being who may be very inconvenienced by the whole matter. In addition, a witness may suffer adverse effects during the investigative process; it's often a lengthy and uncomfortable one. Thus, the investigator should be careful to:

- keep the witness informed of the progress being made in the case;
- keep from unnecessarily inconveniencing the witness;
- make sure that several other investigators aren't interviewing the same witness to secure the same information (this wastes everybody's time);
- inform the witness of the outcome of the case;
- thank the witness for his time and cooperation;
- make sure that the witness is promptly compensated for any expenses he has incurred or any fees he has charged.

The investigator must also be very selective when choosing people to serve as witnesses. There are evidentiary rules which aid him in this task. For instance, a witness must meet specific qualifications before he can give testimony that will be considered admissible in court. He must also be proved to be *competent*.

The investigator should ask himself the following questions (among others; they will vary) before deciding whether or not to use a witness:

- Is the person old enough to testify?
- Does he have any mental problems that might interfere with the validity of the testimony.
- Does he have any difficulty with the language?
- Does the person understand the difference between truth and falsehood? If so, does he realize his obligation to tell the truth on the witness stand?
- Does he have the ability to observe something, recall it, and communicate it?
- Is there some legal reason why the witness can't testify? (For example, is he the defendant's spouse, or priest, or attorney?)

Usually, a person will qualify to be a witness as long as he understands the obligation to tell the truth and is capable of expressing it clearly. In most jurisdictions today, age is a factor only when it can be seen as preventing a witness from preceiving, recollecting, and reporting an incident, understanding his duty to tell the truth, and expressing himself in a way that can be understood by the court.

Usually, a person with a prior felony conviction is not considered to be an incompetent witness simply because of that conviction. Some states, however, disqualify potential witnesses who have been convicted for crimes involving moral turpitude, perjury, and the like.

At common law, husband and wife were disqualified from testifying for or against each other in both civil and criminal cases. Today, husband and wife may testify both for and against each other in civil cases in most jurisdictions. In criminal cases, the husband or wife may testify for the spouse. However, it is generally provided that husband or wife cannot testify *against* their spouse without the consent of the defendant spouse.

(This is not true in all jurisdictions. In some, the spouse may testify despite any objection by the defense. In others, the witnessing spouse may take the initiative and refuse to testify.) The defense usually cannot prevent a spouse from testifying if the case involves a crime committed by one spouse against the other.

A person usually won't be allowed to testify unless he personally perceived the incident under question. As a general rule, *opinions* aren't admitted as evidence, but there are certain circumstances under which *expert opinions* or *lay opinions* will be admitted.

Expert Opinion. An *expert* is a person who is considered to have the power to draw inferences from fact which a jury wouldn't be likely to draw because of their lack of knowledge, skill, or training in a specific area. Two requirements are usually set forth before an expert is allowed to offer his opinion on a matter, however:

- the subject must be so distinctly related to some science, profession, business, or occupation as to be beyond the knowledge of the average person;

- the expert must possess such skill, knowledge, or experience in that field as to make it probable that his opinion or inference will aid the jury in its search for the truth.

Before an expert will be allowed to offer an opinion, a thorough examination into his background and training must be conducted in order to determine his qualificatoins. The expert must be considered to be qualified in every case in which he becomes a witness. For example, the same criminalist may be called upon in many different cases; he must be qualified in *each* case. Similarly, an expert who is qualified to testify in one case may not necessarily be qualified to testify in another.

Lay Opinion. In some situations, *lay* opinion, or the opinion of a person who is *not* considered to be an expert in any specific field related to the case, may be admissible. This kind of testimony will be allowed if the lay person's opinions are based on facts which he has personally observed, or if his opinion is of the kind that the average person is apt to form often and correctly.

Lay witnesses may be called upon to testify even when they can't adequately or accurately describe the facts upon which their opinions are based. In these instances, the lay witness may be allowed to make a complex observation—that is, he may offer his opinion on something even when the matter he observed was too complex or too subtle to describe factually. For example, the witness may give an opinion on a suspect's age, appearance, mental state (Was the suspect calm, or nervous?), sanity (Was the person acting "crazy" at the time of the incident?), or some other relevant factor.

If a lay person is allowed to give his opinion, he will often be asked to justify that opinion. For example, the witness may say that he thought that the defendant had been drunk. The witness may then be asked if he had ever seen an intoxicated person before. Or, if the witness testifies that the defendant was "acting crazy," he may be asked to describe his relationship with the defendant. Does the witness know the defendant well enough to form that kind of opinion?

Thus, while lay opinion may be judged admissible, it must often be qualified. This protects both the courts and the defendant from opinions which may have no basis in fact.

Working Together: The Importance of Relationships Within the Legal System

Not only must the criminal investigator work with suspects and witnesses, but he must also be conscious of the web of relationships that exists within the criminal justice system itself. Each investigation may require the services of several different agencies and types of personnel, and the criminal investigator must be aware of the parts each plays.

Two relationships are especially significant here: the one between the prosecutor and the investigator, and the one between the prosecutor and the police agency as a whole. Needless to say, the investigator's relationship with other personnel in his agency is also important; this was discussed previously in Chapter One.

The Prosecutor and the Criminal Investigator

The prosecutor is the one who presents the state's case against the defendant. And, unless evidence exists to support the state's allegations, there is no case; thus, the relationship between the prosecutor and the criminal investigator is crucial to the success of the prosecution.

The two must not only be willing to cooperate, but they must also trust and respect each other. The prosecutor should feel free to advise the investigator about the strengths and weaknesses of a case under investigation. He should be able to criticize the investigator where necessary and offer praise when appropriate. Similarly, the investigator should be able to advise the prosecutor.

The investigator can learn from the prosecutor which types of cases are apt to result in convictions and which types aren't. This can help the investigator to determine which cases merit an intensive investigative effort. It's a good idea for the prosecutor to conduct an administrative review of those cases which he declines to prosecute, in addition to examining those which the court dismisses; this review process can be useful in channeling the investigator's efforts into more productive areas.

The Prosecutor and the Police

In addition to working closely with the criminal investigator (usually a police officer), the prosecutor also has an important relationship with the police in general. The prosecutor's workload is determined to a great extent by police apprehension policies. And, on the other hand, the ability of the police to prevent crime is largely affected by the prosecutor's policies regarding plea negotiations and other rules and regulations.

Thus, what one does often influences the other: as a result, neither should make a major change without consulting the other. For example, if the prosecutor is thinking about changing prosecution policies regarding certain types of offenses, he should inform the police of this and seek their comments and suggestions. The same holds true when the police are about to make a policy change which will affect the prosecutor's office.

The need for cooperation cannot be overemphasized; misunderstandings and inter-office tensions can prove harmful, and they can be avoided when a continuing, open relationship between the prosecutor and the police agency exists.

Statistical analysis of prosecutorial success or failure in certain cases can highlight the need for improvements in police procedures. For example, it may be decided that better training is needed for evidence technicians, patrol officers, and supervisors, as well as investigators.

An additional advantage to a good relationship between the prosecutor and the police involves the more effective handling of physical evidence.

Evidence Accountability

When an item of evidence is secured from a person, he is often concerned about what will happen to it. In many cases, evidence is private property which has been temporarily "borrowed" by the police and the prosecution. Whenever possible, then, the police should persuade the prosecution to permit evidence to be returned to its owner as soon as possible. This will have a positive effect on police-community relations, in addition to cutting down on the amount of space, time, and paperwork needed for preserving evidence.

Once an item of evidence is seized for use during a criminal prosecution, someone in the criminal justice system becomes responsible for it. For example, if an investigator finds a weapon at the scene of the crime, he is responsible for it until that responsibility is passed on to someone else—such as a laboratory technician. Once the laboratory technician is through with it, he may hand it over to another person, and so on. Regardless of where it is, however, *someone* must be *accountable* for it at all times. The importance of this accountability cannot be stressed too often. A break in the *chain of accountability* may result in the exclusion of an item crucial to the prosecution's case.

From the practical standpoint, the fewer persons who handle the evidence the better. This ensures that the evidence won't be significantly altered in any way, or lost, or damaged—any or all of which can have grave consequences. For example, if an investigator confiscates a narcotic, he should immediately transfer it to a laboratory specialist who will examine it and, if necessary, testify about it at the trial. If the specialist retains it until the time of the trial, the evidence will be handled by a minimum number of persons who can vouch for its presence all during the time when it was in police custody.

The state's case may be significantly weakened if individuals who aren't specifically involved in an investigation take custody of an item of evidence along the way for any period of time. These interventions tend to break the custodial chain and can provide a good reason for the defense to attack the admissibility of the evidence in question. The more people handle a piece of evidence, the greater the chance is that this will happen.

If an item of evidence must be changed in some way—if, for example, a marijuana cigarette must be cut up for analysis—the court will usually accept a reasonable explanation of why this was necessary. It's usually wise if the investigator identifies a piece of evidence by marking it in some way as soon as he secures it.

Conclusion: A Brief Look at the Making of a Good Criminal Investigator

Good criminal investigators aren't born; rather, they get that way because of training and experience. It's a common—and false—assumption that a competent patrol officer, administrative sergeant, or departmental legal officer will make a competent investigator simply because he performs well in a specific area of police work. Often, a person is promoted to the position of investigator without having the vaguest idea about what the job involves. While it may seem that some investigators simply have a "knack" for their profession, the true key is *training*.

Any newly appointed criminal investigator should receive *as a minimum* three weeks of intensive training at the police academy or attend a special school for criminal investigators. At least once every year, he should take a two- or three-week refresher course. In addition, he should also participate in one- or two-day training programs designed to keep him informed of new investigative techniques or changes in departmental rules or procedures. The law doesn't stay the same, and neither do the duties and responsibilities of the investigator. In order to be most effective, both must be in a constant state of flux.

Thus, the good investigator must be aware of the changes that take place in the legal system which may affect his role. He must be willing to take the time to keep his legal knowledge current. New court decisions must be explained to the investigator in detail, along with the impact that these decisions may have on specific investigative techniques. Often, a new or revised statute will mean that a tried and true investigative procedure will have to be altered. The investigator who's unaware of these changes may make grave errors that will destroy a prosecutor's case against a defendant.

A large percentage of the responsibility for keeping investigators informed should rest with the training officer in each police department. he should keep a current file of legal interpretations, laws, and cases, in addition to copying and circulating articles which affect criminal investigative procedures.

Each department should develop a planned schedule of on-the-job training. This might include, for example, scheduled tours of duty in the prosecutor's office. The investigator who spends some time observing and working with the prosecutor can learn a great deal about why supposedly "airtight" cases are rejected or dismissed. The prosecutor will also benefit from the experience of working closely with the investigator on some of the more perplexing problems of developing and gathering evidence.

A good criminal investigator is thorough. As was said in the introduction to this chapter, though, thoroughness isn't the only criterion which determines the success of a criminal investigation. Nor is it an isolated quality; rather, it goes hand in hand with training, experience, and willingness to cooperate with other agencies and personnel, and a working knowledge of the law. No one is born with these qualities, but every good criminal investigator has them.

Summary

No criminal prosecution can proceed without the existence of sufficient evidence to support the state's allegation. Since the criminal investigator is the one who's responsible for seeking and collecting evidence, his role is crucial to the success of the prosecution.

Gathering evidence involves much more than simply going out and picking it up. Many evidentiary rules, which often vary from state to state, have a major influence on how the investigator does his job. The competent investigator is not only aware of these rules—and, because they change frequently, his knowledge must be up-to-date—but is also willing to go along with them.

Evidentiary rules have been made to protect the legal system and the private citizen alike, although it's often assumed that they exist simply to stand in the way of justice. They guard the courts against the possibility of hearing false or meaningless evidence and reaching incorrect conclusions; they shield the citizen from unfair or illegal investigative practices. Basically, a defendant is presumed innocent until proved guilty, and this *presumption of innocence* has served as the basis for several of the evidentiary rules which are a part of the criminal justice system today.

The investigator must not only be familiar with evidentiary rules, but must also be able to distinguish among the various types, or categories, of evidence. While almost anything related to a case can be considered as evidence of one form or another, some kinds of evidence carry more weight than others, depending on the circumstances and on judicial discretion.

Regardless of how much evidence an investigator collects, however, none of it is of any value until it's judged *admissible* by the court. No item of evidence will be admitted for consideration by the trier of fact if it's been collected illegally or without regard for the constitutional rights of the defendant. Even if an item of evidence has been secured legally, however, it still may not be considered admissible. Whether or not evidence is judged admissible depends on several factors, including its *relevancy, importance, materialness,* and *competency.*

Certain quantities of evidence are generally considered to be more convincing than others. Basically, *proof beyond a reasonable doubt* is the major standard in American courts; this means that the trier of fact is nearly one hundred percent certain that the defendant is guilty as charged. The courts will consider other quantities of evidence, however, depending on the circumstances. These include *clear and convincing evidence* and *prima facie evidence,* among others.

In addition to collecting items of evidence during the course of an investigation, the criminal investigator must also work closely with suspects and witnesses. Occasionally, he will be called upon to arrest a suspect. A decision to arrest a person must always be based on *probable cause,* and there are rules which the investigator must follow when performing this task as well as when collecting evidence.

Since witnesses are so important to the success of any criminal prosecution, the investigator must make sure that they meet certain standards, too. Usually, they must have personally seen, heard, or otherwise perceived the incident in question. While *opinions* are generally not considered admissible as evidence, there are exceptions, and the investigator may seek the opinions of experts or occasionally lay persons on certain difficult points of evidence.

The relationship that the investigator has with the prosecutor is another factor which can determine the success of a criminal prosecution. The two are, in essence, working toward the same end, and must be willing to cooperate with one another. The prosecutor should feel free to advise and criticize the investigator, and the investigator should pay attention to what kinds of cases the prosecutor is apt to dismiss, since this will save them both a great deal of time and effort. In addition, the lines of communication between the two should be open at all times; policy changes made by one can very well affect the other.

In short, the investigator's profession is a complex and varied one. It involves many different skills and requires careful training. Experience, of course, is also a factor. Thoroughness, common sense, intelligence, knowledge of the law, and an awareness of the important role he plays—all are qualities which the good criminal investigator possesses and makes use of every day.

Questions and Topics for Discussion

1. Why is it important for the criminal investigator to have a working knowledge of the law? What can happen if he *doesn't*?

2. Discuss some factors which determine whether or not an item of evidence will be judged admissible.

3. Name as many types of evidence as you can and give examples of each, where possible.

4. What are the differences between direct and indirect, or circumstantial, evidence?

5. Discuss some of the problems that may arise when an investigator wants to introduce a tape recording as evidence.

6. Define and discuss what is meant by "proof beyond a reasonable doubt." What are some other quantities of evidence, and how do they measure up to one another?

7. What is the "presumption of innocence?" What kind of effect does it have on a criminal trial?

8. Imagine that the Supreme Court is deciding whether or not to retain the presumption of innocence in the American legal system. You are a Supreme Court judge. What will you decide, and why?

9. What are the basic purposes of a criminal investigation? Of a criminal trial?

10. Discuss some ways in which the prosecutor and the investigator can cooperate with one another to improve criminal investigation techniques. Then consider how their cooperation can help cases to be presented more effectively in court.

11. What is the "chain of evidence accountability?" Discuss its importance. You may want to find out the processes of evidence accountability which are used by a law enforcement agency in your area and present your findings to the class.

12. What is meant by "probable cause" to make an arrest? Why is the probable cause requirement so important to the criminal investigator?

13. What is a warrant? Why is it important?

14. If possible, find out how criminal investigators in your area are trained. What does the training consist of? Is it adequate, in your opinion? Are the investigators trained in legal principles?

Annotated Bibliography

Bailey, F. Lee, and Rothblatt, Henry B., *Investigation and Preparation of Criminal Cases, Federal and State* (Rochester, N.Y.: Lawyers Co-Operative Publishing Co., 1970, with yearly supplement). Written as a handbook to lead the trial lawyer through the preparation phases of criminal cases, this detailed work examines all phases of investigation, from tracing missing witnesses, unearthing public records, and selecting and locating experts, through dealing with and analyzing physical evidence. In-depth chapters discuss particular types of crimes and the techniques and necessities associated with preparing defenses for them.

Felkenes, George T., *Criminal Law and Procedure: Text and Cases* (Englewood Cliffs, New Jersey: Prentice-Hall, Inc., 1976). This book presents the constitutional rules governing criminal procedure in a concise, thorough form. The various decisional mandates are presented through the use of case briefs with explanatory text material. Included in the book are topics such as search and seizure, self-incrimination, speedy trial, plea negotiation, bail, jury trial, confrontation, trial procedures and conduct, cruel and unusual punishments, double jeopardy, sentencing, juvenile procedures, and corrections. Discussion questions are included.

Felkenes, George T., *Rules of Evidence* (Albany, N.Y.: Delmar Publishers, 1974). This book presents a set of valuable rules of evidence used in criminal cases. The author offers a practical approach to the study of evidence while including enough theory to set the background for the rules. Numerous examples are given. Subject areas cover general evidentiary considerations (relevancy, character evidence, reputation); witnesses (qualifications, direct and cross-examinations, impeachment experts, mental conditions); privileges (attorney-client, spousal, governmental, self-incrimination); hearsay rule (admissions and confessions, dying declarations, prior identification, declarations against interest); judicial notice; burden of proof; and the "best evidence" rule. Numerous review questions are provided.

Horgan, John J., *Criminal Investigation* (New York: McGraw-Hill Co., 1974). This book is directed to police science students, officers, and investigators. Discussion is presented on fundamentals, covering guidelines and requisites for investigators; preliminary investigations; collection, identification, and presentation of evidence; modus operandi; interview and interrogation; fingerprints; surveillance; sources of information; and report writing. Discussions of the investigation of several types of major offenses are also included.

IACP, *Criminal Investigation* (Gaithersburg, Md.: International Association of Chiefs of Police, 1971). This book has been prepared by the Professional Standards Division of the IACP and is directed to law enforcement personnel assigned to investigative functions. It is a technical manual for investigation which provides principles of investigation supplemented by techniques of investigation. Various specific crimes are examined for the best methods of approach. Cases are discussed, and each chapter is highlighted by review questions.

Klein, Irving J., *Law of Evidence for Police*, 2nd edition (St Paul: West Publishing Co., 1978). This work is designed as a text and as a casebook for undergraduate study of the law of evidence as practiced in state courts. It contains in-depth discussions of witness examination and trial procedure, opinion evidence, the "best evidence" rule, the hearsay rule (and exceptions to it), privileged communications, declarations against interest, public documents, presumptions, judicial notice, and illegally obtained evidence. Part II contains judicial decisions relating to these categories.

Louisell, David W., Kaplan, John, and Waltz, John R., *Principles of Evidence and Proof*, Second Edition (Mineola, N.Y.: Foundation Press, Inc., 1972). This book includes cases and materials concerning evidence. Fundamentals to inquiry and investigation are presented. The work is organized as a text and is comprehensive in scope. It also contains lists of suggested readings following each segment of discussion.

O'Hara, Charles E., *Fundamentals of Criminal Investigation*, 4th edition (Springfield, Ill.: Charles C. Thomas, 1976). The foundations of investigative work are presented here and are directed to teachers and students in the various branches of investigation. The fourth edition includes a selected bibliography. Discussion covers methodology of investigation and typology of offenses. Includes discussion of the investigator's role in court, specialized scientific methods, and investigative operations.

Waltz, Jon R., *Criminal Evidence* (Chicago: Nelson-Hall Co., 1975). This is a comprehensive work directed toward police and criminal investigators and is written in a style to avoid the lawyer's jargon. Discussion includes such topics as constitutional issues; technical rules of evidence, such as rules against hearsay and the "best evidence" rule; relevancy of evidence; witnesses' testimonial evidence; confessions; burden of proof and presumptions; judicial notice; writings; opinions; and scientific and demonstrative evidence.

CASES:

Mapp v. Ohio 367 U.S. 643, 81 S.Ct. 1684,6 L.Ed.2d 1081 (1961)

Chimel v. California 395 U.S. 752, 89 S.Ct. 2034,23 L.Ed.2d 685 (1969)

Davis v. Mississippi 394 U.S. 721, 89 S.Ct. 1394,22 L.Ed.2d 676 (1969)

Terry v. Ohio 392 U.S. 1, 88 S.Ct. 1868,20 L.Ed.2d 889 (1968)

Wong Sun v. United States 371 U.S. 471, 83 S.Ct. 407,9 L.Ed.2d 441 (1963)

Katz v. United States 389 U.S. 347, 88 S.Ct. 507,19 L.Ed.2d 576 (1967)

Roviaro v. United States 353 U.S. 53, 77 S.Ct. 623 L.Ed.2d 639 (1957)

Gideon v. Wainwright 372 U.S. 335, 83 S.Ct. 792,9 L.Ed.2d 799 (1963)

Argersinger v. Hamlin 407 U.S. 25, 92 S.Ct. 2006,32 L.Ed.2d 530 (1972)

United States v. Wade 388 U.S. 218, 87 S.Ct. 1926,18 L.Ed.2d 1149 (1967)

Kirby v. Illinois 406 U.S. 682, 92 S.Ct. 1877,32 L.Ed.2d 411 (1972)

Miranda v. Arizona 384 U.S. 436, 86 S.Ct. 1602, 16 L.Ed.2d 694 (1966)

Malloy v. Hogan 378 U.S. 1, 84 S.Ct. 1489, 12 L.Ed.2d 653 (1964)

Brady v. United States 397 U.S. 742, 90 S.Ct. 1463,25 L.Ed.2d 747 (1970)

THREE

Conducting Investigations

Chapter Objectives

After reading this chapter, the student should be able to:

☑ Outline what the investigator's managerial responsibilities are.

☑ Identify the basic objectives of an investigation.

☑ Identify the basic processes of preliminary and follow-up investigations.

☑ Summarize the major concepts of investigative procedure.

☑ Describe a model information reporting system for the investigator.

☑ Identify new concepts in crime analysis and describe a program for a closed-loop investigation system.

☑ Recommend strategies for organizing and conducting an investigation.

The Responsibilities
of the Investigator: An Overview

As society has become more urbanized, the investigator's role has dramatically changed. New and greater demands have been placed on the investigator due to technological advances in evidence collection and examination, new interpretations of the law, and the growing numbers of sophisticated perpetrators committing sophisticated crimes. The rising crime rate poses a challenge to the investigator, who no longer can choose to solve a crime by any method but must aim at rendering services to crime victims and the public in an ethical, legal manner.

This changing focus means that today's investigator must not only know the processes of each type of investigation, but must also be able to conceptualize about investigations in general. In addition, he must be willing to relate his efforts to the total team effort of data collection, records storage and retrieval, case assignment, and all the other processes and routines that are necessary to sound investigative practice and successful case resolutions. *Why* a certain investigative methodology is chosen often becomes as important as *how* the process is carried out. Thus, the investigator's role is no longer the narrow, private function of the detective, but rather a more varied and complex one which emphasizes general police service.

The investigator's managerial responsibilities have also increased and now involve two separate mental abilities. First, he must develop his cognitive senses so that the assimilation of details becomes a part of his thinking. Second, the investigator must memorize processes so that no step is omitted during the investigation.

The development of the cognitive senses further dictates *two* types of intellectual awareness. In *divergent thinking* operations, the investigator must think in different directions at the same time, sometimes searching, sometimes seeking alternatives. Not all officers can achieve this type of thinking ability, and management must recognize this fact. The second thinking process, termed *convergent thinking,* leads to *one* right answer or to a recognized *best* or *conventional* solution. This process is usually considered to be much simpler, since it in part depends upon the memorization of processes as they might be outlined in a departmental policy manual.

Not only does the investigator have professional responsibilities, but he has ethical responsibilities as well. He must be concerned with obtaining information that sheds light on the truth of the situation without letting his feelings and opinions interfere. The investigator's efforts may lead to a determination of the guilt or innocence of a suspect, or it may lead to a stalemate in which neither guilt nor innocence can be legally decided. It is the responsibility of the investigator to see that all relevant facts are legally secured and competently presented during a case, and this burden dictates that the assessment and evaluation of the information obtained be done in a meticulous, methodical, and unbiased manner.

The techniques of investigation have historically evolved from "word of mouth," and, as a result, little pertinent documentation on the subject has been available. Two recent studies—the Rochester Study[1] and the Rand Study[2] have been conducted to determine the effectiveness of investigative techniques and practices. For example, the Rand Study seemed to conclude that no single best management system has yet been developed concerning investigations. It implies that a variety of subsystems, when properly applied, may contribute to a better organization for criminal investigation purposes.[3] Thus, it is proposed that concepts be taken from *several* subsystems and integrated into what might be termed a viable "blueprint" for conducting criminal investigations. For example, the model reporting system designed by Project SEARCH (Standardized Crime Reporting System Committee) may be used as a basis for developing an investigative system. (This model is illustrated in Figure 3-1. p. 64.)

In order to integrate any set of processes into one specific system, however, it is first necessary to understand the *objectives* of the criminal investigation.

The Goals and Purposes of Criminal Investigations

The ideal goal of a criminal investigation is to solve a crime if it is solvable and to collect and process information about it in accordance with legal procedure. In order to maintain some stability in the management of an investigation, sub-goals and objectives need to be identified. Four of the most common sub-goals are:

- to identify and collect information that may be used as evidence against suspected law violators;
- to secure evidence that will reveal the innocence of the person or persons under investigation;
- to guarantee a contact for both the victim and the public concerning the retention of material information in a case; and
- to serve both the community and the agency in crime prevention, giving assurances of constitutionality and the deterrence of antisocial acts through education.

Each of these is discussed in detail below.

Figure 3-1. Standardized Reporting System*

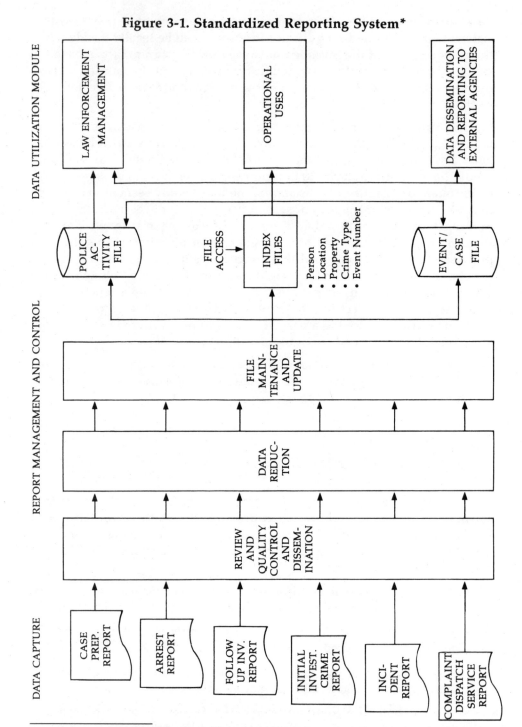

*From *Design of a Standardized Crime Reporting system: Project Search*, Technical Report No. 9, p. 5-5, Crime Technological Research Foundation, December 1973.

The Identification and
Collection of Incriminating Evidence

The traditional objectives of an investigation are concerned with bringing a suspect to justice for a criminal act. While there is little agreement among experts on the best techniques and procedures which may be used to complete this task, some common objectives have been agreed upon. These are implied through the following procedures.

1. The preliminary investigation is conducted for the following reasons:

   a. to determine whether a crime has been committed;

   b. to determine the nature of the crime which has been committed;

   c. to identify the offender;

   d. to locate and apprehend the offender;

   e. to protect the crime scene and preserve evidence; and

   f. to accurately report all events and steps taken during an investigation.

2. The follow-up investigation is conducted to ensure the following:

   a. the follow-through of all information that will lead to the successful conclusion of the investigation;

   b. the apprehension and incarceration of the offender within the economic limitations of the agency;

   c. the maintenance of files and records and the updating of the investigation;

   d. the recovery of missing or stolen property;

   e. the presentation of all evidence to the prosecutor; and

   f. the building of a better image of the police in the public's eyes.

The Securing of Evidence
to Reveal the Innocence of a Suspect

In order to achieve this goal, the same basic procedure should be exercised as are used in the securing of evidence to convict the suspect. A compulsion or need to secure a conviction in a case is not within the purview of the police officer. His attitude should be one of securing and reporting all information about a case in the most effective and objective manner.

Maintaining Satisfactory Contact
with the Victim and the Public

Procedures to achieve a satisfactory contact with a victim include:

1. Initiating reports and keeping complete files on each case.

2. Maintaining personal contact with the victim.

3. Maintaining lines of communication to the public and initiating contacts with the perpetrator.

4. Analyzing data collected and projecting the findings into the agency's central analysis unit for management information.

Crime Prevention

A major function of the investigator is to serve the community in the crime prevention function. Guaranteeing each suspect's constitutional rights while deterring future anti-social acts is a proper role for the investigator. This goal may be accomplished through these procedures:

1. The identification of cases which will not be solved but which may help to prevent other crimes if their study can be used to develop prevention programs.

2. To analyze procedures used all during an investigation to make sure that they are legal. Often, an investigator is the only resource a person has to turn to for assurances of legality.

Conducting Preliminary Investigations

An effective investigation often depends upon many persons and upon the several organizational methodologies that govern their work tasks. In this regard, each agency should set its own procedures and policies regarding case processing. The following material illustrates these concepts:

1. the basic guides and methods for conducting preliminary investigations;

2. some procedures for collecting physical evidence; and

3. the use of official forms for the recording of pertinent events during the investigation.

The Basic Guides and Methods
for Conducting Preliminary Investigations

Preliminary investigations fall into four basic categories. They are:

1. called-for services rendered when an investigator reports to a crime scene at someone's request;

2. investigations initiated by the investigator;

3. undercover investigations; and

4. investigations conducted by paid informants.

Each calls for a different strategy during the preliminary stages.

Called-For Services. This type of investigation projects an investigator into an unfamiliar setting in which he must take command, adjust instantly to a great many different situations, and conduct an investigation with competency in the field. Depending on the investigation and the circumstances surrounding it, the specific tasks the investigator will need to perform will vary. Some management models have provided insights into why it is necessary to employ different methodologies when conducting different types of preliminary investigations. For example, the approach used by the Oakland Police Department, as reported by the Stanford Research Institute (SRI) minimized intuitive judgments in case handling by allocating objective value numbers to case assignments.[4] Using traditional response models, the SRI found that unless relevant information had been located at the crime scene or an offender had been identified, there was little chance of the case being solved at the detective level.[5] And, surprisingly, the study concluded that patrol units were effecting the larger percentages of case clearances. The study also concluded that a major objective of any investigation should be the finding of a large habitual offender population, and that investigations should be geared to this effort. So many crimes are committed by recidivists that the identification of the habitual criminal offender is obviously an important investigative responsibility.

The scope of a preliminary investigation in called-for services may be restrictive or it may include the entire investigation. In any investigation, a case file builds, and is not usually the responsibility of a single investigator. For example, in the "Trash Bag" murders in California, which took place between 1970 and 1977, at least 150 separate investigations were conducted before the case was eventually solved. (How this sort of process takes place is shown in Figure 3-2. p. 68.)

Departmental policies vary. However, the Los Angeles Police Department manual indicates that an officer should continue a preliminary investigation to the point where the delay in investigation caused by the report being processed will not materially jeopardize the investigation.

The Initiation of a Preliminary Investigation by the Investigator. This type of investigation allows for the use of many different strategies. The ones cited are normally used in the investigation of crimes such as conspiracies, organized crimes, and those in which the victim may not be readily identifiable. This type of investigation allows for a more planned and methodical approach than does the response to a crime scene, which is usually more spontaneous. Some general procedures to employ during these types of investigations include the following:

1. A background investigation of suspects, utilizing intelligence data and criminal records files.

2. The assessment and evaluation of available data pertaining to the charge to be investigated. This must be cleared with legal officers or prosecutors in cases where legal advisement is desirable.

Figure 3-2 Steps in the Building of a Case File

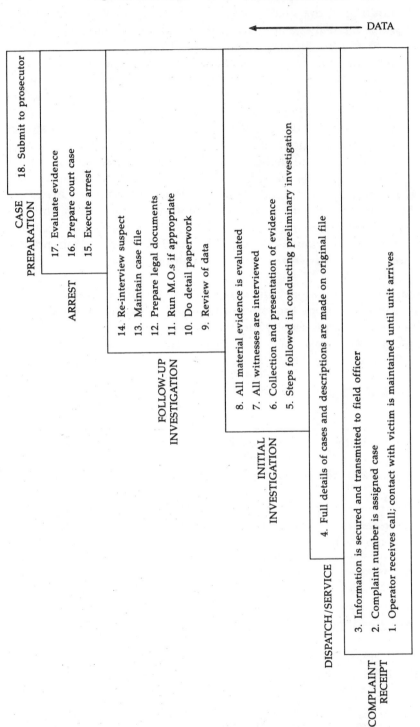

3. The coordination of a plan for action, drawing upon intelligence and evaluation to designate an appropriate scheme. All persons participating in an investigation should have prescribed duties and timetables.

4. The execution of preliminary investigation to determine whether intelligence and other information are valid.

5. The securing of necessary legal documents, subpoenas, warrants, etc., to execute the follow-up investigation.

A schematic of the Intelligence Gathering Process is shown in Figure 3-3. This type of information may be used in all types of investigations. Of course, the investigation should always follow the detailed procedures outlined in his departmental manuals.

Undercover Investigations. In undercover investigations, an investigator is covertly placed in a situation where it is possible for him to observe violations or to receive first-hand information about crimes. The use of undercover officers is considered to be a legal, moral, and ethical way to approach the solution of crimes when other traditional methods are not satisfactory. Preliminary duties in an undercover investigation and operation will vary with each case and are usually covered by departmental policy. A few cautions during the preliminary planning stages are warranted, however. These include the following:

1. Sound criteria for selecting an undercover operator should be established. Stability traits necessary in critical situations should be of prime consideration; therefore, for example, with a little make-up a more intelligent and stable operator may work out better on a case than an individual whose appearance is scruffy enough to fit the investigation. A poorly selected operator may cause embarrassment to the department.

2. A safety cover should be provided throughout an investigation. Positive identification for the role to be assumed by the undercover investigator is imperative. A method of communication checks should also be pre-planned.

3. The collection of background and identification information on suspects being investigated should be a continuing process. When information about a law violation is discovered, and revealing it to other officers will not jeopardize the undercover investigator, it should be promptly referred to officers who can act on the information. The undercover officer should be present when raids are being planned which have resulted from his information.

Investigations Conducted by Paid Informants. An investigation conducted by a paid informant is designed to secure information from within a criminal operation that may not otherwise be available to the investigator.

Figure 3-3. The Intelligence Process*

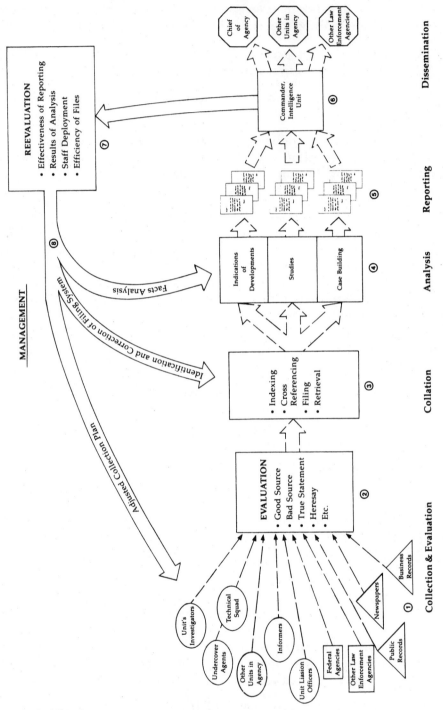

*From *Basic Elements of Intelligence,* Godfrey E. Drexel and Don R. Haris, Department of Justice, Washington, D.C., November 1971, p. 33.

Such investigations are critical to the police if they are going to respond to the total investigative needs of the community. With positive and effective management, these investigations can be most productive in fields where no other method of securing evidence is available. Some of the preliminary considerations for this type of investigation are as follows:

1. The motives of the informant should be known. An informant should be used only if there is some evidence of his integrity and reliability.

2. If the informant's motive is to escape prosecution for lesser crimes, the trade-off must be sanctioned by the court as being in the interests of the community. *Legal requirements must be met* before a paid informant can be used.

3. Money paid an informant should be signed for by the principal investigator, and accounting procedures that ensure fiscal accuracy must be followed.

4. All investigations and operations conducted by a paid informant should be outlined and discussed by the investigator with the responsible administrators in the agency.

Following the preliminary investigation, a case is either closed or assigned to another officer for some form of follow-up investigation. This process is referred to as *case screening and assignment*, and is discussed in detail below.

Screening and Assignment

After the preliminary investigation is completed and there is need for further disposition on a case, an important managerial process must take place. That process consists of *assigning* the case in such a way that a solution to the crime will most likely result.

The methods used for case screening and assignment vary from agency to agency, depending upon the complexity of the investigation, the "political heat" generated by a specific crime, and other factors of a political and economic nature.

During the past decade, case screening and assignment as a process has taken three new directions. Traditionally, the uniformed officer conducted the preliminary investigation and the detective was responsible for the follow-up. Today, however, the following three approaches are more common:

1. the uniformed officer handles both the preliminary and the follow-up investigations;

2. the investigation is initiated by an investigator who is assigned to a centralized, specialized investigative unit; and

3. a decentralized Team Patrol investigator is immediately brought into the case.[6]

The screening and assignment of cases has generally been done by an informal "crime clustering" method. This method clusters groups of crimes—such as crimes against persons, commercial burglaries, and so on—into logical work assignments based on penal code definitions. These clusters often depend on the size of an agency and the agency's ability to support specialized functions. In some agencies, there are overriding reasons why task functions are divided among specialized units. For example, vice units in most urban departments are separated from the traditional investigative units because the vice squads' use of informants often causes internal conflict within the department.

Two major approaches have been suggested for use in developing a screening model. The first involves the development of a listing of *unweighted* criteria for the screening of cases[7], and the second establishes a listing of *weighted* criteria.[8] Each is described in detail in Chapter Twelve.

The Case Analysis Approach.

In this approach, case screening rules are derived, in part, from an analysis of those cases which have been successes and failures.

To determine whether a case should be continued as an active investigation, the answers to these questions need to be secured:

1. Can the complainant or witness identify the offender?

2. Is the offender known to the complainant or witness?

3. Does the complainant or witness know where the offender is located?

4. Is there physical evidence at the scene which would aid in the solution of the case (fingerprints, other physical evidence).

5. Is the complainant or witness willing to view photographs to aid in identifying the offender?

6. Can the complainant or witness provide a meaningful description of the offender (home, address, etc.)?

The criteria cited above all are logical guidelines for establishing investigative processes. In actual practice, however, many other considerations must be made with reference to case screening and assignment regardless of the priority derived from the criteria cited. Case screening and assignment is a complex decision-making process and should be treated as such. *Each agency is encouraged to develop its own screening system.*

Temperament of the Community
Regarding the Agency.

Not all crimes can be solved; thus, a successful investigation may be involved only in the *process* and not the *result*. This is not to say that solutions are not *sought*, however. Due to circumstances beyond police control, the services rendered to the victim and witnesses may be the only tangible result of an investigation. Thus, the investigative function is an important part of community crime prevention, and much of that activity is *not* directly involved in solving crimes.

The relationship a department establishes with the community is often judged according to the type of contact the investigator has with the public. For example, in many agencies throughout the country, investigators are assigned service club activities as a part of their community function. Due to programs like this, the investigator is seen as being less of a "supersleuth" and more of a human contact with an important crime-prevention role in the community.

Once a case assignment has been made, the follow-up investigation begins.

The Follow-up Investigation

There are a variety of ways in which the follow-up investigation may be conducted; each investigation requires a slightly different procedure based upon the circumstances of the crime. Usually, the priority of the case assigned dictates the priority category for the investigation.

In the Rand Study it was observed that the new cases assigned to an investigator can generally be sorted into three categories. Receiving *first priority* are those in which the investigative steps are obvious from the facts related in the incident report. These are the cases in which the victim names the suspect, gives a license number, identifies specific locations where the suspect can be found, or names additional important witnesses who were not interviewed by the responding patrol officer. Investigators are always expected to track down these obvious leads.

Second in priority are those cases which require attention, not because any obvious leads are indicated but because of the seriousness of the offense or the notoriety it receives in the press or in the community. Because investigators want to avoid charges by the community that they are not doing their job (or it may be that an investigator is outraged by the offense and wants to help the victim), additional effort is expected to be made toward solving the case. This may involve recontacting victims and witnesses and going over their prior statements.

In the *lowest category of priority* are the routine cases that offer no indication of additional leads. These cases usually receive nothing more than perfunctory attention.[9]

The fact that different types of cases are treated differently — and, in many instances, *should* be treated differently — deserves further comment. The issue of *investigative priority* — how it's established, how it should be established, who establishes it, and for what reasons — has never yet been clearly resolved. The following observations have been made, however, in an attempt to guide the investigator toward forming a better investigative methodology:

1. Cases are solved by both routine investigative action (shuffling papers) and by unique or special procedures or insights on the part of the investigator. Often, however, the most important function of the investigator is to control the flow of reports and information concerning a case.

2. Good investigative procedures alone are not the solution to curbing crimes. A total managerial plan is necessary, and the investigator is an essential cog in the total system. In a robbery prevention program, for instance, the public relations officers may be more effective than investigators in curbing robberies simply because of a new procedure they may initiate. For example, the rule which states that bus riders must have exact fare—in other words, that bus drivers will carry no cash—has been lowering the number of bus drivers who are robbery victims.

3. Uniformed officers will make most of the arrests in simple cases because they will usually arrive at the crime scene before any other law-enforcement personnel. Conversely, follow-up investigators will probably solve more cases by using teletypes and other investigative resources than patrol officers will. *Who solves the case* should not be a consideration in the measurement of the investigative function. *Who keeps the case together*, in terms of bringing a variety of variables together, is a more accurate description of the investigative function.

4. The solution rate of crimes has no relationship to the numbers of crimes assigned an investigator. One investigator in a given time span may solve 60% of his cases, and at another time solve less than 10% of them. The variables that are not measurable in a case often hinge upon both good investigative techniques and "lucky breaks." The good investigator can usually see the "break" in a case and, as a result, pursue leads that a poor investigator may never discover.

5. Unless he is highly trained in the technical aspects of crime solution methodology, an investigator will make little use of remote or indirect forms of evidence. Many cases are not solved merely because the investigator didn't have the time to pursue all of the leads. Slim leads are usually ignored in favor of leads that appear to have a higher payoff. This "human element" has yet to be eliminated from the art and science of investigation.

6. The data collected by a department is usually not designed to assist an investigator. Historically, such information has been for the benefit of *management*. This is gradually changing with new in-process systems, computerized fingerprints, and automated case records that support the investigative processes.

7. New techniques previously mentioned are limited in use because of the investigator's lack of understanding of software which may be helpful during extensive investigations.

8. Files such as the Los Angeles County Sheriff's Automated Information System, the Los Angeles District Attorney's Prosecutor's Management Information System, and the Los Angeles Probation and Sentencing Sub-system form a computerized network linked through the National Crime Information System that is only recently being extensively used by investigators to bring together the variables in an investigation.

9. The necessary requestioning of witnesses is often difficult or impossible because of investigator time constraints. If there is no time for an adequate follow-up investigation, the investigator should make sure that the officers who originally took the report will call back and reinterview all victims on a regular schedule. For example, a visit with a witness may be scheduled ten days following the initial contact to determine whether new information has developed, and again after about 30 to 45 days. *These steps should be mandatory even though a case has no possibility of being solved.* It puts the investigator in contact with the patrol officer, who in turn is forced to contact the public. These call-backs are the least the public—especially the victims—should be able to expect. The patrol officer has time to make follow-up calls, since he spends about 60% of his field time in fairly unproductive patrol routines. Such contact by the investigator or the patrol officer is often the only satisfaction a crime victim receives. Lack of time is never an excuse; poor management is the only reason such procedures are not in common practice.

Follow-up investigative techniques are usually established in a department manual and evolve during the investigations of specialized crimes. The development of techniques are management responsibilities and will vary from department to department.

In-custody investigation is another vital link in the investigative process.

In-Custody Investigation

This period in the investigation process gives the investigator an opportunity to utilize his training and talent in follow-up contacts with a defendant. The investigator's basic functions at this time include:

1. preparing the case for court;

2. resolving crimes related to the present case; and

3. developing new leads on other cases.

Preparing the Case for Court

Preparing the case for court may be the most important role of the investigator during the investigative process. Often, when a case is submitted to the prosecutor and, in turn, to the court, one of the frequently heard criticisms is that it has not been adequately prepared. Because administrators cannot document this type of activity in terms of case clearances or arrest statistics, it is often conveniently omitted as a legitimate function of the investigator. This is both unfortunate and unprofessional; technical evaluation of cases by a skilled investigator is a necessity.

Each case filed should be reviewed in meticulous detail with the arresting officer, the legal officer, and/or the prosecutor. These duties include, but are not limited to, the following tasks:

1. Working with the probation officer in clearing all crimes that may be connected to the defendant;

2. bringing together all evidence into a logical sequence and ensuring that the chain of accountability is maintained;

3. ensuring that all necessary scientific tests are conducted; and

4. maintaining a continuing contact with the victim, interviewing witnesses, and arranging for special service in cases such as rape and homicides.

An extension of the in-custody investigation is to clear any other crimes that may relate to the case under investigation.

Resolving Crimes Related to the Present Case

Clearance rates are calculated by combining all cleared cases, regardless of which police function is actually responsible for their clearance. According to the Rand Report, there are no department-kept records that enable the clearance rate to be broken down by police function.[10]

The Rand Study also indicated that clearance rates are not apt to vary regardless of the organization imposed upon the investigation function. Experience indicates that the ability to spend time on an arrestee during this critical stage in the case results in a great many clearances, irrespective of the organization. Although the Rand Study did not find a causal connection between training and improved investigation, evidence exists which seems to prove that highly trained investigators produce a better investigative product.

Developing New Leads on Other Cases

This is one of the key functions of the good investigator, although it is seldom addressed as an investigative function in most research efforts. During the course of furthering an investigation, and without jeopardizing his case, the investigator should perform the following functions:

1. Be aware of any co-conspirators who may be revealed.

2. Be willing to talk to the suspect or defendant about other criminals who may be his "enemies." This technique is used in many cases where confidential information may have led to the arrest of the defendant.

3. Be in contact with the defendant periodically so that lines of communication are kept open. A defendant's sense of guilt or remorse can be capitalized upon to clear cases and reveal other crimes. These contacts should be made only in consultation with the prosecutor, and in no way should conversation be carried on against a defendant's wishes.

In-custody investigations offer many opportunities for the investigator that may never again be available. Thus, the expenditure of a certain amount of time at this stage is justified because it allows the investigator to serve as a reference for the defendant, a contact for the probation officer, and an aide to the prosecuting attorney in bringing the case together.

Information Files

The investigative processes used by an investigator are enhanced considerably when he or she is able to fully utilize a number of support systems. Criminal investigation consists largely of assembling the pieces of information necessary to establish the identity of a suspect, according to the standards and procedural guidelines established by the courts. Investigation specialization is thought to facilitate this process by allowing the investigator to concentrate his attention on a particular category of crime. The more familiar the investigator becomes with the modi operandi (MOs) of frequent offenders, the more likely he is to establish relationships between an arrested offender and other past crimes.

To cope with this information-processing workload, all departments have established some basic information files. New information comes into the files primarily from incident or arrest reports which are usually provided in the form of a carbon copy of a report designed for some other purpose. Three basic sources are shown in Figure 3-4. Lack of dedicated clerical help combined with inefficient input procedures, often make these files cumbersome to use, and increase the possibility that important data may often be missed.[11]

A major weakness of criminal investigation as a whole has long been the failure to *standardize* reporting systems so that investigators throughout the United States could communicate on an interstate network. In 1973, the Federal Government recommended a standardized system for all agencies of the criminal justice system.

The Project SEARCH Committee submitted a conceptual systems design that integrated three basic functions of a total crime/event information system. These three functions considered necessary for a beginning automated system, were identified as:

Figure 3-4. Schematic of Data Collection Methods*

COMPLAINT/DISPATCH

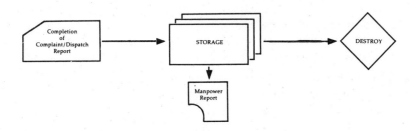

CRIME REPORTS

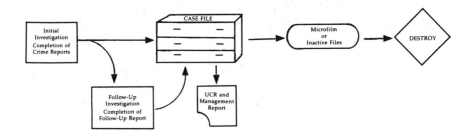

ARREST REPORTS

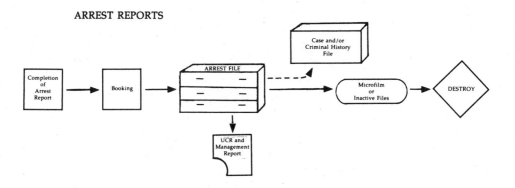

*From *Design of a Standardized Crime Reporting System: Project Search,* Technical Report no. 9, p. 6-1, Crime Technological Research Foundation, December, 1973.

1. data capture;

2. report/data management and control; and

3. data utilization.

A primary goal of the project was to define the data requirements of all users of crime reports and to clarify the provisions by which useful and standardized data could be collected, stored and disseminated.[12] (This system is illustrated later in this chapter.)

The objectives of the project were to:

1. Minimize report preparation time by the reporting officer.

2. Ensure that all required data were collected.

3. Allow increased crime analyses by making available appropriate and standardized data.

4. Create a basic source document for preparation of the Uniform Crime Report.

5. Provide for easy editing and review so as to improve quality of crime reporting.

6. Improve communication between uniformed officers and detectives and between police and prosecutors.

7. Ensure that prosecution functions will be better supported by the receipt of adequate, standardized information from law enforcement agencies.

8. Provide states having appropriate statutory authority with a model reporting system for standard use.

9. Provide a means by which useful and standardized data can be commonly collected on crime and the activities of law enforcement agencies.[13]

The SEARCH Committee established the design for a prototype crime reporting system. At that time, all federally funded information systems were instructed to follow the format of the basic system illustrated in figures 3-4. and 3-5.[14]

As shown in Figure 3-3., the building of a case file is structured upon active data in the system that are instantly available upon inquiry to the computer terminal. The basic input documents of the automated system serve as the backup system in a manual file. The benefits of a standardized system to the investigator are obvious.

Data Capture: The Incident Report

In order to record and obtain the data on a specific event, it's extremely important to have available a document designed for those purposes. The Rochester Model has been selected from among many that serve basically the same functions. Figure 1-1. on page 22 shows the basic reporting document.

The uniqueness of the Rochester, New York, report form is that items on it are ordered in a logical sequence. The form requires that an officer indicate whether he has been able to identify specific "solvability factors"—items of information which might lead to the solution of the case. By asking the officer to check a box if he *cannot* identify a particular factor, the form requires the officer to go through a mental check list of the items he should look for. If an officer does not check a particular box, then he must give some reason why.

This reporting form enables a reviewing officer to decide whether a case merits a follow-up investigation. If any of the solvability factors are present—if any of these boxes do *not* have an "X" in them—then a follow-up is indicated, and the box for "yes" (field follow-up) should be checked. Every report must be signed by a field supervisor indicating his satisfaction with the report and his concurrence with the officer's classification, he must explain why.

Under the Rochester guidelines, any case will be assigned for a follow-up field investigation if there is a significant piece of information which may serve as a lead to follow in order to apprehend the perpetrator. In addition, "if the crime may arouse significant public interest," then a field investigation should be undertaken even if no specific lead exists.[15]

The Rochester Police Department found that some specialized training in using the report was necessary. This is probably true with any reporting system. Regardless of the system it uses, a department should never assign patrol officers to other than patrol duties without first providing them with extensive specialized training. The Rochester system has many good points; however, future reporting systems should be fully automated so that data entered in the field by the preliminary reporting officer can be machine read and reports generated from that process.

The Known Offender File

Known offender files are generally of two types. The first is the regular criminal history file, in which the subject is located by means of his name, social security number, or some other descriptor. This on-line computer filing system has been developed to a high degree of effectiveness during the past decade. To use it, the investigator requests the record of a suspect or a defendant, and a compiled history is immediately available. At the local level, these records are kept in a semi-automated or manual file.

A second system of known offender files allows the investigator to track an offender through the various processes of the criminal justice system. This "subject-in-process" system has limited capabilities, but has been used successfully in some cities (Dallas, for example). The "recidivism model" utilized in Washington D.C. is similar to this system.

The value of maintaining a current file on known offenders is evidenced by the recidivist unit in the Washington D.C. Police Department. That unit

Figure 3-5. Conceptual Relationship of Data System Modules*

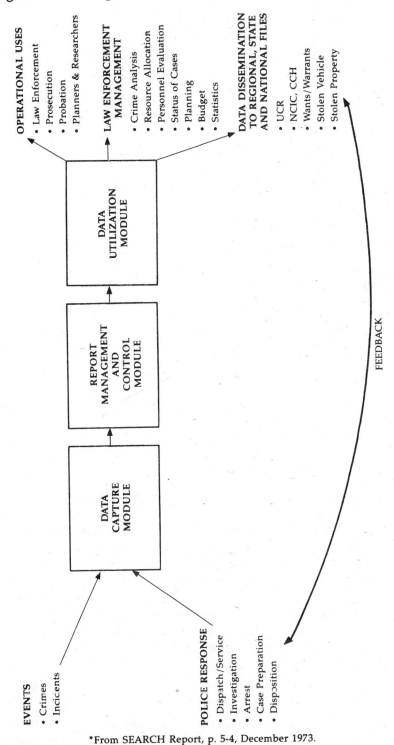

*From SEARCH Report, p. 5-4, December 1973.

monitors and keeps statistics on all people who are arrested while on any form of conditional release such as pre-trial release, post-trial release, furlough from prison, or parole.[16] Other known offender files, like the sex offender file authorized under California Penal Code Section 290, are *specialized*. The major weaknesses of this type of system is the fact that it's often difficult to obtain immediate updated information from the courts.

With the sophisticated automated equipment now available, most agencies are making some inroads into the capturing of large quantities of data to use when comparing or determining modus operandi patterns. Many of the early attempts to utilize this data resulted in some degree of failure. Then failures had several causes. First, many perpetrators do *not* have established behavior patterns, and most engage in many different types of crimes; consequently, law enforcement must deal with repeat offenders across a broad spectrum of crimes.[17] Second, the administration of an agency often tries to implement complex systems without first providing personnel with extensive specialized training. And, finally, no major research has been done by anyone who truly understands investigative processes. These weaknesses are not beyond solution; it is hoped that better research in the future will help to correct them.

The Mug Shot File

Mug shot files come in different forms, but most are very similar to other types of files used by criminal justice agencies. Perhaps no other source of information has been more valuable in solving crimes; few investigations are conducted without the use of the mug shot file.

The manual system of filing photographs by the subject's name or some other identifying factor is perhaps the most common. This system has proved reasonably accessible and simple to use while remaining within budgetary limitations. Trailing a person through an entire filing system via his name, nickname, alias, or MO can be very time-consuming, however; this approach is almost useless when a subject's name is unknown. In an attempt to solve this problem, many departments in the 1960's acquired automated microfilm systems to store photographs and criminal histories. The Kodak Miracode system is one example. It contains complete files on each subject, including his identification sheet, photographs, criminal records, and fingerprint cards. This system has served many medium-sized police agencies well, but it has been expensive to keep current and in many cases has been abandoned for the traditional manual system. In departments where automated systems have been maintained and constantly updated, they seem to be worth the trouble.

Fingerprint File

Fingerprint files are used more than any other sources of information to confirm suspect's identities. They are also consulted when the investigator wishes to check latent prints on file or eliminate suspects from consideration. Although fingerprints are overrated as crime-solving tools — rarely does a perpetrator leave a clear print at a scene, and only 4-9% of those latent prints which are found actually solve crimes[18] — it's rare that a major investigation is conducted without extensive use of the fingerprint file. Such files will remain major instruments of the investigation process, since their importance in making positive identifications is unquestioned. Automating these systems is increasing the numbers of cases which are solved. To make such systems worthwhile, every investigator should know how to perform *primary print classifications* and how to look for latent prints and discover glove and fabric impressions.

The Intelligence File

The value of applying intelligence information to criminal investigation cannot be determined by the number of crimes it solves, but rather by the numbers of leads it offers an investigator who may otherwise lose a case. An intelligence file lists the acquaintances of known criminals; in addition, it reveals *patterns* of criminal behavior which allow specialized investigators to follow-up leads that might otherwise not be clear.

Good intelligence files are especially important when a city does not have a budget to support many specialized details. They are mandatory for handling cases which cross city and state lines. These files are the life-lines to state and federal agencies who must depend upon local agencies for their information sources.

Field Interview File

The field interview, or *FI*, file is a very valuable source of in-house information for the criminal investigator. A field interview takes place when a person is stopped under suspicious circumstances and subsequently released due to the lack of probable cause for arrest. Information about this interview is recorded on an FI card and filed. Many cities maintain their FI files manually, with entries being filed and later located according to the subject's name or the place in which he was contacted. Some cities enter information concerning vehicles into an automated filing system and keep the subjects' names in a manual filing system. In the future, as data banks become more common in police agencies, these files will be automatically retained for a period of time and then erased. FI files are useful for about a year, and after that time can be rendered inactive for one or two years and then destroyed. FI files do not serve as police records per se, but instead are sources of basic information about subjects' movements within particular districts or areas of a jurisdiction.

The Oakland Police Department field contact form illustrates the transition to fully automated FI files (see Figure 3-7.).

Figure 3-7.
The Oakland Police Department
Field Contact Form

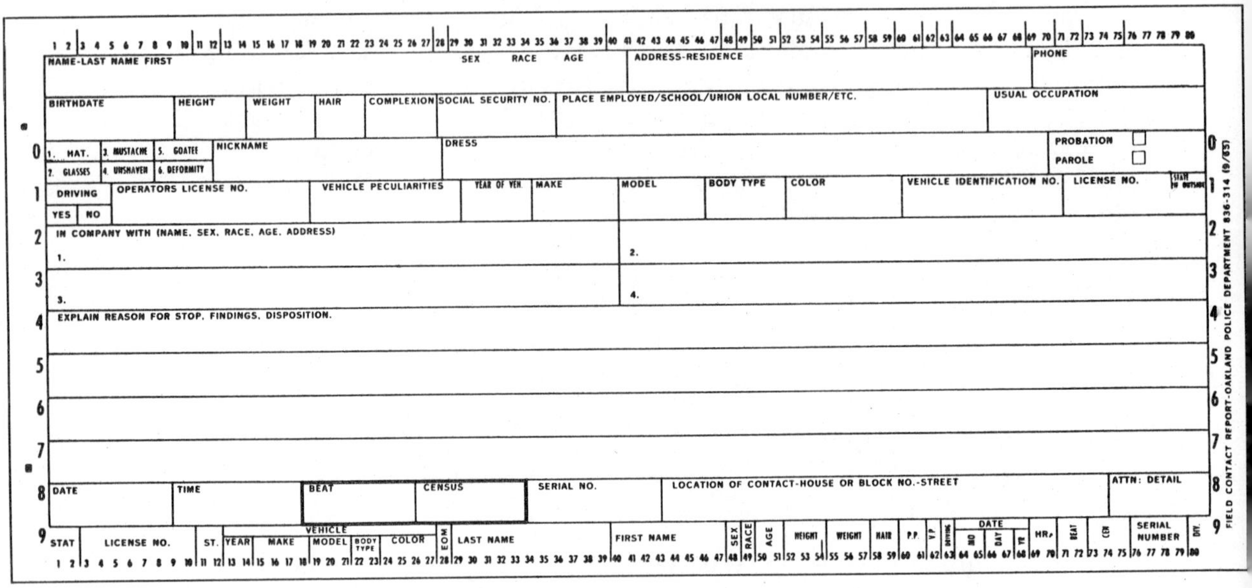
NAME-LAST NAME FIRST | SEX | RACE | AGE | ADDRESS-RESIDENCE | PHONE

BIRTHDATE | HEIGHT | WEIGHT | HAIR | COMPLEXION | SOCIAL SECURITY NO. | PLACE EMPLOYED/SCHOOL/UNION LOCAL NUMBER/ETC. | USUAL OCCUPATION

0 1. HAT. 3. MUSTACHE 5. GOATEE 2. GLASSES 4. UNSHAVEN 6. DEFORMITY | NICKNAME | DRESS | PROBATION ☐ PAROLE ☐ 0

1 DRIVING YES NO | OPERATORS LICENSE NO. | VEHICLE PECULIARITIES | YEAR OF VEH | MAKE | MODEL | BODY TYPE | COLOR | VEHICLE IDENTIFICATION NO. | LICENSE NO. | STATE 1

2 IN COMPANY WITH (NAME, SEX, RACE, AGE, ADDRESS) 1. | 2. 2

3 3. | 4. 3

4 EXPLAIN REASON FOR STOP, FINDINGS, DISPOSITION. 4

5 5

6 6

7 7

8 DATE | TIME | BEAT | CENSUS | SERIAL NO. | LOCATION OF CONTACT-HOUSE OR BLOCK NO.-STREET | ATTN: DETAIL 8

9 STAT | LICENSE NO. | ST. | VEHICLE: YEAR | MAKE | MODEL | BODY TYPE | COLOR | MOE | LAST NAME | FIRST NAME | SEX | RACE | AGE | HEIGHT | WEIGHT | HAIR | P.P. | V.P. | DRIVING | DATE: MO | DAY | YR | HR. | BEAT | CEN | SERIAL NUMBER | DIV. 9

FIELD CONTACT REPORT-OAKLAND POLICE DEPARTMENT 836-314 (9/85)

Stolen Property File

The stolen property file is an important file for the investigator since it is usually automated and numbers, descriptions, and special markings on items of property can be easily traced and verified. Information is available through state files and the FBI's National Crime Information Center (NCIC), which is probably the most comprehensive single filing system available on a national basis. Most agencies are contributors to the NCIC system, and most are regular users. This file fits into the standardized reporting system as illustrated in Figure 3-1.

Crime Analysis

Crime analysis as performed by the investigator has two equally important phases. The first phase is the establishment of an *investigation plan* which includes the development of investigative objectives and an evaluation of how these objectives are being realized. The second phase is the *statistical analysis* of the data collected under phase one and the injection of the results back into the planning process. Together, these two phases form a *closed loop system* of analysis. The processes necessary to complete this closed system are not purely mechanical, but includes the consideration and accomodation of political, geographical, and cultural factors within a community.

The Investigation Plan

The work plan of an investigator is important to consider in the analysis scheme because every police system must be balanced between effectiveness in terms of clearing cases and *protection* of citizens according to the democratic process. An analysis which does not consider the work process is misleading and inaccurate, and often contributes to questionable practices in investigations. Many crimes that may not otherwise be solved can be closed if certain legalities involved in the work process are ignored or not ethically applied. Thus, a case analysis should involve a great deal more than simply counting the hours spent on a case or the numbers of cases cleared.

A major problem in criminal investigation has been the failure to identify specific factors that are utilized in the investigation of a crime. The Management by Objectives (MBO) approach to crime investigation has attempted to identify key factors. This system had been used by police *administrators* for decades when planning investigations. It has not, however, been articulated as a process for the investigator to follow when planning investigations.

There are five basic elements which must be considered when using MBO as a guide in developing an investigative system. These elements include *process, common goals, results, joint identification,* and *assessment.*[19]

Process. The process cannot be the end result of an investigation, but rather must set the tone of the investigative mode by securing solution to crimes. Many steps from MBO are applied to investigative planning; these are conceptualized in the following manner:[20]

a. *What the organization must do to fulfill its basic purposes.* If the basic purpose of an organization is crime solution, what happens to the rights of an individual, and what happens to the idea of protecting a community rather then persecuting its members? It would not be difficult for the police to solve *all* of the crimes committed, but this would have to be done without the basic safeguards now accorded an individual during an investigation. The "crime solution syndrome" should not be given priority over individual safeguards in the investigation process.

b. *How it must be done (the program steps or plan of action required to accomplish it).* This concept provides not only for operational steps in solving crimes, but also for the legal constraints that surround a case. Both of these are agency concerns.

c. *When it must be done (the program steps or plan of action required to accomplish it).* This is often a key factor in crime solution, and an agency should have a defined departmental manual which specifies each function of the investigator at the crime scene.

d. *How much it will cost.* It is difficult to believe that some crimes will not be solved because of budgetary limitation. The sad truth is many cases will not receive the attention they deserve. A sound management plan can help to improve the utilization of personnel and resources.

e. *What constitutes satisfactory performance.* No one has yet come forth with a viable way to put strong management controls on investigations. This is partially the fault of investigators themselves, who in the past have formulated complex plans for crime solutions but have not verbalized these plans. An investigator's ego is threatened when management asks for a plan for an investigation. The basic cause of planning failure on the part of the investigator may be because of the selection process for investigation positions.

f. *How much progress is being achieved.* According to the results of the Rand study and other studies, not much improvement is being made in the investigative function because police administrators are constantly trying to justify their roles based upon case clearance without looking at the managerial processes which control the investigative function.

g. *When and how corrective action should be taken.* For the investigative function, this implies a control device that can be satisfied only by a trained investigator. Current management studies have not attempted to identify the *conceptual* thought processes that go into a good investigation. Thus, no one has decided when cases are solved by luck, or by sound reasoning, or by improved techniques on the part of an investigator.

Common Goals. Common goals are the fundamental endeavors in which an organization is engaged and the results it hopes to achieve. For example, the hostility between plainclothes investigators and uniformed investigators is largely a myth in well-organized agencies. And team policing, contrary to published results, has sometimes *created* rather than solved problems of communication between interagency personnel. Keeping communication open between the investigator and the patrol officer is a constant problem. With good management practices, however, an organization's efforts can be fruitful. If an agency lacks leadership, there is little hope that any system will work.

Results. Each goal is translated into a number of objectives which become measurable targets to be achieved in specific areas. The results achieved can then be compared to stated objectives so that the need for modifying or redirecting efforts can be seen. Objectives should be set for the organization as a whole, and for each unit and each individual.[21]

Although MBO obviously applies to the investigation function, many police agencies insist that there is not enough time to educate and train officers to make these structured plans function. A reassessment of their training priorities is needed.

How the results of an investigation are secured will depend upon how data is sought and pursued. If a social science approach is used instead of the more conventional analysis of crime statistics, a different view of the investigative function will emerge.

Research studies manipulate statistics in an attempt to resolve the crime problem. They develop discrete patterns of crime occurences by location, times of occurrences, the various ways in which crimes are committed and descriptions of property taken. All of these studies can contribute to the efficiency of an agency in a very *limited* manner.

Joint Identification. The MBO approach gives the responsibility for achievement to the superior and subordinate jointly. Both must work together to identify the basic purposes to be achieved and the specific goals which they are attempting to accomplish.

The joint identification of goals and objectives generally produces several positive results in overcoming problems in investigative functions.[22]

These include the following:

1. The plans produced by MBO tend to be more *realistic* than ones generated by other methods. Thus, both the subordinate and superior know each other's roles.

2. By using MBO, subordinates obtain a better understanding of the total situation in which they are involved through consideration of the organization's goals and objectives. Subordinates feel a commitment because the work goals are a product of their efforts. These work goals allow an investigator to have a certain amount of flexibility in determining how a case should be conducted. He takes part in determining what leads are important, what the priorities on personnel and resources are, and other management functions of an investigation.

Assessment. Agreed-upon objectives, translated into policy directives when possible, become the standards against which an investigation may be assessed and measured. This is one way for management to control the investigative function. It is a viable way to evaluate investigative processes, and it has been utilized fairly consistently in better-organized agencies.

The need for rigid controls in the investigative processes has been evidenced by the Federal Bureau of Investigation for the past fifty years. While their methods of control have been criticized, they have also been effective. A system of accountability, reinforced by frequent inspection teams, has kept the investigative processes from stagnating.

Not only must a viable management approach be implemented in order for the investigative function to realize its full potential but data must also be generated that will support decisions made during an investigation. Investigative data have gradually been accumulated over the past decades and, through the evolution of the information systems, some fairly sophisticated information for decision-making is now available in data banks throughout the world.

The Statistical Approach to Investigation Analysis

The traditional approach to statistical analysis, utilizing the FBI Uniform Crime Reporting (UCR) format, has revealed general trends concerning crime events. These general management data have assisted agencies in developing their own forms of management decision-making.

With the development of automated data processing systems, investigators have been provided with an "on-line" system having immediate feedback abilities and the capacity for assessing multiple variables. During the past decades these model systems have emerged in various forms of sophistication, and each succeeding model has been better than the one before. The many sub-systems have become an on-line part of the National Crime Information System.

Some of the basic functions of automated data processing equipment include:

1. Identifying demographic variables so that relationships and patterns may be established;

2. Comparing data from various locations; i.e., a fingerprint found at one location may tie into a suspect arrested at another location;

3. Identifying data elements recorded on a source document, factors which lead to the identification of individuals, and trends in types of crimes, MO's, etc.;

4. Calculating the economic impact of crime and recording identifiers on stolen properties;

5. Furnishing specialized information so that management decisions may be made and projected into the planning process; and

6. Validating all information coming into the system and providing for the comparison of key variables.

From this information an investigator can secure data upon which decisions may be made. The methods of analysis vary from agency to agency and with the outputs desired. The basic scheme suggested here includes but is not limited to these types of data:

1. The numbers of offenses reported by type, time, location, and other information contained in a standardized reporting form suggested by the Rochester Model. This element of the processing makes feasible the scanning of at least one year of field interview information.

2. The numbers of offenses investigated by arriving patrol units, the numbers of follow-up investigators involved, and the numbers by any specialized organizational units involved.

3. Information on how cases were reclassified, assigned, investigated, and closed; i.e., arrest on scene, arrest by follow-up, arrest by other means.

4. The time spent on each phase of the investigation and the duration of the entire investigation.

The data produced from such a system should give the investigator and the manager, in a readable form, all data reported on the crime, including standard reports and inputs from all officers and witnesses in the case.

Because the exact information an investigator will receive from a system will vary, it is impossible to outline the precise data elements that should always be sought or utilized. What *is* important for the investigator to realize, however, is that an investigative plan will work *only* if it is conceived during the management phase and planned through to the final documentation.

Crime assessment is a necessary resource for the police manager and the investigator in the development of work tasks. The assessment methodology based upon crime rate and case clearance has been a poor criterion for measurement, and the sooner police administrators look to better investigative criteria, the better the results will be. The present methods of assessing investigations are inadequate.

Summary

Major studies on what transpires in an investigation have fallen into the trap of counting hours spent on a case and tabulating the clearance rates of crime. Neither of these measures are adequate to describe the complexities of the investigative process. This chapter has described information systems and sub-systems in order to show how an agency might improve the overall investigative process.

There has been no effort to defend present investigative processes, only to discuss them and to reiterate that the investigative process is, and will continue to be, a tool of agency management. The investigator, along with other members of an agency, is a part of the total agency function, designed to support criminal investigations. It has been suggested that Management by Objectives, properly utilized, offers a catalyst to make the investigative function a part of an agency's goals.

Investigative units are groups of ordinary persons, open to human frailties. If the unit has superior personnel, selected on a merit basis, then a better investigative product will be more likely to emerge.

The myth about the "Great Detective" and the solution of crimes by insightful inspiration has been minimized. Emphasis has been placed upon viewing an investigation as a work-oriented, sequential, methodological task based upon a system of team effort for data collection and assessment.

The police officer's role in managing an investigation involves the development of cognitive senses for assimilation of finite details and memorization of processes to insure that no steps are omitted in the investigation.

The objectives of an investigation are outlined to illustrate that the investigative processes seek not only to convict law violators but to protect the innocence of the person or persons under investigation. It is a responsibility of the investigator to assure an official contact for a victim, witness, or other interested person concerned with a case. Also, an important, but often overlooked, function of the investigator is the crime prevention aspect of the investigative unit.

Different types of investigative situations have been outlined and some techniques for conducting each type are cited. For example, called-for services to which a patrol unit would probably respond would require different procedures than would an investigation initiated by an investigator, undercover investigations, or investigations by paid informers.

Techniques for case-screening have been cited. There is no agreement on how this should be done, since crimes are being reported to satisfy management demands for statistics and to provide case solutions by the investigators. Once these questions are resolved, much of the diversity in investigation processes will be standardized.

Steps in the follow-up investigation are stated broadly so that departmental policies in the actual techniques of conducting a local investigation may be developed. Some of the steps are:

(1) Often, the most important function of an investigator is to control the flow of reports and information in a case.

(2) Good investigative procedures must be supplemented by a total plan of prevention.

(3) Whether uniformed officers or plainclothesmen solve a case should not be a consideration in the measurement of the investigative function.

(4) The solution rate of crimes has no relationship to the number of crimes assigned an investigator. The variables used in solving a crime are often not measureable.

(5) There is a lack of adequate professional training in new technology, but the lack of solutions to many crimes rests with the often inadequate time to pursue leads. Time constraints are the investigator's greatest problem.

In-custody investigation is emphasized as perhaps the investigator's most important function. Cases must be prepared for court, and clearing of additional crimes related to the case under investigation and development of new leads in other cases are important.

Information files, including the data capture report (incident report) file, the known offenders file, mug shot file, field interview file, intelligence file, and stolen property file are all important files utilized by the investigator.

The investigative plan for crime analysis is discussed, but not resolved. Some techniques from Management by Objectives produce desired results for management measurement, but these steps are often not applicable to effective investigation techniques.

Statistical analysis systems have been demonstrated.

In conclusion, the chapter was designed to make the student think about the investigative process. A student should view the investigative process as it relates to total agency and community goals in rendering impartial service to any client who becomes the subject of an investigation. There has been an underlying attempt to describe the investigative function as a moral, thinking process directed by just policy guidelines.

Questions and Topics for Discussion

1. Identify and describe the basic functions of an investigation.
2. Obtain copies of the Rand Report and the SRI findings. Study and discuss them with your class. Are any of the findings unusual? Why or why not? Are any of them what you would have expected?
3. In Figure 3-1, trace the route of a file through a standardized reporting system.
4. Identify the four major subgoals of an investigation and their objectives. Are these steps in conducting an investigation proper and needed?
5. Identify four basic categories of preliminary investigations and discuss the need for differences.
6. From Figure 3-2, follow through on the steps in building a case file. Illustrate the importance of each step.
7. Analyze Figure 3-3, describe how intelligence information is processed, and discuss its relative values to many criminal investigations.
8. Why can it be said, "There is no best system of criminal investigation?"
9. Discuss the legal requirements of a case investigation preparation.
10. Why should community attitude toward an agency be an important consideration when that agency is designing its case investigation philosophy?
11. Discuss the importance of in-custody investigation, and point out the dangers of jeopardizing the case that may exist during such an investigation.
12. Identify the major new features of the crime report cited in Figure 1-1, p. 22 and discuss how they affect the investigator.

13. Why must crime analysis be a management procedure rather than just the counting and classifying of crime events?

Footnotes and References

1. Peter B. Bloch and Donald R. Weidman, *Managing Criminal Investigations* (The Urban Institute, Washington, D.C., 1975).

2. Jan M. Chaiken, *The Criminal Investigation Process*, Volume II: Survey of Municipal and County Police Departments (The Rand Corporation, R-1777-DOJ, October 1975).

3. Peter B. Bloch and Donald R. Weidman, *Managing Criminal Investigations* (The Urban Institute, Washington, D.C., 1975), pages 48-49.

4. Bernard Greenberg, Carlos V. Elliott, Lois P. Kraft, and H. Steven Proctor, *Felony Investigation Decision Model—An Analysis of Investigative Elements of Information* (Stanford Research Institute, Menlo Park, California, 1975), p. xvii.

5. *Ibid.*, page xx.

6. For more information on this approach, see Peter B. Bloch and Donald R. Weidman, *Managing Criminal Investigations*, page 48.

7. National Institute of Law Enforcement and Criminal Justice, Law Enforcement Assistance Administration, U.S. Department of Justice, *Managing Criminal Investigations: Prescriptive Package* (U.S. Government Printing Office, Washington, D.C., 1975), pages MM 58-59.

8. *Ibid.*, page MM 59.

9. Peter W. Greenwood, Jan M. Chaiken, Joan Petersilia, and Linda Prusoff, *The Criminal Investigation Process*, Volume III: Observations and Analysis (The Rand Corporation, R-1778-DOJ, October 1975), page 9.

10. *Ibid.*, page 12.

11. *Ibid.*, page 11.

12. SEARCH: Standardized Crime Reporting System Committee, *Design of a Standardized Reporting System: Project SEARCH*, Technical Report No. 9 (Crime Technological Research Foundation, December 1973), page 5-1.

13. *Ibid.*, page 1-2.

14. *Ibid.*, pages 5-4 and 5-7.

15. Peter B. Bloch and Donald R. Weidman, *Managing Criminal Investigations* (The Urban Institute, Washington, D.C., 1975), page 49.

16. *Ibid.*, page 63.

17. Bernard Greenberg, *et al.*, *Felony Investigation Decision Model—An Analysis of Investigative Elements of Information* (Stanford Research Institute, Menlo Park, California 1975), page xxx.

18. Peter W. Greenwood, *et al.*, *The Criminal Investigation Process*, Vol. III: Observations and Analysis (The Rand Corporation, R-1778-DOJ, October 1975), page x.

19. Peter B. Bloch and Donald R. Weidman, *Managing Criminal Investigations* (The Urban Institute, Washington, D.C., 1975) page 144.

20. *Ibid.*

21. *Ibid.*

22. *Ibid.*

Annotated Bibliography

Dienstein, William, *Techniques for the Crime Investigator*, 2 ed., Charles C. Thomas, Springfield, Illinois, 1974. A text illustrating the basic functions of the investigation process. This book outlines the traditional investigative function.

Horgan, John J., *Criminal Investigation*, McGraw-Hill Company, New York, 1974. A comprehensive book dealing with the pragmatic approach to criminal investigations. A step by step approach to all phases of traditional crime investigation.

Leibers, Arthur, *The Investigator's Handbook*, 3rd ed., ARCO Publishing Company, New York, 1972. A practical guide to the traditional techniques of criminal investigation.

McDonald, Hugh C., *The Practical Psychology of Police Interrogation*, Fashion Press, Los Angeles, 1963. Techniques utilized in conducting interrogations. This text uses basic psychological techniques as they apply to criminal interview and interrogations.

O'hara, Charles E., *Fundamentals of Criminal Investigation*, 2nd ed., Charles C. Thomas, Springfield, Illinois, 1970. An indepth and comprehensive text of all phases of criminal investigation including criminalistics.

Osterburg, James, *The Crime Laboratory: Case Studies of Scientific Criminal Investigation*, Indiana University Press, Bloomington, Indiana, 1968. A lab manual for assisting students in relating crime lab processes to the field investigation process.

Pace, Denny F. and Jimmie C. Styles, *Organized Crime: Concepts and Control*, Prentice-Hall, Inc., Englewood Cliffs, N.J., 1975. A discussion of how organized crime is recognized, how it is investigated, and the role the public plays in the control of organized crime.

Russell, Harold E., and Allen Beigel, *Understanding Human Behavior for Effective Police Work*, Basic Books, Inc., Publisher, N.Y., 1976. A text designed to give insight about the origins and complexities of human behavior, the understanding of mental illness and assessing and managing abnormal behavior in the field. A must book for criminal investigators.

Svensson, Arne, *Techniques of Crime Scene Investigation*, 2nd ed., American Elsevier Publishing Company, New York, 1965. A text relating to different concepts of investigation in terms of how investigations are conducted in Europe.

Weston, Paul B., and Kenneth Wells, *Elements of Criminal Investigation*, Prentice-Hall, Englewood Cliffs, New Jersey, 1971. A basic investigation text covering traditional crime investigation. Designed for introductory level investigators.

Vanderbosch, Charles G., *Criminal Investigation*, I.A.C.P. Training Keys, Washington, D.C., 1965. A series of lesson plans covering the basic function of the investigator. Widely used in training academy courses.

FOUR

Investigative Reports: Methods and Meanings

Chapter Objectives

After reading this chapter, the student should be able to:

☑ Explain why good investigative reports are necessary and list some of the different ways reports are used.

☑ Describe what goes into making a good field notebook.

☑ Explain different styles of organizing a field notebook.

☑ Give examples of a useful questioning method.

☑ List the qualities of a good investigative report.

☑ Summarize various ways of preparing and writing an investigative report.

☑ Give examples of various report types and styles and list both their advantages and disadvantages.

☑ Describe some special considerations, hints and standards that can prove helpful during the process of report writing.

Investigative Reports:
The Tools of the Trade

Many people feel that an investigative report is a boring, long-winded document which requires exhaustive research and hours of preparation. It's filled with words that are hard to pronounce, jargon that's difficult to understand, and terms that are impossible to define. The only purpose it serves is to take up an officer's valuable time and keep him or her from performing more important duties—and the only fate it deserves is to be filed on a dusty shelf or in the garbage.

In fact, however, a good investigative report is nothing like the above description. Instead, it's a valuable tool for the criminal investigator (and for many other people as well), and one that he or she returns to again and again.

A report is a means of communicating, of recordkeeping, of sharing experiences and information. It's an accurate, factual account of something which an investigator or an officer has observed, discovered, found out, or thought about. While some reports are written, some aren't (the ones that are will be the main focus here). While some are concerned with a single event, others deal with a series of occurrences. Regardless of the form they take, though, investigative reports are integral to the proper functioning of a police agency at every level of operation. Many are required by law, and for good reason. Human memories can fail; reports help to make sure that information needed both now and in the future will be available in a way that makes sense.

A good investigative report is read, re-read, dissected, discussed, analyzed, and consulted by many persons and agencies for a wide variety of purposes.

- *The officer who compiles it* uses it to document what's happened concerning an incident and to record facts and information relevant to an investigation or case. It helps him or her to outline the kind of further investigation, if any, which is needed before a case can be solved or closed. In addition, a concise, intelligible, accurate report can protect the officer and the department should questions or complaints regarding a case be raised at a later date. It assists the officer if he or she is called upon to testify in court. And, should related or similar offenses occur later on, the report serves as a valuable reference tool.

- *Other officers, technicians, and specialists* use investigative reports during follow-up investigations. They also consult them when interviewing and interrogating witnesses and suspects and when conducting related investigations. In addition, reports are excellent sources of background information which can assist officers in solving future crimes.

- *Supervisors* turn to investigative reports when conducting job performance evaluations, planning future assignments, and responding to questions or accusations about the department's actions.

- *Administrators* use them when deciding what changes, if any, need to be made in a department's policies, procedures, and programs. They also consult them when planning and organizing operational units, estimating budgetary needs, and scheduling officers' tours of duty. Often, reports provide statistical data regarding departmental activities which can help to clarify which areas of the community require more (or less) agency assistance.

- *Other law enforcement, government, and investigative agencies* use reports in much the same way as many of the above do. They also find them valuable when comparing data among agencies and when pooling information which will help to detect and locate persons who are wanted by the police.

- *The FBI and other federal agencies*, in addition to using investigative reports in many of the ways described so far, turn to them when compiling statistics on national and regional crime and criminality.

- *The prosecutor* consults reports when deciding whether or not to prosecute specific cases. If he or she does decide to pursue a case, relevant reports become legal evidence during the trial. The prosecutor also turns to reports as major sources for questions he or she will ask the defendant.

- *The defendant and the defense attorney* use investigative reports when planning their defense. A good report clearly defines the charges and facts of the incident as observed and investigated; it may make the difference between conviction and acquittal.

- *The judge* finds investigative reports useful when determining the dispositions of cases; *the jury and the grand jury* study them when making determinations of fact regarding cases during trials or grand jury hearings.

- *The news media* go to reports when developing stories for print or broadcast. Thus, through the media, reports become communication links between the criminal justice system and the public.

- *Many private citizens* also come in contact with investigative reports. All persons directly involved in an incident have access to reports regarding it, as do their insurance agents when necessary. And, when an individual wishes to prove—to a potential employer, for example—that he or she has no record of serious law violations, reports can help to substantiate his or her claim.

- *Legislatures* study police reports when deciding whether to change statutes or grant salary increases. They also use reports as a way of establishing administrative accountability.

- *Classroom instructors* realize that reports are valuable educational tools, not only when teaching criminal justice administration but also when dealing with report writing and communication skills.

- And, finally, *the community* as a whole benefits from good investigative reports. For example, they can help to indicate which neighborhoods need more police aid and which need less. They can help to convict or acquit a defendant. They can keep the public informed about what's going on in a police agency. They can influence the types of police service the community receives.

Thus, a document as useful as an investigative report deserves a better fate than a dusty shelf. A report doesn't have to be poorly written, or tedious, or impossible to understand—in fact, it's too bad if it is, because it probably won't get the use it merits. A report that's been well written and thoughtfully put together can have a direct influence on the effectiveness of an entire police agency. It can help to determine the future of the officer who wrote it. In short, it can affect the lives of many people.

In order for a report to perform all of its intended tasks, however, it *must* be able to withstand challenges to and attacks on its accuracy, completeness, and validity. It follows, then, that the better an investigative report is, the more thorough an agency will be able to be and the more fairly all persons involved in an incident will be treated.

Of course, report writing can be a chore. It can take time. It requires some effort. But it can—and should—also be looked upon as an art, because it is.

The Field Notebook: The Source of the Investigative Report

An investigative report may be conceived in the mind of the officer—after all, it starts with what he or she perceives or understands or thinks—but it's born on the pages of the field notebook. The scene of an incident such as a crime can be a confusing hodgepodge of information; often, it's difficult to sort it out at a glance or to determine the relative value of each piece of raw data. It's even more difficult to pull the specifics of a scene out of one's memory at a later date, or even at a later hour, if no permanent record is available.

The field notebook serves as that permanent record. It provides a way for the officer to note observations that he or she may never have the opportunity to make again. As a collection of raw data and source material, it's a tool which may be used productively in many ways.

A properly kept field notebook (more about that later) performs the following functions:

- It provides the officer with a detailed, permanent account of the facts of an incident.

- It acts as a memory aid, thus making it easier for the officer to compile final reports and conduct further investigations.

- It documents statements made by the people involved in an incident; these statements can later be compared and are apt to reflect conflicts and variations in the story which can be useful in solving the case.

- It provides clues for further interrogation and interviewing which will assist the officer in formulating questions to ask suspects and witnesses and in evaluating their responses.

- It aids the officer in developing a clear and comprehensive picture of the event in question.

- And, finally, it helps the officer to recall specifics if he or she is called upon to testify in court, in addition to serving as evidence.

Choosing a Notebook

Notebooks are like any other tools; some work better than others, and some people will always prefer one type or brand over all others. Although the selection of a notebook can be a very personal matter, there are certain criteria which can be used when making a choice. Since a field notebook is virtually part of an officer's uniform, it too should fit.

Notebooks come in many sizes and shapes and are available in both looseleaf and bound varieties. Some references suggest that a bound notebook is better than a looseleaf one because it's considered to be more reliable in court. Since it would be immediately apparent if pages were removed from a bound notebook, this type makes it easy to establish that no evidence has been inserted or removed since the original notes were made. This issue is more difficult to resolve if the officer's notebook is a looseleaf one.

On the other hand, some investigators argue that a looseleaf notebook is better than a bound one precisely because pages *can* be removed. This option can ensure confidentiality when it's necessary to do so. Only those notes which specifically relate to a case are admitted as evidence during a trial; other notes may be considered irrelevant and may interfere with the officer's testimony and the value of his or her notes as evidence.

Most police officers seem to prefer a looseleaf notebook with a limp binding, small enough to be carried in a pocket.

Organizing the Field Notebook

A consistent system of notetaking will improve the quality of the field notes taken and increase their usefulness. There are many systems from which to choose; among the most frequently used are the *alphabetical*, the *case report*, the *daily diary*, and the *crossfile*.

In the first system, notes are filed in alphabetical order (by topic or by name) in the field notebook. This method has its advantages in that it's easy to locate notes taken in the past; it requires a great deal of organization ahead of time, though, and if notes are recorded out of sequence they're very difficult to retrieve.

In the case report system, each case is listed separately, and all notes on a case are filed in a specific place regardless of when they're taken. This is a rather cumbersome system and is a difficult one to maintain in notebook form.

In the daily diary system, notes are taken in chronological order. Events are recorded when the officer experiences or observes them. This system is the easiest to organize and maintain and is usually considered to be very efficient. There's no need to organize the notebook ahead of time, and notes can be retrieved according to the dates when they were taken.

The fourth system, which utilizes crossfiling, is the most efficient of all as far as retrieving notes is concerned, but it's also the most time consuming to establish and maintain. This method requires that multiple entries be made—i.e., a main, or primary, entry, and several cross-reference entries which guide the user to the primary material. Reference keys can be made according to dates, names, offenses, modi operandi, and so on.

Styles of Notetaking

Although notetaking is a very subjective matter—each officer will take notes in a way that best suits him or her, according to his or her experience and the requirements of a particular case—there are three styles of notetaking which seem to be most common to police field investigation: *narrative, question and answer,* and *chronological.*

The narrative style tells, in story form, the events of an incident or investigation as the officer experienced them. They progress in a step-by-step, logical sequence that is centered on the situation and describes every pertinent thing that the officer learned or did during the time in question. The style is flexible and adaptable to a variety of situations; it's neither limited by form nor restricted in content. It has its advantages in that a lot of information is apt to be collected and recorded; its disadvantages lie in the fact that the information may be poorly recorded and too lengthy. Meaningful information may be lost among nonessential details; it's often difficult to pull statistical data out of a narrative account.

An example of this style might read like the following:

I first spoke to the accident victim, Miss Evelyn Stewart, at St. Joseph's Hospital Emergency Room, where she was treated by Dr. Baker of the E. R. staff. She had been taken to the hospital in an ambulance and was unable to communicate with E. R. personnel until approx. one and one half hours after the accident. In response to my questions, the victim stated that she . . .

In the question and answer style, both the questions asked by the officer and the answers given by the suspect, witness, or other interviewee are recorded in the notebook. This is a simple way to organize an investigation, and makes it easy to refer to and retrieve information at a later time. One disadvantage it has is that follow-up questions may end up being out of sequence, which may give the notes a disorganized or confusing appearance.

An example of this style might look like this:

Officer Martin: Where were you when the accident occurred?

Evelyn Stewart: I was turning the corner at Fifth Street and Howard Avenue . . .

Chronological notetaking deals strictly with facts and follows a time-centered pattern (*What happened first? And then?*) This method of notetaking is probably the easiest to prepare and use because the information more or less organizes itself. It also results in brief and concise notes. The major disadvantage of this style is that the notes may end up being so brief that they're insufficient or incomplete. Many officers find it difficult to get an overview of an incident and its surrounding circumstances when following this rather restrictive style.

An example might look like this:

1. Accident victim signaled to turn left at Fifth Street and Howard Avenue.
2. She began to proceed across the intersection.
3. The driver of the other vehicle ran the stoplight and entered the intersection at the same time as the victim.
4. The accident occurred.

Helpful Hints for Notetaking

Although every officer develops his or her own way of taking notes, the following guidelines should be helpful regardless of the style chosen:

- The officer's name, telephone number, and home and office addresses should be entered in the front of the notebook.
- All entries should be made with a ballpoint pen or some other writing instrument that will leave a permanent record that won't smear.

- Information which the officer may need frequently—such as hospital, church, and public building addresses and phone numbers, local ordinances, and vehicle codes—should be recorded in the notebook for reference.

- A notebook is *not* a personal diary. In other words, anything which the officer wouldn't want to be read aloud in court shouldn't find its way into the notebook.

- Notes should be taken at the scene and during the course of an investigation, *not* summarized from memory at a later or more convenient time.

- All notes should be retained, and filled notebooks should be filed away with a notation as to the dates when they were begun and ended.

- Events recorded in the notebook should be anchored according to their dates and times. For example, and officer may want to begin each shift with an entry in his or her notebook as to the date, shift, assignment, name of his or her partner, and so on.

- And, of course, if the information recorded in a notebook is going to be useful, it must be legible, well-organized, properly detailed, and accurate.

Deciding What to Record in a Field Notebook

Since the information contained in a field notebook is apt to be used for a variety of purposes, not the least of which is final report writing, the quantity of notes taken is almost as important as their quality. In short, almost everything that an officer notices or observes or finds out about an incident should be considered worthy of writing down, since there's no way to tell which items of information may come in handy later on during an investigation. It's better to take too many notes than too few; irrelevant ones, or those of lesser significance, can be weeded out during the report writing stage.

Basically, names, addresses, work and home phone numbers, and descriptions of suspects and witnesses should all be recorded in the field notebook. In addition, descriptions of items found or noticed at the scene, the results of a search, notes as to when constitutional rights were read, and statements made by witnesses and suspects should all be recorded carefully and completely. The officer should never depend on his or her memory to retrieve facts and information later; anything which seems important to a case should be recorded in the field notebook as soon as possible.

It's often advisable to make sketches of a scene, too, briefly noting where certain items were located. Any damage to objects at the scene, any furniture that looks as if it may have been disturbed, and anything that seems out of place at the scene should be clearly noted and detailed.

In taking statements from several persons, it's wise to take them individually and, if possible, privately. This practice makes it more likely that a statement will be a person's own rather than a product of someone else's influence.

The officer should always focus on recording *facts,* not *opinions.* When opinions seem important enough to be recorded, they should be labeled as such to avoid confusion. When people are quoted, their words should be written exactly as they were spoken; the officer should make no additions or deletions.

Asking Questions

Although a criminal investigation involves many different skills and techniques, and often requires the services of many people and agencies, it is first and foremost a *questioning* process. An officer can find out a great deal about a crime simply by observing a scene, of course, but he or she can find out much more by asking questions—of himself or herself (to aid his or her thinking about a case), of suspects, of witnesses, of associates (who may also be working on the case at the same time), and of anyone else who might know something about a crime or be connected with it in some way.

An officer may ask hundreds of questions during the course of an investigation, some of them over and over again. In many ways, an investigator is like a reporter; he or she must ask the basic *who, what, when, where, why,* and *how* questions common to journalism. An officer will also ask other types of questions, such as *with what, with whom,* and *how much,* which will help to connect specific elements of a crime and aid in putting the pieces together.

Many questions will have concrete, specific answers; others will elicit replies that are more speculative or uncertain or vague. Some will seem obvious, but they should be asked anyway. Again, it's better to find out too much than too little. Information that doesn't seem to relate to a case can be deleted later during the final report writing stage.

It's helpful if an officer asks the who, what, where, when, why, with what, with whom, and how much questions in a certain pattern or order, depending on the circumstances. If questioning becomes a routine matter, the officer is less likely to forget certain important steps in the investigative process.

All information gathered during questioning should be recorded in the field notebook for future reference.

The following sequence of questions is merely a suggestion and can be viewed as a rudimentary checklist. Naturally, each officer will develop a system which works best for him. The questions listed here are usually the kinds which should be answered on a final report. Sometimes, of course, all of the answers won't be immediately available.

Questions About the Crime:

1. Who discovered (and/or reported) it?
2. Who is investigating it? Who, if anyone, has investigated it so far?
3. Who has been questioned about it? Who remains to be questioned about it?
4. Who committed it (if known)?
5. What did the crime involve or consist of? What type of crime was it?
6. What action has been taken on it so far?
7. When did the crime occur?
8. When was it reported?
9. Where did it happen?
10. Why was it reported? (This may seem like an obvious question; sometimes, however, the person who reports a crime has motives of his own that the officer should try to determine.)
11. How was the crime committed?
12. How was it reported?
13. With what tools or weapons was it committed?
14. With what similar crime or crimes does it seem to be connected or associated?
15. How much property was stolen, if any?
16. How much strength was required to commit the crime?
17. How much "inside information" was needed to commit the crime?
18. How much damage was done?

Questions About the Victim(s):

1. Who was the victim?
2. Who are some of his friends or associates?
3. What does he know about the crime?
4. What services (such as medical assistance) did he require?
5. If medical assistance was needed, when did it arrive?
6. Where was the victim when the crime was committed?
7. Where is the victim now?
8. Why was the victim attacked? (What did the perpetrator have to gain?)
9. How was the victim attacked? With what?
10. How much information is the victim able to offer?
11. How much information does the victim seem to be withholding? Why is the victim withholding information, if he is doing so?

Questions About the Witnesses:

1. Who witnessed the crime?
2. Who are some of the witnesses' friends or associates?
3. What do the witnesses know about the crime?
4. Where are the witnesses now? Where were they when the crime was committed?
5. Did they seem anxious or hesitant to talk about the crime? If so, why?
6. How much information are the witnesses offering or withholding?

Questions About the Suspect(s):

1. Who is the suspect (if known)?
2. Who are his associates or friends?
3. What statement has the suspect made, if any?
4. Where was the suspect when the crime was committed?
5. Where is the suspect now?
6. Where was the suspect apprehended? (If he wasn't apprehended, where was he last seen?)
7. How did the suspect get to and from the crime scene?
8. How did the suspect secure the information, tools, etc. needed to commit the crime?
9. How was the arrest made (if the suspect was arrested)?
10. How much information is the suspect offering or withholding?
11. Did the suspect commit the crime alone, or with another person? With whom?

Questions About the Evidence:

1. Who marked and processed the evidence?
2. What does the evidence consist of?
3. What is the corpus delicti? (The corpus delicti is the "body of the crime," or the material upon which a crime has been committed, i.e. the body of a murder victim. Before it can be said that a crime has been committed, factual evidence must be found which determines the existence of a corpus delicti. Documentation of this evidence in a field notebook becomes the foundation of a case.)
4. When was the evidence marked and processed?
5. Where was the evidence found?
6. Where is it now?
7. Why is the evidence important?
8. How was the evidence obtained?

9. How was the evidence marked and processed?

10. How much additional information is needed before the case can be solved or closed?

The Modus Operandi

Many habitual offenders are relatively consistent in their methods; some even have "trademarks" or recognizable techniques. When a particular action or series of actions are considered to be characteristic of a certain offender, he is said to have a *modus operandi*, or way of working—in other words, an *M.O.* or *method of operation*.

If police officers can clearly identify a suspect's M.O., they're more likely to be able to anticipate the suspect's next move and increase the chances that he will be apprehended. If a suspect has already been charged with a crime, another crime which has been committed in a similar fashion can be reasonably connected with him. Thus, it's important that the officer take careful field notes on the *way* in which a crime has been committed.

The following questions are usually asked by an officer in an effort to determine a suspect's modus operandi:

1. What type of crime was committed?

2. When was the crime committed? (Both date and approximate time are important here.)

3. What are some characteristics of the victim? (This means that the victim should not only be identified by name, but also by occupation or some similar distinguishing factor. Is he a college student, convenience store operator, barber? This kind of information can help the police to determine whether the perpetrator seems to prefer a certain type of victim.)

4. How was the victim attacked? (How did the perpetrator achieve or attempt to achieve his goal? What approach was used? Forced entry? Threats? Promises of payment or privileges?)

5. What was the object of the attack? (Why did the perpetrator commit the crime? What did he have to gain? Money? Ransom? Jewelry? Narcotics?)

6. Are there any "trademarks" peculiar to the perpetrator? (Does he have any obvious personal habits or characteristics? For example, does he tend to write on mirrors, or leave candy wrappers around, or damage a specific type of property?)

7. Did the perpetrator say anything or otherwise communicate with the victim? (What was said or written? What were the speech patterns, the sentence structure? Did the perpetrator use any unusual expressions or demonstrate any distinguishing mannerisms?)

8. What type of vehicle did the suspect use? (Was it a bicycle, a car, a van? If possible, the vehicle should be described specifically, with particular attention paid to any unusual features.)

9. What type of property, if any, was stolen? (Not only the type, but specific descriptions are needed here, especially of unusual characteristics or features.)

10. What did the suspect look like? How did he act? (This can include anything that a victim, witness, or officer might recall—such as height, weight, hair color, build, clothing, mannerisms, distinguishing marks or characteristics, and so on.)

Writing the Investigative Report

Report writing is a duty which shouldn't be taken lightly. In many cases, reports are an officer's legal responsibility. Some are required by his agency's administration, while others are mandated by state or federal statute. Deliberate failure to make a report, or evidence of an attempt to falsify the information contained in a report, can result in legal or departmental action being taken against an officer and may even constitute grounds for suspension or dismissal.

Some states' laws require local law enforcement agencies to file daily reports of felonies committed and fingerprints taken. All police agencies maintain a records section; some are simple, while others are extremely complex. In most large police agencies, all information is cleared through a communication center where data is centralized. Many agencies have established a computerized filing system which connects with other local agencies as well as state information centers (such as the ACIC, or Arizona Crime Information Center), in addition to connecting with the NCIC, or National Crime Information Center. Usually, a request to any of these centers for information results in an almost instantaneous response.

The prompt reporting of information on an incident or crime will ensure that the next person who needs it will be able to get it. Reports which are considered to have special significance include those on sex crimes, fire investigations, stolen vehicles, and traffic accidents.

A police report will serve many purposes during its lifetime, and many people will use it and turn to it for information of various kinds. Thus, a report must meet certain important criteria:

- *It must be complete.* A report should leave no unanswered questions; it must be able to stand alone. The officer who wrote it may not always be available to explain or supplement it.

- *It must be accurate.* Inaccuracies can only hurt; enough of them can result in a report's being rendered useless. Even if a report contains evidence necessary to prove a case in court, it may be declared inadmissible if it's full of errors.

- *It must be factual.* There are important differences between *facts, opinions,* and *conclusions,* and the officer must be aware of these differences and what they mean. A fact is objective; it is based on evidence and proof. An opinion is not always objective, nor is it always based on fact; it can be biased and prejudiced. A conclusion is a judgment or a decision which may be based either on fact or opinion. An investigator is a fact-finder and a reporter; he is never a judge, nor should he let opinions or feelings enter into the report writing process.

- *It must be well-organized and well-written.* If the information contained in a report can't be readily retrieved or understood, it won't be as effective as it could be. If a report is unintelligible or confusing, it can cause more problems than it solves.

- *It must be neat and legible.* Spelling and grammatical errors should be corrected. Reports are usually typed, which takes care of the neatness problem in most instances; when they must be handwritten, they should be readable.

- *It must be brief and concise.* A report should present the information to the reader in a clear, simple, easily understood manner. It should contain all of the information pertinent to an investigation—or as much as the officer has been able to collect—while omitting nothing that might be important later on. It should use as few words as possible while still being complete and making sense.

Preparing the Investigative Report

Each police agency requires and uses many different types of reports (the various types will be discussed later in this chapter). One of the most common is the *preliminary investigative report.* Since the uniformed officer is usually the person who conducts the preliminary investigation—he is called to the scene first and observes it before any other police personnel do—this report is considered his responsibility.

There are many ways of preparing a preliminary report, and these will vary from agency to agency. Most agencies use one of the following systems, however:

- The preliminary report is *dictated* by the uniformed officer into a tape recorder or directly to a recording center. At the center, it's transcribed and checked for errors, and a copy of the typed report is distributed to a supervising sergeant or other official for review and approval. Once the report has been finalized, the original is filed in the agency's central records and copies are routed to appropriate details for followup.

- The officer completes the preliminary report in the field in *longhand* and takes it to the station, where it is either typed or filed in handwritten form in central records. Again, copies of the report are routed to appropriate details for followup.

- The officer *types* the preliminary report before completing his tour of duty. It is then reviewed, approved, and filed, and copies are routed.

In one of its 1972 management information publications, the California Commission on Peace Officer Standards and Training described an alternative method for completing preliminary reports called the "One-Write System." Several law enforcement agencies in Oregon have implemented this system and claim that it has increased efficiency and decreased costs of report preparation.

In agencies which use this system, the field officer writes or prints the report immediately after completing the preliminary investigation. The report is written at the scene. The finished report is reviewed by a supervisor and corrections are made if necessary. Once the report is approved, it's delivered to the records section and processed. It is not typed, and duplications are made from the original field copy.

The advantages of this system are that it is faster and cheaper. And, since fewer people are involved in its preparation, the report is more likely to say what the officer intended it to say, and there's less chance that his observations will be misrepresented or altered.

The disadvantages of this system rest largely on the fact that handwriting is often difficult to read. In addition, district attorneys and court personnel prefer typed reports; many people believe that they are more professional in appearance and easier to work with.

A Step-By-Step Procedure for Report Writing

Just as an officer should follow a certain routine when asking questions concerning a crime (whenever possible, that is), it's also wise to follow a procedure or routine when writing an investigative report. Habit helps to ensure that no important steps are omitted. Most agencies use report forms, which make this a little easier; these will be discussed later in this chapter.)

Step One: Planning the Report. If an officer's field notes are complete, there's no need to rush through the actual writing of the report (although, of course, the report should be completed as soon as possible). The notes will serve as memory aids and will help to fill in any blanks.

Report writing, like the investigation itself, can be viewed as a *questioning* process. For example, the officer might want to ask himself the following questions when planning a report:

- What type of report needs to be written about this particular incident or crime?

- Who will read it, and for what purposes?

- Is there a form to follow? If so, what are its requirements?

- Will the material be presented in box form, narrative form, or some combination?

- What sort of information is needed before the report can be considered complete?

This last question leads directly into Step Two.

Step Two: Gathering Facts. Again, the officer might want to ask himself questions like the following:

- What pertinent facts are contained in the field notes and can be drawn from that source?
- What evidence has been marked and processed? What does the evidence consist of?
- Have all leads been followed up? Are statements, fingerprints, and so on complete and available?
- Have the facts been clearly documented?
- Is there any information which doesn't have to be included in this report but should be saved in case it's needed later?

Step Three: Organizing the Material. Once the necessary facts and information have been located and are available for the purposes of the report, the officer should organize them *before* beginning to write the report itself. This will save time, in addition to making sure that nothing important is left out. Questions like the following will prove helpful:

- What's the best order in which to present the facts? (This will depend on circumstances and, if a form is being used, on the dictates of that form.)
- How can the facts be presented in a way that makes them simple and clear?
- Which are the primary, or most important, facts? Which are the secondary or supplementary ones? (This can be especially important when a form is being used and space is severely limited.)

Step Four: Outlining the Report. This, too, is an organizational step, and makes the final writing easier.

If the report will be in narrative form, outlining in advance will improve the quality of the final report. If it will be in box form, the outline will already be there and the officer will simply have to fill in the blanks.

Information should first be divided into *major topic areas*, then into *subtopics*, and then into *details*.

Step Five: Writing the Report. The outline may be used as a guide during the actual writing process. Since the facts will have been established and the structure will have been determined, the officer will be able to concentrate on structure and content. Hints for report writing are given below.

Step Six: Evaluating the Report. After the officer has finished writing the report, he should look it over at least once before submitting it for final approval. Again, a series of questions can help:

- Do the words chosen represent the facts—or do they instead convey opinions or judgments?

- Is the report clear?

- Is it easy to understand?

- Is it complete?

- Does it say what I want it to say?

- Is it objective and concise?

Helpful Hints for Report Writing

How a report is written can sometimes be as important as what it has to say. A report can contain all kinds of relevant information; if no one can read or understand it, though, it won't serve its purpose and may even be detrimental to an investigation.

A sentence should contain a *single thought*. The shorter the sentence, the less likely it is that the reader will miss the point. A paragraph, on the other hand, should support a *single theme*. It may be long, or it may be short, but it should express only *one* dominant idea.

The writer should concentrate on *specifics* and avoid *generalities*. For example, instead of writing "The woman had some packages with her," the officer should instead write, "The woman was carrying three packages in her arms." And, rather than saying "It's cold today," the idea could be more accurately expressed by the words "Today the temperature is 30⁰F." "He was of medium build" won't be nearly as helpful as "He was 5'10" tall and weighed 152 pounds." Sometimes, specifics won't be available, and the officer will have to approximate, where they are, however, they should be recorded as precisely as possible.

Sentences should be worded so that they make *positive* rather than *noncommittal* statements. For example, "John wasn't very sober" should be replaced by "John was intoxicated," and "The suspect seemed to be in a hurry" would be more effective if written "The suspect ran out the door."

An investigative report is meant to be a vehicle for sharing information; thus, it should be written in a manner that's *simple* and *to the point*. There's no need to impress the reader with fancy language or *overstatement*—nor is there any need to keep him in the dark with vague descriptions or *understatement*. For example, "I observed the young man as he ran swiftly down the dark alleyway, careening against the garbage cans that lined his treacherous path" may work well in a detective novel, but it doesn't belong in a police report. Nor does "He ran" serve the purpose. "The suspect ran down the dark alley, bumping into garbage cans" gets the point across without belaboring it. When adjectives are relevant and necessary, they should be used; when they don't do anything but decorate a story, however, they should be deleted.

Slang and *jargon* have no business in a police report; not everyone is familiar with the "inside" language common to a particular agency, and its use may confuse the reader.

A report is *not* the place to moralize or editorialize. The police officer is an impartial observer; the reader should be allowed to form his own opinions.

In a handwritten report, the officer should be careful when writing numbers and letters which may be confusing. For example, a sloppily written Z may look like a 2, and vice versa; so will a 9 and a 4. The reader shouldn't have to stop midway through a report and try to decipher the officer's handwriting.

Until recently, the first person pronoun, "I," was seldom used in report writing. It was considered more professional for an officer to refer to himself as "the undersigned officer" or "this officer." Instead of writing "I observed the car," the officer would say "This officer observed the car." Third person references are sometimes awkward and unclear. Today, most agencies are focusing on simplicity, conciseness, and direct communication, and officers are being encouraged to use "I" when appropriate. It's both easier to read and to write.

Standardization:
Some Useful Techniques for Report Writing

Every law enforcement agency has developed some standardized procedures for reporting items which are common to most investigative reports. This can improve the clarity, accuracy, and consistency of agency reports, in addition to speeding up the process as a whole. Although each agency will formulate its own set of standards according to its own requirements and needs, most have developed fairly simple procedures for reporting the following ten items:

1. *Names.* Proper names should be spelled out in full, last name first, followed by first name and middle initial. The last name is usually printed or typed in capital letters. Women's names are followed by Miss or Mrs.; military service personnel are identified by rank and serial number. Examples: SMITH, Miss Susan; ANDERSON, John.

2. *Addresses.* Addresses should be specific, including the street number, apartment, suite, room number, or whatever other type of unit number is applicable. If a person's permanent address differs from his current address, both should be recorded and a notation made as to which address is the temporary one.

3. *Telephone numbers.* Numbers, area codes, and extension, where applicable, should all be noted. Home and work telephone numbers should be recorded and identified.

4. *Dates.* Many agencies prefer that the number of the day be written first, followed by the first three letters of the month and the last two

digits of the year; for example, *22 Jan. 78.* Where a span of days is indicated, a dash should be placed between the first and last dates: *11-22 Jan. 78.*

5. *Witnesses.* Information regarding witnesses should be as complete as possible. Sex, race, and age should all be recorded, using standardized abbreviations like the ones listed below.

6. *Sex, Race, and Age.* These characteristics should be noted for suspects and witnesses alike in as accurate a way as possible. This information should be obtained tactfully, however; the officer can gather most of it by simply observing the person. Standardized abbreviations for these categories include:

    Sex: Male = *M*, Female = *F*.

    Race: White (Caucasian) = *W* (includes Mexican and Latin).

    Negro = *N*;

    Chinese = *C*;

    Japanese = *J*;

    American Indian (Native American) = *I*;

    All unknown = *X*.

The age of the person on his most recent birthday should be recorded; if age is estimated; the approximate spread of years should be indicated; for example, *30-35.*

7. *Occupation.* A person's occupation consists of the line or lines of work by which he ordinarily earns a livelihood. This information should be noted on the report form, even if the person is unemployed.

8. *Values.* Property which has been lost, stolen, or recovered should be itemized and described as fully as possible. Its approximate value should also be noted. Stolen vehicles are figured according to current wholesale "Blue Book" figures. Checks, securities, and non-negotiable instruments receive no dollar value estimate. All other types of property should be estimated at approximately 40% of their cost of replacement.

9. *Descriptions of household articles, clothing, jewelry, and other property* should include the maker's name or brand name, serial and model numbers, size, color, and approximate value. Identifying marks should be noted. Where special identification techniques have been used (such as "Operation I.D." numbers, which are furnished to property owners by the police in certain cities), these should also be noted.

10. *Descriptions of persons* should be detailed and complete. In addition to recording a person's name, nickname, alias(es), and permanent and temporary addresses, the description should also include:

    a. sex (M or F)

b. race (using the common abbreviation)

c. age (an estimate is acceptable if the exact age is unknown)

d. height (can be obtained by comparison with others present)

e. weight (can also be obtained by comparison with others present)

f. build (explanatory terms are appropriate here, such as "slim," "husky," "athletic," and so on)

g. hair color (such as *Lt. Brn.* for Light Brown, *Blk.* for Black, *Dk. Brn.* for Dark Brown, and so on); hair types (straight, curly, kinky); style and/or condition (frontal baldness, total baldness, crown baldness, type of haircut, possibility of a wig)

h. eyes: shape (round, oval); color (*Bl.* for Blue, *Brn.* for Brown, and so on); description of glasses, if the person was wearing them; contact lenses if they're obvious

i. beard, if the person wears one, or other facial hair

j. any peculiar or distinguishing characteristics (such as tattoos, scars, etc.)

k. clothing (should be described in order, from headgear down to shoes. Each item should be identified in as much detail as possible.)

There are abbreviations other than the ones noted above which are also commonly used in police reports. When selected carefully and used correctly, they can add to the brevity and clarity of a report. They should *never* be used when an officer is unclear of their meanings, however, or if it's possible that the reader might misunderstand them.

Table 4-1 lists several abbreviations often found in police reports.

TABLE 4-1 Common Abbreviations

Names of Agencies and Proper Names

Department of Motor Vehicles	DMV
Department of Public Safety	DPS
Federal Bureau of Investigation	FBI
National Council on Crime and Delinquency	NCCD
National Crime Information Center	NCIC
Police Department (with local name)	___PD
Uniform Crime Reports	UCR

Ranks and Titles

	Abbreviations
Captain	Capt.
Colonel	Col.
General	Gen.
Investigating Officer	I.O.
Lieutenant	Lt.
Lieutenant Colonel	Lt. Col.
Major	Maj.
Officer	Off. or Ofc.
Sergeant	Sgt.
Watch Commander	W.C.

Direction Indicators

East	E
West	W
North	N
South	S
Eastbound	E/B
Westbound	W/B
Northbound	N/B
Southbound	S/B
Right Front	R/F
Right Rear	R/R
Left Front	L/F
Left Rear	L/R

Common Words or Phrases

All Points Bulletin	APB
Also Known As (for aliases)	Aka
Apartment	Apt.
Approximate	Approx.
Avenue	Ave.
Background	Bkgd.
Boulevard	Blvd.
Broadcast	B/C
Building	Bldg.
Crossing	x-ing
Date of Birth	DOB
Dead on Arrival	DOA
Division	Div.

Common Words or Phrases	Abbreviations
Does Not Apply (or Not Applicable)	DNA or (NA)
Driving While Intoxicated	DWI
Estimate	Est.
Felony	Fel.
Field Interview (or interrogation)	FI
Freeway	Fwy.
High School	H.S.
Hours	Hrs.
Identity	ID
Information	Info.
Juvenile	Juv.
Maximum	Max.
Minimum	Min.
Miles Per Hour	MPH
Miscellaneous	Misc.
Misdemeanor	Misd.
Month	Mo.
No further description	NFD
Passenger	Pass.
Pedestrian	Ped.
Penal Code	PC
Private	Pvt.
Place of Birth	POB
Registration	Reg.
Report	Rpt.
Residency	Res.
Station	Sta.
Temporary	Temp.
Unknown	Unk.
Vehicle Code	VC
Warrant	Warr.
With	$\bar{c}$
Without	$\bar{s}$
Witness	W (or Wit.)
Year	Yr.

NCIC State Abbreviations

Alaska	AK	Montana	MT
Alabama	AL	Nebraska	NE
Arizona	AZ	Nevada	NV
Arkansas	AR	New Hampshire	NH
California	CA	New Jersey	NJ
Colorado	CO	New Mexico	NM
Connecticut	CT	New York	NY
Delaware	DE	North Carolina	NC
Florida	FL	North Dakota	ND
Georgia	GA	Ohio	OH
Hawaii	HI	Oklahoma	OK
Idaho	ID	Oregon	OR
Illinois	IL	Pennsylvania	PA
Indiana	IN	Rhode Island	RI
Iowa	IA	South Carolina	SC
Kansas	KS	South Dakota	SD
Kentucky	KY	Tennessee	TN
Louisiana	LA	Texas	TX
Maine	ME	Utah	UT
Maryland	MD	Vermont	VT
Massachusetts	MA	Virginia	VA
Michigan	MI	Washington	WA
Minnesota	MN	West Virginia	WV
Mississippi	MS	Wisconsin	WI
Missouri	MO	Wyoming	WY

Canada	CD	Mexico	MM

An Overview of Report Types

The average police agency uses a number of different types of reports. Many, of course, are based on the information contained in the officers' field notebooks.

There are five basic types of *presentation categories,* or ways in which reports are compiled and written:

1. *Narrative reports* are situation-centered and written in story form with no predetermined pattern or outline. These can include *summary reports* (which summarize the important facts and details of an incident) and *supplementary reports* (which add to the information contained in the original summary reports).

2. *Chronological reports* are time-centered, concise, brief, and organized in the sequence in which the events of an incident occurred. Examples of these include *inspection reports* and reports on routine agency matters.

3. *Specialized reports* summarize the past or plan for (or project) the future. These might include surveys and summaries of reports made earlier.

4. *Form reports* are printed and standardized. They are used in those instances when it's of primary importance to elicit responses which are consistent and easily retrieved. They include *traffic accident reports* and *service reports,* among others. (Form reports are discussed in detail below.)

5. *Combination reports* can be a combination of any two or more of the above. They might include *juvenile reports* and *felony reports,* where cases are complex and require various investigative steps.

Forms and Formats

A report *form* provides the officer with a specific, restricted, formal outline within which to record data regarding an incident or crime. Categories of importance are preestablished, and no other information is desired or requested. A *format* provides the officer with guidelines to follow when reporting information, but leaves the specifics to his discretion. Most law enforcement agencies utilize a number of standardized forms and formats which police officers use in report writing.

Usually, the information categories which lend themselves to box form are located at the top of the report; these include, for example, the victim's name, address, and phone number, the date and time of the crime, the date and time when the crime was reported, the value of the property taken, the type of offense, the suspect's date of birth, place of birth, nickname, and aliases, and so on. The remainder of the report form is usually left blank for narrative information; sometimes, the format guidelines are printed just above this section.

The narrative part of the report usually requires both space and flexibility. The officer may find it necessary to reconstruct the crime, describe additional suspects, summarize related details, describe evidence, and include pertinent, objective opinions and conclusions. One of the best guides to use when organizing a narrative section is a list of the categories of information considered pertinent to this section. If the department doesn't provide such a list, the officer may find it helpful to design one for his own use.

The three types of report forms which are most frequently used are the *arrest, accident,* and *incident* forms. An example of each is included in Appendix A.

Some Advantages and Disadvantages of Report Forms

Most police agencies are concerned with seeking out the same general types of information. Forms can help to guarantee uniformity in reporting. They can ensure that pertinent categories of information won't be overlooked, and that the data required will be specific, brief, and clear. In addition, it's easy to tell when a box form report is complete and when it isn't; no item should be blank. Those which don't apply to the particular investigation being reported are so indicated by a straight line or N/A written in the appropriate spaces.

There are some dangers inherent to form reporting, though. Pertinent information that isn't specifically requested in one of the boxes may be omitted entirely. And, while brevity is usually considered an advantage, the form may be so brief that the information included won't give a clear picture of the event or incident being described.

Other Report Categories

Police reports may also be labeled according to the stages of the investigative process.

- *Preliminary reports* relate the facts of the initial investigation in terms of what's been done, what's been learned, and what follow-up, if any, is recommended.

- *Supplementary reports* are continuations of original investigations or additions to original reports.

- *Addenda* contain materials pertinent to an investigation and are usually attached to preliminary or supplementary reports. They might include photographs, sketches, diagrams, or special reports.

Some reports are written to meet specific agency requirements. For example:

- *Internal business reports* are required in agency management. These might include reports on personnel and equipment, and may draw from letters written to or from the agency on certain business matters.

- *Technical reports* are concerned with specialized subjects and detailed specifications. Examples include *systems analysis reports* and *research reports*.

- *Summary reports* collect data for public or intelligence information. For example, a summary report may detail an officer's overtime activities.

- *Operational reports* are concerned with police investigations, arrests, traffic offenses, and other subjects directly related to officers' assignments and tours of duty. These might include reports on misdemeanors, felony arrests, and vehicle damage.

Police officers most frequently write operational reports, or day-to-day accounts of what occurs on the job. They also, of course, write preliminary reports. Detectives and specialists, who are usually responsible for follow-up investigations, write most supplementary reports. Any police officer, whether uniformed or specialist, may attach addenda where appropriate.

Report Writing: Special Considerations

Even when a fairly straightforward form is used, report writing still requires some thought. Sometimes, information must be included even when no space is allotted for it; at other times, certain types of information *shouldn't* be included even though it's requested or required.

Informants

Informants are persons who provide leads to the police during the pre-liminary and follow-up stages of an investigation. An informant may be someone who happens to know something about a case and approaches the police to share that information, or someone who regularly helps the police and is paid for his efforts. An informant may be a law-abiding civic leader, or a known criminal who is currently involved in criminal activities. He may or may not be known to the suspect; he may speak in confidence or openly, he may be willing to testify, or may refuse to; he may or may not need police protection. Regardless of the myths which give the informant the unpleasant reputation of being a "squealer," then, an informant can be anyone; thus, each one deserves special consideration.

When working with informants, the police officer should keep the following special considerations in mind:

1. *The informant's motive.* What does he hope to gain by cooperating with the police? Understanding an informant's motive can help the officer to weigh the validity of the information received, consider how it might best be used, and decide how much police protection, if any, the informant needs. Of course, an officer should never make "deals" with an informant which might compromise his integrity or that of the agency, nor should the officer ever get involved in illegal activities simply to extract information from an informant.

2. *The informant's identity.* An informant should never be named in a police report; this could put his life in danger. His whereabouts should also be concealed. Written information regarding the inform-ant should be kept separate from the central files and shared with a very limited number of other persons.

3. *The information itself.* Often, an informant is so afraid of testifying that he will only reveal information anonymously. Since it's very difficult to prosecute a case which is based on information gained from a source who can't or won't testify, it's wise to treat information received from informants as *opinion* or *hearsay* rather than as *factual*

evidence. Independent follow-up of information received in this manner will often develop other sources of evidence which can be used in court and which won't be dependent on corroborative testimony from a concealed informant.

Statements

Statements made by witnesses and suspects can be documented *in substance* (that is, they can be summarized) or *verbatim* (that is, in the person's exact words), depending on how they will be used later. If a statement will be used merely to give substance or clarity to a story, it can be recorded in substance in the field notes and mentioned briefly in the investigative report.

Statements which are important as legal evidence should be recorded verbatim, however. Once it has been written down, a statement must be read, verified, and signed by the person who made it.

In addition, statements must be *legally obtained* in order to be considered as valid evidence. Initially, a statement can be recorded on tape or taken by a stenographer, but it must be transcribed, verified, and signed before it will be admitted in court.

Evidence

Any evidence discovered during an investigation must be clearly described and documented *in detail* in the report itself. The questions *who, what, when, where, why, how, with what, with whom,* and *how much* must be answered as thoroughly as possible in each instance.

Evidence can include, among other things, test results (for example, the findings of a Breathalyzer test for intoxication), fingerprints, photographs, sketches, tools or weapons found or used at the scene, physical evidence found at the scene or on the suspect's person, and impounded vehicles. Since the facts about an item of evidence must be recorded in such detail, it's usually best to follow the narrative form when discussing them in the report. For example:

> Two shots were fired by Matthews toward the victim. One shot struck the victim in the right wrist. The other shot missed the victim and was recovered at Minnowland, 2472 E. Broadway, where it was found lodged in the east wall five feet from the floor and three feet from the south wall.
>
> The gun used by Mathews was a .22 caliber automatic revolver, serial #15367. It was registered in the name of John A. Smith. Two .22 cal. bullets were in the magazine.
>
> The gun, unfired bullets, and slug were tagged by Ofc. Jones for identification and booked at the Crime Lab Property Section.

All pertinent sketches, photos, processed laboratory findings, and related materials should be included as addenda to the completed report.

A Few Last Words from the Rand Corporation Study

In the final analysis, just how important are investigative reports? According to the Rand Reports, which resulted from a study supported by a grant from the National Institute of Law Enforcement and Criminal Justice, they can significantly affect the outcome of criminal cases and are seldom as good as they should be:

> In relatively few departments do investigators consistently and thoroughly document the key evidentiary facts that reasonably assure that the prosecutor can obtain a conviction on the most serious applicable charges [page viii] ... Police failure to document a case investigation thoroughly may have contributed to a higher case dismissal rate and a weakening of the prosecutor's plea bargaining position [page ix].

When an officer is careful to record and document facts and information essential to a case—in other words, when he takes the time and makes the effort to complete a good investigative report—fewer cases are dismissed and pleas to original charges are more frequent. The criminal justice system functions more smoothly and efficiently.

Thus, the often-heard complaint that police and prosecutorial efforts are wasted because too many cases are never solved—either due to insufficient evidence or to some legality—may well be countered by the application of a little more effort to good reporting. This is a duty and a responsibility which must be accepted by every police officer today.

Summary

Although it's often assumed that police reports are boring technical documents which are of little or no use to anyone, the opposite is in fact true. Many persons and agencies—including police administrators, investigators, the FBI, judges, private citizens, and the media, among others—turn to police reports for various reasons. Basically, a report is a way of communicating and recording facts and information related to a case. It can make the difference between a continuing problem and a ready solution; it can also help to ensure that all persons involved in a case are treated fairly. In addition, it can serve to defend a police department's actions and policies should criticisms or questions arise.

Frequently, a police report is based on the information which the officer collects and records in his field notebook. There are many different types of notebooks available, and the notebook itself can be organized in various ways, including the *alphabetical*, the *case report*, the *daily diary*, and the *crossfile* methods. Among the many styles of notetaking which are practiced by police officers, the most common are the *narrative*, the *question and answer*, and the *chronological.* Each officer's notebook will reflect his own personality and preferences; regardless of the type, organization, and style chosen, however, the notebook should contain complete and detailed notes on all aspects of the investigation with which the officer becomes involved.

The investigative process is a questioning process, and there are certain types of questions which should always be asked about the crime itself, the witnesses, the suspect, the evidence, the suspect's modus operandi, and anything else which might shed some light on the case under examination. The questions an officer asks during an investigation will be much like those a reporter asks while writing a story; they will include the basic *who, what, where, when, why* and *how,* in addition to *with what, with whom,* and *how much.* An officer who follows a general routine when asking questions about a case is more apt to get the kinds of information which will prove helpful later. In many instances, an officer only has one chance to observe a scene and should make sure that the information gathered at that time is as complete as it can be.

The actual writing of the police report (which is the officer's legal responsibility in many cases) doesn't have to be a difficult or time-consuming task. Again, a routine can prove helpful. A six-step process has been suggested: the steps include *planning the report, gathering facts, organizing the material, outlining the report, writing the report,* and *evaluating the report* prior to submitting it for final approval.

A good report is complete, accurate, factual, well-organized, well written, neat, legible, brief, and concise. It contains neither opinions nor judgments. Its style can be almost as important as its content; a sloppily written report that's hard to read and full of grammatical errors simply won't look as good or carry as much weight as a carefully compiled and written one. Most agencies have developed a series of abbreviations and standard policies which can help to make the process a bit easier; an officer should never use shortcuts unless he is absolutely sure of what they mean, however.

Each agency uses several different types of reports in its day-to-day functioning, and each type has its own set of requirements. Many are written on forms which request specific categories of information, no more and no less; these can do a lot of the officer's work for him and simplify the report writing process, but they have disadvantages in that they may not always leave sufficient space for detailed replies or ask all of the right questions. Even when a form is used, then, the officer must frequently use his own best judgment when deciding what to include and what to omit when compiling the final report.

Every report, regardless of how insignificant it may seem, is important to the effective functioning of a police agency. And *every* officer must take the responsibility for writing complete, factual, readable reports which will be useful to the many persons and agencies who will turn to them both during and after an investigation.

Questions and Topics for Discussion

1. Discuss some of the many ways in which police reports are used. Who turns to them, and why? How does the quality of a report affect its usefulness?

2. What is a field notebook, and why is it important? What are some ways in which a notebook can be organized?

3. As an ongoing project, you and your class may want to follow a criminal case which is being reported on in your local newspapers. Imagine that you're an officer involved in the case, and set up a field notebook. What kinds of questions will you ask? How will you set up your notebook? What style of notetaking will you choose?

4. You and your class may want to conduct a series of role-plays based on the investigative process. Work together to formulate the details of a "crime." What kinds of questions will you ask about the victim, the witnesses, the suspect(s), the evidence, the crime itself? After the role-plays have been completed, write a final report based on your "findings."

5. What is a "modus operandi?" Why is it important for an investigating officer to determine a suspect's M.O.?

6. Briefly discuss the qualities of a good investigative report. Why is each important? What could happen if an officer were careless when writing a report?

7. What are the six basic steps involved in report writing? Briefly discuss each.

8. Why is a report's *style* almost as important as its content? Name some things which could harm a report's effectiveness and credibility.

9. If possible, obtain a copy of a completed police report from a local agency. Analyze and discuss its style, content, form and format.

10. Work together as a class (or individually) to develop an efficient report form. Then compare it with an actual form obtained from a local police agency.

11. Name and discuss some common report types. What are some of the advantages—and disadvantages—of form reports? If possible, interview a police officer to get his opinions of report forms.

12. Imagine that an informant has just contacted you about some information you need to solve a criminal case. What will you attempt to find out about the informant? What precautions will you take, both when dealing with the informant and when compiling your final report? Why? How will you present the information the informant supplies you when you're called upon to testify in court.

You may want to consider two types of informants. One, for example, may be a local druggist who thinks he knows something about a crime and is willing to testify in court. The other may be a former girlfriend of a man who's suspected of committing a murder.

Annotated Bibliography

Board on Police Standards and Training (Salem, Oregon): " 'One Write': A System for Efficient Report Writing." Originally published by the Commission on Peace Officer Standards and Training, State of California, September 1972. This text describes an alternative system of report writing and discusses its implementation in Oregon. Includes a discussion of the system's advantages and disadvantages.

Bloch, Peter B. and Weidman, Donald R., *Managing Criminal Investigations*, Washington, D. C., U. S. Department of Justice, June 1975. Includes a discussion of how whole police departments contribute to the success of criminal investigations. Gives examples of how to improve the investigative process.

Dienstein, William, *How to Write a Narrative Investigation Report,* Springfield, Ill., Charles C. Thomas, Publisher, 1964. This monograph in the Police Science Series describes the principles and methods involved in writing narrative reports.

Gammage, Allen Z., *Basic Police Report Writing*, Springfield, Ill., Charles C. Thomas, Publisher, 1961. This guide to police report writing describes the purposes, values, and principles involved in the process. It also includes suggestions for writing and form preparation.

O'Hara, Charles E., *Fundamentals of Crime Investigation*, Springfield, Ill., Charles C. Thomas, Publisher, 1970 (second edition). This text has been one of the standards in the field for many years. It focuses on achieving operational effectiveness in investigative work.

The Rand Series: *The Criminal Investigation Process*, vols. I, II, and III. Santa Monica, Cal., The Rand Corporation, October 1975. Volume I: *Summary and Policy Implications*, by Peter W. Greenwood and Joan Petersilia. Volume II: *Survey of Municipal and County Police Departments*, by Jan M. Chaiken. Volume III: *Observations and Analysis*, by Peter W. Greenwood, Jan M. Chaiken, Joan Petersilia, and Linda Prusoff. This text, a part of Prentice-Hall's "Essentials of Law Enforcement" Series, presents the essential elements of criminal investigation simply and systematically.

FIVE

Interviewing
and Interrogation

Chapter Objectives

After reading this chapter, the student should be able to:

- ☑ Identify people who may be important sources of information for the criminal investigator.
- ☑ Identify and briefly explain the significant Supreme Court decisions which have directly affected police interrogative procedures.
- ☑ Define the terms *interview* and *interrogation.*
- ☑ Discuss the ethical and moral considerations of interviewing and interrogation.
- ☑ Explain the importance of communication during both interviewing and interrogation.
- ☑ List the criteria for the selection of interview and interrogation sites.
- ☑ Explain the importance of preparation as it concerns both interviewing and interrogation.
- ☑ Discuss several different types of interview and interrogation subjects.
- ☑ Give a general overview of both the interrogation and interview processes.

People: Sources of Information
for the Criminal Investigator

Any investigation—whether scientific, technical, scholarly, or criminal—may be viewed as a process which aims at solving a problem. This process usually consists of five very basic steps:

1. identifying the problem;
2. collecting and recording information related to the problem;
3. evaluating data;
4. choosing a course of action; and
5. eventually resolving the problem.

During a criminal investigation (which aims, of course, at solving a crime), the investigator is most often the person who's responsible for carrying out the second step of this process. Before a crime can be solved, a great deal of information, or evidence, must first be collected. Without this information, the process cannot continue and the problem cannot be resolved.

Part of the information gathered during a criminal investigation will be physical; that is, it will be able to be seen, or touched, or picked up, or photographed. Physical evidence may include a murder weapon, a broken window, a fingerprint, stolen property, a threatening letter, or anything else which might be noticed at a crime scene, retrieved from a suspect, or contributed by a witness or victim. The majority of information collected by an investigator will be verbal, however; it will be obtained by talking to people who are related to the crime or know something about it. Witnesses, suspects, victims, complainants, and informants will all contribute to the body of knowledge by means of which a crime will be solved. This people information will be gathered through techniques known as interviewing and interrogation.

While the two are similar in that both require communication skills on the part of the officer, they are also very different. Interviewing can, in most cases, be taught. It is a science which can be passed on to others without too much difficulty. Usually, it involves give-and-take on the part of both the investigator and the person being interviewed, who is more often than not a willing participant in the process.

Interrogation is another matter entirely. No one enjoys being interrogated; it can be both frightening and intimidating. The investigator has to work within, around, and in spite of the resentment and resistance of the person being interrogated, and this requires more than communication skills alone. Interrogation is a creative process which calls upon insight, sensitivity, a wide background of knowledge, innovation, logic, a grasp of facts, and an understanding of human nature. Many of these traits or talents are abstract; they simply can't be taught. Most can be acquired, though, through observation and experience. Ultimately, an officer learns how to interrogate not by attending classes or reading textbooks, but by performing interrogations and watching others perform them.

There are aspects of interrogation which can be passed on, however. For example, some techniques have proved more effective than others. Some settings have seemed to be more conducive than others to successful interrogations. Many of these aspects and others like them will be dealt with here as we explore how people can be valuable sources of information for the criminal investigator.

Interviewing, Interrogation, and the Law

Interviewing and interrogation have a common goal: obtaining information which will help to solve a crime. How this goal may be realized is in large part shaped by laws which have been drawn from the provisions of the Fifth and Sixth Amendments to the United States Constitution, which protect people's individual rights in several specific ways.

For example, the Fifth Amendment provides that no person can be required to give evidence against himself, and that no one can be "deprived of life, liberty, or property without due process of law." The Sixth Amendment ensures that the individual has the right to be represented by counsel (among other rights). These protections guard against the dangers of self-incrimination and help to determine the value or worth of confessions. (While some confessions are voluntary—and even these are affected by law—we will be concerned here with those which are made during interrogations.) In addition, the Fourteenth Amendment, enacted after the Civil War, guarantees that no state can "deprive any person of life, liberty, or property, without due process of law." All three of these Amendments, while seeming fairly straightforward, have been subject to a great deal of interpretation since their passage.

For example, it used to be that the admissibility of a confession was questioned only if the confession seemed "untrustworthy;" in other words, its content was more apt to be examined than the context in which it was made or the circumstances under which it was obtained. Gradually, the courts began to realize that confessions which resulted from physical torture were questionable in nature; only later was psychological coercion seen as a matter for concern.

Prior to the passage of the Fourteenth Amendment, the Federal courts had no jurisdiction over how the individual states went about administering justice. The widespread use of physical force to extort confessions was well documented, and the problems that went along with it were noted: "The third degree brutalizes the police, hardens the prisoner against society, and lowers the esteem in which the administration of justice is held by the public." It took a while before the Fourteenth Amendment had any real effect; the above statement, taken from the Wickersham Commission Report on Lawlessness, was recorded in 1931—sixty-three years after the Fourteenth Amendment had been ratified. In 1936, five years later, the U. S. Supreme Court made a landmark decision which helped to extend the protections of the Fifth Amendment to state interrogations. In *Brown v. Mississippi*, the Court reversed the convictions of three black defendants whose confessions had been obtained by means of systematic beatings. This decision, like most others up until that time, dealt with physical rather than psychological coercion.

Other Supreme Court decisions affecting confessions and the interrogative process followed. In 1940, *Chambers v. Florida* held that the undue detention of suspects for the purpose of obtaining their confessions violated their right to due process of law:

> The very circumstances surrounding their confinement and their questioning . . . were such as to fill the petitioners with terror . . . To permit human lives to be forfeited upon confessions thus obtained would make of the constitutional requirement of due process of a law a meaningless symbol.[1]

Again, the Court was concerned more with physical than psychological pressure.

The decisions culminated with four major ones during the 1960's: *Massiah v. the United States, Escobedo v. Illinois, Miranda v. Arizona,* and *In re Gault.* The first, *Massiah*, in 1964, went a long way toward protecting the rights of the accused, specifically the Sixth Amendment right to counsel. Massiah was out on bail, he had been indicted, and counsel had been retained. Meanwhile, law enforcement officers convinced one of Massiah's friends to engage in a conversation with him and contrived to overhear it. Not only was this eavesdropping, but it also deprived Massiah of his right to counsel by getting one of his friends to perform the function of a law enforcement officer without Massiah's knowledge or that of his lawyer. Massiah's conviction was subsequently overturned.

Within a month of the *Massiah* decision, in June of 1964, the Court ruled in *Escobedo v. Illinois* that Escobedo's conviction would have to be overturned because the defendant had been denied counsel during questioning and the questioning had gone on anyway. Even though Escobedo had asked for his lawyer several times, his request had been denied; in addition, he was never informed of his right to remain silent. These facts caused the Supreme Court to reverse the conviction even though the defendant had *not* been under indictment at the time.

The rights which were stressed in *Escobedo*—the right to counsel and the right to remain silent—were further detailed and strengthened in *Miranda v. Arizona* in 1966. Since that time, law enforcement officers have been required by law to advise a suspect of his rights while in a custodial interrogation situation. This decision set forth the following:

1. The accused must be advised of his right to remain silent, and that whatever he says can and will be used against him in a court of law.

2. The accused must be advised of the right to counsel and the fact that an attorney will be appointed for him if he can't afford to retain one. This right must be explained to include the right to have the counsel present during any questioning and at all stages of the criminal justice proceedings.

3. The accused must be advised that if he agrees to answer any questions, he can change his mind at any time and the questioning will stop.

4. The accused must give an affirmative indication that he understands each of these rights, and must make an affirmative waiver before questioning may proceed.

Even though the *Miranda* decisions seemed quite specific, there were some questions which were not answered and which still remain open. For example, what exactly constitutes a "custodial interrogation situation" was not clarified. There are other elements which remain foggy, but one is absolutely clear: Whenever an officer fails to properly advise a suspect according to the requirements of the *Miranda* decision, and questioning results in information which may aid in incriminating the suspect, that information is apt to be declared inadmissible by the court. This has been called the "fruit of the poison tree" concept. An example will help to illustrate it: If an officer discovers through questioning that the suspect has hidden a weapon used to commit a crime, and the hiding place is revealed, the subsequent introduction of the weapon as evidence against the suspect might be supressed *if* it can be shown that the officer failed to advise the suspect of his rights according to *Miranda*. In other words, an officer who ignores the results of this decision and refuses to advise a suspect of his rights is flirting with the possibility that any evidence discovered or any statement made by the suspect during an interrogation won't be admitted as evidence.

Miranda has had a direct and significant effect on the interrogative process. The decision itself is full of references to law enforcement literature on the subject of interrogation. Chief Justice Warren, in writing the 30,000 word decision, named and quoted various police literature sources which supplied the basis for his decision on the psychologically coercive nature of the police interrogation. Thus, at least in part, police writers attempting to deal with the more *creative* aspects of interrogation actually contributed to the Court's thinking as it wrestled with the critical issues of the case. The following, taken from the Court's decision, indicates the impact that these police writings had upon the Justices during their deliberation:

> Interrogation takes place in privacy. Privacy results in secrecy and this in turn results in a gap in our knowledge as to what . . . goes on in the interrogation rooms. A valuable source of information about present police practices . . . may be found in various police manuals and texts. . . . These texts are used by law enforcement agencies themselves as guides. . . . By considering these texts . . . it is possible to describe procedures observed and noted around the country.[2]

Some of the authors named in the *Miranda* decision are held in high esteem in law enforcement and educational circles today. It's important to note that these writers had explored the psychological aspects of interrogation and had given precise examples of strategies and tactics which are freqently used to give the police an advantage. Thus, it seems as if it's becoming more and more clear to the courts and police officers alike that neither physical nor psychological force is a desirable tool to use during interrogation.

Miranda was carried one step further in 1966, when *In re Gault*, the fourth major decision of the 60's, extended these rights to juveniles and succeeded in substantially altering the juvenile justice system. Other related decisions followed. In *Michigan v. Mosley*, determined in December of 1975, the Court dealt with several important issues. First, the defendant, Mosley, had refused to answer questions during an initial interrogation on one charge, and questioning had ceased. Two hours later, he was questioned by another officer about a second charge, and this time he confessed. In both instances, Mosley had signed *Miranda* waivers, and at no time had he requested counsel. Although the Court ruled in favor of admitting the confession and sustaining the conviction, it would appear that *Mosley* has strengthened *Miranda* in the following ways:

1. After invoking his right to remain silent, a suspect should not be questioned a second time about the *same* offense unless he requests such questioning or volunteers such information.

2. Upon invoking his right to remain silent on one offense, a suspect should not be questioned about other offenses without a lapse of about three hours, at which time he must be readvised of *Miranda*.

3. If state law requires that the accused be brought before a magistrate "without unnecessary delay," this should be done immediately after the first interrogation and prior to further questioning.[4]

It's interesting to note that most of the rights concerning interrogations and confessions with which the Court has been struggling to define have been in existence since 1791, when the Bill of Rights was declared to be in force. Unfortunately, none of these rights is as simple or as straightforward as it seems; many aspects are still open to interpretation. It might be said that the police and the Supreme Court are working together to define and clarify these rights. Until they are perfectly clear—which doesn't seem very likely in the near future, if at all—they'll have to continue working together in the simultaneously frustrating and creative process of interpreting the rights of the people as stated in the Constitution.

Ethical and Moral Considerations

Before continuing with more detailed discussions of the interviewing and interrogation processes, it's necessary to sidetrack for a while in order to emphasize the ethical and moral considerations which must be taken into account during these processes. While interviewing and interrogation are often perceived as routine matters, this perception can be both dangerous and wrong. There are other issues at stake than legal ones, and the Supreme Court's decisions discussed earlier reveal their awareness of these issues. The officer must be aware of them, too.

One reason why the courts and the police are constantly struggling with the problems of interpreting human rights is the fact that the needs of society at large don't always correspond with or complement the freedoms guaranteed to each individual. It's been said that one person's freedom extends only as far as the next person's nose—in other words, when one person threatens another by exercising his rights, questions are raised which aren't easy to answer or resolve. The Constitution is an eloquent attempt to set forth both those individual freedoms and the means for maintaining an equilibrium between personal rights and the welfare of society in general. It's more than a mere legal form; it also incorporates the ethical perceptions of a society as they related to basic human liberty, and in this sense the Constitution can be seen as having a moral character as well as a legal one. Rather than being static, it is ever changing and alive. This has its disadvantages as well as its advantages.

While it would be nice to be able to turn to the Constitution as the last word in every legal matter, its moral nature makes this difficult to do. Rather than being perceived as a handbook of legal do's and dont's, the Constitution must be seen as incorporating all other legal writings while at the same time transcending them. It literally stands apart from other legal pronouncements or codes while simultaneously serving as their foundation and source. This is admittedly a paradox, but one which leaves room for improvements, which an absolutely rigid Constitution wouldn't do.

For every law, there's an exception; the moral nature of the Constitution makes its possible to take these exceptions into account. But, because it's now and always has been (and probably always will be) virtually impossible to come up with a moral code that satisfies all people in our society—or that means the same thing to everyone —the struggle between individual and societal rights will simply have to continue. And the police will continually be called upon to get in the middle of it. Here is where the two-sided nature of the Constitution—legal vs. moral, straightforward vs. vague, definite vs.

indefinite, constant vs. changing, clear vs. paradoxical—can be seen as causing problems rather than paving the way for solutions, depending on one's perspective.

The police officer's occupation as a law enforcer means that he works in an atmosphere that is legally oriented, and there's always the danger that legality will be confused with morality. That is, what's legal may be superimposed on or considered more important than what's moral. This is easy to understand, since the law can be perceived as definite, or objective, while morality is another matter entirely. To make the issue even more confusing and volatile, an officer's views are often conditioned by the laws of the particular state or jurisdiction in which he operates. The laws of one state concerning a certain matter may differ radically from the laws of another—and, in many instances, the Constitution is seen as a hindrance to the enforcement of the everyday legal codes with which the officer comes in constant contact. Sometimes, the police fail to view the Constitution as being a statement of both the legal and moral nature of society and its members. They fail to give the Constitution priority over codified statutes. It's difficult to determine which is more important—the law, or the exception. Some people assume that police officers would have a much easier time of it if they would simply believe in the essence of the Constitution itself and view it as *the* statement of the indelible principles of human existence in this country, but this is easier said than done.

Any interrogation must be perceived as a combination of moral and legal issues. The basic protections of the rights of the accused set forth in the Constitution are protections which are fundamental to the concepts of personal freedom. That document grants certain rights to the people to which they're entitled. These rights don't have to be earned, nor do they have to be deserved. They are privileges which belong to the individual merely because he is a human being. They can't be abridged either legally or morally. Police behavior that aims at circumventing, denying, or destroying these rights amounts to unethical—in short, immoral—behavior.

The officer's job is made even more difficult by the fact that two aspects of morality can be said to exist, and both affect him strongly. First, there is the personal, or subjective, morality which belongs to the individual and tends to be relative. Something is either "good" or "bad," depending on a person's opinions and feelings. Secondly, there is an institutional morality—a structured value system which tends to reflect morality in a less relative, more stable context. The police field is an institutionalized setting, and there are occupational moral values that exist in that institution. More often than not, an officer's personal morality won't conflict too much with the institutional morality he works within. Usually, an officer will rely on police institutional morality as the basis for the moral decisions he will have to make in the occupational setting. The problem lies in that neither personal nor institutional morality is one hundred percent correct.

An example may serve to clarify this concept. Suppose that the prevailing attitude in a police department says that crime is going up, the guilty are going free, and the victims are suffering with no relief in sight. Suppose the argument continues, stressing that much of this is due to "softness" on the part of the police during interrogations. The effect might be that police institutional morality would condone and possibly even encourage officers to behave in a manner that would deny individuals their constitutional privileges within the police interrogative situation. Such an approach might very well expedite criminal convictions and case clearances, and this would serve to support by practical results the institutional morality which actually emphasizes immoral conduct. In other words, morality would become immorality; conduct considered ethical would really be unethical. This type of perversion, regardless of its results, is wrong. The end simply doesn't justify the means when human rights are at stake.

When the police recognize that certain rights have been given to the people by virtue of the Constitution, then they, acting as agents of the state, have the greatest responsibility and obligation to ensure the protection of these rights. This means that not only must they work their hardest to prevent crime, but must also make a concerted effort to prevent police misconduct as well, even when this misconduct is seen as furthering the goal of crime prevention.

In the final analysis, if the police don't protect the rights of the accused at every stage of the criminal justice process, the Constitution becomes no more than a piece of paper. The professional police officer represents the Constitution where it counts the most—on the streets. He must not only respect and abide by the legal and moral considerations set forth in the Constitution; he must also embody them.

The Interview: A Definition

Police work is people work. Of all the methods available for the collection of information during a criminal investigation, interviewing remains the officer's primary tool. Interviews will occur more often than any other means of gathering information. They will develop additional sources of information, too, including physical evidence and the identification of suspects. The criminal investigator will generally perform more interviews than interrogations, and the success of an interrogation will in large measure depend on the effectiveness of the interviews that preceded the officer's contact with the suspect.

One point needs to be made here. Recently, the term "interrogation" has been avoided somewhat by law enforcement personnel. Admittedly, it has negative connotations, and it's beginning to be replaced by the less precise term "custodial interview." While it's true that criminal investigators may well find it advantageous to refrain from mentioning "interrogations," especially when they're on the witness stand, there are significant differences between interviews and interrogations which have to be acknowledged. An interview is not the same as an interrogation, and vice versa. Using a single term to define both of them isn't only inaccurate, it's deceptive. Changing the name of the interrogation doesn't change its nature.

Basically, an interview is a *conversation with a purpose.* It may or may not be formal, depending on what setting the officer feels will work best and what's available. The aim of any interview is to direct the conversation in such a way that the person being interviewed will feel either comfortable or willing to provide the officer with useful information.

This general purpose may be divided into three specific categories:

1. First, the officer is concerned with simply accumulating any information which relates to a crime or an incident. He will seek to discover and learn from the subject anything at all that will assist in painting a clear picture of what happened or corroborate information already known.

2. Second, the officer will attempt to identify or locate evidence or loot. He will try to learn from the subject whether evidence or loot in fact exists and, if so, where it can be found.

3. And, finally, the officer will use the interview to discover victims, witnesses, or suspects. Many cases are cleared because of information obtained during an interview. It provides the officer with an opportunity to identify the existence of additional victims, determine the identy of any other persons who might also be witnesses, and maybe even apprehend a suspect.

There are other goals which the interview may achieve, in addition to the ones stated above. For example, while talking to a victim or a witness, the officer has the chance to evaluate that person's potential as a witness in court. He can usually get a pretty good idea of how that person will function in a courtroom setting. The alert investigator can also pick up clues during an interview which can help to determine the defenses that the suspect may use later on. He can then forewarn the prosecutor of any defense advantages the suspect might have and alter his own approach and direction during the investigation in an attempt to overcome the possible defense through evidence or testimony.

Choosing Subjects for Interviews

Generally speaking, interviews are most often utilized to gain information from victims or witnesses—people who are in some way connected with or related to a crime or an incident. The basic assumption is that this type of individual will be willing to communicate with the police. It's quite possible, however, that a victim or a witness will be reluctant to talk to the police; he may even be hostile. In these instances, the investigator may be forced to alter his techniques.

There are other types of people who may be interviewed even though they're not directly connected with a crime. These include representatives of other agencies, both public and private; keepers of records; business community representatives; and other people to whom the investigator may turn in order to discover facts relevant to an investigation.

Many people interviewed by the police will be either *complainants* or *informants*. A *complainant* is someone who officially requests police action and may or may not have any actual evidentiary information to provide. (For example, if a juvenile is a victim of a crime, his parents may be the complainants.) Often, a complainant will only be able to point the investigator toward other people who have more specific knowledge that can be used in court. A complainant may be concerned about something which has raised his suspicions without being able to furnish the police with any concrete facts.

Although the term *informant* conjures up all kinds of undesirable images, they are often incorrect. Some informants are criminals who are paid by the police for the information they supply, but most aren't. Generally, an informant is a person who simply comes forward out of the community to provide information that might not otherwise be uncovered during the course of an investigation. Contrary to myths surrounding the informant, he seldom meets the police secretly on the fifty-yard line of an empty stadium after midnight. A person may act as in informant only once or twice during his lifetime. Usually, he isn't sought by the police—the police may not even be aware of his existence. Instead, an informant is simply someone who's willing to share something he knows and approaches the police with that information.

Over a period of time, a criminal investigator will interview a wide variety of persons with an equally wide variety of backgrounds and positions in the community. Some will be highly successful and important business and professional people; other will be former suspects. Some will belong to the working class; others may be unemployed or on welfare. They will include both old and young people with very different ethnic and cultural backgrounds. If interviewing is a science, then the community is the laboratory; thus, the successful interviewer will be fully capable of communicating effectively at all levels and with all types of people.

It's a good idea for the officer to give some thought to the type of person being interviewed before the actual interview takes place.[5] This may be difficult for the uniformed patrol officer who tends to come into contact with people without the benefit of pre-interview processing; the criminal investigator, however, often has the time to think about the people he will be talking with and consider some of their motives and the psychological factors involved. These are often dependent on *role expectations*.

A *role* is the position that life circumstances have placed a person in at a given time and which cause him to behave in certain ways. For example, our society expects fathers to behave differently from mothers, employers differently from employees, poor people differently from rich people, and so on.

Similarly, an interview subject perceives a role that he must play, and the officer has certain expectations of the subject. If the expectations of the subject and the officer are radically different, the officer may need to alter his approach. This is one reason why the same opening line won't work in every interview situation. Thus, it's important for the interviewer to be flexible and willing to tailor his approach to fit the circumstances.

The interviewer can more or less expect certain things of certain types of subjects, however. For example, children entering early adolescence tend to be good witnesses. Their senses are sharp and their memories well-developed. Adolescents are another matter, though. While their physical and mental faculties are at a prime point of development, many of them are wrapped up in their own problems and may not be effective witnesses.

Older people, especially the elderly, make excellent witnesses and should not be overlooked. The retired person very often has a wealth of knowledge about what's been going on is his neighborhood simply because he spends a lot of time walking around and talking to others in the area.

The shy or nervous person represents a difficult witness, since the officer usually has to pull the information out of him in bits and pieces. Conversation may be difficult; questions are apt to be answered in short sentences. When dealing with shy or nervous people, the interviewer must simply be patient.

Very young children are often witnesses to or victims of crime. They won't always make good interview subjects, however, due to their age and lack of experience. For example, a child who says that he saw something happen "last week" may not have any idea of what a week really represents in terms of time. The investigator can use certain "icebreakers" to determine a child's basic knowledge and level of maturity. The officer might ask the child questions like, "Can you tie your own shoes?" "Do you know when your birthday is?" "What's the name of your school, the name of your teacher, your room number?" "What grade are you in?" "Where do you live? Can you tell me your address or telephone number?" "Where do your parents work?" "Do you know how to tell time?"

In order for a child to be sworn as a witness in court, it must be shown that he has an understanding of the concept of veracity; that is, that he knows the difference between the truth and a lie. An investigator can discover whether a child possesses this concept by framing a question in the negative; for example, "What happens to a person who tells a lie?" The answer must be one that indicates the child's knowledge that something bad will happen if a person lies. This demonstration of understanding is usually all that's needed in order for a child to be qualified to take the oath as a court witness.

Generally speaking, a child under six years of age will have difficulty being judged as a competent witness. Even the six-year-old may cause some difficulty. Thus, if the star witness is a very young child, the officer will have to be fairly certain that he will later qualify as a witness in court.[6]

Most victims and witnesses will be cooperative and will want to help the police. Some won't, however, and may even be hostile. The hostile witness may resist giving information to the police for a variety of reasons. He may have a personal interest in the suspect, for example. This resistance supports the use of interrogative rather than interviewing techniques.

The investigator should always keep in mind that interview subjects are human beings with human weaknesses. Not only are they unable to remember every detail of a crime perfectly, but they are also affected by their backgrounds, previous experiences, emotions, and personal biases. What they recall can further be altered by the types of questions the investigator asks. It has been established that eyewitness testimony can be altered by the use of certain questions or words. For example, a witness will usually respond affirmatively in a significant number of instances if asked whether he saw *"the* gun" or *"the* suspect" as opposed to *"a* gun" or *"a* suspect."[7] Leading questions can help, but they can also hurt. The officer should be aware that even seemingly harmless words or phrases can elicit false or useless information from a subject.

Recently, attention has been given to the use of hypnosis as a means of assisting recall. While this has been utilized in the past with suspects as a tool of the defense, it's currently finding favor at the investigative level with witnesses and even investigating officers.[8] Although the value of hypnosis as an investigative tool can be uncertain, it should not be overlooked in priority cases as a possible means of increasing a subject's—or an officer's—ability to recall details.

Communication: The Essence of the Interview

Communication involves more than meets the ear. In the first place, words are symbols which can be greatly affected by feelings. After all, communication is nothing more than a behaviorial process of interaction, and most people act according to their emotions. Therefore, words are only a small part of communication. Most of the message is conveyed by clever combinations of two other communicative tools: intonation and non-verbal means.

Intonation involves the use of various inflections, the raising and lowering of tones, and the speed or slowness of speech. It's often portrayed in written form by use of underlining, italics, boldface print, exclamation points, parentheses, and the like. An officer's intonation during an interview can have a definite effect on the subject; to use an extreme example, the officer who politely asks "What do you think happened?" will get a much different response than the officer who shouts it.

Non-verbal communication contains three separate types of behavior which are often combined. First among these are facial expressions. These can be used by the interviewer, but perhaps more importantly, they can be interpreted by the interviewer when they're used by the subject. Second among these behaviors are gestures. Certain gestures are symbolic and culturally important; these include the military salute, obscene gestures, and even the simple handshake. Others are subtle and unique to the individual. Again, the interviewer can use gestures to express himself while interpreting those of the subject. And, finally, positioning or pose must also be taken into account. For example, police officers tend to walk and stand in certain ways after pulling a driver to the side of the road. Similarly, interviewees may sit with their bodies facing in a certain direction or take definite revealing positions. All three of these nonverbal behaviors—facial expressions, gestures, and positioning—have been combined under the now accepted heading of body language.[9]

Effective communication is essential to both interviewing and interrogation, of course. Since the investigator will normally do far more interviewing than interrogating, however, the interview provides the best (and perhaps the least crucial) area in which to develop the necessary skills.

Choosing the Site of the Interview

A lot of attention has been paid to where the interview should take place—perhaps too much. An interview is a situation in which the subject is no more than marginally reluctant to participate; he seldom offers outright resistance. Thus, there's seldom any need for secrecy or elaborate preparations of the interview site. Three very general criteria can be used when making this decision, however; they will simply help to ensure that the interview will go as smoothly as possible. They include privacy, limited interruption, and comfort.

Privacy is necessary for several obvious reasons. For one, there may be times when the victim or witness won't want certain facts to be widely known. As an example, an officer may contact a married adult who witnessed a fight at a local bar. This person may be more than willing to help the police but reluctant to have his spouse know that he had been frequenting the bar. There are also instances in which a witness or victim may live in a high-crime area and fear criminal retaliation. If witnesses and victims are going to feel free to express themselves, the location of the interview must allow for a semblance of privacy. This is especially true in cases where the details are sordid or ugly; a rape victim isn't going to want to tell the whole story to an audience, and a parent may hesitate to provide information about a vicious attack in the presence of his children. In addition, children may hesitate to talk to the police if they think that this will get them in trouble with their parents or other adults in their lives.

When possible, the officer should interview subjects one at a time. Otherwise, a third party observer may end up answering the questions directed at the subject. This can be frustrating to everyone concerned. The classic example of this sort of thing occurs when the person to be interviewed is questioned in the presence of a close family member, such as a spouse or a parent. The third party may have no direct knowledge of the offense but feels compelled to talk about it anyway; this wastes everybody's time.

The second criterion, that of limited interruption, simply means that the investigator can't conduct a successful interview in a distracting environment. It's hard, for example, to talk to a subject in a room where children are watching television, or in a business office where the subject is constantly being interrupted by phone calls or other employees.

It's questionable whether an officer should ever interview a subject at the subject's place of work. Few employers like the idea of the police coming into their businesses to talk with their employees; in addition, an employee who's been asked for an interview may have been contacted through the personnel office and may well worry about what other people in the organization are thinking and saying about him. On the other hand, highly placed executives, various business and professional people, and representatives of other governmental agencies sometimes prefer being contacted at the office. To facilitate matters, then, the investigator should always ask the subject where he wants to be interviewed and go along with his wishes as much as possible. An officer who simply marches into a person's office without making an appointment ahead of time may find that a willing subject has become an unwilling or even hostile one. The officer may win a symbolic victory in getting into the person's office, but the quality of the information obtained will be substantially reduced. Those investigators who frequently complain that persons who occupy positions of importance in the community "don't want to be bothered" are often more at fault than their subjects are.

The third criterion, the degree of comfort, has both physical and psychological aspects. For example, if a person is interviewed on the job and feels as if his boss is timing the interview, he is apt to be very uncomfortable. Or, if a person being interviewed at home knows that the neighbors are all peeking out between their curtains at the police car parked out front, he may become tense and unwilling to communicate.

The physical aspects of the interview may seem very obvious, but they're too often ignored. A subject shouldn't be expected to spend a great deal of time standing up or enduring too much heat or cold. If the subject doesn't smoke, an officer who does can create an unpleasant atmosphere. These are all very basic points; naturally, the officer doesn't have to provide the subject with plush surroundings but should merely use some common sense and courtesy. A subject shouldn't have to miss dinner or lose sleep. He is apt to be anxious during the interview, and this may increase his need to go to the bathroom; if an interview is going to be lengthy, the officer can at least make sure that bathroom facilities are available. These and other reasonable considerations can influence the willingness of the subject to participate.

In terms of locations, familiar surroundings are often the best. The home is a good place in which to contact many people. A lot of them are used to talking about serious matters around the table they eat at; thus, the dining room or kitchen is an excellent and informal place for the home interview. People in higher economic groups may prefer the living room; the officer should again ask them to express their preferences and abide by their wishes. In poorer homes, subjects may be very self-conscious, and the officer should avoid patronizing them or others in their homes. Nobody needs to be judged or catered to by a police officer. The best all-purpose approach to any home interview is simply "When in Rome . . ."

Another good location for an interview that is often overlooked is the police vehicle. While the subject is apt to consider it a fairly neutral area, it's actually a very personal extension of the officer. People are intrigued by the police, and the act of entering this sanctuary is interesting without being overwhelming. A person who's had a great deal of police contact as a suspect may also prefer this location; it will be a novelty to be able to enter it and then leave it freely at the end of the interview.

Hints for Effective Interviewing

People in America are used to answering questions. They do it when interviewing for jobs, applying for credit, or responding to opinion surveys. Thus, many are apt to see the investigative interview as simply another question and answer session, an opportunity to speak their minds. The investigator who behaves during the interview as if it's a perfectly normal occurrence can further help to put the subject at ease.

Most witnesses' experiences can be divided into stages, and a knowledge of these stages will also prove helpful. First is the act of *observing* an incident or crime, which involves no more than the sensing of the environment and what's going on in it. This is followed by *perception*, or the mental process of interpreting the information furnished by the environment during observation. The third stage involves *mind-fixing*, which includes the development of bias, the association of ideas, fantasy, and personal judgment. These all work together to influence the way in which the person memorizes the incident. Later, usually as a result of some external stimulus, the person recalls and recounts what he perceived. Recall, however, isn't a precise skill; it's often contaminated by other experiences, thoughts, and imagined occurrences.

The fact that these stages are known to exist support the contention that the interview should take place as soon after the incident as possible. Recall and memory begin to fade or change dramatically with time; the sooner a person is interviewed, the more accurate the information he has to offer is apt to be.

At the beginning of an interview, it's best if the officer asks broad, open-ended questions rather than specific ones. These permit the person to respond with large quantities of narrative, some of which won't be specific and much of which may seem irrelevant. Some subjects may interject extraneous material simply to impress the interviewer. At any rate, this opportunity for the subject to give a general overview of the incident will assist the interviewer in determining what type of person he is dealing with and allow for the interview setting to become more relaxed. After the subject has finished with his original description of the incident—and the officer should let the subject finish—the interviewer can begin asking questions that may fill in specific gaps.

Often, an investigator may fail to ask important questions; this is another reason why the subject should be allowed to talk freely for some time. The person being interviewed probably won't know exactly what information the police are after, and even though it may seem tedious or time-consuming, it's better if he talks too much than too little.

This leads to a discussion of a skill which the good investigator simply can't do without. In short, he must learn to be a good listener. Most people are poor listeners, particularly police officers. The police are used to telling other people what to do, and it's difficult for them to keep quiet while another person is telling them something.

Young people and poorly educated people have the tendency to use a lot of personal pronouns while telling stories. The officer may have trouble distinguishing one "we" from another. Without seeming to scold or getting impatient, the officer should either casually interrupt the subject for clarification or question the person again more specifically after he has finished talking. The officer should interrupt the speaker as little as possible.

Preparing for the Interview

It's absolutely essential for the officer to prepare for an interview ahead of time. Although this topic may have been overworked, many investigators still enter into interview sessions without having the foggiest idea about the case circumstances, what direction the interview should take, or what the person being interviewed is like. In some situations, of course—especially during the early phases of the investigation—time constraints, workload, and lack of information won't permit for thorough preparation. As the investigation proceeds, though, the investigator should be more and more careful in this regard.

Even during the earlier stages of an investigation, there are informal resources that can quickly provide the investigator with additional insights and background information. These include, among others, conversations with the first officer to arrive at the scene; departmental records, as well as those of other agencies; and public information sources, such as vital statistics, voter registration, and city/county directories. The officer who fails to follow up on details which are readily available is usually either lazy or inefficient; the sources are there if the officer will take the time and make the effort to use them.

A little research prior to an interview can help the officer by telling him something about what to expect from the subject. For example, a potential witness who has just completed jury duty may not want to get involved in a process that could lead him back into a courtroom. If a person was once a victim in a case, and lost the case, he may very well have negative feelings about the criminal justice system as a whole. If a subject lives in a high-crime area, he may legitimately fear retaliation. A person's relatives or friends can also affect his willingness to be interviewed.

Often, a simple check of public records—including jail records—can help in locating a potential subject and save the investigator a great deal of time. More than one officer has spent several days on the streets trying to locate a witness or a suspect who's securely locked in the local jail.

The more facts an investigator acquires prior to an interview, the more able he will be to control the conversation. It's very important that the officer be familiar with the crime scene, for example. If the investigator was not the first officer to arrive at the scene, he should take the time to visit it and become fully acquainted with its layout. Then, when a witness says something like, "I think it was the third house on the right," the officer will be able to relate that description to what he has actually seen without having to interrupt the speaker.

Thorough preparation can help the officer in the following ways:

1. It can provide him with a sense of the basic purpose of the interview. Many interviews fail because the officer has no idea of what he wants to achieve or of what information the witness may be able to supply.

2. It can reduce the need to rely on a "fishing expedition"—a series of aimless questions that, with luck, will result in some useful answers.

3. It can help to cut down on the number of long pauses that make the subject uncomfortable and embarrass the officer.

4. It can help the officer to determine whether information provided by the subject will have to be corroborated by other testimony.

5. It will aid the officer in better understanding the time element involved in the incident. Often, words or phrases used to describe concepts of time differ from person to person and from one social group to another. For example, some people may call the noon meal "dinner" while others refer to it as "lunch." The interviewer must try to narrow the subject's concept of the time element involved in the crime or incident; if the officer doesn't himself know precisely when it took place, the information received from the subject may seem to be confusing or misleading.

Preparation will also help the officer with another aspect of successful interviewing—assimilation of information. An interview isn't just a conversation; it's an opportunity for the officer to evaluate the statements that the subject is making and analyze their importance. If the officer is prepared for the interview ahead of time, he will have a basis upon which to make judgments like these.

Interrogation: A Definition

The police interrogation is an adversary situation. Rather than being a give-and-take circumstance like the interview, it's a mind-matching competitive interaction between the officer and the suspect. The officer is trying to find out something that will incriminate the suspect, and the suspect is doing his best to keep the officer from doing just that. Thus, an interrogation can be a demanding and exhausting process, physically, mentally, and emotionally. The police interrogator must be prepared for an experience that may be both draining and frustrating.

An interrogation may be defined as a systematic questioning in a formal situation where the subject is resistant or unwilling to participate. The fact that the person being questioned has a strong vested interest in keeping information from the police is what distinguishes an interrogation from an interview.

The general objective of any interrogation is to discover the truth. However, the truth is not always that the suspect is guilty. The officer must be as interested in discovering innocence as he is in establishing guilt. Whenever an interrogation results in a discovery of the truth, it must be considered successful, whether or not a prosecution follows.

More specifically, the objectives of the interrogation include obtaining a confession or admission; gaining information to support a prosecution; and determining such additional facts as the identities of other participants in the crime, the location of additional evidence, and the whereabouts of loot or stolen property. Other objectives may include uncovering information to clear the suspect of additional offenses, to corroborate information previously learned from other witnesses, and to preview possible defenses.

It's important that the investigator understand the differences between a confession and an admission. A confession is a voluntary statement which describes the details of the corpus delicti, including the intent to commit the crime, and leaves no room for the possibility of innocence. Thus, the mere statement, "All right, I did it!" doesn't stand as a confession. An admission, on the other hand, is a statement of fact from which an inference of guilt may be drawn; in itself, it doesn't stand as fully incriminating. For example, a suspect may admit to having been at the scene of a crime while actively denying having had anything to do with the crime itself.

One type of admission, termed the negative admission, is often overlooked by the novice interrogator. When, for example, a suspect continually denies that he has ever been inside of a particular building, and continues to deny it—even if the investigator has evidence of the suspect's fingerprints from inside the building—the suspect is making a negative admission. This can help the state to prove that the suspect is prone to lying, which can help to lead to a guilty verdict.

Choosing the Site of the Interrogation

Due to the adversary nature of the interrogation, it should be held on grounds that are familiar to the investigator, thus giving him the psychological advantage. This "home ground" concept is still valuable even when the physical conditions of the area used for interrogations may not be the best.

The place of the interrogation should provide some degree of privacy, and it should limit distractions. Interruptions must be kept to a minimum. Either there should be no telephone in the room, or all calls should be held until the interrogation is over. Routine messages should also be held. Interruptions should only be permitted when their content bears directly on the information necessary for a successful interrogation. Interrogation rooms should not have windows, fancy drapes, excessive furniture, knick-knacks, or wall ornaments—in other words, anything that the suspect can concentrate on to avoid answering questions.

Many interrogation rooms are located within jails, and while this can be very convenient it can also cause problems. Although this seems so obvious as to almost be ridiculous, the officer must be especially careful that the person brought to him for interrogation is the right person. It's much too easy to bring the wrong person from the cell block when the jail is either large or busy. It isn't only embarrassing to discover that the wrong person is being interrogated, but it usually takes time before the fact can be recognized. And, more important, this error may funnel confidential information back into the inmate population and forewarn persons who may be interrogated in the future.

Preparing for the Interrogation

Earlier in this chapter, it was emphasized that the investigator should be prepared before conducting an interview. Preparation is even more important to successful interrogations. To go into an interrogation "cold" is at best a gamble and usually results in less than desirable outcomes. In fact, many interrogative failures can be traced directly to inadequate preparation on the part of the investigator. The interrogator needs all the data he can gather, *both* about the offense itself and about the suspect.[10] An interview is likely to be informal; an interrogation is usually formal. An interview subject will probably be willing to cooperate with the police; an interrogation subject will probably be the opposite. In an interview, the subject should be made to feel as if he has the floor and can talk as much as he wishes; in an interrogation, the investigator must take the upper hand. All of these differences between interviewing and interrogation serve to emphasize the importance of preparation.

Most crucial is the interrogator's knowledge of the crime scene. Whenever possible, his acquaintance with the geography of the scene, compass directions, and the location of items such as loot and evidence should be complete. He should be ready to cite specifics. Often, an interrogation subject will cooperate only if he is made to feel that the police already know the answers to the questions they're asking. Thus, preparation is the foundation from which all other aspects of the interrogative process will flow.

An Overview of Interrogation Subjects

Although an interrogation isn't a pleasant situation, and no one can be said to enjoy it, there are some subjects who will be willing and able to participate. There are a variety of reasons why some people are easy subjects for interrogation. Some are simply very open or naive; others may lack intelligence or experience. Many young offenders have one or more of these characteristics. In addition, a majority of juvenile offenses are committed within a peer group setting, and this increases the chances of encountering a willing interrogation subject. Even when adults work in groups, an individual may be willing to implicate his partner, especially if he had less to do with the actual crime than the partner did. For example, a lookout may be willing to talk sooner and more freely than the person who actually broke into a building and took the major risks. Risk-takers are people who are either quite calculating (an indication of intelligence and experience) or somewhat daring. Those suspects who assume criminal tasks that call for less risk involvement are usually easier interrogation suspects; this is especially true if the suspect can be made to feel that the authorities are really "after" the risk-taker instead of him.

Another willing subject is the "hard con" or "big fall" who knows that he is either wanted for a more serious offense or by another state. In effect, this type of suspect will be "shopping" for the best deal. He will probably have to do some time, and realizes this, but may have some say about the where and when if he cooperates during the interrogation.

An interrogation is like an interview in that it, too, is more than a mere conversation. The interrogator will have to be very observant of not only what the suspect says but also of how he behaves and what his dominant feelings or emotions seem to be. A youth who's unwilling to participate may become more willing if the officer can determine that the youth is concerned about how his parents may be feeling and brings this into the interrogation setting. A young person who indicates anxiety about court experience, incarceration, probation, or a police record can be nudged toward the need to reconcile himself with society.

Subjects who are embarrassed in the eyes of their families or communities; those who wish to spare their families any further suffering; and those who have become institutionalized due to numerous periods of incarceration may all be willing to provide statements for differing but significant motives. When things seem to be going very badly for them, and they see themselves as causing problems for many other people whom they care about, they may wish to resolve the immediate difficulty more quickly by cooperating with the police.

Naturally, suspects who are convinced that the police have the full story and are in possession of enough evidence to sustain a conviction against them will be more motivated to talk. They may hope that their willingness to share information with the police may result in easier sentencing. A fingerprint discovered at a significant place in the crime scene can often turn the tide, as can solid witness testimony. Again, the need for the interrogator to be in possession of this type of information—in other words, to be prepared—cannot be overemphasized.

The value of an interrogation subject's statement is in part dependent upon whether it can be admitted or supressed in a courtroom. Some subjects are simply inadequate. If it can be shown that they don't understand their own rights and the nature of the charges against them—that is, if it can be shown that they lack certain mental faculties—there's a good chance that their statements won't be judged admissible. The voluntariness of their statements will be tested, and important evidence may be supressed. This can result in an otherwise solid case being lost.

Persons who might be considered incapable of competently waiving their rights or voluntarily answering questions during interrogation tend to fall within three distinct categories:

1. those who are severely mentally retarded, very immature, or extremely psychotic;

2. those who abuse drugs or alcohol, and are under the influence during the interrogation; and

3. those who are physically ill, injured, or excessively fatigued.

Each of these categories merits further explanation.

While a person might not be so severely retarded that he can be legally excluded from criminal responsibility, he may be judged incapable of freely and voluntarily providing information during an interrogation. The same holds true for the psychotic person; he might be capable of intending to commit a crime but not of providing a voluntary statement in a custodial interrogation.

Lack of maturity applies directly to the concept of *tender age*. A child may not be considered sufficiently mature to waive his rights without adult counsel. It should be noted that while many decisions have tended to uphold the theory that the general juvenile population is sufficiently mature to waive their rights in an interrogative setting, many local courts have ruled the opposite. And, when tender age combines with retardation or psychosis, the question of voluntariness becomes pronounced.

While the police routinely question persons who are under the influence of alcohol or drugs, the reliability of these subjects' statements may be challenged. A defense counsel has a great deal on his side in this type of situation. These persons should be interrogated after they've overcome the effects of alcohol or drugs, not while these effects are still obvious.

Any individual who's injured or physically ill will have a built-in reason for explaining away later any incriminating statements made to the police during an interrogation, as will anyone who claims serious fatigue. Quite simply, a person can claim, "I just wanted to get the police off my back;" if he can be shown to have been under a lot of strain, or too tired or sick to respond voluntarily, any statements he makes may be questioned.

Whenever the voluntary nature of a statement can be challenged, there's a high probability that the court will supress it. This fact should serve as a rule of thumb for the interrogator.

Many subjects will simply be unwilling to cooperate with the police in any way. An infinite array of factors will have combined to form a resistance level that's difficult to overcome. These factors can be grouped under two major headings: *attitudes* and *motivators*.

A person who harbors antisocial attitudes as a basic part of his personality will tend to act out these attitudes in negative forms of behavior. The interrogation is merely another setting in which such behavior can be demonstrated. Negative attitudes toward the police in general, or toward the interrogator in particular, can significantly reduce the officer's ability to obtain information from a subject.

Threats—whether real or perceived—give rise to increased stress in the individual being interrogated. The fear of incarceration, anxiety over loss of status, or fears about the reactions of co-participants in the crime can cause a suspect to simply refuse to participate in an interrogation, especially if he sees no way out of the problem.

A subject can be influenced to resist by a number of motivators as well. One in particular is that of not wanting other people to know the full extent of one's involvement in a crime. A suspect may feel that if he refuses to talk, his spouse or parents or friends won't find out about what he has done.

The competition arising from a confrontation with respresentatives of law enforcement, or "the system," can also provide the motivation necessary for a subject to resist interrogation. Trying to "beat the rap" may be the only significant stimulus the suspect perceives. The investigator who has a grasp of the fundamentals of human behavior—including some insight into his own behavior—will have a better chance of directing the course of the interrogation toward a more successful conclusion.

The length of a suspect's record of previous arrests and convictions doesn't serve as a reliable indicator of how willing or unwilling he can be expected to be. A subject who's served several long prison terms already may be very cooperative and want to clear up other criminal matters, while a first offender may be much more stubborn. Again, the better an officer understands human behavior, and the more flexible he is willing to be, the better chance he has of conducting a successful interrogation.

Appeals: The Tools of the Interrogation

Persuasion plays an important role in the interrogation, especially if the subject is less than willing to cooperate. The persuasive strategies used during interrogation can be divided into two major categories: appeals to logic, and appeals to the emotions. The two aren't mutually exclusive, however; it isn't uncommon to discover them being used alternately or even simultaneously. Again, interrogation is a creative process, and the interrogator can be viewed as a sort of artistic director who shouldn't insist on following the same old routine time after time.

Appeals to logic or reason are basically attempts to make the subject see that it's in his best interests to clear up the matter at hand and move on in the criminal justice process. This method amounts to the "We already know, so you may as well tell us about it" approach. By using straightforward, factual arguments, the investigator can attempt to strike a rational chord within the suspect. For example, the investigator might say, "We know you were at the scene. We have two witnesses and a fingerprint to prove it." The investigator might then try to direct the subject's attention to the futility of further resistance by saying something like, "Since we have both evidence and witnesses to prove you were at the scene, it doesn't make much sense to keep insisting you weren't there."

Generally, the logical approach seems to work best in situations where the police already have enough information to move toward a prosecution—and where the subject possesses above average intelligence. That is, this type of appeal seems most effective in the face of rational unwillingness to cooperate rather than mere stubborness or fear.[11] To achieve maximum success with this approach, the officer must combine two levels of communication: the informative, and the interpretive.[12] In other words, the officer must both communicate information and interpret that information in a way that makes sense to the subject. He or she must cite factual data and evaluate it with the subject in a logical, rational manner, using judgment and opinion as a way of opening the subject's mind to the advantages of cooperating with the police.

The appeal to the emotions, on the other hand, utilizes gut level communication and aims at the subject's vulnerable areas. It strikes out at weakness, fear, or anxiety. It's usually considered a more direct approach than the logical method.

It's interesting to note that an appeal to logic will usually be more effective if it's mixed with an appeal to the emotions. Using both facts and fears is often more successful than either approach alone. If only one approach is used, however (and this is often the case with novice interrogators), the emotional appeal format seems to be more successful with Americans than the logical one.[13]

The emotional appeal begins with a content cue—something couched in a phrase, a word, or a bit of information—that arouses a state of emotional tension within the subject. This is then followed by a reassuring recommendation embedded in the communication which more often than not helps to bring about a desired response. The systematic use of the cue, reassurance, and expectation of a response can be developed into a sort of chain of communication, where a new emotional cue follows the resolution of each previous one and leads the subject along.[14] It's important that this balance between emotionalism and reassurance be maintained. Threats alone tend to make the individual so anxious that he internalizes his stress by simply withdrawing. Thus, threats should be mixed with offerings of "ways out" in order to keep the subject from becoming even more resistant.

Effective emotional appeals usually begin with an attempt to get the individual to see the effect his behavior is having on other people in his life—such as family, friends, or peer group. There are other tactics which also seem to work. With men especially, for example, an attack on their sense of pride or masculinity can bring about desired results, as can a demonstration that their friends are on the "outside" and that they're "taking the rap" for the people they're protecting. In any case, the subject must be offered a way out of the dilemma. The interrogator must communicate this reassurance very carefully, however, without ever implying a "deal" or a "payoff" as a result of cooperation. This demands that the officer have well-developed communication skills; in addition, he must never lose sight of the fact that a confession or admission must be voluntary in order to be accepted by a court.

Dos and Don'ts for
Successful Interviewing and Interrogation

Both interviewing and interrogation are processes of communication which attempt to achieve a common goal: obtaining information that will be useful in solving a crime. Although there are many important differences between the two, there are also enough similarities to make a series of general guidelines like the following useful. Some of them can be taught; others must be learned by experience and observation.

Dos

- *Let the subject talk.* One of the most glaring mistakes novice interrogators make is to not allow the person being questioned to express himself. Officers either interrupt too much or actually change the direction of what the person is trying to say, and important information is never given the chance to emerge.

- *Learn to listen.* Many officers are such poor listeners that they never actually hear what the subject is saying. Often, an admission is made that goes right by the investigator. If the subject has the floor, the officer can learn a great deal simply by paying attention.

- *Clarify information.* There are two sides to this. First, the officer should always ask the subject to explain a point or a detail if it isn't at first clear or if it seems confusing. (The subject shouldn't be interrupted while speaking unless it's absolutely necessary, however.) On the other hand, though (and this is especially relevant to interviews), the officer shouldn't get so carried away with his own presumptions or theories of what happened during an incident that he leads the subject in only one direction. Sometimes, a witness won't provide an important piece of information simply because he doesn't realize its importance. If the officer is busy pursuing one point to the exclusion of all others, vital information may never be revealed.

- *Expect denials and even outright lies.* Some officers fall into the trap of emotionally reacting to obvious denials or lies. This reaction is a combination of personal feelings and the fact that most police believe that the public respects police authority and would never knowingly deceive a law enforcer. The officer should simply assume that the majority of people will attempt to reduce their roles in criminal actions out of sheer self-defense and avoid getting caught up in an equally emotional response.

- *Use open-ended questions.* Basically, the interviewer (and sometimes the interrogator) will want to encourage the subject to talk as much as possible. Open-ended questions tend to result in narrative, detailed answers. A general question like "What happened then?" tends to move the process forward while allowing the subject to respond in some detail. Again, it's better if the subject talks too much than not enough.

- *Use non-directive questions.* This approach is especially useful during interrogations. It involves nothing more than repeating the last point made by the subject in question form; in this way, the officer avoids directing the subject's answers while still requiring him or her to respond. The following is an example of a conversation utilizing this tactic:

SUBJECT: "I went in through the window."

OFFICER: "The locked window?"

SUBJECT: "Naw, it was open and I just climbed through."

OFFICER: "Climbed through?"

SUBJECT: "Yeah, into the kitchen."

OFFICER: "The kitchen?"

SUBJECT: "Well, I didn't stop there. I went on to the bedroom to look around."

OFFICER: "To look around?"

SUBJECT: "You know, for money and stuff."

- *Relate time elements to alibis.* The officer should always allow the suspect to fill in all details of an alibi, even when the suspect seems confused and supplies an alibi for a different time than that during which the crime was committed. Basically, this allows the suspect sufficient rope to hang himself. Detailed questioning will result in his not being able to come back with a new alibi when it's pointed out that although the alibi sounds good, it doesn't cover the time when the offense occurred.

- *Utilize the hypothetical approach.* Sometimes it's useful during an interrogation to present hypothetical situations that parallel actual circumstances. This can help the subject to see what he is up against and begin to understand why it's to his benefit to cooperate.

- *Make sure that the right person is being questioned.* This point has already been discussed; it's important enough to merit repeating, however. A mistake is surprisingly easy to make.

- *Obtain a verbal statement if necessary before trying to record it.* The interrogation process is a delicate balance (as are some interviews); if a suspect seems ready and willing to make a statement, and the officer nervously says, "Hold on a minute, I have to record this," the statement may never be made because the suspect will take the opportunity to reconsider. The full statement should be obtained whenever the subject is willing to give it rather than at the officer's convenience.

- *Watch for signs of deception.* This requires the officer to have some knowledge of body language. The narrowing of the eyes, the tightening of the stomach, and sudden nervous movements on the part of the subject can all tell the officer that he isn't being entirely truthful or that the officer is getting close to the real issue.

Don'ts

- *Never promise a witness that he won't have to testify.* Unless the officer is prepared to go to any length to protect the source of the information, he should never offer this kind of reassurance to a witness.

- *Don't ask too many personal questions of a witness or suspect.* Much of this information will be available from various public records; there's no need to waste time or increase the anxiety of the witness or suspect by asking questions that can be answered by other sources.

- *Don't give a witness or suspect more information than the witness or suspect is offering.* Often, an investigator finds that a subject is the one who's asking all the questions. These should be routinely fielded with noncomittal answers, and the officer should take control of the questioning immediately. Many investigators give more data than they receive.

- *Don't ask questions that can be answered with a simple "yes" or "no."* In the search for information, the good interviewer or interrogator will be after specific details from the subject, not mere affirmations or denials. Questions that imply their answers will also be ineffective.

- *Never get involved in a meaningless argument.* Even though it seems ridiculous, officers often end up arguing with interview or interrogation subjects. "Yes, you did!" and "No, I didn't!" shouting matches don't add up to meaningful communication.

- *Don't make idle threats.* Many suspects are wise in the ways of the law, especially if they've been suspects before. Thus, a threat from an officer to "lock you up and throw away the key" will simply cause the subject to doubt the competency of the investigator.

- *Don't bluff in such a way that the subject gains from it.* An implied bluff is all right and can be an effective tool, but it's a big mistake to go out on a limb that can be sawed off. If an officer claims to have a suspect's fingerprint from inside of a building when the suspect was merely a lookout and never actually entered the building, the suspect will have the upper hand.

Summary

In many criminal cases, people evidence can be more important and valuable than physical evidence. The criminal investigator will collect this people evidence through the processes of interviewing and interrogation. Although the two are similar in many ways—both require that the officer possess skills in the areas of communication and human relations, for example—they are also very different. An interview subject will normally be willing to cooperate with the police; thus, an interview setting can be informal and tailored as much as possible to the needs and preferences of the subject. An interrogation, however, is most often a formal situation in which the subject would much rather not be involved. He will probably offer a great deal of resistance. Each approach, then, calls upon different talents and techniques; neither can be considered purely routine.

The interview can be viewed as a sort of training ground for learning how to conduct a successful interrogation. Often, interviewing can be taught; interrogation, on the other hand, must be learned through experience and observation. Interrogation is generally considered the more creative of the two processes and the most demanding. Changes in the law have increased these demands. The officer must not only be aware of the laws pertaining to confessions and admissions, for example, but must also comply with them. The Constitution, upon which the laws are based, is a moral as well as a legal document; it's important, then, that any facts related to a case be obtained ethically as well as legally. Several recent Supreme Court decisions have emphasized the rights of the subject primarily because these rights have often been ignored or disregarded in favor of solving a crime by any means.

Communication is the essence of any successful interview or interrogation. Communication involves more than just words; it also encompasses facial expressions, gestures, and poses. A good investigator must have some knowledge of how body language can be read and interpreted. During an interview, the officer will want to let the subject talk as much as he wants to; during an interrogation, the officer will want to take the upper hand more obviously and direct the questioning into certain areas considered important to the case. In any event, the officer will have to know how to listen as well as how to talk in order for real communication to take place.

An interview should be held as soon as possible after the incident. This is because most people go through a series of stages—observation, perception, mind-fixing, memorization, and recall—and each is more subjective than the last. Human beings have human memories which can fail or change over time and are affected by many different factors and influences. The investigator shouldn't be in such a big hurry that he neglects to prepare for the interview, though. Lack of preparation can only hurt. An officer who goes into an interview without having the vaguest idea about the particulars of the case wastes everybody's time. Preparation is also important because witnesses usually don't know what specific information the police are after and may not offer a particularly important piece of information simply because the police don't ask for it.

Preparation prior to an interrogation is even more essential. The more an officer knows, the less likely a subject will be able to deceive the police or successfully downplay his role in the crime. Many interrogative techniques—such as bluffing and presenting hypothetical situations—require the officer to have a solid grasp of specifics.

Both interview and interrogation sites should be carefully selected. During an interview, a subject should be made as comfortable as possible; this will make him more willing to communicate. During an interrogation—which is usually an adversary situation—there should be no distractions or interruptions to interfere with the process. Communication in any event is facilitated by a semblance of privacy and mutual respect.

Regardless of how experienced an officer is in interviewing witnesses or interrogating suspects, he must never forget that every subject is a human being with human rights and weaknesses. True, an officer can have certain reasonable expectations of how people will behave, depending on their ages, backgrounds, social circumstances, and the like, but he can never be *sure*, and this requires a certain degree of flexibility and openness to change. Each person is different; each case is different. There will always be variables which will have to be dealt with.

In short, the investigator is no better than his ability to acquire information. Most of this information will come directly from people. A lot of effort has gone into defining police work as a science, but it is basically and most importantly people work. Whether on the streets, in a witness's home, in an interrogation room, or in a courtroom, the investigator is a human being responsible to—and responsive to—other human beings.

Questions and Topics for Discussion

1. Discuss the major differences between interviewing and interrogation. How do the subjects differ? How should the officer's approach differ?

2. Name and briefly discuss some Supreme Court cases that have significantly affected police interviewing and interrogation.

3. What are the differences between a confession and an admission? What is a "negative admission?"

4. Discuss some of the ways in which the Constitution may be considered a moral as well as a legal document. How do these moral considerations affect the investigator? What is "institutional morality?"

5. If a criminal investigator attempts to get around having to advise a suspect of his *Miranda* rights, what might be the outcome? Briefly discuss the determinations made in the *Miranda* case that specifically affect the suspect.

6. What is a "custodial interview?" When, if ever, should that term be used?

7. What is the purpose of an interview? Of an interrogation? Discuss in detail.

8. What is an informant? A complainant?

9. Imagine that you're interviewing a child in an attempt to determine what kind of witness he will make. What specific types of questions will you ask? Define the "concept of veracity" and discuss how it relates to very young witnesses.

10. Name and define the three major tools of the communication process. Discuss the three major types of non-verbal communication.

11. What are the criteria an officer should use when selecting a location for an interview? An interrogation?

12. Name and discuss the stages a witness will go through regarding a crime or an incident. Why is it important to conduct an interview as soon as possible?

13. Why is it so important for the officer to prepare for an interview? An interrogation?

14. Should an interrogation be considered successful even if a suspect is found to be innocent?

15. Why are some subjects willing to be interrogated? Why are others unwilling or even resistant?

16. Discuss some factors which may contribute to making an interrogation subject inadequate.

17. How can the concept of "tender age" affect an interrogation and its outcome?

18. Discuss the two different types of appeals used during an interrogation?

19. What are some signs of deception that an investigator may observe during an interrogation?

20. With other members of your class, role play both an interview and an interrogation. You might want to research a case currently being considered in your local courts and tailor your role play to that case.

Footnotes and References

1. *Chambers v. Florida*, 309 US 227, 1940.
2. *Miranda v. Arizona*, 384 US 436, 1966.
3. *Ibid.*
4. Charles E. Travelstead, "Miranda and Custodial Interrogation," *Illinois Police Officer*, Vol. 7, No. 3 (Summer 1976), pp. 43-57.
5. Samuel R. Gerber and Oliver Schroeder, Jr., *Criminal Investigation and Interrogation* (Cincinnati: Anderson, 1972), pp. 274-396.
6. C.J. Flammang, "Interviewing Child Victims of Sex Offenses," *Police*, Vol. 16, No. 6 (February, 1972), pp. 24-32.
7. Elizabeth F. Loftus, "Reconstructing Memory. The Incredible Eyewitness," *Psychology Today*, Vol. 8, No. 7 (December 1974), pp. 117-119.
8. Martin Reiser, "Hypnosis as a Tool in Criminal Investigation," *Police Chief*, Vol. SLIII, No. 11 (November 1976), pp. 36-59.
9. Julius Fast, *Body Language* (New York: M. Evans, 1970).
10. Gerber and Schroeder, 1972, p. 396.
11. Philip G. Zimbardo, *et al.*, "Communicator Effectiveness in Producing Public Conformity and Private Attitude Change," *Journal of Personality*, Vol. 33, No. 2 (November 1965), p. 254.
12. John Powell, *Why Am I Afraid To Tell You Who I Am?* (Chicago: Argus, 1969), pp. 55-56.
13. George W. Hartmann, "A Field Experiment on the Comparative Effectiveness of Emotional and Radical Political Leaflets in Determining Election Results," *Journal of Abnormal and Social Psychology*, Vol. 31, No. 3 (June 1936), p. 100.
14. Ralph L. Rosnow and Edward J. Robinson, *Experiments in Persuasion* (New York: Academic Press, 1967), p. 147.

Annotated Bibliography

Aubry, Arthur, *The Officer In The Small Department*, Springfield: Thomas, 1961. This text includes an excellent basic chapter dealing with sources of information in a clear, concise manner. A separate chapter presents the funadmentals of interviewing and interrogations without cluttering the material with elaborate writing style. An easy to read, worthwhile reference.

Bristow, Allen P., 2nd ed., *Field Interrogation*, Springfield: Thomas, 1972. Although the main emphasis of this text is on the patrol task, Chapter VI deals effectively with the interrogation. The material covers aspects of special subjects to be questioned; e.g., juveniles, the intoxicated, females, and others. There is a discussion of interrogative techniques under specific headings. The material includes illustrative dialogues used as emphasis.

Creamer, J. Shane, *The Law Of Arrest, Search, And Seizure*, Philadelphia: Saunders, 1968. A well-written book that contains a very simplified, complete, and direct presentation of the Miranda requirements and the Constitutional foundations applied to police application.

Dudycha, George J., *Psychology for Law Enforcement Officers*, Springfield: Thomas, 1955. An old standby that provides an excellent basic development of material for the understanding of behavior. There is an effective chapter describing the interview process and the criteria of that setting. The book also contains a good discussion of the psychology of deception.

Fast, Julius, *Body Language*, New York: Evans, 1970. The primary text on the principle that the body does not lie. Written for lay understanding, the book is an outstanding introduction to non-verbal communication.

Flammang, C. J., *The Police And The Underprotected Child*, Springfield: Thomas, 1970. A good chapter dealing with both the interview and the interrogation as tools of criminal investigation. Special attention is paid to the importance of interviewing, including problems encountered with young children.

Fricke, Charles W., rev. by LeRoy M. Kolbrek, 6th ed., *Criminal Investigation*, Los Angeles: Legal Book Store, 1962. An excellent analysis of witness characteristics and traits, coupled with an extended discussion of statements, admissions, and confessions. (NOTE: Predates *Miranda*.)

Gerber, Samuel R. and Oliver Schroeder, *Criminal Investigation and Interrogation*, Cincinnati: Anderson, 1972. Includes eleven chapters dealing with various aspects of interrogation and written by different contributing authors. The material includes information on the polygraph, use of truth serum and hypnosis, and the interrogation as used in England. Particular interest should be paid to the chapters addressing the social-psychology of interrogation and the semantics of interrogation.

Kirk, Paul, *Crime Investigation*, New York: Interscience Publishers, 1960. An authoritative work that covers the crime scene search, evidence potential, and the crime laboratory in an unparalleled manner. Thorough, complete, and academically sound, this book should serve as a background reference for the interviewer-interrogator.

McDonald, Hugh C., *Police Interrogation*, Santa Ana: Townsend, 1963. This book applies the psychology of the interrogative interaction to specific typological crime categories, as well as supplying the basics of both interviewing and interrogative techniques. The text has an excellent chapter dealing with mental blocks to memory and willingness to respond.

Nedrud, Duane R., *The Supreme Court And the Law Of Criminal Investigation*, Chicago: L E Publishers, 1969 (with yearly supplements). An outstanding overall presentation of the legal aspects of the investigative process, including an in-depth analysis of the factors affecting interview- and interrogations. Well written and aimed at the police audience.

O'Hara, Charles E., *Fundamentals of Criminal Investigation*, 3rd ed., Springfield: Thomas, 1973. This is an extensive effort to cover the totality of criminal investigation. Part III contains six chapters directed at the interview and interrogation and sources of information. The material is written in relative language and is easily understood. Actual dialogues appear as examples and sample forms are presented as guides to written statements. An overall pertinent text for the criminal investigator.

Thayer, Lee, *Communication*, Washington, D. C.: Spartan Books, 1967. One of the most complete volumes on the communicative process that is readily available. This book is somewhat academic and theoretical, but covers the full range of current communicative thinking. Very pertinent to the investigator are the chapters dealing with cross-cultural communication that represents an area in which officers often find difficulty.

Vanderbosch, Charles G., *Criminal Investigation*, Washington, D. C.: International Association of Chiefs of Police, 1968. A total section is aimed at the interview and interrogation. The book is a no-frills approach, easily assimilated by police officers. Two chapters deal with legal aspects of the interrogation, including Miranda, and there is a good discussion of witness perception in another chapter. The book includes a general presentation on the fundamentals of obtaining information from people.

Wicks, Robert J. and Ernest H. Josephs, *Techniques In Interviewing For Law Enforcement And Corrections Personnel*, Springfield: Thomas, 1972. A very basic and easily digested self-paced instructional book dealing with the interview process. The material includes non-verbal communication, a discussion of the interrelationships inherent in the interview, and the characteristics of the unproductive interview. It is easy to read and easy to use.

SIX

Processing the Crime Scene

Chapter Objectives

After reading this chapter, the student should be able to:

☑ Describe the key features of a thorough and complete crime scene investigation.

☑ List and describe the basic steps in a crime scene investigation.

☑ Explain why the first acts taken in investigating a crime scene are crucial in importance.

☑ Define police responsibility in protecting, examining and recording a crime scene.

☑ Describe what actions the first officer at a crime scene should take and what actions the scene investigator should take. Identify factors involved in a decision to seek outside help during the investigation of a crime scene.

☑ Describe methods of conducting crime scene searches with regard to specific types of evidence that may be encountered.

☑ Explain the special requirements of outdoor searches.

☑ Describe special techniques for conducting investigations of fires and explosions.

☑ Explain the importance of a quality police laboratory.

The Scene of the Crime:
A Definition

The crime scene is proof that a crime has been committed. It contains many or all elements of the corpus delicti and often holds evidence which connects a suspect or suspects to the crime. In most cases, it serves as the starting point for the criminal investigation. It reveals and conceals countless aspects of the crime, and as such must be carefully protected and processed. These are police responsibilities; how effectively and efficiently these responsibilities are carried out will directly affect the outcome of the case.

The act of processing a scene can be broken down into a number of sequential *steps*. Many of these should be completed *before* the scene is actually examined. Once an item of evidence has been altered or destroyed, it isn't possible to restore it to its original condition; thus, these preliminary steps are among the most important ones in the investigative process.

While each department may vary the sequence somewhat, depending on its own policies and procedures, the following order is usually considered basic:

1. Any victims present at the scene are cared for immediately.

2. The scene is protected from outside influences and forces which may damage or destroy the evidence it contains.

3. The dimensions of the scene are determined.

4. A scene investigator is assigned.

5. A preliminary examination of the scene is made.

6. A decision is made to either continue or terminate the investigation.

7. A scene recorder is assigned.

8. A decision is made regarding outside help.

9. Floors and entryways are processed for trace evidence.

10. Photographs and sketches of the scene are made.

11. The scene is processed for fingerprints.

12. A thorough search of the scene is conducted.

Each of these steps will be discussed in detail.

Caring for the Victim

If there's an injured victim at the scene, the first officer to arrive (usually a patrol officer) must see to it that this person is cared for immediately. While the scene should be protected as much as possible so that valuable evidence isn't destroyed or damaged, saving the victim's life should be the officer's primary concern.

Another officer should accompany the victim in the ambulance if the victim needs to be taken to the hospital. This officer should try to get a statement from the victim and make sure that the sheets used by ambulance personnel on the victim are kept for trace evidence examination. (Trace evidence can include, for example, hairs, fibers, and body fluids which were transferred from the perpetrator to the victim and then from the victim to the sheets.) The officer should also see to it that all clothing taken from the victim remains in police custody and is properly dried and packaged for later examination. Hospital personnel usually won't worry about preserving evidence and may even cut the victim's clothes off; the officer should try to retrieve the material in the best possible condition without interfering with medical procedures. The officer should also try to salvage anything which may have caused the victim's injury, such as bullets and other projectiles.

Protecting the Crime Scene

The importance of protecting and preserving the scene of a crime cannot be overemphasized. Before it can even be determined that a crime has been committed, a corpus delicti must be established. If evidence is damaged, destroyed, or removed, the corpus delicti may never be established, missing links may never be found, suspects may never be identified and apprehended, and the crime itself may never be solved.

The police officer who first arrives at the scene has the greatest responsibility for protecting it. This is a primary rule in every police agency. The first official acts taken at the scene will either help to bring the investigation to a logical conclusion or will have a negative effect on all future investigation and prosecution of the crime. Thus, much depends on the actions and reactions of this one person.

There are many people and factors which can either singly or in combination do serious harm to a crime scene. These include:

- *the weather.* Especially when a crime scene is located out-of-doors, much evidence may be subject to change or erasure by wind, rain, snow, harsh sunlight, and/or extreme temperatures.

- *persons who have committed the crime or are connected in some way with the suspect.* They may attempt to remove or destroy incriminating evidence.

- *newspaper and television reporters, photographers, and other members of the media.* Their main concern will be that of gathering news; their goals can conflict with those of the investigation.

- *curious citizens, souvenir collectors, and thieves.* They can introduce confusing fingerprints and alter the condition of important evidence; in some instances, they may simply steal it.

- *other members of police agencies who aren't assigned to the scene but come along anyway to "help."* They may contaminate and/or destroy valuable evidence because they don't know what they're doing; they can also get in the way.

- *victims or other persons who have been affected by the crime.* They may be so sickened by the sight and condition of the crime scene that they may try to clean it up or put it back the way it was before the crime occurred.

The first officer at the scene may even have to guard against his own overzealousness. Sheer curiosity, or the desire to impress superiors by being the first to discover important evidence, may result in undue curiosity or haste.

The only type of evidence the first officer at the scene should actually attempt to collect is eyewitness evidence. He should get the names and addresses of witnesses for use in the future for interviewing purposes. If possible, witnesses' statements should be taken immediately and recorded in the field notebook. This information should be obtained discreetly, of course; incidents have been observed where witnesses were asked to reveal their names, addresses, and phone numbers within earshot of suspects.[1]

There are numerous variables involved in protecting a crime scene. If the crime took place in an enclosed area with only one entrance, the officer's job is made much simpler. He merely clears the scene, detains witnesses (and possibly suspects) for questioning, and guards the entrance until help arrives. It's much more difficult to protect the scene if it's located in the middle of a busy street, however. The officer must be able to quickly and objectively evaluate the scene, determining which evidence seems most important or vulnerable to contamination or erasure. He must then go about salvaging and preserving as much evidence as possible. This can be accomplished by roping the scene off or by erecting portable traffic barriers. The officer's primary responsibility is that of protecting the scene, though, not cordoning it off; if necessary, he should stay at the scene and enlist the help of others to locate and erect ropes and barriers.

When the crime has taken place out of doors, and it becomes clear that steps must be taken to shield the evidence from the elements, the officer must decide whether to cover the evidence and leave it at the scene or to remove certain items to places of shelter. If the latter option is chosen, any steps taken to move evidence must be carefully recorded and reported to the scene investigator when that person comes to take control. This should only be done if it's clear to the first officer at the scene that evidence may be rendered useless if it's left there.

Determining the Dimensions of the Crime Scene

A crime will either be in progress or over with by the time the first officer arrives at the scene. In any case, the dimensions of the crime scene will have been laid out by the perpetrator, and the officer will be responsible for discovering and defining them. This should be done in a reasonably short time and with as few errors as possible.

In a purely technical sense, the crime scene begins at the point where the perpetrator initially changed intent into action. It continues through his escape route and the disposal of any evidence in his possession. For example, a patrol officer may surprise a burglar in the act. The burglar may flee, hiding or discarding stolen property along the way. Although a getaway car may be located nearby, the burglar may be forced to leave by some other means. The actual crime scene, then, will extend to the furthest point at which evidence was discarded or hidden and include the getaway car.

There are clues which will tell the officer whether a criminal was surprised in the act. For example, a burglar may leave a personal article at the scene, such as a hat, jacket, flashlight, or pair of gloves. Valuable property which is easily portable and which was left behind may also indicate that the job wasn't completed. The officer may even hear glass breaking as the burglar makes an unplanned-for escape. The presence of clues like these will alert the officer that the surrounding area should immediately be searched for a getaway car, tools, and stolen items.

The first officer who arrives at the scene, then, will be primarily responsible for protecting it and determining its dimensions. He should not do any examining of its contents unless specifically instructed to do so. If other officers, technicians, and personnel have been notified, they will usually reach the scene fairly quickly. By the time they arrive, the first officer should have stabilized the scene so that they can perform their jobs without any interference or difficulty.

Conducting the Preliminary Investigation of the Crime Scene

The title and rank of the person assigned to conduct the preliminary examination of the scene will vary from department to department, depending on policies, procedures, and the availability of personnel. The one who is eventually designated as the *scene investigator* may be the uniformed officer who gets there first, or a detective, or an evidence technician, or a criminalist from the laboratory. In any event, that person will usually continue in the role of scene investigator for the duration of the processing.

The scene investigator is the only person who should be involved in the preliminary examination of the crime scene. He should first find out as much as possible about the crime and the scene from the first officer who arrived there and from any available witnesses. The relationship between the scene investigator and the patrol officer is an important one, then:

> . . . [C]ooperation between detectives and patrol officers is essential to improving success *in investigations.* The two reasons most often cited are the crucial importance of the preliminary stage in many investigations and the fact that patrol officers are potentially one of the best sources of information for detectives.[2]

The initial phase of the preliminary examination should be one of thinking and planning rather than acting. The key words at this stage of the search are observation and recording;[3] before doing anything else, the scene investigator should pause to look closely at the scene without disturbing it. According to one authority,

> . . . [N]othing [should be] touched, picked up, or moved until it has been photographed, located on a sketch, and minutely described as to location, and any other pertinent observation.[4]

The scene investigator is as capable as anyone else of destroying evidence or rendering it useless due to carelessness or haste. His primary objective, then, should be that of assimilating all possible knowledge about a crime without in any way coming in contact with the evidence. The scene investigator must take sufficient time to absorb the details of a scene before beginning to sort through and analyze the evidence; errors committed in the safeguarding and examination of the crime scene can never be rectified.[5]

The first officer at the scene should waste no time in securing and protecting it; the scene investigator should take as much time as he can to observe it before anything further is done. These are the first two steps of processing the crime scene, and perhaps the most important.

Determining Whether to Continue the Investigation

After the scene investigator has conducted a careful preliminary examination and reviewed the facts known so far with the first officer to arrive at the scene, a significant decision will have to be made. This decision will consist of two basic choices: Should the investigation be canceled, or continued? Inadequate evidence or uncooperative witnesses or victims may make it necessary or wise to cancel the investigation at that point.

Recording the Crime Scene

If it's decided that the investigation should be continued, someone within the police agency will have to be designated as the *recorder*. Sometimes, the scene investigator also takes this role; at other times, another person is assigned it. Once a recorder has been chosen, all arrivals, observations, evidence discoveries, and removals or transfers of evidence—in short, anything at all that has to do with the scene or the investigation—must be carefully recorded. Complete and accurate reports will provide the main body of the investigation; the discovery and retrieval of evidence in and of itself isn't sufficient to bring a case to its logical and satisfactory conclusion:

> In order for an evidence recovery system to be successful, several principles of quality control must be addressed. The provisions which are made for documenting the activities of an officer at the scene and his decisions relative to the collection of evidence are extremely important. Not only must these reports establish the "chain of evidence" but they should also provide a basis for subsequent evaluation of the individual technician's efforts by those in supervisory positions.[6]

A lack of accurate documentation can only help the defense attorney. There's no substitute for complete records—especially not memory. The investigation should be recorded as it happens, not later when it seems more convenient. (Chapter 7 contains a thorough discussion of this topic.)

Seeking Outside Help

The scene investigator should be able to tell from looking at the scene whether or not outside help will be needed. If the crime under investigation is a fairly common one in that jurisdiction, it's likely that departmental policy will specify what assistance may be used. Occasionally, the scene investigator may feel that outside help is needed even if it's out of the ordinary to request it. For example, the crime may be rare or extremely complex. The agency conducting the investigation may not have the necessary experts in its own ranks. In this event, all action at the scene should *stop*, except in cases where evidence may deteriorate and should be protected or collected.

Often, because of influences such as internal pressure or departmental pride, an officer will continue to investigate a scene even though he isn't qualified for it and may not be able to fully cope with it. Once he realizes that outside help is needed, it may be too late. This type of situation not only harms the agency responsible for the investigation but may also adversely affect the experts who are ultimately called in. If the experts realize that much of the evidence has been destroyed or damaged and refuse to take part in the investigation, they're apt to be labeled as "uncooperative." If, on the other hand, they agree to help, they may find that the odds have been stacked against them by the very people who have approached them for assistance. This is a "no win" situation all around, and it can usually be avoided. The scene investigator must have a realistic understanding of the investigative capabilities of his own department. Again, there's usually only one opportunity to do the job well. The decision of whether or not to request outside help must be made *before* the scene is disturbed.

Examples of crimes for which outside assistance may be necessary include bombings, arsons involving homicides, major burglaries, multiple homicides, execution-type homicides, and kidnapings. Every department, especially smaller ones, should keep on hand an updated list of names, addresses, and phone numbers of knowledgeable personnel who may be called upon for assistance. The list should also contain information about what equipment and personnel are available from other local, county, and state departments, and how their services may be obtained. For example, if it's believed that a gun used in a crime has been tossed into a lake, and the department doesn't possess an underwater magnet, the list should specify where one is available and how it can be procured. Or, when a crime has been committed out of doors and an aerial photograph would do the best job of describing the scene, the list should provide information about where the services of a pilot and an experienced aerial photographer can be obtained. Preplanning pays off time and again, especially since the police frequently work under heavy public scrutiny and must at least act as if they know what they're doing.

If it's decided that departmental personnel are capable of proceeding with the investigation without outside help, the scene investigator must determine which resource people are necessary and make sure that they and their equipment will be at the scene as soon as possible. This means that the examiner will also be responsible for keeping the investigation under control and flowing smoothly.

The Importance of Coordinating the Investigative Team

Depending on the size and policies of the department and the nature of the crime under investigation, the investigative team may consist of one generalist or a whole group of specialists. This group may include artists, photographers, fingerprint experts, coroners' physicians, and criminalists, among others. If a group is called in, their work must be coordinated in such a way that evidence won't be damaged or eliminated and the investigation will proceed without interference or delay. If group members end up working against one another simply because they're not being well managed, the scene investigator won't be able to put everything back where it was for a new start; thus, the designated scene investigator should be clearly in charge of the investigation. Ideally that person should have no other responsibilities during that time.

Examining the Crime Scene

In some cases, it may be necessary to process floors and entryways for trace evidence before proceeding any further with the investigation. This can be especially important when police personnel will be entering and leaving the scene frequently.

The scene investigator may decide that general scene photographs should be taken. The photographer(s) should not only take pictures of the overall scene and its elements but should remain there to photograph evidence as it's located. The scene should also be sketched and its measurements recorded.

After the scene has been photographed and/or sketched, the investigative team should search for traces of transferred evidence according to a pattern or method established by the scene examiner. If no pattern is set forth, the search effort may become chaotic and large segments of the scene will be gone over several times while others will be neglected entirely. At this stage of the investigation, no member of the team should touch anything at the scene if at all possible, nor should anyone discard cigar or cigarette butts, chewing gum, candy wrappers, or any other refuse; these will only serve to confuse the issue.

If the scene contains a body, the body should be searched for traces of transferred evidence. As preparation is made for removal of the body, a careful search of the area immediately beneath it should also be made:

> . . . [T]he best physicial evidence is normally found at or near the site of the most critical action that was taken by the criminal against property or the victim. Thus it is most likely to find important physical evidence in the immediate area surrounding the body in a homicide case than at some distance away.[7]

The body should then be placed on a stretcher and covered with a clean sheet; the sheet should be preserved as evidence for processing in the laboratory. All clothing and other possessions on the body should be carefully preserved for processing in the laboratory as well; a special effort must be made to avoid cross-contaminating items of evidence.

At this stage in the investigation, the scene investigator may call on fingerprint experts to process the scene for prints. After this has been accomplished, a thorough investigation of the scene can begin.

Methods for Conducting a Thorough Search of the Crime Scene

Transferred Evidence

Much of the evidence discovered during a criminal investigation will consist of transferred evidence, or trace evidence. This will include evidence transferred to the scene or to the victim by the perpetrator, as well as that which has been transferred to the perpetrator by the scene or by the victim. While corpus delicti evidence establishes the existence of the crime, transferred or trace evidence tends to place a suspect at the scene. Thus, the discovery and processing of this evidence is a major part of the investigative process.

Transferred evidence may include such items as latent fingerprints, hairs, fibers, and body fluids. Some of it may not be visible except under magnification or infrared light; much of it is likely to be fragile and located in places where it can easily be destroyed or contaminated. The preservation and protection of such evidence is of utmost importance since it may serve to place a specific suspect at the scene or even help to prove that the suspect had definite contact with the victim. The search for transferred evidence requires the investigator to have infinite patience, a sense of curiosity, and dedication to the job at hand.

Several categories of transferred evidence will be discussed in detail.

Hair. People are constantly shedding hair, and it's easily pulled out of the scalp or skin. Thus, it's reasonable to expect that human hair will be found at a crime scene, especially if the perpetrator came in violent contact with the victim or had to exert any effort at all in committing the crime.

Hair may be found in many different places around the scene. For example, the perpetrator may have bumped his or her head when crawling through a window or some other opening, snagging hair on the upper part of the entryway. Or, he may have physically assaulted the victim, and hair may be found on the victim's clothing or clutched in the victim's hands.

The use of a flashlight and/or oblique lighting will help in the search for hair. Floors and floor coverings should be examined before anyone else walks on them. All cloth furniture and bedding should be searched; hair adheres to fabrics. Crawl spaces which may have been used by the perpetrator should be thoroughly examined. Low-hanging branches, fences, and other protrusions out of doors which may have been part of the crime scene should also be gone over carefully.

A color photograph should be taken of every place where hair is found, and the hair itself should be put into a clearly marked container. Although hair alone can't positively identify a suspect, it can greatly help the investigator by reducing the number of suspects (a suspect may be eliminated, for example, if the hair found at the scene has been dyed and his hasn't been). It will also reveal many other facts that will assist in furthering the investigation.

Fibers. Fibers from drapery, carpeting, upholstery, clothing, and other materials at the crime scene may be found on a suspect's clothing, especially if the suspect has spent a great deal of time at the scene or engaged in some sort of violent struggle or activity. The scene investigator should collect small bits of every type of fabric at the scene to serve as standards for laboratory use; these will later be compared with fibers found on the suspect.

The best way of collecting fibers is with a filter-equipped vacuum cleaner. Anything drawn into the vacuum cleaner should be placed in a clean evidence container and clearly marked. For each new area vacuumed, a new filter should be used to avoid cross-contaminating the evidence.

Footprints. A perpetrator will often walk through grease, oil, freshly painted floor areas, and sometimes blood before entering smooth surfaces. Photographs of resulting prints should be taken as standards for later comparison. If the prints are reasonably clear, they should be measured to determine their size and width. (An investigator should never fit his own shoe into a print in an attempt to determine its size; this will only succeed in destroying the evidence.)

Wet, snow-covered, or muddy shoes will also leave prints. The investigator can examine them to determine how many people were involved in the crime and can sometimes tell from their arrangement whether the perpetrator has any peculiar ways of walking that can be cited later as identifying characteristics.

Footprint impressions made on soft or muddy ground should also be photographed and measured. A plaster casting may be made of such impressions if there's a chance that they may be washed away or otherwise damaged or eroded.

Cloths, Snaps, and Buttons. Pieces of cloth, threads, snaps, and/or buttons may be torn from the perpetrator's clothing during the crime. The search for such items should center around points of breaking and entering and points of escape, in addition to those areas where violent physical activity occurred. Occasionally, a perpetrator may leave cloth patterns when kneeling or resting parts of the body—such as knees, shoulders, and elbows—on soft surfaces. Evidence like this should be photographed and then placed in clearly marked containers. Cloth imprints should be photographed and, if possible, plaster castings should be made of them.

Definable Dust and Wood Particles. When breaking into a building, a perpetrator will often cut through brick, cement blocks, plaster, or drywall. The dust created by such actions is considered definable; that is, it can usually be identified with a fair amount of certainty. Samples of dust should be taken from the scene and labeled for future comparison with any that's found on the suspect's clothing. Saw dust and wood chips should also be collected and saved for later comparison.

Tool Marks. Tools and other hard objects used to commit a crime will leave their own peculiar "fingerprints" at the scene. These "fingerprints," or distinctive marks, will generally be of two basic types: negative, and generated. Negative marks are those which are made when one surface is hit by another; generated impressions, or striae, are made when one surface moves past a series of points on another.[8] Sometimes, a tool will leave a combination of these two types of marks.

Some marks reveal class characteristics; that is, they can be examined to determine the specific kind of tool which made them. Others, while less specific, are still valuable to the investigator.

- Screwdrivers, jimmies, crowbars, pipes, and other prying tools will leave negative impressions, or indentations, which may reveal the type of tool used and its condition.

- Hammers, ball peen hammers, sledges, and other striking tools will leave either negative impressions or a combination of negative and generated impressions. Their size and shape may reveal the type of tool used and its condition.

- Axes, knives, shears, bolt cutters, wire cutters, chisels, and other cutting tools will leave generated marks. These will be covered with grooves, or striae, which will help to indicate the angle and direction of the cut. It may be difficult to determine the type of tool used, however, since a generated mark is made by moving a tool across a surface and no definite impressions may remain.

- Wrenches, pliers, clamps, and other holding tools will leave negative impressions where the tool bit in and didn't slip, and generated impressions where the tool slipped.

Tool marks may also indicate an implement's irregularities. Marks left on the tool during manufacture, sharpening, use, and disuse may be readily apparent in the impression left. For example, an axe blade may have been nicked by a rock, and the image of that nick will transfer to the surface of a cut made by the axe. While irregularities are often visible to the naked eye, they're far clearer under low magnification.

Frequently, a perpetrator works with tools that weren't meant for the job. This fact can often help the investigator. As a result of misuse, tools may break and fragments may be left at the scene—sometimes imbedded in the object which was attacked, and sometimes lying nearby. Tool fragments can readily be matched with the tool of their origin and as such make excellent evidence.

When a tool is used on a painted surface, paint chips may remain on the tool. If at all possible, the tool mark should be cut out of the surface the tool was used on and sent to the laboratory where suspects' tools can also be examined for the presence of similar paint chips.

The investigator is not responsible for comparing, matching, or figuring out tool marks—this is the laboratory's job. The scene investigator should *never* attempt to fit tools into pry marks or duplicate any other type of mark at the scene; such actions will tend to make the real evidence useless.

Body Fluids. Body fluids found at the scene—such as blood, sweat, semen, urine, tears, and the like—can provide very useful evidence. The investigator's responsibility is *not* to evalute it, though, but to collect and preserve it, submitting it to the laboratory in the best possible condition.

Blood. Blood is the most common body fluid evidence found at crime scenes—and it's also the most frequently mishandled and misunderstood. Often, the investigator will have to use his imagination and experience when collecting blood evidence. The way in which it's collected and preserved may depend on how close the nearest crime laboratory is. A local laboratory can be given wet bloody clothing; a regional, state, or federal laboratory should only receive clothing that's been carefully dried and packaged. Heat, humidity, and bacteria can combine to break down blood evidence and render it useless. Wet stains will deteriorate rapidly if they're packaged and sealed for a long period of time. Thus, the investigator must exercise care and common sense when handling this very important type of evidence.

Wet bloodstains on floors, cement, automobiles, and the like may be soaked onto clean cloth, cotton swabs, or (in an emergency) paper towels. The soaked stains should be allowed to air dry before packing. All stains should be kept separate, since they may originate with more than one person. Whenever possible, a stain that's already dried on an object should be submitted to the laboratory intact on the object itself. If this isn't feasible, it can be scraped onto clean paper which should then be folded and placed in a labeled envelope. The stain shouldn't be scraped directly into the envelope because the particles tend to become trapped in corners and are extremely difficult to remove. A moistened cotton swab or paper towel will loosen a dried stain and soak it up if the stain is fairly fresh.

Wet bloodstained clothing or fabrics shouldn't be folded until they're dry, as this will transfer the stains from one area to another. Dried clothing, swabs, and other evidence must all be packaged and labeled separately to avoid cross-contamination.

Other Body Fluid. Some people's blood group substances are contained in all of their body fluids and tissues. These persons are known as secretors. Their sweat, tears, saliva, urine, hair, skin, fingernails, and organs will all contain this information, in addition to other substances a laboratory will be able to detect.

Most evidence of this type will be found dried. Garments containing such evidence should be carefully packaged, as these stains tend to be fragile.

At this point in time, body fluid evidence can't be used to positively identify an individual. However, it is considered good circumstantial evidence which, when combined with other types, can place a person at the scene, corroborate a witness's statement, or exclude a suspect. Often, the most desirable ways of collecting and preserving this evidence won't be immediately available, and the investigator will have to make do with resources at the scene.

Conducting Outdoor Searches

Although the general techniques of crime scene investigation are fairly constant regardless of the location of the scene, there are special considerations which must be taken into account when a crime occurs out of doors. First, the scene may not have clearly defined perimeters. Surfaces will be rough, irregular, and easily altered. The "floor" may be made up of rises, valleys, gullies, and bodies of water. Weather variables can also cause problems. If rain or snow have fallen since the crime occurred, much evidence may have been changed or simply washed away. The investigator must use points of reference which are available in the field even though they may be considerable distances apart. The overhead aerial photograph is an excellent way to record an outside scene and include all points of reference used in sketches. It provides an opportunity to view the entire scene that can't be duplicated by photographs taken from the ground. Whenever possible, then, the investigator should procure aerial photographs of the scene.

Transferred Evidence

Pollen, Vegetation, Seeds, and Earth. The investigator must be aware that pollen, vegetation, seeds, and earth are possible items of transferred trace evidence. If a perpetrator walked through or hid in a flower bed on his way to breaking into a house, for example, traces of earth, vegetation, and pollen will probably be found on his shoes, clothing, and maybe even ears and hair. Similarly, traces may be found on the victim's body.

Specimens of earth, vegetation, and pollen should be collected for later comparison with evidence found on the suspect or victim. Each item should be individually packaged and labeled. If an approach or escape path can be determined, specimens of vegetation and earth should be collected from that area as well.

Flower bed earth can be excellent evidence. An owner may make his own soil, for example, using exact amounts of humus and loam. Fertilizers may be analyzed and traced. Insecticides may also be identifiable. Any type of earth that appears to be at all special or unusual, then, should be collected for later examination and comparison.

Trees and Shrubbery. All shrubbery, low-hanging tree limbs, fencing, and any other outside object with a rough surface should be carefully examined for traces of cloth fibers, threads, and human hair. Such transferred traces should be recorded, preserved, and labeled for later comparison with the suspect's and/or victim's clothing.

Foot and Tire Impressions. The scene investigator should pay close attention to any foot and tire impressions left on soft surfaces at the scene of the crime. Their locations should be recorded and sketches and photographs should be made. After these tasks have been accomplished, impressions should be shielded from accidental disturbance and the weather by protective coverings. The coverings should be identified so they won't be discarded later.

Impressions which appear to show class characteristic and/or individual irregularities require the attention of a casting specialist, who should make individual plaster casts of each impression. Any earth that adheres to a casting can be used as the standard for that specific location.

Oil and Crankcase Traces. When vehicles are driven through tall grasses or weeds, traces from the underside of the vehicle may be brushed off and remain at the scene as evidence. Adequate standards should be collected for later comparison with the dirt on the underside of the suspect's vehicle.

If an older vehicle is left standing for a period of time, it will tend to drip oil. Any such drippings should be collected and preserved for later examination and comparison.

Searching the Victim

Regardless of whether a victim is living or dead, the goals of the search are the same. Often, it takes a great deal of professional objectivity to make a thorough search; it isn't always easy for the squeamish person, especially if the victim is dead.

Searching a Living Victim

The main purpose in searching a victim is to examine the clothing and body for transferred trace evidence. The victim should be asked to stand on a clean sheet of paper and cloth, and the outer clothing should be carefully gone over for the presence of hair, snaps, buttons, or pieces of thread. The clothing should then be thoroughly vacuumed with a filter attachment; transferred traces will later be compared with those found on an assailant or at a particular location.

Fingernail scrapings should be taken if the victim struggled with or came into physical contact with the perpetrator. If the victim's clothing was removed at any time during the crime, his underclothing and body should also be examined. How such an examination is carried out will depend entirely on the nature of the crime and the investigation at hand; the investigator should keep in mind, however, that he is working with a human being, and one who may very well be upset or frightened; a little consideration will make the process easier for everyone concerned.

Searching a Dead Victim

Although this process can be very trying for the investigator, it's nevertheless necessary to the progress of the investigation and must be carried out. The investigator should simply be as objective and professional as possible, seeking help when and where it's needed.

A body search is carried out in much the same way as a scene search. First, a very careful preliminary visual examination must be made. The initial recording should include information on the position and condition of the body and the condition of the victim's clothing. (Was it buttoned or unbuttoned? Are there any rips or tears? Is the clothing twisted?) Any stains which are discovered should also be recorded.

Following this visual examination, transferred traces should be collected and recorded. The clothing should then be vacuumed, after which any apparent cuts or tears should be measured. The shoes should be examined for traces of earth and dust. The shoes should be taken off of the victim and carefully placed in evidence containers, one for each foot, to avoid the possibility that evidence may be lost in transit.

Fingernail scrapings should be taken and packaged. When something unusual is noticed under a fingernail—such as skin, hair, or blood—careful note should be made of both the hand and the specific finger. Freshly broken fingernails or teeth should also be examined; a suspect, or a suspected area of criminal activity, can then be searched with these in mind.

After the victim's outer clothing and the exposed portions of his body have been examined, the body should be placed on a stretcher in its original position, if at all possible. The stretcher cover should be clean so that evidence which might transfer from the body will be easily seen. Once the body has been lifted onto the stretcher, the area immediately under where the body was found should be carefully searched; if that area has a fabric surface, it should be vacuumed.

The medical examiner or pathologist will normally be the person who's called upon to search the interior of the victim's clothing and the covered portions of his body. The investigator should make him aware of all aspects of the case known so far.

Searching a Body Found Outdoors

When a body is discovered outdoors, regular scene investigation techniques should be followed. The thoroughness of the investigation may be seriously limited, however. The weather may have deteriorated the evidence, or animals may have helped to destroy it.

A murder may be committed at one location and the victim's body left at another. The scene investigator will have to attempt to determine if the crime took place where the body was first discovered. The area and the victim's clothing should be examined for evidence of dragging or rolling, and the surrounding area should be searched for signs of struggle. The victim's clothing should be carefully examined and vacuumed or brushed for trace evidence. When the body is moved by the police, the area immediately under it should be examined thoroughly, since it will have been shielded from the weather and may be in a fairly original state. Any stains on the ground should be collected and tested.

If the victim's clothes or shoes are soiled, specimens of the soil should be collected for later comparison with soil standards taken from several locations in the immediate vicinity of the body.

Conducting Vehicle Searches

There can be any number of reasons why an investigator may want to search a vehicle. He may simply want to establish its legal identity. It may be possible that contraband has been hidden there; in this case, the investigator will estimate the smallest unit size of the contraband and its consistency (whether powder, solid, vegetation, or liquid) and then follow a search pattern while examining any cavity or container which might be concealing the contraband. Or the investigator may suspect that the vehicle was used in a hit-and-run.

In searching for hit-and-run evidence, the investigator must first know all the available facts about the case. He should then look to see whether the front end of the vehicle has been damaged. Cloth impressions, pieces of thread and fabric, hair, blood, and even palm prints may be discovered. In cases of high-speed accidents, there may be evidence on the top and trunk lid as well. When it appears that the victim was run over, the underside of the vehicle will also have to be searched; this is best accomplished if the vehicle is driven over an open pit (or raised up) which provides for an unobstructed view of the entire undercarriage and permits the use of lighting at all angles.

In an open-pit search, the vehicle should first be placed *half* over the pit. The preliminary examination should begin at the leading edge of the underside and proceed from front to rear. Once the preliminary examination has been completed, a more thorough search should be conducted in which each part of the undercarriage is carefully studied. Particular attention should be

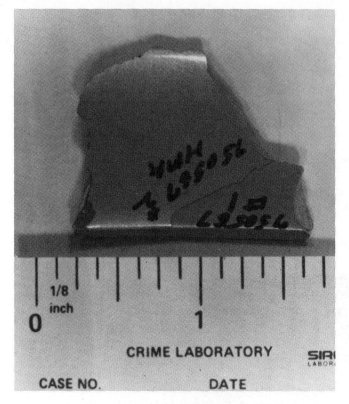

Figure 6-1. The paint chip on the right was found at the scene of a hit and run accident. The matching chip was taken from a suspect's vehicle. (Photo courtesy of Lorain County Criminalistics Laboratory, Elyria, Ohio.)

Figure 6-2. These two pieces of radiator hose were found to be a perfect match in a case involving a vehicle theft. (Photo courtesy of Lorain County Criminalistics Laboratory, Elyria, Ohio.)

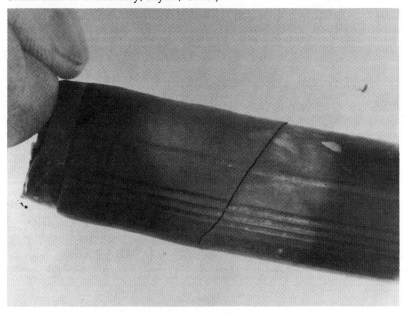

paid to protrusions. Fabric, hair, blood, and impressions should be recorded and photographed; evidence should be removed with tweezers and placed in clearly marked containers. Blood should be scraped into an evidence container and dirt from the same location scraped into another container to serve as a standard; this will later be compared with dirt found on the victim's clothing.

A vehicle may also be searched in an attempt to discover whether or not a suspect or victim has been in the vehicle at any time. This search also requires a sequence. First, the outside should be processed for prints. The inside should then be searched for transferred trace evidence. The investigator should be very careful not to touch the vehicle any more than necessary so as to avoid confusing the laboratory with an extra set of prints.

After this part of the search has been completed, the vehicle should be vacuumed—with filters—a section at a time, beginning with the left front floor and moving to the left front seat, the left rear floor, the back of the left front seat, the left rear seat, and the rear ledge. The same procedure should be followed through the right interior portion of the vehicle. If the investigator has reason to believe that the trunk was also used, it too should be vacuumed.

Once the vacuuming has been completed, the interior should be processed for prints, starting with the left front dash and moving to the rearview mirror, steering column, windshield, and other smooth surfaces. Seatbelt buckles are also good possibilities.

Special Cases: Fires and Explosions

Some types of crimes require special investigative methods. Two of the most prominent of these types are fires and explosions. Most other crimes will leave the scene fairly intact, and the investigator will be able to determine its dimensions, examine a great deal of evidence which has been left in a natural state, and proceed with a normal scene investigation. Fires and explosions, however, will totally or at least partially destroy most of the materials—hence, most of the evidence—at a crime scene. Evidence must be found to establish that a structure was burned or damaged by explosion with *criminal intent* in order to overcome the presumption that its origins were accidental. This type of evidence is frequently available if the investigator will take the time and make the effort to look for it.

Fires

When a fire of suspicious origin is reported to the police, the decision to investigate must be made while the fire is in progress or at least while the burned area is still hot. (The investigator may want to take the time to change into coveralls or some other work clothing to avoid ruining his street clothes.)

The investigator's primary purpose will be to establish whether evidence of arson exists and, if so, what that evidence consists of. Thus, he must attempt to determine the origin or origins of the fire. The investigator should not be concerned at this time about the extent of the fire, since this will only serve to confuse the issue.

Conducting the Preliminary Investigation of a Fire. The preliminary investigation should focus on the *exterior* of the burned structure. For example, were doors, windows, or skylights left open or broken prior to the fire? After looking over the exterior, the investigator should attempt to get an overview of the entire scene with respect to the vertical and lateral spread of the fire, the presence of articles foreign to the building, debris, and levels of burn.

Conducting a Thorough Investigation of a Fire. Every fire begins with a small flame, whether it originates with a match, a torch, a lighter, or some other device. In order for it to grow, *fuel, air,* and *ventilation* are all necessary. The arsonist is intent on causing a small flame or spark to grow; thus, he must supply fuel at the origin and make sure that sufficient air and ventilation exist to feed the fire. The accomplished arsonist will carefully choose his place of work by making sure that adequate air and ventilation are available; the novice, on the other hand, may see to it that air and fuel are on hand but neglect the need for ventilation.

The fuel itself may consist of trash, crumpled newspapers, wood scraps, and other burnable materials. Since this in and of itself usually doesn't generate sufficient heat quickly enough to cause a major fire, some sort of liquid flammable will normally be used as an *accelerant*. This liquid will be poured onto the fuel prior to ignition. In searching for the point at which the fire originated, then, the scene investigator should concentrate on locating the *lowest initial points* of flame. Fire generates heat, and heat travels upward, causing more fire if fuel and air are present. If one can find the lowest point of the fire, and it can be determined that it was the *initial* low point, the origin of the fire will have been located. Generally speaking, if more than one point of origin is discovered, there's little question that arson was the cause of the fire.

Another characteristic of fire that's useful to the investigator is the fact that it burns gases on the *surfaces* of solids. Thus, piles of trash and other fuels used to start a fire may be charred and burned on the outside but almost untouched inside. Large samples of paper, trash, or other fuels found at or near the point of origin should be collected in airtight metal or glass containers and delivered to a laboratory, where it can usually be determined what type of liquid flammable was used to start the fire.

If an excessive quantity of accelerant was used, it may have worked its way through cracks or holes in the floor before igniting. Burn marks along the cracks and on the underside of the flooring will make it obvious that an accelerant was used; in addition, some of the flammable liquid may have flowed to a lower level of the structure and be waiting in a puddle there for discovery.

The search for the point or points of origin and the gathering of laboratory samples must be accomplished as soon as possible, or much of the evidence is apt to literally evaporate into thin air. The investigator should also search for possible fuse bypasses, ignition devices, electric irons, and other heat and flame generating implements.

Fraud Fires

Fraud fires—those which are deliberately set, or for which arsonists are hired, in order to collect on insurance policies—are becoming increasingly more common. If it appears that a fire was set for purposes of defrauding an insurance company, the investigator should collect samples of the burned items for later comparison with the items claimed on the inventory held by the insurance company. Chances are that silver, crystal, furs, and expensive furniture listed there will have been replaced with inexpensive items prior to the fire. A laboratory will be able to determine, for example, if a mass of metal that had once been cutlery is really silver; pieces of furniture fabric will also probably be intact and can be examined to determine whether cheap furniture was substituted for the expensive items claimed. In addition, television sets and other appliances can usually be checked via their serial numbers.

Most or all of the contents of the building may have simply been removed before the fire; in that case, the remnants won't correspond with the insurance company's list. It may also be discovered that the claimant removed the insurance policy from the building shortly before the fire occurred, or called his agent ahead of time to check on the conditions of the policy.

Explosions

Explosions often occur during fires. If the contents of a burned building normally included containers of flammable liquids or other materials which might have exploded when heated, the explosion can usually be considered incidental to the fire. If, on the other hand, such materials were not usually in the area, then they may have been put there deliberately to further accelerate the fire.

Explosions are usually grouped into two distinct categories: *low* explosions, and *high* explosions. In a low explosion, the sides of a building will be pushed out and the superstructure will collapse. A high explosion tends to radiate force out from a central core; extensive local shattering of glass will result, and a crater will be left.

A low explosion may result from a gas leak or gasoline vapors. Since gasoline vapors are heavier than air, related explosions will tend to occur in the lower half of the structure or room; these are difficult to dismiss as accidental unless gasoline was often used in the area in large quantities. A gas leak, however, usually involves natural gas, which tends to rise and accumulate near ceiling areas. A careful examination of an explosion which takes into account both its appearance and its odor can normally indicate whether a gas explosion was accidental or deliberate.

A high explosion necessitates an explosive and a detonation device. Unless explosives are routinely used in an area where an explosion has occurred, the investigator should assume that criminal intent was involved. Remnants of the detonation device and of the type of explosive used can usually be discovered within the perimeters of the explosion area; these can often be reconstructed with favorable results.

The "molotov cocktail" - a combination explosive/fire-setting device—is in wide use today. Typically, it's thrown through a window in an attempt to set a fire. Molotov cocktails leave obvious evidence; remains of the glass container are usually available and should be collected carefully to preserve possible fingerprints.

A Final Note: Choosing a Laboratory

The laboratory plays a crucial role in the scene investigation. At many points in this chapter, it was said that the evidence collected—whether at the scene, from the victim, from the suspect, from any vehicles which may have been used during the crime, and so on—should be sent to the laboratory for further processing. This is because the investigator is usually responsible for collecting evidence, *not* for evaluating it or performing detailed and technical testing. These are all part of the laboratory's job. Thus, the scene investigator must have first-hand knowledge of where evidence should be sent for examination and comparison. And, as much as possible, he should have some say in the selection process.

The most important consideration for the investigator to keep in mind when choosing a laboratory is *turn-around time*. Will the lab be able to process evidence quickly enough to be useful? Will the report be complete and accurate? The second consideration should be that of *expertise*. Will the laboratory be qualified to process the evidence it receives? Will it know what to do with it? For example, there are few qualified document examiners. Some laboratories may be able to perform firearms comparisons but aren't fully competent in the ballistics area. Some may be better at processing blood and urine evidence than others. Some may simply not handle arson evidence. Police agencies must be aware of the capabilities and limitations of the laboratories to which they send evidence for analysis and must make their selections on the basis of these qualifications.

INTERDEPENDENCE OF PHYSICAL EVIDENCE

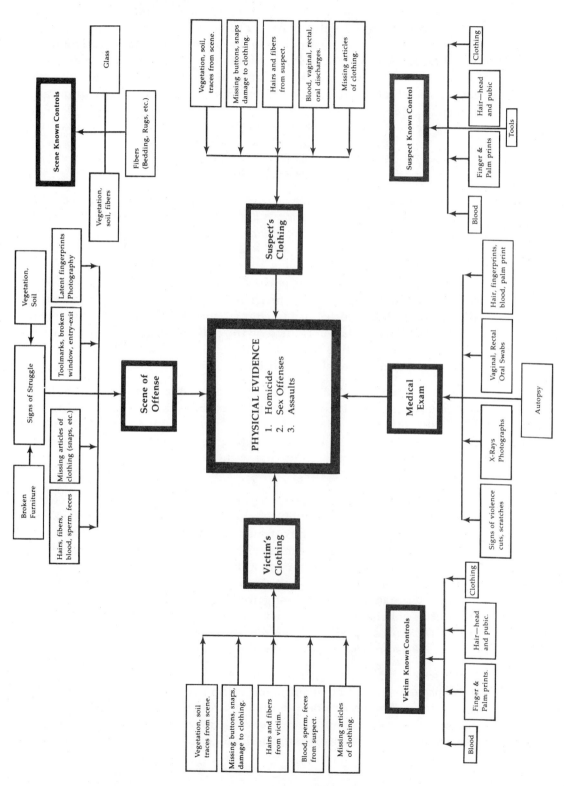

Many federal and state laboratories specialize in specific fields of examination while not getting involved at all in others. For example, one federal laboratory concentrates solely on drug-related work. A state lab may emphasize blood and urine analysis. At any rate, most criminalistics laboratories—whether federal, state, or local—provide police agencies with detailed information on the services they're able to provide, and it's up to each agency to keep that information current and make sure that its personnel are informed.

Summary

How a crime scene is processed can directly affect the outcome of a criminal case. This puts an enormous amount of responsibility on the first officer at the scene—who, in many instances, can make or break a case—and on the scene investigator. Much of the weight of the investigative process rests on these two persons' shoulders. If they don't know what they're doing, or if they don't do what they're supposed to do, evidence may be damaged or destroyed and the case will not reach its logical conclusion. Thus, even though the best laboratories in the country may be available for evidence analysis, what they get is determined by the police officers in the field. And what these officers provide to the laboratories is determined by their training, expertise, and personal capabilities.

The many and varied steps of processing a crime scene are carried out with one goal in mind: to discover evidence which can be used to bring an investigation to a close. This evidence will not only help to prove that a crime has been committed, but will also tend to connect a certain person or persons to the crime. A case isn't a case without evidence, and much of that evidence is found at the scene.

Corpus delicti evidence is necessary before it can be established that a crime has been committed. For example, a victim's body and evidence of violent death can be used to establish the corpus delicti of a homicide. Tool marks at the door and theft of property from a building establish the corpus delecti of a burglary. Bodily injury to a person, a threat, and a weapon establish the corpus delicti of aggravated assault. This type of evidence, then, is of primary importance to the scene investigator. It will provide the foundation on which a criminal charge against a defendant will be based. Thus, it must be safeguarded, processed, and delivered to the court without error. The closer it remains to its original condition, the more valuable it will prove to be.

Transferred trace evidence is that which tends to prove a case against the person charged. It must be of sufficient value to convict that person. Thus, while trace evidence may not be initially as obvious as corpus delicti evidence, and may require much more work to discover, it's just as important. These two types of evidence, then, are the focus of any scene investigation.

One can discuss endlessly the processes and systems used during an investigation, but the fact remains that an investigation is carried out by human beings and as such is far too often subject to human error. Recently, it's been proposed that the problem can be handled by training and assigning more evidence technicians to police agencies. This may be fine for larger agencies with more resources, but there are approximately 13,000 local and county agencies across the country which can't support any type of specialist at all. These agencies must make do with what they have, call on outside help when it's needed (and when it's available), and rely on criminalistics laboratories.

Although this picture may appear bleak, it isn't as bad as it seems. Continued and continuous training of patrol officers can make the process of collecting evidence more of a skill and less of a random endeavor. Even though each scene differs from any other, the objectives and methods of scene processing remain fairly constant. There are routines which can be followed, procedures which can be abided by, steps which can be taken in some semblance of order. This chapter has suggested several different ways of going about particular types of investigation; these will change according to the nature of the crime and the needs of the agency.

Regardless of the system used, however, a single goal remains true to them all. *Evidence* is the key to the successful investigation. How carefully and thoroughly it's gathered will depend not only on how knowledgeable the officer or investigator is, but also how dedicated he is to the job at hand.

Questions and Topics for Discussion

1. Why is the scene of the crime so important? What types of evidence might be found there?

2. If you were the first officer to arrive at a crime scene, what would you do? If the scene were located in an apartment building? On a busy highway? In a field? How would your actions differ in these various situations, and why?

3. Name some things which might interfere with the protection of the crime scene. How should each be handled? Consider the following examples. (You and your class may want to role-play some of them.)

   - The crime scene is located in a suburban yard, and a storm is about to break.

   - A reporter has shown up at the scene. He or she has a reputation for being hostile toward the police.

   - A rape victim has contacted the police, but wants to take a bath before being examined.

   - Three other officers have arrived at the scene to offer assistance. The scene has not yet been secured.

- You've been designated as the scene investigator. Your department supervisors have been putting pressure on agency personnel to gather evidence as quickly as possible and cut down on the time spent on scene examinations. You realize that outside help should be called in, but it might not be able to arrive for some time.

- What are some of the things *you* could do to damage or harm scene evidence? How could you avoid doing them?

4. Why is cooperation between patrol officers and scene investigators so important?

5. When might it be best to cancel an investigation rather than continue it? Discuss some of the factors which may be involved in making this decision.

6. You're the first officer to arrive at the scene. You've also been designated scene investigator—*and* scene recorder (there's a personnel shortage in your department). What should you do first? Why? Discuss the series of steps you would follow in carrying out your responsibilities.

7. Conduct a role-play with your class. Set up a "crime scene" and discuss its elements in detail. One person should be designated as the scene investigator. Several other persons can play "outside help" roles. How should the investigative effort be coordinated?

8. What are negative tool marks? What are generated tool marks? Which is usually easiest to read, and why? Discuss what is meant by "class characteristics."

9. Discuss the various ways of handling body fluid evidence.

10. What are the differences between "transferred" evidence and "corpus delicti" evidence? Is either type more important than the other? Why or why not?

11. Why are investigations of fires and explosions different from searches of most other crime scenes? Discuss the steps important to each.

12. Find out from your local police department which laboratories they use for analyzing and processing evidence. If one is located nearby, and it's mutually convenient, arrange a visit.

Footnotes and References

1. Frank J. Cannavale, Jr., and William D. Falcon, *Witness Cooperation* (Lexington, Mass.: Lexington Books, 1976), p. 3.

2. Peter B. Bloch and Donald Weidman, *Managing Criminal Investigations* (Washington: United States Department of Justice, 1975), p. 3.

3. Richard H. Fox and Carl L. Cunningham, *Crime Scene Search and Physical Evidence Handbook* (Washington: United States Department of Justice, 1973), p. 15.

4. William Dienstein, *Technics for the Crime Investigator* (Springfield: Charles C. Thomas, 1968), p. 21.

5. Arne Svensson and Otto Wendel, *Techniques of Crime Scene Investigation* (New York: American Elsevier, 1970), p. 2.

6. Joseph L. Peterson, *The Utilization of Criminalistics Services by the Police* (Washington: United States Department of Justice, 1974), p. 38.

7. Fox and Cunningham, 1973, p. 11.

8. Julian S. Hatcher, Frank J. Jury, and Jac Weller, *Firearms Investigation and Evidence* (Harrisburg: The Stackpole Company, 1957), p. 439.

Annotated Bibliography

Arthur, Richard O., *The Scientific Investigator*, Springfield: Charles C. Thomas, 1965. A text on the basics of the application of scientific investigation for police officers.

Battle, Brendan P., and Weston, Paul B., *Arson: A Handbook of Detection and Investigation*, New York: Arco Publishing Company Inc., 1970. An all-embracing book outlining the detection and investigation of arson. Actual cases are used to illustrate proper and effective detection of arson.

Bloch, Peter B., and Weidman, Donald R., *Managing Criminal Investigation*, Washington: United States Department of Justice, 1975. This is a prescriptive package dealing with the observations and conclusions of a research project based on an examination of the investigative practices of six selected police departments.

Cannavale, Frank J. Jr., and Fallon, William D., *Improving Witness Cooperation*, Lexington: D.C. Heath and Company, 1976. Includes research and findings of important implications for prosecutors and police officers on witness management.

Chaiken, Jan M., *The Criminal Investigation Process: Volume II*, Santa Monica: The Rand Corporation, 1975. A research report on the responses of police departments with more than 150 employees to a national survey on the investigation process.

Dienstein, William, *Technics For the Crime Investigator*, Springfield: Charles C. Thomas, 1968. A source book notable for its basic approach to the problems and obstacles confronting investigators. Outlines basic techniques essential to the investigator.

Fox, Richard H., and Cunningham, Carl L., *Crime Scene Search and Physical Evidence Handbook*, Washington: United States Department of Justice, 1973. A handbook which provides investigating officers with a practical guide to techniques that will help them to fully realize the value of physical evidence and the support available from a criminalistics laboratory.

Greenwood, Peter W., Chaiken, Jan M., Petersilia, Joan, and Prusoff, Linda, *The Criminal Investigation Process: Volume III: Observations and Analysis*, Santa Monica: The Rand Corporation, 1975. A research report on investigative organization and contributions of police in the criminal justice process. The project attempted to determine the effectiveness of new technology and reveal how investigative effectiveness is related to organizational differences.

Greenwood, Peter W., Petersilia, Joan, *The Criminal Investigation Process: Volume I*, Santa Monica: The Rand Corporation, 1975. A research report on a two-year study of police criminal investigation practices and their impacts on the justice system.

Hatcher, Julian S., Jury, Frank J., and Weller, Jac, *Firearms Investigation and Evidence*, Harrisburg: The Stackpole Company, 1957. An in-depth reference on the study of firearms, ammunition, tool marks, and ballistics. Particularly helpful in explaining the methods and means of comparing markings on bullets and casings with weapons for identification.

Heffron, Floyd N., *Evidence for the Patrolman*, Springfield: Charles C. Thomas, 1965. A basic reference on criminal evidence written with the police officer in mind.

Kirk, Paul L., *Crime Investigation*, New York: John Wiley and Sons, 1974. A text on crime investigation written with the interests of both the criminalist and the field investigator in mind.

National Advisory Commission on Criminal Justice Standards and Goals, *Police*, Washington: United States Department of Justice, 1973.

O'Brien, Kevin P., and Sullivan, Robert C., *Criminalistics: Theory and Practice*, Boston: Holbrook Press, 1972. This text supplies the student with a fundamental source of instruction; it also offers practical advice and help to the detective at the scene.

Osterburg, James W., *The Crime Laboratory*, Bloomington: Indiana University Press, 1968. A laboratory workbook designed for the student in criminalistics, including case studies of criminal investigations and practical exercises.

Peterson, Joseph L., *The Utilization of Criminalistics Services By the Police*, Washington: United States Department of Justice, 1974. An analysis of the physical evidence recovery processes used by police.

Soderman, Harry and O'Connell, John J., Revised by O'Hara, Charles E., Modern *Criminal Investigation*, New York: Funk and Wagnalls, 1962. An excellent source text and reference for student and practicioner alike, it treats the application of the natural sciences to the investigation of crime.

Svensson, Arne and Wendel, Otto, *Techniques of Crime Scene* Investigation, New York: American Elsevier, 1970. An in-depth treatment of scene examination and the traces which can be found there, this is an excellent text for introducing police officers, detectives, and criminal investigators to scientific crime detection.

Taylor, William W., *Case Investigation*, San Francisco: Aqueduct Books, 1965. Explores the general practices of criminal investigation and their applications to specific crimes, as well as makes clear the investigator's role as a witness.

SEVEN

Recording the Crime Scene

Chapter Objectives

After reading this chapter, the student should be able to:

☑ Explain why careful scene recording is important.

☑ Describe various methods of scene recording, including note-taking, sketching, photography and videotaping.

☑ Give examples of the different ways of sketching a crime scene.

☑ Explain the need for careful log preparation during each phase of the recording process.

☑ List the basic elements of a photographic log.

☑ Outline the chain of accountability as it concerns scene recording, especially photography.

☑ List the photographic techniques which might be used in specific types of cases.

☑ Identify the many uses for videotaping in the criminal justice field.

☑ Outline some videotaping techniques which might be used in specific types of cases or under specific circumstances.

☑ Explain the necessity for qualified scene recorders who are willing to keep up with new developments in their fields.

The Importance of
Careful Scene Recording

A crime scene furnishes much of the evidence and information necessary to a successful criminal investigation. It may contain the corpus delicti itself, in addition to clues as to the modus operandi of the perpetrator, evidence which tends to connect a suspect or suspects to the crime, and other types of evidence which can be examined by the investigative team. Regardless of how much an investigator notices at a crime scene, though, or of how carefully he analyzes or processes or searches the scene, his efforts may be in vain if every step of the investigation isn't carefully recorded and documented.

Well-kept and complete scene records are invaluable during the follow-up investigation. They can help the scene investigator to recreate the scene and decide what further steps need to be taken in order to bring the case to a logical conclusion. They can help him to remember certain aspects and details of a case which might otherwise be forgotten or misunderstood. In addition, they can serve to substantiate the prosecutor's case in court. Poor records—or no records at all—can only help the defense attorney. An officer's testimony that begins, "I think I saw..." or "I seem to remember..." or "In my opinion, this is what happened..." carries little or no weight in the courtroom unless comprehensive records are also available.

Records offer proof that a crime occurred, that certain types of evidence were discovered, that witnesses and suspects were located. They can range from simple notes written in a field notebook to sophisticated videotapes encompassing an entire scene, from its exterior to the mere shadow of a fingerprint. Their quality—and quantity—can make or break a case. Thus, their importance can never be overemphasized and should not be underestimated.

Note-Taking:
The First Step in Scene Recording

There are many different ways of recording a crime scene. Some are highly technical and utilize complex equipment; others require the services of specially trained personnel. Such equipment and personnel may not always be available when they're needed, however. Thus, the officer's main recordkeeping tool should always be his field notebook. The field notebook is not only the primary source of the investigative report (see Chapter 4); it's also an excellent medium for recording the elements of a crime scene.

A properly kept notebook is a wealth of knowledge, facts, and data. It often proves indispensable when an officer is trying to reconstruct a scene and analyze it to determine follow-up procedures. Since scene recording primarily involves taking down information about the evidence present at the scene, the officer will want to ask a number of related questions. These might include the following:

- Who found the evidence?
- Who booked the evidence?
- Who handled the evidence?
- How was the evidence disposed of or stored?
- Where was the evidence logged?
- How was the evidence marked?
- When was the evidence discovered?
- What condition was the evidence in when it was found?

Naturally, the order in which the officer asks questions like the ones listed above and how he decides to record them (along with their answers, of course) will vary according to his own way of going about the investigative process. One aspect of note-taking that's important to keep in mind, though, no matter what particular method is followed, is that it should always reflect a *professional* attitude on the officer's part. Subjective comments or notes which don't pertain to the case shouldn't be included in the notebook; it could be embarrassing if they were read aloud in court. Therefore, only that information which is considered relevant to an investigation should be recorded in the field notebook.

Even in instances when sophisticated equipment and trained personnel are available for technical recording purposes, the officer should still take down necessary information and facts in his notebook. This should always be the first step—and a continuing one—of the scene recording process.

Sketching the Crime Scene

Most crime scenes are both sketched *and* photographed. While photographs are taken so that all of the visible elements of a crime scene can be clearly shown, a sketch can be more selective and specific. It can highlight those elements which are most important—such as the location of a victim's body, or the presence and condition of physical evidence—while simply deleting those which might prove irrelevant or distracting.

Several sketches may be made of a single scene; each must be identified by specific types of written information. If a sketch contains too much written information, however, it can confuse the viewer. Thus, many agencies have established standards, or guidelines, which help the officer to determine what should and shouldn't be written on a scene sketch. The following are usually considered sufficient to identify a sketch:

- The name and position of the investigator who made the sketch;

- The date and time at which the sketch was made;

- The classification of the crime (for example, was it a burglary? a homicide? an assault?);

- The agency's case number;

- The names of any persons who assisted in taking measurements of the scene;

- The precise address of the crime scene;

- Reference points used during sketching, along with compass directions;

- The scale (for example, 1″ = 5′) at which the sketch was made; and

- The location and identification of specific items of physical evidence found at the scene. The investigator may wish to use symbols or numerals rather than trying to write lengthy descriptions or explanations on the sketch itself. Of course, a *key* to any symbols used should also be supplied if they aren't standard among agency personnel.

Methods of Sketching the Crime Scene

A crime scene sketch may be made in one or more of several ways. Each involves the use of specific techniques which are fairly easily learned. The way in which an officer will choose to sketch a particular scene will depend on his own preferences and skills and on the nature and requirements of the scene itself.

- The *coordinate sketching method* involves measuring the distance of an item of evidence from *two* fixed points. For example, a *baseline* may first be determined (this might be a wall for which the exact measurements are known); the distance will then be measured between the item of physical evidence and the baseline at right angles to the baseline. In Figure 7.1, the baseline is found to be 5′2″ and the body of the victim is 3′4″ away from the baseline at right angles to it. These measurements serve as *coordinates* which place the victim's body in an exact location at the scene. This method of sketching is especially useful where identifiable and permanent reference points exist, such as a wall or a window.

- The *triangulation method* is most frequently used in outdoor investigations where identifiable reference points are few and far between. Two points are selected, and the item of physical evidence is located along a straight line from each of these points; the two points are also joined by a line on the sketch, and a three-sided figure is formed. In Figure 7.2, the two reference points are 5′ apart and the tail segment is located 39′ and 37′ from each of the two reference points, respectively.

Figure 7-1 An Example of the Coordinate Sketching Method

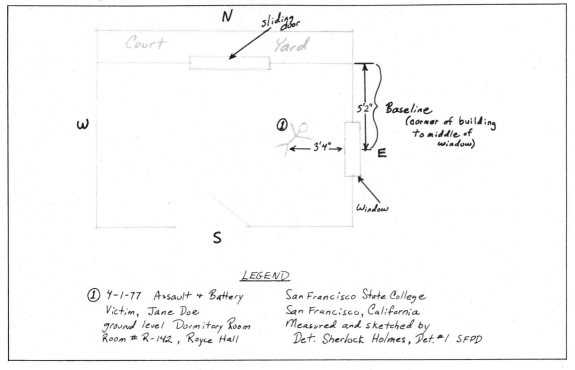

Figure 7-2 An Example of the Triangulation Sketching Method

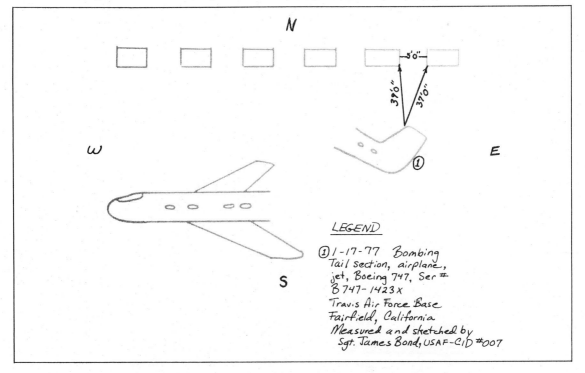

- The *cross-projection method* is used primarily when the evidence is located indoors. The sketch includes all doors, walls, and windows, all of which are drawn as if lying flat on the floor. No attempt is made to create a three-dimensional effect.

- Sometimes, an investigator may use *polar coordinates* alone when compiling a sketch. Items of physical evidence are located and referenced to the polar designates north, south, east, and west.

Any of the above methods may be used when making either *rough* or *smooth* sketches. Rough sketches are usually done at the scene; the investigator may use graph paper and indicate proper measurements right on the sketch. Smooth sketches are usually made by someone with drafting knowledge, who transfers the figures from a rough sketch to a precise scale drawing. Smooth sketches are the best type to present in court, since they have a more professional appearance. Figure 7.3 is an example of a smooth sketch.

Figure 7-3 An Example of the Smooth Sketching Method

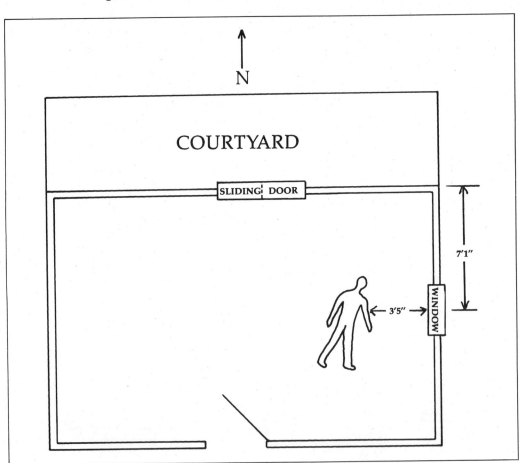

Photographing the Crime Scene

The goal of any criminal investigation is the discovery of *evidence* which can be used to bring the case to a logical conclusion. Briefly, this evidence usually falls into four categories:

- corpus delicti evidence, which establishes that a crime has been committed;
- modus operandi evidence, which reveals how the crime was committed;
- evidence which tends to prove the identity of the perpetrator; and
- evidence which tends to connect a suspect or suspects to the crime.

A typical crime scene contains a great deal of all of the above types of evidence. Thus, it's necessary that it be recorded accurately and impartially. Photographs of the scene are among the best records which can be made. And, because much evidence can change over time, it's important that scene photographs be taken as soon as possible.

Often, a photograph can depict a scene more clearly than a witness can; it may contain significant elements that the witness didn't notice or simply forgot about. It can help to refresh a witness's memory, and add weight and credibility to his testimony. It can also assist jurors in understanding various aspects of the scene.

In order for a photograph to be considered admissible during a criminal trial, it must satisfy several criteria. These include:

- It must be established that the photograph will aid the jurors in reaching a decision without misleading or prejudicing them.
- It must be authenticated by witness testimony—preferably that of someone who was at the scene when the photograph was taken.
- And, finally, the photographer must be able to identify the subject matter on which the photograph focuses and testify conclusively that everything in the photograph is accurately portrayed.

Photographs can be among the most useful forms of evidence during a criminal trial. They can be judged inadmissible under certain circumstances, however. The judge makes the final decision; the investigator can do his part by making sure that any photographs introduced as evidence have been carefully taken and processed and are properly identified.

Identifying Scene Photographs

Often, many photographs are taken at a single crime scene. They may be taken at different times and, in certain circumstances, by different photographers. To avoid confusion, then, a comprehensive log must be kept of all photographs taken at a crime scene. In court, a written log carries much more weight than an officer's memory.

The log should answer the basic *who, what, where, when, why,* and *how* questions common to the investigative process by carefully detailing the following information about *each* photograph taken at the scene:

- the date and time when the photograph was taken;

- the name of the person who took the photograph, along with his position and title within the department;

- the type of equipment used in taking the photograph (such as 4x5 Crown Graphic, 35mm, videotape, and so on);

- a complete description of any special or out-of-the-ordinary equipment that was used to take the photograph;

- the location of the subject of the photograph (this might include a brief description of where the evidence was in relation to a fixed object. For example, a description might read: "Photograph #20 shows a homicide victim facing northbound approximately 2' from the north living room wall");

- a listing of all technical details pertinent to the specific photograph, such as the F-stop used, the speed used, and the rating of the film;

- a description of the angle at which the photograph was taken (in relation to the subject); and

- any necessary clarifying comments. (For example, were there any problems during the photographic session? Did the camera jam at any time, or were there any other technical difficulties? Did the weather have any effect on the session? Was it foggy, or raining, or snowing?)

Again, it's important that the log contain complete identifying information on each and every photograph taken at a crime scene.

Scene Photographs and the Chain of Accountability

Often, scene photographs are considered to be just as important as other items of physical evidence. Thus, they should be handled as carefully and professionally as, for example, a murder weapon or a tool used to commit a burglary. A photographer may have only one opportunity to take a specific photograph, and that photograph may carry a great deal of weight during the remainder of the investigation and the trial. Once a photograph has been taken, then, someone must be *accountable*—or responsible—for it at all times. Who has it at what stage during the investigation, where it's stored, who receives prints, where negatives are kept—all information of this type should be recorded in detail and readily available.

A typical chain of accountability for a scene photograph may be much like the following:

1. The police photographer takes the photograph on location.

2. He then logs the photograph.

3. After the proper identifying information has been logged, the photographer stores the film in a photographic carrying case and takes it to the police photographic laboratory for processing.

4. The laboratory then becomes responsible for the film, at least for the time being. Laboratory personnel keep another separate log of their own which contains the following information:

   a. who turned the film in, and when;

   b. what occurred during processing (complete notes should be taken at every phase);

   c. how many prints were made, and who received them (such as the detective bureau, the identification bureau, and so on);

   d. where the negatives have been stored (all negatives should be kept in specially designed envelopes; all envelopes should be marked with the case number, the type of crime photographed, and the type of photograph taken); and

   e. which unit of the police agency received the negatives and prints if they weren't stored at the laboratory, and when this transfer occurred.

Each officer or unit within an agency receiving photographs for investigative purposes should also keep careful logs as to when the photographs were received and who was assigned possession of them.

In some cases, many authorized persons may have access to the negatives and prints made of a particular scene. Regardless of how many people actually end up handling scene photographs, however, a log should record *each* time a photograph is transferred or stored. The photographer—or the investigator in charge—must be able to give a precise account of where a photograph was during all stages of the investigative process should a defense attorney decide to question the validity of a photograph by challenging the accountability chain.

It isn't always possible to send film taken at a scene to a police laboratory. In some instances, negatives may have to be processed at a local commercial laboratory instead. At times like these, the department must first make sure that the individual or company responsible for processing the film is reputable. Such an individual or company must also be familiar with any court requirements which might pertain to the developing and printing processes. The number of people handling the film should be kept to a minimum, and a log must be made which details every step of the processing, including the names of all persons who came in contact with the film. Again, photographs are valuable evidence which must be protected and preserved.

Taking Photographs in the Field

What kinds of photographs a photographer decides to take of a specific scene, and how he decides to take them, will depend in large part on the type of crime which was committed and the circumstances surrounding it. There are some basic guidelines which can be helpful when making decisions like these, however:

- Important items of evidence should be photographed individually as they appear at the scene.

- A log should be kept of each photograph taken.

- It's generally better to take too many pictures than too few. The quantity of photographs taken will often be determined by two factors, though: the seriousness of the crime itself, and the departmental budget.

- The type of equipment used should be selected according to the photographer's experience and the availability of such equipment. The scene investigator should first talk with the photographer to determine what equipment is considered necessary and then make sure that it's available when needed.

- Overall photographs of the scene should be taken *before* the scene is searched—that is, before anything is moved or removed for processing.

- Closeup photographs should be taken of all items of physical evidence. Closeups should also be taken of a victim's wounds, bruises, scratches, skin punctures, and any other identifying marks.

- A ruler or some other measuring device should be placed in the photographer's field of vision and photographed along with the subject. Prints can be made later either with or without the measuring device showing.

Whatever guidelines a department or agency follows concerning scene photography, there's one which should stand as a rule under all circumstances: evidence should *never* be picked up or moved until *after* it's been photographed.

Specific Photographic Techniques: The Arson Scene

As was discussed in Chapter 6, arson can cause special problems for the criminal investigator. It can also make the photographer's job more difficult. Since much of the evidence in an arson case may literally go up in smoke, it's essential that the photographer arrive at the scene as promptly as possible, while the fire is still burning, and that photographic equipment be kept in a state of readiness at all times. Equipment used to photograph fires might include a 4x5 Crown Graphic camera with holders equipped with black and white film, in addition to holders equipped with color film; a 35mm camera with color capabilities may also be used. If the department has a portable videotape ensemble, this should be taken to the scene without delay.

Color photography is gaining recognition as a valuable tool for the arson investigation. Color shots can record the progress of a fire and reveal its intensity, for example. An intense fire will usually move from red to yellow to white; color film can record this progression. In addition, color photographs of the smoke and vapors which emanate from the fire can reveal, in some cases, the nature of the *accelerant*, or the substance which was used to help the fire along. Some accelerants give off their own definite colors which may show up in both flames and smoke; records of these colors can aid the investigator in determining what kinds of accelerants were used and whether the fire really was started by an arsonist. For example,

- *White smoke* may reveal the burning of a phosphorous substance.

- *Black smoke* may indicate that the burning material has a petroleum base. Turpentine, rubber, tar, petroleum, and coal all give off black smoke.

- *Grayish smoke* may indicate that the incendiary substance consisted primarily of straw or hay.

- *Reddish-brown or yellow smoke* may reveal the presence of nitrates or a nitrocellulose-based material. Accelerants which burn with these colors include nitric acid, photographic film, and some types of gunpowder.

The photographer should keep in mind that *factual* photographs are more useful—and tend to be more admissible—than *sensational* ones. Over-dramatic photographs may be seen as prejudicing the jury. It's a good idea to take a series of photographs recording each step taken by the fire department in fighting a fire, for example. Photographs should also record the size of the flames, the upward flow of the fire, and the direction in which the fire is traveling.

In most cases, the first photograph of a fire should be taken at a distance using a telephoto lens. This will enable the photographer to capture details which will show the overall picture and later prove valuable to the investigator. When possible, it's best to photograph an arson scene from a point higher than ground level; this will provide an overview of the scene and give the investigator a greater sense of perspective. And, since studies have shown that arsonists often return to the scene of a fire to view the results of their efforts, pictures of the crowd in the vicinity of the fire should also be taken.

Videotapes are being utilized more frequently during arson investigations, and with good results. Their instant replay capability makes them especially useful. Once a crowd is taped, for example, the investigator can immediately play back the tape on a monitor located at the scene and look carefully at the people in the crowd, observing their actions and reactions to the fire. This technique has proved helpful in at least one arson case. A fire inspector noticed that the modus operandi of a still-buring fire seemed similar to that of an earlier fire, and requested that videotapes from the first fire be brought to the scene. He then taped the crowd at the second fire and played back the tapes from both fires, looking carefully at the crowd in each instance. One person appeared on both tapes. The inspector confronted this person, who, after being shown the two videotapes, confessed to having set both fires. As a result, many hours of follow-up effort were saved. Before videotaping equipment became available, still photographs had to be processed and printed prior to examination; as a result, the perpetrator often left the scene without being discovered.

Once a fire has been extinguished, the photographer should begin to take pictures of the exterior of the burned structure. Usually, it's considered most efficient to take several views of the scene from diagonally opposite corners of the building. Additional views can then be taken from higher positions so that the total extent of the fire can be recorded and evaluated later during the investigation. In major arson cases, the photographer should also take aerial shots from an adjacent rooftop or, when possible, from a helicopter.

The scene investigator should work with the photographer to determine which photographs should be taken inside the building and direct the photographer accordingly. Again, nothing should be moved until after it's been photographed. Usually, interior walls are recorded first, followed by pictures of the furniture and any other equipment found in the room. Anything which might have been used in starting the fire—such as metal or glass containers, trash, or pools of accelerant—should be photographed where they're found without being touched or moved. When possible, items of physical evidence should be photographed in relation to fixed objects. If latent fingerprints are found, closeup photographs should be taken. Care must be exercised so that evidence isn't contaminated or destroyed. In some special cases, the scene investigator might think it wise to suggest to the firefighters that they not aim their fire-retardant chemicals at certain areas of the scene. Of course, scene investigators and photographers should never interfere with the job that fire department personnel are trying to do.

Finally, a photographer at a fire scene should keep a careful log containing the following information:

- what type of camera or videotape equipment was used;

- what model of equipment was used;

- what aperture settings were used;

- what type of film or videotape was used;

- what type of lens was used;

- any special problems which came up during the photographing of the scene;

- details of the items of evidence which were photographed; and

- angles at which photographs were taken.

Specific Photographic
Techniques: The Burglary Scene

Burglaries are often difficult to solve simply because the perpetrator usually leaves the scene before the crime is discovered. Photographic evidence showing the corpus delicti and the modus operandi can be especially helpful in bringing a burglary case to a successful conclusion. Sometimes, suspects are released from custody because the police neglected to obtain essential photographs of the scene. Scene photographs, then, can be very useful to the prosecutor, and the photographer's role is thus an important one.

Although how a photographer goes about recording a burglary scene will depend on a number of factors, the following sequence of steps is usually considered basic:

- First, the photographer and the investigator work together to analyze the situation. What items are critical to the investigation? How should they be photographed? With what types of equipment? In what order?

- Second, the exterior of the area in which the burglary occurred should be recorded via distant, middle, and closeup shots.

- Third, photographs of the point of entry should be taken. A detailed photographic sequence can help to depict how the perpetrator entered the premises and might include shots of pry marks, channel lock marks, broken glass doors, and so forth.

- Fourth, photographs of each room from which property was stolen should be taken. At this point, the photographer should work even more closely with the scene investigator to determine the *search pattern* to be followed and the number of photographs to be taken. If the burglary involved many items of high cost, then a larger number of photographs is usually justifiable. The use of a wide-angle lens may prove more economical than other types of lenses since it allows the photographer to take fewer pictures of the scene without leaving anything out.

- And, finally, photographs should be taken of the perpetrator's exit, if known.

Any items left behind by the perpetrator—such as tools, pieces of clothing, hairs, and so on—should also be photographed and logged. Photographs should always be taken in relation to other fixed objects at the scene. When taking pictures of footprints, glove prints, small articles, tool marks, and hair, for example, a ruler should be placed in the photographer's field of vision to serve as a reference. Special lighting—such as oblique lighting—can be helpful when photographing minute pieces of evidence, cloth impressions, and prints.

The photographer's primary responsibility when recording any scene is, of course, to assist the prosecutor and the investigator in establishing the elements of a crime by permanently documenting evidence. This can best be accomplished if the photographer and the scene investigator work together closely and help each other during every step of the investigative process.

Videotaping the Crime Scene

Many judicial and law-enforcement personnel today acknowledge that videotaping is an excellent and accurate way of recording a crime scene. It often provides a more "realistic" feeling than still photographs alone and can capture many important details that other recording processes may easily miss. In particular, a videotape can record an entire crime scene while stills may unavoidably neglect some crucial areas. A videotape also provides a sense of immediacy and tends to capture the "atmosphere" of a scene more readily than still photographs can; this is enhanced by the presence of narration. As was mentioned earlier in this chapter, the instant replay capability is also useful. And, when still photographs are desired, they can be reproduced directly from the videotape.

Videotaping is best accomplished by a team of investigators. In a typical team, one individual acts as the technician who operates the equipment, and the other functions as the narrator who describes and documents exactly what he wants the technician to tape, in addition to providing a verbal and contemporary account of the scene. The coordination of team members is thus very important. While this may at first seem like a complex and time-consuming task, it pays off. Training, practice, and experience with the equipment in the field can all help team members to coordinate their efforts. Ideally, videotaping equipment should seem as commonplace to the officer as the field notebook; the less sensationalized and more matter-of-fact videotaping becomes, the more valuable it is as an investigative tool.

Portable videotape technology has made significant advances in recent years. For instance, the standard ½" reel-to-reel, which was often troublesome and difficult to use, has been replaced by the more sophisticated and manageable ½" cassette. Some types of equipment incorporate a date/time display within the television monitor and the camera itself, thus relieving the photographer of the responsibility for constantly authenticating or recording the date and time when a tape is made. Many of these built-in features can't be tampered with and thus are less apt to be questioned by defense attorneys.

The admissibility of a videotape as evidence is usually determined by the same standards used when determining the admissibility of still photographs. Nevertheless, the police or security agency which wishes to utilize videotaping equipment and taped evidence should check local and state requirements pertaining to their legality. For example, the voluntariness of a videotaped statement may come under scrutiny, and the investigator will have to be certain that a suspect who makes such a statement is aware that he is being taped and has been informed of his rights.

Videotaping techniques must be practiced before they can be perfected. Long shots followed by closeups should be taken in a slow, systematic manner. Photofloods or other artificial light sources should be used in dark areas or those which may be difficult to see for whatever reason. "Panning" may also be used; this involves shooting from left to right in a steady, smooth process. The less "jumpy" a videotape is, the easier it will be to view and examine later and the more respectable it will look in court.

Other Uses for Videotaping

In addition to recording the crime scene itself, videotaping can be useful during many other stages of the investigative process. These include, among others:

- recording witness testimonies and depositions;
- recording evidence;
- recording lineups; and
- recording trials.

Juries are becoming more willing to accept videotaped testimonies and depositions in cases where witnesses can't appear personally in court. And, in certain cases, a "dying declaration"—literally, a statement made while a victim is dying—can be videotaped and later used in court. This type of evidence can be invaluable in that it reveals the date and time at which the statement was made in addition to presenting the condition of the victim in a fairly unquestionable way.

Videotaping can also be used to accurately and clearly record tangible physical evidence found at the scene, such as bloodstains, fingerprints, footprints, and other impressions left by the perpetrator. Oblique lighting can help to highlight the ridges in a fingerprint and improve the clarity of the exposure. Once a print is videotaped, it can be stop-framed on the television monitor and a photograph can be taken off of the monitor for identification purposes. Closeups of this type of evidence should first be taken using a telephoto lens and then be followed by the closeup lens. The use of powders can also help to highlight details of small and hard-to-see items of evidence.

In recording evidence, it's important that the narrator and technician work closely to precisely describe the nature of the evidence and its location at the scene. Of course, the chain of accountability applies to videotapes as well as to still photographs.

Videotapes of lineups are helpful for identification purposes and also aid the court in determining whether proper lineup procedures were followed by the police agency. It's wise for the agency to seek the advice of counsel prior to taping a lineup, however.

In the area of trial recording, it's expected that videotaping will be used in the near future to parallel the official court reporter's transcript. Trial proceedings could later be viewed by authorized personnel. Many judges have expressed interest in being able to supplement their study of a transcript with a videotape. In cases where the validity or accuracy of a court transcript is questioned, the videotape could serve to back it up. The jury may also find such tapes useful when they're attempting to reach their final decision. In addition, potential judges and lawyers may use videotapes to review key trials and analyze segments of court proceedings for instructional purposes.

Videotaping is also being used as a teaching tool in criminal justice classrooms. The instant replay feature allows simulated circumstances to be replayed and discussed for purposes of analysis.

Specific Videotaping Techniques:
The Vehicle Accident Scene

Vehicle accidents are difficult to record and investigate since they usually occur out in the open on busy streets where moving traffic and curious spectators may inhibit the investigative process. As was stated in Chapter 6, it's up to the first officer who arrives at the scene to secure it so that investigators and photographers can do their jobs without interference.

The videotape team should reach the scene promptly—before witnesses have had a chance to leave and before evidence has been altered or destroyed. Depending on traffic safety requirements, nothing should be moved until after the scene has been recorded. (The exception to this rule in any case, of course, is the victim who needs medical assistance.) This is another reason why the videotape team should arrive at an accident scene without delay; a public thoroughfare should be returned to its normal state as quickly as possible to lessen the chance of further accidents occurring.

In addition to recording the scene as a whole, the technician and narrator should also concentrate on obtaining views of the scene from the perspectives of the drivers involved in the accident and the witnesses who observed it. Tapes which attempt to record approximately what the driver or witness actually *saw* at the scene from his point of view can be powerful evidence during a trial and very useful during a follow-up investigation. The technician should be careful when videotaping a scene to include in it some permanent reference point such as a telephone pole, a curb marker, a fire hydrant, a house number, and so on.

The videotape team should also try to "recreate" the accident as much as possible. This involves first taping the scene from approximately 100 feet away to give the investigator some idea of how the scene may have appeared to the first driver just prior to the accident. Were traffic signals obstructed? Did any abnormal weather conditions exist? How heavily traveled is the area? The team should then take another similar picture from the viewpoint of the second driver. Shots of the area about 20-30' away from the probable point of impact should be taken next; these will help to establish the presence of traffic controls, skid marks, and other items of evidence. Again, scenes should be shot at eye level to give them a more realistic appearance.

Specific Videotaping
Techniques: Victims and Suspects

When viedotaping a victim for purposes of recording his condition and conducting an interview, the narrator must first identify himself, his agency, the case number, and the type of case involved. He must then make sure that the victim knows and acknowledges that the videotaping is taking place. After these initial steps have been taken, the technician can then take an overall long shot of the victim followed by closeups of the victim's face and any bodily injuries. All camera movements should be slow and smooth; care should be taken that the camera doesn't jump from the subject's face to his feet too quickly, for example. Naturally, videotaping should never interfere with necessary medical care.

Before photographing a dead victim, the videotaping team should work with the scene investigator to analyze the scene, determine the best search patterns to follow, decide on which views of the scene should be recorded, and prepare some idea of the direction the narration should take. Depending on the technique chosen for searching the victim, the investigator and the narrator may wish to engage in a recorded dialogue. Long shots should be slowly and systematically followed by closeups. During the investigation, the photographers and the detective should search for other types of evidence which might bear latent fingerprints of the perpetrator. All videotaping must show the physical evidence in relation to some stationary object, in addition to recording the person who first located the evidence.

It's especially important to videotape the body as it's first being turned over by the coroner's investigator or detective. Closeups of all evidence located beneath the body should be obtained. Spent bullets, weapons, broken debris, and other evidence may well be found there.

When videotaping a suspect, special attention should be paid to the suspect's demeanor. He may demonstrate certain types of body language which could give the investigators valuable clues; for example, if the suspect constantly wrung his hands, or perspired heavily, or wiped his forehead, the photographer would want to capture these gestures for later evaluation and analysis. The suspect must always give his permission prior to the videotaping; an exception to this rule might involve an intoxicated driver who's taped while being given the sobriety test either at curbside or at the police station.

A Note on the Professional
Qualifications of Scene Recorders

The professional qualifications of scene photographers, videotape technicians, and investigators are often heavily weighed in court. The more qualified an officer is, the more credible his testimony is apt to seem. And, of course, a qualified individual is better able to carry out the steps of an investigation with greater skill and professional expertise, making fewer mistakes and performing the various responsibilities involved in the process more efficiently and quickly. There's little room for error during an investigation. Evidence is fragile; suspects tend to be evasive or hostile; witnesses may not always be cooperative.

Training is especially important in order for an investigator to do his job well. Police photographers, for example, can begin their training by taking basic courses in physics and chemistry to learn the fundamentals of optics and become acquainted with the chemicals used in developing and printing photographs. Specialized training in crime scene photography, evidence photography, and x-ray photography can be obtained through various schools; other specialized classes may be taken through state police academies, colleges, universities, and the FBI. The type of training the individual decides to pursue should depend on his own career goals, along with the needs and policies of the department.

Education is also a major consideration, especially for those officers who are involved in the technical aspects of investigation. In many areas of the United States, a high school degree is no longer considered sufficient. The Bachelor of Science degree is often required—and occasionally even the Master's Degree; since more officers are obtaining advanced degrees, competition for preferred positions is getting stiffer, especially in larger police departments. Degrees can also enhance an officer's reputation; when giving court presentations and testimonies, for example, an individual with advanced degrees is more likely to be recognized and respected as an expert in his particular field.

Experience is still an excellent teacher. Where specific types of experience aren't readily available in the field, internships can often be arranged to train the officer in specialized or technical areas. Persons seeking careers as police photographers are usually expected to have substantial amounts of experience in developing and printing photographs; this can only come after long, hard hours of work in the darkroom. During a trial, a defense attorney may often ask specific questions and expect the photographer to answer them quickly and correctly. For example, the photographer might be asked questions like, "What type of chemicals were used in processing the prints?" "What type of paper was used?" "What photographic books or periodicals have you read lately?" Experience—and a constant awareness of the changes taking place in the field—can keep a photographer prepared both when performing on the job and when responding to questions in court.

In many cases, a police officer who wishes to testify as an expert witness in a certain area of criminal investigation must posses the *credentials* which vouch for his credibility. For example, he may belong to such organizations as the American Forensic Society, the Association of Criminal Justice Educators, the International Association of Identification, the Handwriting Association, the International Association of Chiefs of Police, and/or other professional organizations or groups which require their members to have certain qualifications and abilities.

The expert witness must also be able to *identify* and *account for* all stages of the evidence processing. Again, the chain of accountability is of utmost importance. He should be careful when testifying, however, to make sure to use language that the jury can understand. Although he may use many technical terms on the job, they should be kept to a minimum in the courtroom.

The police officer's *demeanor* and *bearing* are also significant in the court setting. Confidence—without an excess of ego—can help to convince a judge and a jury that an officer knows what he is talking about. Dress and speech should reflect the witness's professional attitude. Any dress code set forth by the individual's department should be conformed to.

Training, education, and experience are all ongoing processes. The fields of forensics and evidence investigation are constantly expanding, and the investigator must be willing to keep up with new developments. This might mean that he will need to take courses on a regular basis, both to be informed of recent advances and to be reminded of standard techniques and procedures. The skills involved in scene recording necessitate more than just *doing*; they also require the investigator to learn, to question, to seek out new information, to keep up with the times. This willingness to grow is the most important professional qualification an investigator can possess.

Summary

Recording the crime scene is a major facet of the criminal investigation process. Carefully kept records can authenticate and improve upon a witness's testimony, refresh the investigator's memory, help to determine follow-up procedures, and provide valuable evidence during the criminal trial. They can also establish the chain of accountability which is so important to a successful criminal investigation. The absence of records—or the presence of poorly maintained records—denotes a lack of professionalism which can only hurt the police agency.

There are many ways of recording the crime scene. The most common among these include the field notebook, sketches, photographs, and videotapes. Each has its own set of requirements. Field notes should be clear and concise, and should only contain information on cases under investigation. Personal opinions or feelings should never be written in the notebook. Sketches should be made according to one of the accepted methods, such as the coordinate method, the triangulation method, the cross-projection method, and the polar coordinate method. Each sketch should be identified with the officer's name, the particulars of the sketch, the date and time at which it was made, and other significant identifying features. Every photograph taken at a crime scene should be precisely logged and must be accounted for during every step of the investigation. Videotaping should be accomplished by a coordinated team of investigators who conform to the legal requirements of that recording method.

No two crimes are alike; thus, the way in which the investigator decides to record a particular scene will depend on a number of factors. He will need to ask and answer a number of questions before beginning to record a scene. These might include: What are the particular circumstances surrounding this scene? What did the crime involve? How much time and money can be used for the recording process? What items of evidence are of special significance? What methods of recording the scene will prove most useful to the scene investigator and the prosecutor? What types of equipment are available for use at this time, and what additional personnel, if any, should be called upon? Although scene recording should be begun as soon as possible after a crime has occurred—while an arson fire is still burning, for example—this doesn't mean that the scene recorder should simply rush to the scene and begin working without giving it any thought. It's generally a good idea for the scene recorder to spend a few moments with the scene investigator in deciding how the scene should be recorded and in what order photographs or videotapes should be made. In any case, a scene should always be recorded before evidence has been moved or removed. Photographs, sketches, or tapes made at this time will serve to preserve and present the scene *as it was,* which will never again by possible during the course of the investigation.

The investigator should keep in mind at all stages of the investigation that factual information recorded objectively is more valuable—and more admissible—than sensational or biased information. The investigator must be concerned with gathering and recording *evidence* that will bring a case to its logical conclusion. The more evidence he discovers and records, the more likely it is that the case will be efficiently handled. And, the more carefully evidence is recorded, the more apt a court is to accept and consider it. The investigator will decide along the way what types of evidence need the most attention and how they should be recorded and processed. These decisions will depend to a large extent on his experience and the nature of the crime itself. The investigator will never be responsible for determining the outcome of a case, however; that decision always rests with the court. Thus, he must gather information about a case without judging it.

The effective criminal investigator is always concerned with updating his qualifications and skills. Training, education, experience, and the willingness to keep learning are all necessary in order for an investigator to establish—and maintain—expertise in his particular area. And, finally, his professionalism must be evident at all times—whether on the streets, at a crime scene, or in court.

Questions and Topics for Discussion

1. Why is scene recording such an important aspect of the investigative process? What could be the outcome of an investigation for which records were poorly kept or insufficient? How could this affect the follow-up investigation, the court proceedings? Discuss at length.

2. Work together with your class to determine some of the elements of an imaginary crime scene. (Or, you may want to research a crime which occurred in your area.) Then practice sketching the scene according to the methods outlined in this chapter. If someone in your class has drafting experience, have him compile a smooth sketch of the scene.

3. What types of evidence are apt to be discovered at a crime scene? How should each type be photographed? When should each be photographed? Discuss the importance of coordinating the efforts of the police photographer and the scene investigator.

4. Look again at the crime scene you and your class described for Question 2 above. Then work together to decide what types of photographs should be taken of the scene. Compile a photographic log. If someone in the class is knowledgeable about photography, he can contribute technical information to this discussion. Or, you might want to arrange to have a police photographer come to your class and give a presentation of the methods he uses to photograph a crime scene and keep a log.

5. In this chapter, specific techniques for photographing arson and burglary scenes were discussed. How do you think a police photographer might go about photographing a homicide? An assault? A bombing?

6. Discuss ways in which a videotaping team might be coordinated. What types of training might be involved?

7. If you can, come up with some other ways in which videotaping might be used within the investigative process. Try to formulate some ways that aren't mentioned in this chapter. If possible, meet with members of your local police agency to find out how they utilize videotaping equipment during an investigation. You might be able to set up a viewing of some videotapes made by agency personnel.

8. Do some research in your local law library to find out the latest court decisions regarding the use of videotape during the criminal investigation. Do there seem to be any trends? What precedents have been set? Have there been cases when videotaped evidence has been judged inadmissible? Why do you think this happened? On the basis of your findings, determine some of the legalities an investigator must keep in mind when utilizing videotape equipment.

9. How might the beginning investigator prepare himself to become an expert in a specific field? Find out what types of courses are available, for example, to train a police photographer or a videotape technician. You might want to consult local police personnel to determine what training they have pursued during their own careers.

10. Interview at least four investigators to find out what investigative techniques they normally use and how they usually record crime scenes. How do their methods differ? How are they alike? Why does each choose the methods he does?

11. Research one or more recent criminal cases that have been investigated in your area. What types of evidence were discovered? How were they recorded? How did they affect the outcome of the case?

Annotated Bibliography

California State Department of Justice, *The Physical Evidence Manual* (General Services Documents, Sacramento, Cal.: 1975). A physical evidence manual for investigators; contains information on various aspects of investigations.

Moenssens, Moses, *Scientific Evidence In Criminal Cases* (The Foundation Press, Inc., 1973). A legalistic reference book for investigators who seek guidelines regarding major court decisions on crime scene investigations.

Sansone, San J., *Modern Photography for Police and Firemen* (W. H. Anderson Company, 3rd printing, 1974). A reference book of technical and photographic techniques utilized by police officers and firefighters.

Walls, H. J., *Forensic Science* (Praeger Publications, Inc., 2nd edition, New York, 1974). A reference book which discusses in detail the various crime scene investigation techniques which are beneficial to investigators.

U. S. Department of Justice, LEAA, National Institute of Law Enforcement and Criminal Justice, *Video Support in the Criminal Courts* (U. S. Government Printing Office, Washington, D. C., 1975). A reference book including the latest technological developments and laws regarding the use of videotaping equipment in courtrooms and during investigations.

EIGHT

Processing Evidence Found at the Crime Scene

Chapter Objectives

After reading this chapter, the student should be able to:

- ☑ List and define the various classifications of physical evidence.
- ☑ Identify the types of crime laboratories and give reasons for their increasing numbers.
- ☑ List the different steps involved in the process of identifying evidence and determining its characteristics.
- ☑ Give reasons why a criminalist's role is important as both an examiner and as a witness.
- ☑ Describe the various ways in which specific types and categories of physical evidence are processed both by the investigator and in the laboratory.

The Crime Scene:
A Study in Uniqueness

No two crimes are ever alike, so no two crime scenes are ever identical. Even though a perpetrator may follow a certain pattern, or modus operandi, when committing a number of crimes, each will be different in some way from all of the others. For this reason, the scene investigator must be imaginative, flexible, and often ingenious. Although he or she will be expected to perform certain prescribed tasks regardless of the type of crime under investigation, he must also approach each situation as if it has its own personal set of characteristics and elements—because it does.

No scene can be examined as if it's the same as one that was searched yesterday or a week ago or ten years ago. Each poses new problems which the investigator will be called upon to respond to and deal with. The perpetrator may have a favorite modus operandi when doing his job; the investigator cannot. When he arrives at a scene with the attitude that it's a strictly routine matter, evidence unique to that scene may be unintentionally destroyed or simply overlooked. This is not to say that criminal investigation is a purely random endeavor, however; rather, it's a very creative one.

The success of an investigation is often determined by the first few acts taken at the scene. All other persons who join in the investigation effort at a later time will be directly affected by the initial actions taken and decision made by the scene investigator. It's clear, then, that the investigator plays a crucial role. How he or she handles and evaluates the evidence discovered at a crime scene can literally determine the outcome of a case.

Some investigators are directly involved in the technical aspects of evidence processing, such as analysis and testing. Others merely decide which items of evidence should be processed and which shouldn't. In any case, the investigator invariably has a strong influence on all the subsequent steps taken during a criminal investigation.

The Importance of
Evaluating the Scene

Any crime scene, regardless of the nature of the crime, contains a great deal of evidence. Before beginning to process any of the evidence present at a scene, however, the investigator should first take a few moments to look carefully at the scene and evaluate it. This step can lessen the chance that errors will be made while at the same time adding to the investigator's knowledge of what the crime consists of and how it may have occurred.

Basically, the crime scene will contain evidence which reveals the *fact* that a crime has been committed (corpus delicti evidence), evidence which reveals the *identity* of the perpetrator (such as fingerprints), and evidence which can aid the investigator in mentally reconstructing the criminal act in an effort to understand how and why it took place and how it can best be resolved. Each item of evidence can be classified before it can be processed. Evidence classification can help the investigator to determine which types of evidence deserve the most attention and are apt to prove the most valuable.

Classifying Evidence

Evidence concerning a crime may be grouped into two general categories:

- *direct evidence*, which includes statements made by eyewitnesses, confessions obtained from suspects, and so on; and
- *indirect*, or *physical*, evidence, which includes those items or objects found at a crime scene.

The latter type will be the focus of this chapter.

Indirect evidence can be identified according to class and individual characteristics if these characteristics can be differentiated. Class characteristics are those which are common to a group of objects. Evidence materials having observable class characteristics can normally be further identified according to subclasses. For example, the heel of a shoe belongs to a certain class of items. Subclasses might include the brand of the shoe and its size.

If an item of evidence can be identified according to subclasses, its probative value—that is, the likelihood that it will aid in proving some aspect of a criminal case—usually increases. If it's possible to identify an object so thoroughly that all other similar objects are excluded from comparison, then that item is said to have been individualized and has a particularly high probative value. For example, if an investigator is sure that certain marks found at a scene could only have been made by one specific screwdriver, then that screwdriver will have strong probative value as evidence in court.

The scene investigator should be aware of which types of evidence are apt to prove most useful in court. The following list describes several categories of indirect evidence, beginning with fingerprints, which have the highest probative value, and ending with hairs and fibers, which in most cases have the lowest probative value since they're difficult to precisely identify.

1 Fingerprints are the source of what's technically termed friction ridge evidence. Natural debris (such as oil or perspiration) or foreign material (such as blood or ink) collect in the ridges at the end of the finger and are transferred to some item at the scene. The ridges form a swirl

pattern, and no two patterns are alike; thus, friction ridge evidence is the only common type of evidence which allows for the total individualization of human beings. There are other parts of the body—for example, the feet, the lips, and the palms of the hands—which also have unique characteristics which allow for individualization, but their impressions are less frequently found.

2. Physical matches exist when two or more pieces of an item which has been broken or torn are found and can be demonstrated to fit together. Sometimes, for example, a burglar may break a tool and leave part of it at the scene; if that part can be matched up with one found in his or her possession, the individuality of that item is established. Other examples of possible physical matches include glass and/or paint chips, torn paper, paper matches removed from a matchbook, or pieces of tape.

3. Hitting one object with another, leaning on something, or otherwise putting pressure on an item will often leave an impression. Impressions are grouped into three categories:

   • two-dimensional;

   • three-dimensional; and

   • three-dimensional combined with striae, or markings which indicate the movement of one surface across another.

Two-dimensional impressions might include dust prints of shoes on smooth, hard surfaces; cloth marks on dusty or greasy surfaces; typewriting; and handwriting. Three-dimensional impressions might include shoe prints or tire tracks in dirt or mud; indentations made by a striking tool; and bite marks. Striae can result when a projectile, such as a bullet, passes through a grooved barrel, or when a hard metal tool is slid across a softer metal surface.

Impression evidence may be individualized if enough distinctive marks can be found at the scene and matched up with their sources. When it's not possible to individualize an impression, it can usually still be identified according to its class characteristics.

4. Trace evidence consists of small or microscopic particles which can't be physically matched with others. Trace evidence may be individualized only if it's very unique. For example, a multi-layered paint sample may sometimes be individualized, as can mixtures of unusual portions or ingredients, such as a gasoline mixture.

Most often, however, trace evidence cannot be individualized. Some items can be grouped according to class characteristics (which have less probative value, of course, since they're less specific). For example, a paint sample found at a hit-and-run scene can be identified visibly and chemically as being exactly the same as one that's been taken from a known vehicle, but it can't always be assumed that this vehicle is the only place in the whole world where this particular paint can be found.

5. Physiological fluids such as blood and semen are undoubtedly unique to their sources, but at this point in time they can only be identified according to subclasses. Thus, physiological fluids found at crime scenes cannot be individualized. They can provide valuable information to the investigator, however, especially if their geographic arrangement at the scene can be properly interpreted. In many instances, blood patterns can help to explain the sequence of events associated with a crime.

6. Hairs and fibers generally lack the characteristics necessary for individualization. Unique combinations or qualities occasionally permit the exclusion of other sources, though. Hairs and fibers found at a crime scene should always be retained and processed since at the very least they can be used to exclude certain suspects.

The Crime Laboratory and the Criminalist: An Overview

The Growing Number of Crime Laboratories: Meeting a Need.

Much of the physical evidence found at a crime scene ends up at a crime laboratory for processing. This wasn't always the case, however; laboratories were simply too few and far between. The past decade has seen an increase in the number of laboratories supplying information to the criminal justice system. This increase is usually considered to be the result of three major factors: changes in the law, the rising crime rate, and the availability of more funding and more personnel. Each of these factors will be discussed here.

Changes in the Law. Two Supreme Court decisions in the 1960's—Chimel v. California in 1965, and Miranda v. Arizona in 1966—placed severe restrictions on police search and interrogation practices. Prior to Chimel v. California, a police officer was permitted to search all areas under a suspect's control when making an arrest. This meant that an officer could search a suspect's entire house if he wanted to. The Court's decision limited the area that could be searched to the suspect's body and the area immediately surrounding him—usually interpreted as an arm's-length distance. Before making a more extensive search, an officer would have to obtain a search warrant. Thus, the police no longer had access to much of the evidence they used to be able to collect as a matter of course. They had to depend more on the evidence found at the crime scene, and much of this required careful laboratory analysis.

The *Miranda* decision made it imperative that police officers warn a suspect of his constitutional rights prior to arrest or interrogation. A confession obtained without the benefit of a *Miranda* warning was illegal and therefore inadmissible as evidence. This meant that it was no longer a good idea to rest an entire case on direct evidence, and the police began to rely more on indirect evidence found at the scene. Naturally, crime laboratories were called upon to evaluate and analyze much of this evidence.

The Rising Crime Rate. The growing crime rate also added to the laboratories' workloads. One type of violation in particular became more common: the illegal use or sale of restricted drugs.

A prosecutor can issue a criminal complaint only after he has been convinced that reasonable cause exists to believe that a particular individual has committed a crime. In drug cases, reasonable cause doesn't exist until a substance found in the suspect's possession has been identified as a restricted drug. Once a substance has been procured from a suspect, it must be analyzed within a reasonably short period of time. In California, for instance, a complaint must be issued within 48 hours of an arrest or the suspect will be released. Since a number of drug violators tend to be transient, the police might find it difficult to locate a suspect if it takes a long time to find out that a drug found in his possession is in fact a restricted substance. Before the number of laboratories increased, the ones that were in operation had to give this type of analysis priority, and other investigations simply had to wait. This put pressure on a number of areas in the criminal justice system, and it was obvious that more laboratories were needed.

The Availability of Funds and Personnel. Many local authorities, recognizing that their laboratory needs were not being met, took their problems to the federal level. In response, the Omnibus Crime Control and Safe Streets Act was passed in 1968. Under this act, the Law Enforcement Assistance Administration (LEAA) was created in part to coordinate the actions of the various law enforcement agencies. Federal funding was made available, and some of it was channeled into grants for crime laboratories. At approximately the same time, the space program was winding down somewhat and many of its associated projects were being terminated. As a result, a number of scientists and technicians reentered the job market and many found positions at crime laboratories.

Laboratory Systems

Today, there are two systems of crime laboratories operating within the United States: central and core/satellite laboratories. A central laboratory concentrates all services in one location that's convenient to the majority of its users. It's ideal for areas that are small in square miles but large in population. Usually, a central laboratory is located near the judicial building, the morgue, and as many separate investigative agencies as possible.

Core/satellite laboratories best serve those areas in which the population is spread out over many square miles. For example, the State of California has seven core laboratories (each of which is, in effect, comparable to a central laboratory) and fourteen satellite laboratories (each of which provides limited services). The core laboratories are located central to areas with large populations; the satellites are scattered throughout the state in areas of medium population density. In addition, many large California cities and/or counties have their own full-service laboratories and use the State system only as backup.

Laboratory Equipment

In order for a crime laboratory to be able to properly analyze and examine evidence, it must have access to a great deal of highly technical (and frequently very expensive) equipment. For example, a fully-equipped central laboratory should possess the following:

- microscopes (of several different kinds; see Figure 8-1 p. 218 for an example of a scanning electron microscope);
- cameras which can be used in conjunction with the microscopes;
- spectrophotometers;
- spectrometers (see Figure 8-2 for an example);
- spectrographs;
- chromatographs;
- sophisticated photographic equipment of various types;
- balances;
- programmable temperature-controlled hotplates;
- ultrasonic cleaners; and
- assorted glassware and chemical apparatus.

Every laboratory should also have a complete reference library and enough clerical personnel and laboratory assistants to free the evidence examiners for more technical responsibilities.

In the event that a local laboratory doesn't have a specific piece of equipment that's needed to complete an analysis, a nearby university can usually be counted on for assistance.

The Identification of Evidence: A Process and a Concept

Every item, no matter how large or how minute, has its own specific identity. The criminalist's job is to determine that identity as closely as possible. In some instances, this can be accomplished by simple visual comparison. In other cases, it may appear as if one item is indistinguishable from another when it really isn't. The naive examiner may assume that just because he or she can't tell two items apart, they have a common origin. This assumption is very risky.

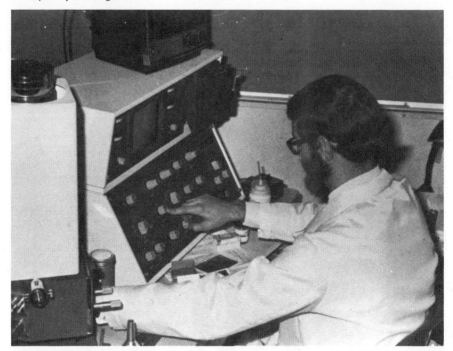

Figure 8-1. *The Scanning Electron Microscope.* This is one of the newest analytical tools being used in crime laboratories. Capable of up to 100,000x magnification, it can also be coupled with an X-ray fluorescence spectrometer to analyze an item of evidence according to its elements.

Figure 8-2. *The Gas Chromatograph/Mass Spectrometer.* This instrument is capable of separating complex mixtures into their pure components and then identifying each component individually.

The aware criminalist realizes that precise information must be discovered, developed, and evaluated before an item of evidence can be clearly and correctly identified. He is also aware of the limitations which influence the success of this process. These might include:

- his own lack of experience or education in a particular subject area;
- the lack of certain necessary equipment in the laboratory; and
- the nature of the item of evidence itself. It may have been improperly handled during collection, for example, or damaged or contaminated during storage. Or, it may simply be so common that absolute individualization is impossible.

The Search for Identity. The identification of a particular item of evidence is accomplished by an orderly series of steps. Each step has an exclusionary effect; that is, once it's been satisfactorily concluded there are fewer items which must be carried over to the next step.

For example, blood is first examined to determine its type. Once a sample's type has been established, a large number of possible donors can be eliminated from consideration. Even if it's found to be of the most common type, about half of the population can theoretically be eliminated. (When the investigator is working with a select group of suspects, it may be possible to eliminate one or perhaps even all of them.) Once the next step in the examination process has been completed, even more suspects can be eliminated from the group of possibilities, and so on.

Thus, if an examination is carried out properly, each additional step adds to the certainty of the identification. When a step-by-step procedure has eliminated all but one of the possible origins of an item of evidence, individualization has been achieved.

Determining Evidence Characteristics. As was mentioned earlier in this chapter, all materials have two types of characteristics: class and individual. In many cases, individual characteristics of a specific item may be too remote to recognize; this doesn't pose a problem, however, if class characteristics are all that need to be determined. Usually, for example, it's sufficient to identify a restricted drug according to its class characteristics if other facts surrounding its use and confiscation are known.

When it's extremely desirable to individualize an item of evidence, though, and this can't be achieved, the criminalist must be satisfied with determining class characteristics alone. For example, a great deal of research has been performed in an attempt to individualize such biological materials as blood, semen, and hair, but this individualization isn't yet possible. The research has established many procedures that can be used to identify subclass characteristics of these substances, however, so it has been very useful.

It's important that the criminalist be able to recognize and distinguish independent from dependent class characteristics. For example, an automobile manufacturer may paint a large number of automobiles with a black primer under the outer layer. Each time an exemplar paint sample from that maker is examined the same combination is observed. These two paint layers are not two independent class characteristics. Since the manufacturer made the decisions to always use the same combination, these two layers represent but one independent characteristic. The fact that there are two layers, each of different color, can be considered a subclass characteristic. In the center of the damage all the factory paint may be removed during the repair process. The original paint may remain in the undamaged area surrounding the repair. When the surface is repainted, this remaining original paint now is covered with two or more new layers. This makes these specific locations on this specific vehicle unique from all other vehicles in the original class. This paint has both class and individual characteristics. Since it is remotely possible that two vehicles from the original class could be damaged and repainted with the same replacement paint, six or more identical layers are desirable before common origin is proposed. Further, it is of the utmost importance to examine the history of the vehicles involved in the investigation. Consider a fleet of vehicles whose owner repaints the entire fleet once or twice a year. These vehicles may all have identical multilayered paint.

Sources of Evidence Material. Items of evidence can also be grouped into two more categories. These categories are dependent on the sources of the items. If the origin of an item is known for a fact, the item is called a standard. If it isn't known, it's called questionable evidence. Standards serve as a basis for comparison; that is, a standard can be compared with a questionable item to determine the latter item's origin.

For example, paint scrapings taken from a burglary victim's door are standards because their precise source is known. These can be compared with questionable paint chips found on the tip of a pry bar in a suspect's possession. Or, the investigator may obtain rolled ink impressions of a suspect's fingerprints; these standard prints can then be compared with latent prints found at a crime scene. The careful investigator will collect standards from many different locations and objects at a crime scene.

Forensic Certainty and Confirmation: Two Goals for the Criminalist. **Forensic certainty** may be defined as the confidence that an item of evidence is what the criminalist says it is—without question and without doubt. This certainty can be achieved only after a series of careful examinations. For example, a number of tests may determine that a white powder is indeed cocaine to the exclusion of all other materials. Or, if the material submitted for analysis is human blood, it can be determined with forensic certainty that the blood is of a specific type, Rh factor, and so on. Forensic certainty has nothing to do with speculations about the origin of the item or how it arrived at the crime scene; it's concerned only with the identity of the material itself.

Usually, before forensic certainty can be achieved, some form of confirmation must also be conducted. Confirmation, in general, consists of a second analysis which is carried out to confirm the qualitative and quantitative results of an original analysis. The second analysis may be a simple duplication of the first one, and it may even be conducted by the same examiner. Ideally, more complex items or samples require that the second analysis be conducted by a different examiner using an independent method.

The following examples illustrate possible confirmation procedures:

- An examiner determines via the Lattes slide procedure that a blood sample retrieved from a crime scene belongs to a certain blood group. Another sample from the original quantity of evidence is then tested by the absorption-elution procedure. If the second analysis gets the same results as the first, confirmation has been achieved.

- A tool mark found at a scene is examined by one investigator under a comparison microscope. After he has completed the examination, the same tool mark is re-examined by a second criminalist who is not told the results of the first examination.

The Responsibilities of the Criminalist as an Expert

Once a criminalist has finished analyzing and examining an item of evidence, he must generate a report based on his findings. This report carries a great deal of weight and must be right the first time. Of course, a correction can be made later, and an opinion can even be changed, but only after the original report has been carefully scrutinized by the courts and attorneys involved in the case. An error is a serious matter; it can interrupt the freedom of an innocent person, free a guilty person, and affect the reputation of the criminalist and the agency which he represents.

Thus, the criminalist should always take the firm position that regardless of external pressure he will not be rushed into a conclusion or form an opinion for which there is no proper basis. He will also take care not to release a report that could be misleading or misrepresented by anyone who uses it.

The criminalist who is called upon to serve as an expert witness assumes an awesome responsibility and must be constantly aware of this fact. Judges, juries, and attorneys often assume that just because the criminalist is a scientist his testimony is bound to be accurate and true. This misconception is based on another greater one: that science is foolproof. Nobody's testimony should be accepted without question, regardless of his reputation or position within an agency or community.

Some evidence examiners have exploited the respect that others have for science. For example, one evidence examiner actually falsified his university credits, lied about his on-the-job training, and incorrectly reported his "findings" on several cases in which he testified. He was eventually detected, but not until his behavior had seriously affected many lives and his disregard for the truth had had a lasting effect on the profession he claimed to represent.

Processing Specific Types of Evidence

It should be clear by now that the outcome of an investigation depends heavily on cooperation among investigators and laboratory criminalists. The scene investigator will initially respond to the scene, evaluate it, and select the items of evidence which will go to the criminalist for examination and analysis. If he ignores or overlooks important evidence or handles it carelessly, the criminalist will be severely limited in what he can do. On the other hand, if the investigator is careful to see that the criminalist receives sufficient amounts of evidence—both standards and questionable items—and the criminalist makes errors or incorrectly performs his end of the examination process, then any further steps the investigator (and the prosecutor) can take will be restricted or even futile. A successful investigation, then, is a result of the investigator and criminalist acknowledging the interdependency of their roles and working together as professionals.

The examples of evidence processing discussed in the remainder of this chapter will highlight this mutual give-and-take arrangement. The investigator discovers and retrieves the evidence; the criminalist examines and analyzes it. A look at each example which follows will reveal just how complex this process can be and how important it is that each step be taken with caution, intelligence, and awareness.

Processing Friction Ridge Evidence

As was mentioned earlier in this chapter, fingerprints, the most common type of friction ridge evidence, have higher probative value than any other type of physical evidence. Although palm prints, footprints, and lip impressions are also able to be individualized, they are found less often; thus, fingerprints will be the focus of this discussion.

Fingerprints are made available to the investigator—and, in turn, to the criminalist—via two distinct ways: documentation and discovery. Ink impressions (for which a person's fingers are inked and then rolled across a clean surface) are often collected by enforcement agencies for a number of reasons. For example, prints may be collected from a person who is applying for a job, someone who wants to be bonded, or someone who is being arrested for a criminal violation. These prints are retained and kept on file as standards: they have been documented and are readily available for investigative use.

The investigator may also, of course, discover prints which have been unintentionally left at a crime scene by the perpetrator. These can be categorized according to three subgroups: latent prints, visible prints, and plastic prints.

Latent, or "hidden," prints are by definition not visible to the naked eye. They are made when the perpetrator (or anyone else, for that matter) touches some object at the scene and thereby transfers to that object bodily secretions such as perspiration or sebaceous oils. Perspiration is constantly being excreted within the friction ridge structure, especially during times of stress; sebaceous oils are picked up by the fingers when touching the face—a common gesture. These substances are left on an area much as inked rubber stamp leaves an impression on a receptive surface; all or most of the details of the friction ridge are transferred. (In today's vocabulary, incidentally, all prints found at a scene—whether visible or not—are usually referred to as latents.)

Visible prints are able to be seen by the unaided eye. They are made when the perpetrator touches some foreign material—such as blood, paint, grease, makeup, or chalk—before touching some item at the scene.

Plastic prints are created when the perpetrator touches some soft, pliable surface, such as fresh paint, putty, clay, or butter.

Discovering Prints at the Scene. In order to discover the maximum number of fingerprints left at a crime scene, the investigator must first use his imagination to "reconstruct" the scene, or determine within a reasonable degree of probability how the crime occurred. This will help him to determine which areas should be processed. The investigator should take time to mentally reconstruct how a crime was committed *before* the scene is thoroughly searched; otherwise, many prints that aren't readily visible (and even some that are) may be unintentionally destroyed or damaged.

The investigator should first examine suspected areas simply by looking at them and shining a light on them. If the light source is placed very close to the area being searched and held at an oblique angle to that surface, even a very slight change in the surface should be noticeable. Visible and plastic prints can often be located using this technique. Physical and/or chemical methods must be used to process prints that are not visible, however, or to make indistinct ones more clear.

Physical and Chemical Processing. Physical methods of processing latent prints (this includes both those that are visible and those that aren't) generally involve dusting the suspected areas with powder. The powder adheres to the ridges of the print and makes them visible. (Plastic prints are an exception. These are normally cast, after which a rolled ink impression is made of the casting and then compared to documented prints already on file.) Chemical methods, on the other hand, cause chemical reactions to take place on the suspected surface which expose any fingerprints left there. Which method the investigator chooses (he may sometimes choose both) will depend on a number of factors. It's usually best to attempt to get results via dusting first, however, since some chemicals can permanently damage certain types of fingerprints, especially oily ones.

Before beginning to dust for prints, the investigator should carefully examine the surface in question with the following considerations in mind:

- *Is the surface dry?* If not—if it's wet with water, for example—it must be allowed to dry completely at room temperature before dusting. If the surface is wet with an oily material, then dusting may not be possible, at least for the time being. If other foreign materials are present—such as blood, ink, dust, or some other substance—this should be recorded in the official scene notes. A series of photographs should also be taken to document the condition of the surface being examined. If this foreign material is thought to be valuable to the investigation, it should be lightly brushed to one side and collected. (Blood should be allowed to dry first, of course).

- *What is the surface made of*? Some building materials, for example, don't respond well to dusting, such as unfinished wood, stucco, and the rough side of frosted glass. Smooth surfaces are the most receptive.

- *What is the color of the surface*? A powder which contrasts with that color will reveal the most information. For example, if the surface is white, a black carbon-base powder should be used. If it's black, white or gray powder will give the best results. (Iron dust is also occasionally used as a powder.)

Once the investigator has decided that a surface is ready for dusting and has selected the appropriate powder, a small amount of the powder should be taken up onto a camel's hair, fiberglass filament, or feather brush that's been specially prepared for fingerprint development work. Excess powder should be removed by lightly flicking the brush. The brush should then be lightly applied to the surface in question. A mask should always be worn as a precautionary measure. More powder can be added as needed. (See Figure 8-3.)

The powder should be applied to the print according to the flow of the pattern which begins to develop. Crossing the flow at right angles can damage the print. After the print has become as visible as it's going to get, excess powder should be removed. A closeup photograph which includes a ruler or some other measuring scale in its viewing area should then be taken; a 1:1 camera is preferable since the final image on the negative is life size. If a contact print is made, the print should also be life size. Some grades of finish paper may stretch or shrink during development; this is one reason why it's important to include a measuring device within each photograph. Distortion can be discovered by simply comparing the original ruler with the photographic print.

Once the area has been photographed, a piece of transparent lifting tape should be placed over the processed print in order to protect it (see Figure 8-4). Other areas of the scene surrounding the print can then be safely searched (see Figure 8-5). After the investigator decides that all possible prints have been located, an overall photograph of the area should be taken to further document the collection procedure. All steps taken during fingerprint processing, all observations made, and any conclusions reached at the time should be included in the case notes.

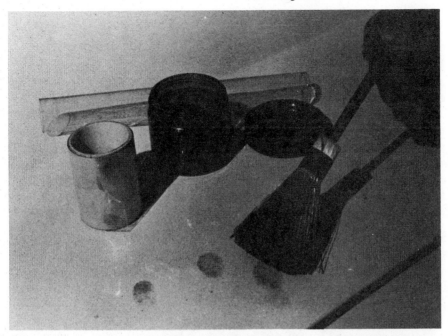

Figure 8-3. *Fingerprint Dusting.* The basic materials required for dusting fingerprints are a brush, powder, and lifting tape. In this photograph, black carbon dust is being applied with a fiberglass brush.

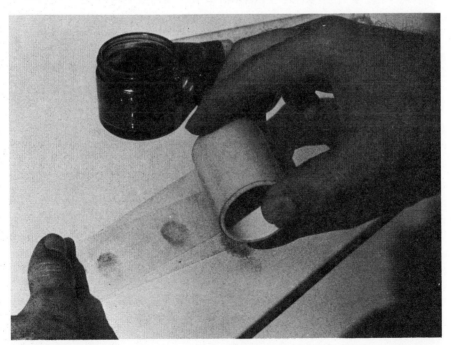

Figure 8-4. *Preserving Fingerprints.* Once fingerprints have been made visible by dusting and have been photographed, a section of lifting tape is stretched out over them. The tape is then pressed down to the surface to secure it, beginning with the cut end.

After a scene examination has been completed, the lifting tape can be pulled away from the surface and the print transferred to a clean, contrasting 3x5 card (see Figure 8-6).

If dusting proves unsuccessful, chemicals can be applied to surfaces or objects at the scene by spraying, dipping, or brushing. All chemicals are potentially dangerous; thus, the importance of following safety precautions cannot be overemphasized. The area being chemically treated should be properly ventilated, with the airflow constantly moving away from the investigator. Protective clothing must also be worn, especially gloves. The investigator should be careful not to let any of the chemicals being used come into contact with his skin; if contact is inadvertently made, the affected areas should be flushed with cold water immediately.

Silver nitrate solution is the most frequently used chemical for print developing. It's especially convenient when many large surfaces, such as several cardboard cartons, need to be searched, since it can be applied with a brush. Silver nitrate reacts with the sodium chloride present in perspiration to form silver chloride; after exposure to light, silver chloride turns black, and the friction ridge pattern becomes evident. If time is at a premium, the surface can be exposed to light to hurry the developing process along; this won't increase the quality of the print, but it won't hurt it either.

If silver nitrate comes in contact with the skin, it causes black spots to appear. This reaction indicates a poor handling technique; remedial training in the use of chemicals may be called for.

Nihydrin can be applied by spraying, dipping, or brushing. An area that's been treated with nihydrin will turn contrasting colors of light red, especially in the presence of heat. These shadings will reveal the characteristics of fingerprints in the area.

If nihydrin comes in contact with the skin, the affected area will turn purple. Disposable gloves will not protect the hands against nihydrin discoloration. Again, remedial training may be necessary.

Iodine is applied by enclosing the object under scrutiny in a cabinet or container and then heating the iodine crystals until fumes are created (See Figure 8-7). Iodine becomes gaseous without first passing through an intermediate liquid phase. The gaseous vapors are dark brown, and when they come in contact with an oily print a temporary contrast becomes evidence. Since it is termporary, a photograph of the print should be taken immediately. Once it starts to fade, however, it can be enhanced by breathing on it.

The investigator should keep in mind that all chemical methods have some limitations and drawbacks. In summary, then, the following general procedure is recommended for print processing:

1. The investigator should first evaluate the scene and mentally reconstruct how the crime happened. Visible and plastic prints can then be observed by the use of oblique lighting.

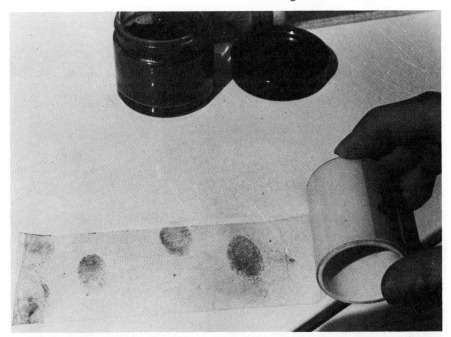

Figure 8-5. *Getting a Clear Image on Tape.* The tape is then pressed down on all of the developed prints. This is accomplished by running the thumb along the tape. If air bubbles form, they should be *carefully* rubbed out.

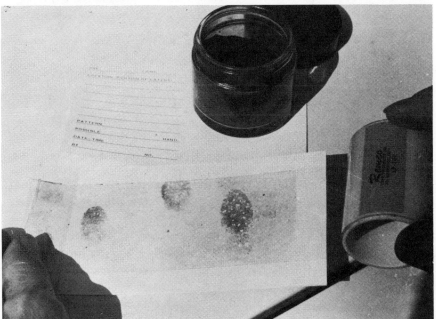

Figure 8-6. *Removing Prints from the Scene.* Once the transfer of the prints to the tape has been accomplished and documented, the tape is pulled away from the surface of the roll end so that the last area attached is the cut end. Then, when approximately 1/2" of the tape is still stuck to the surface, a clean 3x5 card is inserted under the transfer area. The tape is then pressed onto the card and the roll is cut away.

Figure 8-7. *A Fume Hood Containing an Iodine Fumer.*

2. All suspected prints that aren't immediately visible should be dusted.

3. If prints still aren't clearly visible, suspected areas should then be chemically treated. In other words, this process should be undertaken only if eye detection and dusting fail to produce the expected results of the examination.

Processing Physical Matches

Establishing that two pieces of an object or item "fit" together appears to be the simplest type of laboratory examination. It can usually be determined fairly quickly whether a physical match between two items exist. This type of match is normally considered to be absolute; anyone can recognize the fit, and no one can (usually) challenge the opinion that two pieces of an item were at one time joined together. Figures 8-8 through 8-12 illustrate examples of physical matches.

Almost anyone can perform a physical match, but only a qualified examiner should attempt it. This is simply due to the fact that an examiner who knows how to handle evidence and what to look for is less likely to damage

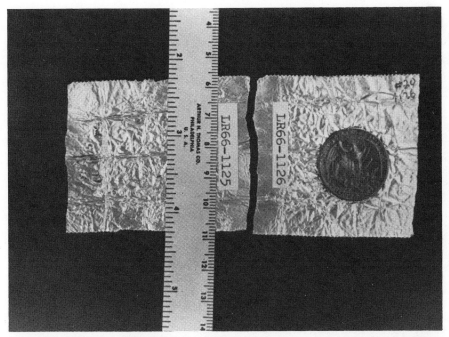

Figure 8-8. *Aluminum Foil Bindles Containing Heroin.* A suspect was accused of selling bindle 66-1125 and four other similar bindles. He denied it. A search of his residence revealed additional bindles made of aluminum foil. The bindles were found to have common edges and thus could be physically matched.

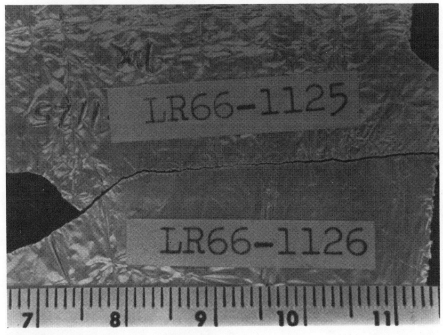

Figure 8-9. *A Closer View of Two Other Bindles.*

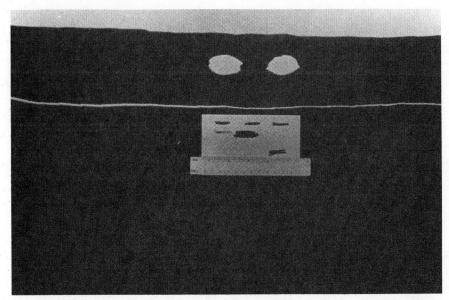

Figure 8-10. *A Mask Found in the Possession of a Suspect Accused of a Crime.* An alleged accomplice claimed no knowledge of the crime. A search of the accomplice's residence, however, disclosed a large piece of cloth which seemed identical to that from which the mask was made. The two pieces were found to have a common edge and were physically matched.

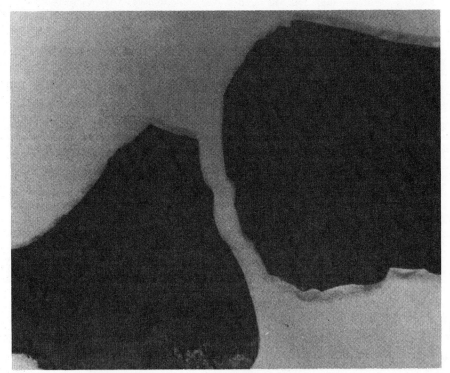

Figure 8-11. *Paint Chips.* The upper paint chip shown here was removed from a suspect's vehicle. The lower chip was collected from the scene of a hit-and-run accident.

Figure 8-12. *The Same Two Paint Chips Reversed.* The striae indicate that this area of the vehicle had been repaired at least once before. Matching striae complement the common edge evidence.

it or make errors. Physical matches are a good place for the beginning investigator or examiner to start; however he should always be supervised and directed and his findings confirmed by an expert.

Processing Impression Evidence

Impression evidence can be separated into three categories: two-dimensional, three-dimensional, and three-dimensional with striae. Tool marks, for example, will usually fall into one of the three categories as follows:

- A two-dimensional impression is formed when the surface characteristics of one object are transferred to another without penetration. For example, a rubber stamp makes this type of impression.

- A three-dimensional impression is made when one object actually penetrates another. When the host material is plastic in nature (that is, when it's soft or pliable or otherwise receptive), it may retain the characteristics of the penetrating object.

- A three-dimensional impression with striae is made when one object penetrates another and is then withdrawn laterally or moved around. This leaves a series of parallel lines or ridges.

Most tools—which can include anything from common tools to shoe heels to teeth—are capable of making any of the marks described above. In most cases, the host surface is damaged; occasionally, the reverse is true. In some situations, both the tool and the host surface is damaged; this can happen when a perpetrator uses a tool to do a job it wasn't made to do, for example.

Evaluating Evidence According to Class Characteristics. Although it's certainly convenient if the perpetrator leaves his tools behind at the crime scene, this rarely happens. Thus, the investigator must learn how to evaluate impressions to determine their class characteristics. Impressions can reveal valuable information like the size of the tool, its shape, and, in some instances, its brand name.

Impressions can also reveal facts about the perpetrator. Shoe prints, for instance, can indicate abnormalities in his walk. Teeth impressions in a bite mark can be used to build a model of the perpetrator's dental characteristics. (Skin is a very plastic surface, however, so teeth impressions often don't last long enough to prove especially useful.)

Precise identification of an impression may require the investigator and the criminalist alike to perform a long series of investigative steps. For example, if the size of a perpetrator's shoe must be determined, the following will probably be necessary:

1. First, if a complete sole and heel pattern is available at the scene, it should be photographed. A measuring scale of some sort should always be included in the photographs.

2. Second, photographs should be compared with sample shoes in an attempt to identify the brand of the sole and heel.

3. Once the brand has been determined (an impression may often reveal the letters or numbers stamped into the sole or heel, for instance), the manufacturer should be contacted. Sole or heel manufacturers commonly sell their products to several different shoe makers. The manufacturer will usually be able to provide the investigator with information about how many soles and heels were produced and how they were geographically distributed.

4. Following this step, a commercial source of the manufacturer's product—that is, a retail outlet—should also be contacted. The investigator should have an idea of the approximate size of the shoe which left the impression at the scene. For the purposes of this explanation, let's say that the impression measured 11¼" long. Several pairs of shoes should be obtained from the retail store. It's best if the investigator can arrange for 10-20 pairs in five sizes: the size which comes closest

to the measurement of 11¼″, along with the next two smaller sizes and the next two larger sizes. It may be necessary to visit more than one outlet in order to locate this many shoes.

5. If the impression left at the scene was that of the right shoe, for example, then each right shoe from the pairs obtained for examination should be measured. Ideally, the measurements will reveal five distinct sets of characteristics, since five different sizes are being included in the comparison.

6. The impression found at the scene should be compared to each element in the five categories. Ideally, the questioned impression will correspond to the elements of only one category. When the impression's measurements fit more than one category, each possible size must be reported. This is due to the fact that factory substitutions have been known to take place. A shoe may be a different size than its markings would seem to indicate. For instance, the inner surface of a shoe may be marked according to a specific size; once it's cut open, however, it may be discovered that the sole is a different size altogether. The possibility of this occurring must be considered in each case. (See Figure 8-13.)

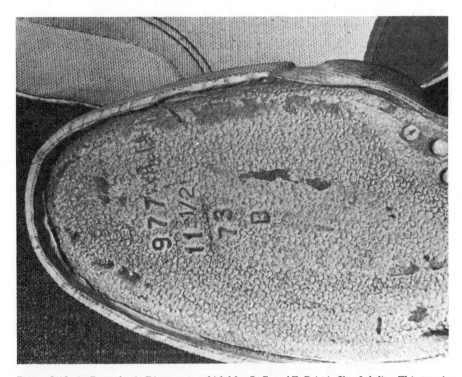

Figure 8-13. *An Example of a Discrepancy which May Be Found To Exist in Shoe Labeling.* This tennis shoe was purchased as a size 12—the size indicated in the lining. When the shoe was cut open, however, it was found to have a size 11½ sole—a difference of ⅛″.

7. Once the evidence print can be shown to correspond with only one sample size, it can be assumed that the class characteristic of size has been established.

Note that all of the steps above are necessary to determine this *single* class characteristic. Others, of course, must be determined by still more tests and examinations.

Most tools will wear with use. Defects will become obvious, along with specific markings that result from use or abuse. Before the investigator can be certain that a specific mark within an impression is an individual characteristic—in other words, that it's unique to the particular tool that was used to make the impression—the source or cause of that mark or defect should first be established.

The initial step in this process again involves locating and contacting the manufacturer and supplier of the tool in question. Once this has been accomplished, a large number of apparently similar tools can be examined. A mark that may at first appear to be unique may in fact be present on all or many of the tools examined. In this case, the mark in question would turn out to be a class characteristic rather than an individual one.

Generally speaking, it's dangerous to make assumptions about the origins of a particular impression or mark within an impression before sufficient research has been conducted. Each case must be considered individually. All possible sources of a mark must be taken into account before any positive identification is possible.

Sometimes, of course, the tool itself is available for examination. A burglar may have been surprised in the act, for example, and left the scene in a hurry, neglecting to pick up his tools. Or, a suspect may have been apprehended, and his shoes will be available for comparison with impressions found at the scene.

Such an examination should closely conform to guidelines like the following:

1. First, the tool (again, let's say "shoe" for the purposes of simplifying this explanation) should be examined for foreign matter that may have value as evidence. For example, a suspect's shoe may be soiled or bloody; samples of the soil or blood should be taken from the shoe and examined by a criminalist. Its presence should also be documented by a series of photographs.

2. If practical, the shoe (or tool) should then be examined for fingerprints.

3. Any shoe impressions found at the scene should be compared with a series of new impressions made by the examiner using the suspect's shoes. These new sample impressions should conform as closely as possible to the original. Thus, if the questioned impression was made in dust, the sample impression should also be made in dust; if the

questioned impression was made on glass, the sample impression should also be made on glass. If the impression was made in blood, fingerprint ink should be substituted.

It can be very difficult to get a sample print that precisely matches the condition of an evidence print. One way of doing this that seems to work fairly well is the following:

a. A strip of butcher paper approximately 10-20 feet long is placed on the floor.

b. A liberal amount of fingerprint ink is applied to the bottom of the suspect's shoes.

c. An assistant who's approximately the same size and weight as the suspect then puts the suspect's shoes on.

d. The assistant then duplicates the perpetrator's movements at the scene as closely as possible. If the impressions found at the scene indicate that the suspect had been running, then the assistant wearing the inked shoes should run along the length of the butcher paper. If the perpetrator seemed to have walked around the scene, the assistant should walk along the butcher paper. Eventually, this process should result in a sample that's close enough to the questioned impression to be considered successful. The process can then be repeated on cellulose acetate or some other transparent material which can be used as a direct overlay on a one-to-one photograph of the original evidence print.

Each type of impression will possess class characteristics and in most cases individual characteristics. The impression may be submitted to the laboratory in its entirety, e.g., a damaged safe. When the impression is not portable, a replica may be submitted in the form of a cast, lift of a photograph. If the field investigator has been thorough, a combination of the above will be submitted. For example, a three-dimensional impression should be photographed with a scale included in the field of view. This type of photograph must be taken only when the camera is parallel to the subject's surface. After adequate photographs are obtained, then a cast should be made of the impression. When the original impression is two-dimensional, such as a dust print on a tile floor, the impression should be photographed as above and then a lift should be obtained. Lifting material is available from commercial sources for this type of collection. If it is unavailable at the time, a series of slightly overlapping strips of fingerprint tape may be substituted. In either case, the field investigator should practice his technique on nonessential test surfaces prior to attempting the real thing.

Processing Physiological Fluid Evidence

Although any body fluid may have value as evidence, blood, semen, saliva, and perspiration are of special interest simply because they're the most frequently found at crime scenes. Information derived from body fluids can be divided into two distinct categories:

- First, careful examination of the location of the fluid at the scene and its distribution pattern on objects or materials found there can aid the investigator in reconstructing the events of the crime. Blood patterns, for instance, may be the only reliable means of reconstructing the behavior of both the perpetrator and the victim.

- Second, laboratory analysis may identify many genetic characteristics present in the fluid that can help in determining the identity of the perpetrator. These factors have varying degress of probative value.

Thus, the investigator should first evaluate the scene thoroughly before conducting any examinations that may result in important physiological fluid evidence being inadvertently destroyed or damaged. Once this has been accomplished, the fluid samples should be collected and handed over to the laboratory for analysis.

Processing Fluid Samples in the Laboratory. For the purposes of simplifying this discussion, blood will be the only physiological fluid dealt with here.

Once a questioned blood sample is submitted to the laboratory, the criminalist must ask three questions about the sample:

1. Is the material really blood?

2. If so, is it human blood?

3. And, finally, if it can be identified as human blood, what genetic characteristics can be determined from the sample?

There are a variety of procedures which can be used to answer the above questions. Unless the laboratory has the capability to answer all three, however, none of them should be attempted. Whether or not these questions will be able to be answered in a certain laboratory or by a certain criminalist depends on a combination of factors, including the criminalist's own qualifications and the availability of certain necessary types of equipment and instruments. The inexperienced examiner can severely damage the evidence and permanently restrict its value. Or, even worse, he can misinterpret his findings; this may result in an innocent person being implicated in a crime or a perpetrator being released.

The following procedure is recommended for the examination and analysis of blood samples:

1. Before the investigator removes the sample for transfer to the laboratory, he should first see to it that color photographs are taken of the sample in its original condition at the scene. A ruler should be included in at least one close-up photograph.

2. Once an adequate series of photographs has been taken, some (or all, if necessary) of the sample can then be removed from the scene. How the investigator chooses to accomplish this removal will depend on how much material is present in the sample, how old the sample is (if known), where the sample is located, and what it's been exposed to so far (if known).

3. The sample is then transferred to the criminalistics laboratory.

4. Once a sample has been received at the laboratory, a routine examination is conducted. This usually involves the following steps:

   a. First, a presumptive test is conducted which results in a color-producing reaction.

   b. Second, heme tests indicate the presence of hemoglobin residue.

   c. Third, a precipitation test is conducted, during which a solution of the questioned material is exposed to a variety of anti-species sera. A visible precipitate results when the questioned material comes in contact with the appropriate anti-serum. (The above three tests establish that the substance in question is really human blood.)

   d. Fourth, the sample is tested to detemine its blood group. For example, Type A blood contains A antigens (carbohydrates which are attached to the walls of the red cells) and anti-B antibodies (free-floating proteins). Type B blood contains B antigens and anti-A antibodies. Type AB blood contains both A and B antigens but no antibodies; type O contains both anti-A and anti-B antibodies but no antigens. Each person inherits his blood type, and thus it serves as a specific genetic marker.

   e. Next, the blood sample is tested to determine its Rh group.

   f. Tests are then conducted to determine what enzymes it contains.

   g. And, finally, a series of tests are performed to determine any other distinguishing or individualizing characteristics that might be present in the sample.

Each of these tests is aimed at determining yet another characteristic of the sample. The more characteristics the criminalist can discover, the more positive the identification of the source of the sample is apt to be.

It isn't always possible to conduct many of the above tests on a particular blood sample. It may be too small in quantity, or simply too old. The protein molecules present in blood have a very limited lifespan; once the blood has dried and been exposed to the elements for a time, many of these characteristics are likely to disappear or become indistinguishable.

Processing Trace Evidence

Trace evidence is generally defined as including any small particles or materials found at the scene or on a suspect that lack the potential for absolute individualization. Thus, they're usually examined for their class characteristics alone. Two questions are usually asked about trace material when it's submitted to the laboratory for analysis:

- What is it made of? and

- Can it be established that its origins are common to either the scene or the suspect?

For the purpose of this discussion, trace evidence will be identified as being too minute to have a common edge—too small, in other words, to be said to establish a physical match. Examples of materials which may be considered as trace evidence include bits of glass, metal, paper, minerals, plastic, plaster, paint, plant material (such as wood), and chemical materials like gasoline or drugs.

Trace evidence should be photographed and documented before it's touched or moved, of course. It should then be examined microscopically and, if desired, removed from the scene.

The criminalist's role in processing trace evidence will depend on a number of factors, including the nature of the trace evidence itself; the equipment available in the laboratory for analysis purposes; and his own abilities to not only conduct the examination but also interpret its results. Careful laboratory examination of trace evidence should *not* be attempted if the proper equipment isn't available or if the examiner lacks the expertise to fully explain the results. A partial examination may be misleading and its results may be misinterpreted; in addition, the evidence may be destroyed or altered. As was stated earlier, the aware investigator recognizes his own limitations. If he feels incompetent to handle a particular examination, another laboratory or nearby resource should be consulted.

Processing Hairs and Fibers

At this stage in the development of criminal investigation and examination techniques, hairs and fibers can only be relied upon to reveal class characteristics. Although human hair is undoubtedly unique to its source, the capabilities for distinguishing individuality have not yet been achieved. Hairs and fibers can be valuable to the investigator as circumstantial evidence or to prove a point, however.

Ideally, the examiner should be familiar with many different types of hair prior to analyzing a particular sample. This includes human hair of all races and both sexes from the head and body alike, in addition to many different species of animal hair. In most instances, human hair can quickly be distinguished from animal hair; this type of determination should be confirmed by careful examination under a microscope. Unfortunately, complete hair evaluations are often too time-consuming and nonproductive to be worthwhile.

At best, hair can be examined in an attempt to exclude certain sources from consideration. Only when a very limited number of sources exist is it possible to eliminate all but one.

Fibers can be divided into two groups: natural, and synthetic. Natural fibers include wool, silk, cotton, linen, and asbestos (a mineral); synthetic fibers include rayon, acetate, nylon, polyester, and orlon, among others. Visual examination is usually sufficient to determine a fiber's color and general appearance; more extensive testing should always be undertaken to determine its chemical and physical properties in order to provide as complete a classification as possible. Class characteristics are usually all that can be distinguished with any certainty.

Summary

The crime scene investigator must be prepared to deal with a variety of situations. Each crime scene is different. If he allows himself to accept a new crime scene as a "routine investigation" the chances of overlooking important evidence increases greatly. The scene investigator must retain his imagination, flexibility and ingenuity.

It is unlikely that any error made by the scene investigators will ever be overcome by follow-up investigation or by laboratory analysis of the evidence. In fact, improper collection of evidence can render that evidence totally useless.

Crime scene investigators and laboratory personnel must be aware of the relative value of evidence. Evidence can be used to prove a crime actually was committed and in some cases, who committed the crime. Evidence can be used to reconstruct the actions of the crime itself.

Physical evidence is considered a form of indirect evidence. Physical evidence will always have class characteristics and will usually have distinguishable individual characteristics. If evidence can be individualized it has a greater value in proving a point. Friction ridge information (fingerprints) has the highest probative value while fibers generally have the lowest value.

The need for Crime Laboratories has grown rapidly in the last decade. A continuous increase in the number of crimes combined with many changes in the law has forced law enforcement to utilize physical evidence rather than confessions to establish the guilt of the suspects. Fortunately, funds, personnel and other resouces have been made available.

Two types of laboratory systems have been developed. They are the Centralized System and the Core/Satellite System. Either system may be used depending on the population densities of the area.

Regardless of the type of laboratory system utilized, the laboratory must have a wide variety of analytical instrumentation. No one should be expected to do a job without the proper tools.

The processing of evidence should only be performed by an aware examiner who recognizes his own weaknesses. These weaknesses may be in training or in available equipment. It is also possible that the weakness may be the nature of the material being examined.

When the original sources of evidence is known to the investigator the evidence is called *standard* material. When the source of the evidence is not known then it is called *questioned* material.

The identity of questioned evidence material is established by an orderly series of examinations. Each successful examination excludes members of the class of evidence being examined. Ideally, at the conclusion of the examination all similar materials will be excluded leaving only one source.

Eventually the conclusions and opinions of the criminalist must be presented to the courts. He must rely on truth, not on reputation.

The processing of specific types of evidence follows a similar pattern. This pattern includes note taking and photography of relevant observation.

There is a common bond between successful crime scene investigator and evidence examiner. The primary ingredients of the bond are mutual understanding and cooperation, communication, and a genuine interest in each others success. Individually, successful law enforcement personnel, of all types for that matter, are achievers that maintain a high level of integrity, flexibility, ingenuity and most important of all, always keeps an open mind.

Questions and Topics for Discussion

1. Discuss the importance of evaluating the crime scene before beginning to process any evidence found there.

2. What is meant by "probative value?" Discuss the relative probative value of the various classifications of physical evidence. What contributes to the probative value—or the lack thereof—of each?

3. Name the major source of friction ridge evidence and discuss in detail some ways in which it can be processed at the scene.

4. Name and discuss the two distinct ways in which fingerprints are made available to the investigator.

5. When should chemical means be used to process prints found at a crime scene? What precautions are necessary when using chemicals?

6. Name the three types of impressions which might be found at a crime scene, and discuss some of the possible sources of each. Then go into detail about how impression evidence should be processed.

7. How have changes in the law affected the number of crime laboratories? Name specific cases which have proved influential.

8. Which particular crime has contributed to this increase in the number of crime laboratories? Why?

9. Discuss the types of equipment which are considered basic to the complete crime laboratory. If possible visit a nearby laboratory and tour the facility. Arrange for a criminalist to provide explanations and, if possible, demonstrations of the various types of equipment. Afterward, do some research in the library to discover how and when various types of equipment were invented and what their functions are in specific criminal cases.

10. How do class characteristics differ from individual characteristics? Which tends to have more probative value? How might each prove useful to the criminal investigator and the prosecutor?

11. Many people believe that science is infallible—that scientists can't make mistakes. How might this belief affect a criminal trial? Discuss the criminalist's responsibilities as an expert.

12. Why is it necessary to confirm laboratory findings? What's meant by "forensic certainty?" What could be the outcome of an improperly conducted laboratory analysis or an incorrect evaluation of the findings?

13. Discuss the two systems of crime laboratories operating within the United States at the present time.

14. If possible, arrange for a police investigator to visit your class and conduct demonstrations of the various ways of processing fingerprints.

15. This chapter discussed in detail ways in which shoe impressions might be processed. How might a cloth impression—made, for example, when a perpetrator leaned against a dusty shelf—be processed?

Annotated Bibliography

Abbott, John R., Germann, A. C., *Footwear Evidence* (Springfield, Charles C. Thomas, Publisher, 1964.) The text expresses the views of the author regarding the individuality of feet. All Criminalists should be aware of the potential of this form of evidence.

Culliford, Bryan, J., *The Examination and Typing of Bloodstains in the Crime Laboratory.* (Washington, D.C., U.S. Government Printing Office.) A compilation of laboratory methods stressing electrophoretic techniques. The emphasis is on various enzyme grouping and some other polymorphic protein systems.

Davis, John E., *An Introduction to Toolmarks, Firearms, and the Striagraph.* (Springfield, Charles C. Thomas, Publisher, 1958.) A collection of fundamental procedures for striation evidence. The striagraph, though not widely used, has an interesting application.

F.B.I., *Handbook of Forensic Science* (Washington, D.C.—U.S. Government Printing Office, 1975.) This handbook is more than an outline of services provided by the FBI, although service is offered. Many techniques are presented.

F.B.I., *The Science of Fingerprints*, Washington, D.C.—U.S. Government Printing Office.) Primarily covers classification of fingerprints but several field and laboratory techniques are discussed.

Goddard, Kenneth W., *Crime Scene Investigation* (Reston, Virginia, Reston Publishing Company, Inc., 1977.) The emphasis of this text is collection of evidence. Since no laboratory can function without proper collection procedures, these fundamentals are essential.

Kind, Stuart, Overman, Michael, *Science Against Crime*, (New York, Doubleday and Company, Inc., 1972.) An overview of Forensic Sciences, past and present. Many basic principles are explained in non-technical terms.

Kirk, Paul L., Bradford, Lowell W., *The Crime Laboratory* Sprinfield, Charles C. Thomas, Publisher, 1965.) Basic organization of a laboratory.

Kirk, Paul L., *Crime Investigation*, Second Edition. Edited by Thornten, John I. (New York: John Wiley & Sons, 1974). A rewrite of Kirk's classic text; provides an excellent discussion of almost all forms of physical evidence.

MacDonell, Herbert L., Bialousz, Lorraine, F., *Laboratory Manual on the Geometric Interpretation of Human Blood Stain Evidence*. (Laboratory of Forensic Science, P.O. Box 1111, Corning, New York, 14830). A blood analysis manual suggesting many experiments to study blood spatter patterns.

O'Hara, Charles F., Osterburg, James W. *An Introduction to Criminalistics*. (The MacMillan Company, New York, 1952, Revised edition, Indiana University press, 1972). A basic text containing many useful techniques. Some procedures are obsolete, but provide good historical information.

Siljander, Raymond P., *Applied Police & Fire Photography*. (Springfield, Charles C. Thomas, Publisher, 1976.) A wide variety of photographic problems are discussed. Many techniques can be used in the laboratory as well as in the field. Lacks technical information.

Svensson, Arne, and Wendel, Otto, *Techniques of Crime Scene Investigation*, Second Revised American Edition. Edited by Nicol, Joseph D. (New York, American Elserier Publishing Company, 1965.) This text covers a wide variety of techniques. It emphasizes scientific investigation and would be useful for police physicians (pathologists), investigators and criminalists. Although field examination is stressed, many of the same principles apply in the laboratory.

Walker, Leila J., Taub, Howard, *Fundamental Skills in Serology* (Springfield, Charles C. Thomas, Publisher, 1976.) Many common serological procedures are outlined in a workbook, self-study foremat. Not all apply to Criminalists.

NINE

Sources of Information for the Criminal Investigator

Chapter Objectives

After reading this chapter, the student should be able to:

☑ Explain the ethical and legal considerations of conducting an investigation.

☑ Describe how constitutional considerations limit the information-gathering process.

☑ Identify what persons and agencies can serve as resources to the investigator.

☑ Identify local, state and federal sources of documented information.

☑ Explain the importance of verbal as well as documented information.

☑ List general suggestions for conducting an investigation.

Information Gathering and the Conflict
Between Rights and Responsibilities

Foremost in the mind of the investigator should be the respect for the Constitutional Rights and Right of Privacy of those persons and their activities he is caused to investigate.

Sam J. Ervin, Jr.

For better or for worse, each of us leaves behind a large number of documents containing all kinds of information about ourselves and our lives as we pass from birth to death. Almost every important event requires the completion of one kind of form or another. We fill out personal histories when we're admitted to grammar school, junior high, high school, and college. A visit to a doctor, hospital, or counselor requires the filling in of innumerable forms. We apply for an insurance policy, credit, purchase a home, get married, join the military, become employed, quit our job, look for another—and each of these actions demands that more personal histories be recorded and filed away. If we're poor, or manage to get ourselves arrested, the number of forms, records, and dossieres kept on us increases dramatically.

There are several billion files scattered about the country which contain information on over 212 million people. In 1974, the United States Senate Subcommittee on Constitutional Rights published a report which revealed that a total of at least 54 agencies were keeping up-to-date files on American citizens in 858 data banks. Seven hundred and sixty-five of these data banks were reported to hold 1,245,699,494 individual records; the other 93 computer centers simply failed to provide information in response to the Senate Subcommittee investigation.

It's impossible to even imagine how many other records are kept in state, county, and city offices, or how many there are in the data banks and file cabinets of credit companies, public utilities, personnel offices, insurance companies, hospitals, private associations —and the list goes on and on. Every day, thousands of new files are added to the billions already in existence. Every hour of the day, new entries are made in old dossieres.

Many of these information sources are of great value to the criminal investigator. They shouldn't be viewed as unqualified blessings, however, because they aren't. The government's passion for collecting enormous amounts of information on its citizens isn't always consistent with its simultaneous emphasis on democratic ideals. Similarly, one questions why the private sector is permitted to collect the amounts of information it does. As in all cases involving the rights of citizens, the issue boils down to the need to protect society and individual rights. Which merits the most protection—society's rights, or human rights? Whose needs are more important—those of the criminal investigator who suspects an individual of committing a crime, or those of the person who may or may not be guilty? The debate is one which will probably never be resolved, and obtaining the proper balance between all of the people and agencies involved seems an impossible task. The fact remains, however, that these sources are invaluable to the criminal investigator. In most cases, crimes simply couldn't be solved without them. As such, the investigator must be aware of how to locate these sources and how best to use the information they contain.

While it's doubtful as to whether all the records kept in our country really need to be kept, it's true that careful record-keeping and voluminous files can help to solve and, in many instances, even prevent crimes. The focus of this chapter will be on how these resources can be utilized by the investigator in performing his job. We live in an age of rapid transportation and increasing population mobility. The police officer employed in a large urban department usually won't know either the perpetrator or the victim of a crime on a personal basis; records can assist him in going about finding a solution. Even a small-town officer, who may be acquainted with the victim of a crime, probably won't know the identity of the perpetrator. Thus, the police officer must know where and how to find information that may be needed on a moment's notice. This chapter discusses many of these resources and their importance to the investigative process.

Constitutional Limitations on Information Gathering

The investigator who wishes to collect information on a specific person or group of persons is faced with two problems at the outset. The first concerns the question of where the information can best be found. Which is the most complete source? Which is the most reliable, the most efficient? What form are its records in? How old are they? How complete? Can the information be assumed to be accurate? The second concerns the constitutional limitations which must be considered whenever one person goes about trying to find out something about another. In a case where a crime has been committed, a suspect is presumed innocent until proved guilty; in order to prove someone guilty, however, the investigator must work closely with the prosecutor and other persons within the criminal justice system, in addition to both public and private agencies, in order to collect and evaluate information about that person. If this information is to have any value, it must be obtained both legally and ethically. Mere lip service to either of these qualifications may result in important evidence being judged inadmissible by the court. Ignoring them—or refusing to comply with them—is both unprofessional and wrong.

The Fourth, Fifth, Sixth, Eighth, and Fourteenth Amendments to the Constitution have set forth certain guarantees for the purpose of protecting people's rights. These guarantees—and the ever-changing interpretations of them—have a definite influence on what an investigator can and can't do. Each jurisdiction or state may have its own laws regarding certain specific cases or instances, but these Constitutional guarantees apply to every case, whether at the county, state, or federal level.

Briefly, the Fourth Amendment is primarily concerned with guarding citizens against unreasonable searches and seizures. The Fifth Amendment protects people from being compelled to witness against themselves. The Sixth Amendment sets forth the right to a speedy and public trial, the right to confront one's accusers, and the right to counsel. The Eighth Amendment prohibits excessive fines and cruel and unusual punishments. And, finally, the Fourteenth Amendment clarifies the fact that no state can deprive any individual of life, liberty, or property without due process of law. This final amendment and its interpretations have been the basis for most of the restrictions placed upon criminal investigators by the Supreme Court, which has the power to enforce it.

Each of the guarantees mentioned above is a constitutional right, and thus there's no getting around it. The investigator's personal feelings must play no part in how an investigation is conducted. It doesn't matter whether an individual investigator approves or disapproves of a particular constitutional right or a certain Supreme Court decision; he must abide by the laws which define these rights and the decisions which clarify them regardless. In simple terms, the Constitution is the law of the land and as such must be obeyed. Every police officer takes an oath of office upon entering the police service to uphold this law, and this oath should take precedence over the desire to take any unethical investigative shortcuts, no matter how appealing they might appear to be.

All evidence in a criminal case must be obtained legally. When the law permits, many records are available for the asking. If more than a simple request is required, the subpoena powers of the court may be utilized.

Government Sources of Documented Information

Municipal Police Agencies

Most city police departments keep a variety of records. Depending on departmental policy and organization, the majority of these are found in two units, or divisions: the Bureau of Criminal Identification, and the Bureau of Information. The investigator can usually assume that he will have ready access to these sources.

The Bureau of Criminal Identification. Sometimes called the Record Bureau or the Criminal Identification Section, this unit is responsible for collecting and maintaining files on felony and misdemeanor arrests, along with related fingerprints and photographs. In addition, numbers given to arrested persons for identification purposes are also kept on file in this division.

In most jurisdictions, the criminal identification unit also receives and retains duplicate copies of warrants and wanted notices from other law enforcement agencies. An alphabetical listing of suspects' and criminals' nicknames is also maintained; these lists have proved very useful in more than one instance.

The majority of metropolitan police departments also keep another type of record in their Bureau of Criminal Identification. When persons are released from prison and intend to take up residence in a particular area, copies of their records, fingerprints, and photographs are usually forwarded to that jurisdiction's criminal identification section. If an individual has previously been arrested in that jurisdiction, this data is kept in his file. If he has no record of previous arrest in that area, the information is indexed and filed under his name.

The Bureau of Information. This bureau—also called the Information Unit or the Information Section—is probably the most comprehensive source of information for the investigator. Not only are all records of arrests and accidents kept here, but files of general information that can be very useful for follow-up purposes are also maintained.

In most cases, an alphabetical index is kept in this bureau which contains a card on every complaint and/or suspect. Normally, an index card contains the suspect's name, address, the type of case he was believed to be connected with, a correspondence number (if any correspondence was involved) for cross-referencing, and specifics on the squad to which follow-up action, if any, was assigned. The index may also contain AC's ("Aid Cards") made out by police officers who rendered assistance at an accident, and FI's ("Field Interview Cards") made out by officers who have conducted interviews in the field.

The Bureau of Information also keeps gun permits, applications, or registrations (filed both alphabetically and by the last three numbers of the gun), and lists of those lost or stolen articles which bear serial numbers or engraved identification markings. Pawn shop files are also found there; these contain information on the serial numbers of all pawned or pledged items received by local pawn shops. The license numbers of all towed and repossessed vehicles and the circumstances surrounding these incidents are also kept in this division of the police agency.

Occasionally, this section maintains a Business Information File (although in some departments this information is kept elsewhere). This file contains a listing of all the businesses in the city, their addresses, phone numbers, and business hours, and the owners' addresses and emergency telephone numbers. Other information which may be found in this bureau includes records of stolen cars, bicycles, and vehicle parts, along with a listing of the traffic citations issued by the agency.

Other Sources of Information Within the Police Agency. The Traffic Division is usually responsible for maintaining accident files. In most instances, the traffic clerk keeps a master log containing the names of drivers, property owners involved, the type and location of each accident, and the names of any person who have been cited or charged. Many jurisdictions also maintain a file of drivers' names which contains their birthdates and physical descriptions. A similar record is kept of all persons injured in accidents that have been investigated by the police.

Although the State Motor Vehicle Bureau is the primary source of information on an individual's driving status, large cities maintain supplementary data within the traffic bureau on people whose licenses have been suspended by the courts, along with records of court dispositions in traffic violation cases. The traffic bureau will usually also keep records of people who might be wanted for questioning about hit-and-run accidents and records of suspected hit-and-run vehicles.

In practically all jurisdictions, taxicab drivers are granted permits by the police department. Records of these permits are found in the traffic bureau, along with full biographical data on the drivers, their photographs, permit numbers, and fingerprints.

In addition to all of the above, metropolitan police departments often maintain units which deal specifically with organized crime. Since individuals involved in organized crime tend to move about frequently, it's important that their movements be followed as closely as possible. This information is often shared with other federal, state, county, and city agencies.

The Forgery Squad, sometimes known as the Check Detail, keeps on hand a file of the names of local bad check passers and forgers, as well as a list of establishments from which checks have been stolen or to which bad checks have been written. This file contains all known information about persons suspected of having passed bad or forged checks, and includes any statements or notes made by the officers who have worked on these cases. In some units, the check detail is part of the confidence, or "bunco," squad, which investigates the numerous con games that operate in larger cities.

City Government Offices

In many cities, the City Clerk's Office is the hub of all municipal operations. The clerk, by virtue of his position, serves as liaison officer between the governing officials and the taxpayers, and between the executive and general bodies of municipal personnel. The duties of a municipal clerk vary from city to city and from state to state; there are, however, some duties which are consistent in nearly all city clerk's offices.

For example, most cities require applicants for certain types of licenses to fill out application forms which are then retained and indexed by the city clerk. In some cities, city clerks furnish the police department with a duplicate of every license application received. In some instances, the police may even be called upon to recommend whether or not an applicant should be granted a specific type of license. In other cases, the police may simply want to have the information on hand for regulatory purposes.

Various other city departments and offices can also provide valuable information to the criminal investigator. Briefly, these include the following:

- the Office of the City Attorney;
- the Office of the City Treasurer;
- the Street Department;
- the Building Department;
- the Office of the City Planner;
- the Office of the Personnel Director; and
- the Department of Sanitation.

County Agencies

County Sheriffs' Departments. Most county sheriffs' departments or police forces are similar to the police departments of small- or medium-size cities. There are exceptions, of course; for example, the Los Angeles County Sheriff's Department has one of the largest police forces in the state of California and in the entire United States as well. When deciding whether or not to visit a county sheriff's office, the investigator should keep in mind that the smaller the department is, the better the chance will be that the officers there will know something about the subject of the investigation.

The county sheriff's office usually contains an Identification Bureau which acts as the central source of most of the county's recorded law-enforcement information. The two main files in the Identification Bureau are the criminal records and the traffic records.

Criminal records are usually broken down into three categories: those which are concerned with crimes against persons, such as murder, rape, assault, sex crimes, and robbery; those which are concerned with crimes against property, such as burglary, shoplifting, theft, and auto theft; and those which contain a large variety of miscellaneous reports. In some jurisdictions, county police officers compile history sheets on persons who have been convicted of crimes. These can be of value to the investigator since they contain information on the families, friends, and associates of persons who have been arrested within the county.

Although the average county police department usually doesn't have separate detective squads for vice, forgery, auto theft, and missing persons, as large city departments do, it usually does have a unique Juvenile Bureau. The juvenile records kept by this bureau contain a great deal of information about the background, family life, and associates of each juvenile offender in the county.

The Traffic Records Division within a county department maintains separate cards on file for each accident reported. Each card includes the name, address, license plate number, driver's license number, and arrest number (if there is one) of a person involved in an incident. It also contains information on the subject's date and place of birth, sex, color, age, occupation, height, weight, complexion, hair color, and eye color, along with notations on any distinguishing marks, scars, or features. In addition, the charge and the facts of the arrest (again, if one occurred) are included here. If there was any indication that the person was under the influence of alcohol while driving, an alcoholic influence report is also filled out which gives the where, what, and when of the subject's drinking, along with any observations made by the officer or witnesses. (If a person is arrested for a traffic offense of such a serious nature that he is fingerprinted, these records are kept in the criminal files rather than the traffic files.)

In some sections of the United States, the sheriff is still the dominant law-enforcement authority figure in the county, although the sheriff's functions and responsibilities vary from state to state. In any case, sheriffs can be of great assistance to the investigator. They are particularly helpful in suggesting individuals who might be able to aid an investigator with his inquiry.

The National Sheriffs' Association puts out a directory of its members which contains photographs of the association's national officers and names of its state officers. A page or part of a page is usually devoted to each state and federal enforcement agency and includes information on its territorial jurisdiction and the names of the county sheriffs and associate members of the association. The investigator might find it useful to have a copy of this directory on hand for reference purposes.

County Government Agencies. The National Association of Counties (NAC), located at 1001 Connecticut Ave. N.W. in Washington, D.C., maintains a staff which assists county agencies by supplying them with numerous technical reports and study reports, information about conferences, and advisory bulletins. Partially due to the NAC's influence, most counties now prepare annual reports which describe the duties and functions of each of the county offices and often includes pictures of the county officials. The annual report can be a good starting place for the investigator who wishes to find out how each county office functions and what its organization consists of. In addition, nearly all counties have an Office of Public Information, and personnel in this office can usually be called upon to supplement the data contained in the annual report. The employees of the Office of Public Information are also responsible for issuing county press releases and are usually acquainted with the newspaper reporters in the area.

In some counties, the Office of Public Information and the Office of Economic Development are one and the same. Office of Economic Development personnel are excellent sources of reference information on the business people in a county, especially the real estate developers. Other county departments or offices which the investigator may find helpful include:

- the Board of Election;
- the Department of Public Welfare;
- the Department of Inspection and Licenses;
- the Clerk of the County Council;
- the Fire Department;
- the Department of Finance;
- the County Purchasing Department;
- the Department of Public Works; and
- the Department of Agriculture and Home Economics.

State Agencies

State Law Enforcement Agencies. Although it's difficult to generalize about state police departments, since their scopes of authority and responsibility vary from state to state, there is one function which seems to be common to all of them: the collection and clarification of information on crimes and criminal offenders. In most states, there are statutes which require all law-enforcement agencies to report criminal acts either to the Identification Bureau of the state police or to the State Bureau of Criminal Identification and Investigation. Where no such laws exist, many municipalities and penal institutions furnish these reports voluntarily.

The central records section of a state police headquarters will normally keep records on criminal cases, criminal intelligence, inflammable liquid installations, firearm registrations, investigations they've conducted for other departments, traffic arrests, and motor vehicle accident investigations. They may also have many noncriminal fingerprint records which can be very useful to the investigator. Noncriminal fingerprints are often taken from persons who wish to apply for certain types of professional or private licenses, such as state dental licenses, check cashiers' licenses, licenses to sell firearms, licenses of private detectives and their employees, game licenses, taxi licenses, liquor licenses, concealed weapons permits and renewals, canvass permits, and others. In addition, employees of establishments which serve or sell liquor, members of the bar, school employees, and all applicants for state employment may also be required to file their fingerprints with the state police. Thus, the investigator who wishes to inquire about a subject who at any time applied for a position with a public police force, for example, or with the police force of a state institution will usually find the subject's fingerprints and photograph on file with the state police.

In order for state police agencies to be able to obtain noncriminal fingerprints from persons in certain occupations, however, a state law or local ordinance must exist which allows them to do this. For example, a municipal ordinance may demand that all bartenders be fingerprinted; this ordinance must be passed before the state police will be allowed to require and process these prints. On the other hand, many private citizens voluntarily submit their fingerprints to state police agencies for identification purposes.

Firearms registration records are maintained in many state police identification bureaus. Some states make such registration mandatory, while in other states it's still voluntary. In Pennsylvania, for example, the Uniform Firearms Act requires the Pennsylvania state police to administer the regulations of the act, enforce its provisions, and register all firearms, whether a person has obtained a license to carry firearms or to sell them in a retail establishment. Currently, there are more than 1.5 million firearms registered in Pennsylvania.

New Jersey has a voluntary firearms registration policy; in addition, all gun clubs in the state send annual lists of their members to the New Jersey state police. Each list includes the birthdate of each member, along with other relevant information.

The photographic section of a state police department usually has a "rogues' gallery," where photographs of everyone arrested in the state are filed according to race, sex, height, and crime. These photographs are forwarded to the state police by local law-enforcement agencies and penal institutions. A complete name index file, including the subjects' aliases, is also maintained. The photographs are made available to law-enforcement agencies across the state so that crime victims may view them for the purpose of identifying suspects, and so that the police may refer to them when conducting inquiries about crime suspects.

In nearly all states, the state police are responsible for supervising the flammable liquid business, particularly in the areas of transportation and storage. An investigator who wants to find out about a certain official of a liquid petroleum gas company, for example, can obtain objective reference information about him from the state police. Some states also have an arson division which monitors the control of inflammable liquids. In Pennsylvania, for example, the state police maintain a Fire Marshall Division, and the Commissioner of the Pennsylvania State Police is empowered to appoint certain local officials whose duties include submitting full details involving every fire occurring in their respective districts, reporting the existence and location of fire hazards, and otherwise cooperating with the Fire Marshall Division in the enforcement of its regulations.

Many state police organizations now have aviation units which investigate violations of state aviation rules and non-carrier civilian aircraft accidents. Members of this unit inspect airports to determine whether they are complying with rules and regulations and to ensure that adequate safety equipment is available.

Many state police departments also contain a fish and game division which is responsible for seeing to it that violations of fish and game laws are kept to a minimum. In Oregon, for example, this division made almost six thousand arrests in a one-year period; some of these violations carried heavy fines.

State police agencies also keep a wealth of information on their own personnel. Training academy files, for instance, contain considerable information about the students (which may also include officers of county and municipal departments), and personnel records are kept up-to-date.

State police perform many functions besides simply keeping records, of course. Often, a state police department conducts investigations at the request of some other state office. These might include investigations into pollution violations, violations of laws concerning the support of minors and the receipt of unemployment compensation or public assistance, and character investigations of employees of state commissions.

State Government Sources. The files of any state government are full of all kinds of information. In order to be able to seek it out, though, the investigator should have two essential references at hand. The first is the telephone directory of state offices, which usually also lists the addresses of the various departments, divisions, bureaus, branches, units, and sections. The second reference which the investigator will find very useful is the State Blue Book, Almanac, Red Book, or Manual (obviously, the name of this publication differs from state to state). This source not only presents short summaries of the functions of the various departments, but in many instances includes excellent biographical writeups of state officials. Many of these publications include photographs of the state senators, legislators, and judges, along with the governor, governor's staff, and other officials. Most public libraries have copies of these publications. A sample listing includes:

- The California Almanac;
- The Illinois Almanac and Fact Book;
- The Maine Register;
- The Montana Almanac;
- The Nebraska Blue Book;
- The New Jersey Legislative Manual;
- The New York State Red Book;
- The North Carolina Manual;
- The Oklahoma Almanac;
- The Oregon Almanac; and

- The Pennsylvania Manual.

Other state agencies can provide certain specialized types of information to the investigator. For example:

- The Department of Agriculture keeps records on individuals in the milk farm, livestock, and plant industries.
- The Department of Banking and Insurance has considerable data on individuals and companies involved in banking, insurance, and associated fields.
- The Department of Civil Service has employment information on most state, county, and municipal employees and applicants for civil service positions.
- The Department of Conservation and Economic Development has information on people engaged in any occupation that touches on natural resources and their conservation, such as water supplies, fish and game, and state and regional planning.
- The Department of Education sets forth the regulations for teachers and administrators, some state colleges, state libraries, and state museums. This department keeps short form records on professional employees of the school systems as well.
- And, finally, the State Highway Department is responsible for constructing and maintaining state highways and roads. Highway Department employees also examine and study the facilities of the various commuter and passenger systems. This department keeps records on those people who have been displaced (forced to move) because of highway construction.

Other state departments include:

- The Department of Health;
- The Department of Institutions;
- The Department of Labor and Industry;
- The Department of Law and Public Safety;
- The Department of State;
- The Department of the Treasury; and
- The Department of Public Utilities.

Federal Agencies

The departments and agencies of the United States Government keep varied and numerous records. Some sources are more general than others, like the Veterans Administration and Selective Service records; some tend toward more specific types of information, such as the Department of the Interior, which maintains records on Deputy U.S. Game Wardens.

There are several reference works available with which the beginning investigator might find it wise to become familiar. These include The United

States Government Organization Manual and The Congressional Directory. Every department and agency of the federal government puts out its own telephone directory, too. Another handy reference tool is the Chart of the Organization of Federal Executive Departments and Agencies, which has been prepared by the Committee on Government Operations of the U.S. Senate. This chart is helpful to the investigator who wants to know the exact name of an office, division, or bureau, and the place it occupies in the organizational structure of a department or agency.

The Department of Agriculture. An investigator who's introduced to the myriad activities of the U.S. Department of Agriculture for the first time might understandably be bewildered and not know where to begin using the resources available within that department. A good place to start is at the Office of the Inspector General. This first stop serves a dual purpose:

1. A check of the files of that office will reveal whether the subject's name has ever come up during the course of any other investigation; and

2. Even if there are no records of that subject in that location, the inspectors in the office will be able to direct the investigator to other sources within the department.

This agency, by the way, has the third largest investigative unit in the federal government.

The Department of Commerce. Many sources of information on individuals and companies are kept by the bureaus and offices of the U.S. Department of Commerce (USDC).

• The Commercial Intelligence Divsion has considerable data on many foreign firms and individuals.

• The Office of Export Control maintains an index which includes the names of persons and companies believed to be involved in suspicious shipments of strategic goods.

• The Trade Missions Division has full background information on individuals who have been considered for membership in trade missions to foreign countries.

• The Patent Office has information on inventors, attorneys, and agents who represent inventors.

• The Maritime Administration has information on principal officers of subsidized U.S. shipping lines, applicants for ship mortgage or loan insurance, applicants to practice before the Adminstration and the Maritime Subsidiary Board, and people in the shipping world who have been investigated for whatever reason.

• The Office of Audit and Investigation of the Bureau of Public Roads has data on individuals believed to have been involved in any irregularities concerning highway projects receiving federal aid.

- The Great Lakes Pilotage Administration contains complete background information on Great Lakes pilots.
- The Personal Census Branch (in Pittsburg, Kansas) of the Bureau of the Census maintains the personal census records that are collected every ten years.

The Department of Defense. The Department of Defense (DOD) collects and maintains a considerable amount of information that can be of value to the investigator:

- The Office of Special Investigations of the Air Force has prepared a handy guide to the location of frequently-checked records.
- The Defense Industrial Security Clearance Office in Columbus, Ohio, keeps industrial security clearance records for all elements of the DOD and many other departments and independent agencies of the U.S. Government.
- The Office of Industrial Access Authorization Review of the Office of the Secretary of Defense keeps a card record on every case which is forwarded to this office for adjudication as to whether an access authorization should be granted or refused.
- The Office of the Chief Media Accreditation and Tours of the Office of the Assistant Secretary of Defense for Public Affairs keeps excellent records of news personnel who have applied for authorization to visit military installations.
- The Foreign Liaison Offices of the Army, Navy, and Air Force have information on military attaches posted to the U.S., along with records on foreign visitors to military installations and defense contractors.

The Department of Health, Education and Welfare.

- The Food and Drug Administration of the Department of Health, Education, and Welfare (HEW) maintains district offices that gather information on people engaged in most phases of the drug industry.
- The Bureau of Education Assistance Programs of the Office of Education of HEW keeps records of teachers, school administrators, librarians, and educational media specialists who have applied for admission to one of the programs of the National Defense Education Act of 1964.
- The Division of Research Grants and the Office of International Research of the National Institutes of Health (NIH) has records of U.S. citizens, permanent resident aliens, and foreigners who have received research grants from NIH.
- The National Library of Medicine has considerable information on people involved in the broad field of medicine.

The Department of Housing and Urban Development. The Department of Housing and Urban Development (HUD) is composed of the Office of the Secretary, two constituent units (the Community Facilities Administration and the Urban Renewal Administration), and three constitutent agencies (the Federal Housing Administration, or FHA; the Public Housing Administration; and the Federal National Mortgage Association, or FNMA). Regional offices of the Department are located in New York City, Philadelphia, Atlanta, Chicago, Fort Worth, San Francisco, and Sanurce, Puerto Rico. The offices that are of most interest to investigators are those of the Compliance Division of the Federal Housing Administration.

The Department of the Interior. The various bureaus and offices of the Department of the Interior contain a great deal of information which can be of value to the investigator:

- The Office of Survey and Review is the principal investigative arm of this department and concerns itself with investigating irregularities.

- The Bureau of Land Management maintains records of public lands and administers the leasing and licensing of these lands.

- The Office of Minerals Exploration of Geological Survey has information on firms and individuals who apply for government assistance to finance mineral exploration.

- The Branch of Loans and Grants, Bureau of Commercial Fisheries, Fish and Wildlife Services, has information on commercial fishing enterprises that apply for various types of financial assistance.

- The Bureau of Sport Fisheries and Wildlife Service has considerable information on all U.S. Deputy Game Wardens.

- The National Park Service has information on concessionaires at national parks.

The Department of Justice. In the Department of Justice, three agencies contain a tremendous amount of information that the investigator will find helpful: the Federal Bureau of Investigation; the Drug Enforcement Administration; and the Immigration and Naturalization Service.

The Immigration and Nationalization Service has recorded data on nonimmigrants, immigrants, naturalized citizens, and some native-born citizens. The Foreign Agents Registration Section has records of individuals and principal officers of companies representing foreign governments and agencies. The Office of Alien Property Custodians has information on property taken over by the U.S. Government during times of emergency and the individual and corporate claimants of this property. The Records Administration Office of the Administration Division keeps the files on all actions handled by the various divisions of the department.

The Federal Bureau of Investigation, or the FBI, has one of the largest personal identification units in the world. This section, known as the Identification Division, maintains a file of about 160 million fingerprint cards. Access to these has been made easier by the recent addition of an automatic fingerprint reader system which reads and records fingerprints through the use of computerized optical scanning equipment; this system is known as FINDER.

The identification system also maintains a card index section divided into criminal, civil, male, and female files. Aliases are also listed.

This unit is unquestionably one of the most important resources for law enforcement personnel. In one recent year, this unit processed over 6 million fingerprint cards, handled over 2 million fingerprint identifications, and identified over 40 thousand fugitives.

One of the most important functions of the FBI is their management of the National Crime Information Center. The following information on this center has been taken from "NCIC—A Tribute to Cooperative Spirit," FBI Law Enforcement Bulletin, 41:2, February 1973, pp. 2-5; and National Crime Information Center, Washington, D.C., FBI n/d.

The NCIC's computer equipment is located at FBI Headquarters in Washington, D. C. The present equipment includes rapid access storate units, popularly known as the memory, with a capability of accommodating nearly two million records representing criminal activities. In a matter of seconds, stored information can be retrieved through equipment in the telecommunications network. Connecting terminals, placed near the radio dispatcher, are located throughout the country in police departments, sheriffs' offices, state police facilities and Federal law enforcement agencies. These dispatchers can respond quickly to requests from the men on the street. NCIC, as well as operating statewide systems, furnishes computerized data in a matter of seconds to all agencies participating in the centralized state systems.

NCIC Headquarters with its computerized system might be compared to a large automated "file cabinet" with each file having its own label or classification. Such a cabinet of data contains information concerning:

Stolen, Missing, or Recovered Guns,

This valuable file contains a listing of stolen or missing guns identified by make, caliber, type and serial number. To enter these guns in file, it is essential you have the date of theft, the identity of the agency holding the theft report, and that agency's case number, in addition to the identifying data. To search the gun file the serial number and the make of the gun should be furnished the computer. If a gun has been recovered and an NCIC inquiry reveals there is no theft report, the weapon can still be entered into the file as a recovered gun. In the event a theft report is later made, a search will immediately reveal that the weapon has already been recovered.

Stolen Articles

A listing is contained in this file of items of property not designated under the other classifications. Articles are described in terms of types, brand names, serial numbers, and models. The date of theft, the identity of the police agency holding the theft report and that agency's case number are also included in an article entry. Such a file is useful to you because of the wide variety of stolen property listed. A value criterion exists for entering stolen property in this file; however, local discretion based on investigative experience and sound police judgment is the controlling factor in making entries of articles regardless of the value. In making inquiries of this file, the computer should be furnished the serial number and the type of article.

Wanted Persons

Included in this file are the names of persons with identifying data against whom charges are outstanding and warrants issued for extraditable offenses. To make an inquiry it is essential to furnish a person's name and date of birth or some other numerical descriptor peculiar to him. It's helpful to furnish his social security number, military serial number, or similar identification known. Information such as height, weight, and hair color cannot be searched in this file, but in entering the record of a wanted person, these items must be set forth. In addition, it is essential to furnish the offense for which an individual is wanted, the date of the arrest warrant, the identity of the law enforcement agency holding the warrant for this person, and that agency's case number. If he owns a vehicle and is known to be using it while a fugitive, the identifying number of the vehicle and the license plate number should be entered into his record. In the event inquiry is made concerning this vehicle, the wanted person's record will be revealed.

Stolen/Wanted Vehicle and Stolen License Plate Files

These two files are closely related to each other with the only difference being separate methods by which NCIC receives data to be placed in storage. For entry into the stolen vehicle file, the information needed is the automobile make and model, the vehicle identification number, the license plate number, the state of registration of the license number, the type of license plate (truck-trailer-taxi-dealer), the color of the automobile, the car's date of theft, the identity of the agency holding the theft report along with that agency's case number. The license plate file requires the same information; however, no vehicle is involved. To search these files all that is needed is the vehicle identification number or the license number and state of registration.

Stolen/Embezzled/Missing Securities

This file contains serially numbered identifiable securities which have been stolen, embezzled, or are otherwise missing. Securities, for the purpose of this file, include currency (paper money—both real and counterfeit) and those documents which are of the types traded in securities exchanges—stocks, bonds, etc. Also included in the file are warehouse receipts, travelers' checks, and money orders. Personal notes and checks, cashiers' checks, officer's checks, and certified checks are not included in this file.

Securities are basically described in terms of type, serial number, denomination, issuer and owner (and social security number if owner is a person). Other descriptive expressions which are helpful to identify securities are readily available from observation of the security and are termed "sinking fund," "series A," "collateral trust," "cumulative," "convertible," etc. The date of theft, the identity of the police agency holding the theft report, and that agency's case number are also included in a security entry.

This file is useful to you because of the mobility of security thieves and the speed with which NCIC can advise on the receipt of an inquiry whether a questionable security has been entered in NCIC as having been stolen or embezzled or as missing. To make an inquiry it is essential to furnish type, serial number, and denomination. A special provision makes it possible to obtain information containing securities taken from one person by inquiring by type and owner and/or social security number of the owner.

The Department of Labor. The Office of Labor-Management and Welfare Pension Reports of the Department of Labor has information on labor and management officials, who must submit data about themselves in accordance with the Labor-Management Reporting and Disclosure Acts and the Welfare and Pension Plans Disclosure Act. The investigation unit of this office maintains records of frauds and embezzlements in violation of these acts.

The Bureau of Employees' Compensation has considerable pertinent information on all people covered under the various federal compensation laws. The Bureau of Apprenticeship and Training has established Joint Labor-Management Apprenticeship and Training Committees which have information on apprentices and trainees in numerous trades. The Department of Labor has also published a directory of national and international unions in the United States.

The Postal Inspection Service. The Postal Inspection Service consists of a group of postal inspectors who have been commissioned by the Postmaster General. Their duties are divided into two general categories:

1. criminal investigations relating to all types of offenses against the postal establishment; and

2. service investigations which require a determination of whether postal venues are being properly protected, appropriated funds are being economically expended, and the service itself is being prorated in conformance with the law and in the best interests of the public.

The activities of postal inspectors include investigations of people who steal mail, embezzle postal funds, rob mail carriers, burglarize post offices, forge money orders, and/or use the mails to defraud; those who send bombs, poisons, or pornographic materials through the mails; those who engage in extortion; and those who write poison-pen or threatening letters.

The Department of State.

- The Passport Office has millions of applications and photographs of applicants for passports.

- The Visa Office maintains data on certain types of visa applicants.

- The Office of Munitions Control has information on manufacturers, exporters, and importers of items on the U.S. Munitions List.

- The Bureau of Public Affairs has information on past and present foreign correspondents accredited to the Department of State.

- The Office of International Affairs keeps records on foreign correspondents accredited to the United Nations.

- The Bureau of Educational and Cultural Affairs has information on Americans who have studied abroad and foreigners who have studied in the United States under educational exchange programs, and on performing artists and specialists who visit foreign countries under U.S. Government-sponsored programs.

The Department of the Treasury. The primary sources of information in the Treasury Department are the law-enforcement agencies that come under the jurisdiction of the Secretary of the Treasury. These include the Bureau of Customs, the U.S. Secret Service, the Intelligence Division of the Internal Revenue Service (IRS), the Alcohol and Tax Division of the IRS, and the Inspection Service of the IRS.

Other offices of the Treasury Department will have information of value to federal investigators:

- Income, estate, gift, and other tax records are maintained in the district, regional, and national offices of the Internal Revenue Service.

- The Office of Domestic Gold and Silver Operations will have considerable information on individuals and companies in the industries.

- The Surety Bond Branch, Bureau of Accounts, Fiscal Service will have data on surety companies.

- The Bureau of the Public Debt will have information on holders of subscription-type Treasury Bonds and the various issues of U.S. Savings Bonds.

The General Services Administration. The General Services Administration (GSA) has offices in most major cities across the country. It is charged with broad responsibilities in the management of government property, supplies, records, defense materials, and services.

Within the GSA the investigator will find the Transportation and Communication Service, which provides advice and assistance in transportation and traffic management, supervision, and operations of telecommunications for civilian agencies, in addition to the management and utilization of public utilities.

The GSA maintains too many other records to mention them all here. An interesting historical source which might prove useful in tracking some of them down is the National Archives and Records Service.

The Interstate Commerce Commission. An investigator seeking information on an individual who has been an officer, director, or employee of a transportation firm which is engaged in interstate commerce will probably find a great deal of data in the records of the Interstate Commerce Commission (ICC) in Washington, D. C. (Other ICC offices are located in most major cities across the country.) To obtain a license as a freight forwarder, water carrier, or motor carrier, for example, an individual or company must file an application with the ICC. Anyone opposed to the granting of a particular license can have his testimony made part of the record. If there is a public hearing on the application, a docket is maintained; such dockets are public information.

In addition to the documented information available through the ICC, most safety inspectors of that commission have personal knowledge of supervisory employees of the various carriers in their regions.

On the local level, for instance, the License Inspector is a good source of information on all forms of transportation which require licenses, including local trucking and passenger transportation.

The safety regulations of the ICC require all truck drivers to take a physical examination at least once every three years. The prescribed form for this examination asks for the driver's address, Social Security number, and date and place of birth, as well as a part of the results of a complete physical examination. The report must be signed by the examining physician. The same regulations require every motor carrier to have in its files at its principal place of business (or at a regional or terminal office, if such has been approved by the ICC) an eligibility certificate or photographic copy thereof for every driver employed or used by the carrier. This certificate must be completed by a licensed doctor based on a physical examination. The safety regulations also require that every driver have in his possession such a certificate or copy while on duty.

Private Sources of Documented Information

Utilities

In conducting neighborhood inquiries, it's sometimes desirable for the investigator to check the records of private and or public utility companies which serve the area where the subject of the investigation either lives or has lived. The records of gas, electric, water, telephone, and sewer companies are particularly helpful in finding out about those areas for which city directories are not published.

Most private and/or public utility companies keep their records according to the street addresses of their customers. The value of these records can be shown by an illustration of a fictional investigation of "Charlie Brown." Let's say that Charlie Brown moved from his residence at 123 Peach Street in Farmdale. The records of the electric company in Farmdale, for example, would show the date when service for Charlie Brown was turned off and the date when the final bill was mailed to his new address. Of course, these records would also show the new address: 200 Spruce Street in Springfield. In Springfield, the electric company would add Brown's name to the 200 Spruce Street address card directly under the name of the former subscriber at that address. His place of employment and his former address in Farmdale would also be listed on the card. An investigator who wanted to learn Charlie Brown's former address(es) could review these cards and trace them back until he reached a point where a card had been filed and destroyed. (In some areas, utility companies still keep a record of subscribers listed by name, but the majority keep their records according to street addresses.)

In a few areas, new subscribers must apply in person for utility services and fill out forms containing considerable data about themselves. In most areas, however, the new subscriber merely gives the required information over the telephone. The utility company usually doesn't conduct inquiries as to the authenticity of the information obtained.

The records of utility companies can also be helpful in finding people who lived in the same apartment house as the subject of the investigation or who lived next door during a specified period.

Street Indexes and Directories

In the hands of a trained researcher, a city directory can provide the answers to many different types of questions. The Association of North American Directory Publishers, 60 East 56th St., New York, N.Y. has published a four-page brochure, "Imagine A City Like This," which points out that a city directory can answer these questions:

About an Individual:

- How does he spell his name?
- Is he married? If so, what is his spouse's name? If a woman has been widowed, what was the name of her husband?
- Does the person own his home?
- Does the person have a telephone? If not, who has the nearest telephone?
- Who are the person's neighbors?
- What does the person do for a living?
- Is he the "head of the house," or a resident?
- How many adults are there in the person's family?
- Does the person own a business? If so, is he a member or a partner?
- Is the person an officer in a corporation?
- What are the names of some others who are in the same business or profession?

About a Business Concern:

- What is the correct name of the business?
- What is its correct address?
- What type of business is it?
- Is it a partnership or a corporation?

- Are there other business in the area which operate along the same or similar lines, or provide the same services or products?
- What is the business's specialities?
- Are there any branches? Is so, where are they located?
- If the business is located in an office building, what rooms does it use?

About a Section of the City:

- What's the quickest way to get there?
- How do the streets run?
- Where on a block is a specific address normally located?
- Who lives at a given address?
- Is there a telephone at that address? If not, where is the nearest telephone located?
- What is the character of the neighborhood?
- Does the area consist primarily of houses or apartment buildings?
- What is the nearest street corner?
- What is the nearest store, church, school, or garage?
- Where are offices and public buildings located?
- Where are hospitals, nursing homes, and other care facilities located?

About Clubs, Societies, Associations, Churches, Schools, and Cemeteries:

- What is its complete name?
- Where is it located?
- Where is its headquarters?
- Who is its secretary?
- When are the regular meetings held (if at all)?
- If it's a school, who is the principal?
- If it's a cemetery, where is it located and what is its name?

Back issues of city directories can answer questions like, "How long did a certain individual work for a specific company? How long did he live at the same address? Who were his neighbors in a particular area? Back issues are very valuable when urban renewal has made it necessary to tear down an entire area of a city. A check of back directories will provide the investigator with the names of people who resided near a subject before the area was demolished; the current city directory will give the present addresses of some of these former neighbors.

The Association of North American Directory Publishers also puts out a catalog of the city, county, and state directories which are published in North America (it costs about $1).

It provides information on publishers of directories, the territories they cover, dates of issue, and contents, with an accompanying code covering the contents.

Offices of the investigative arm of a government department or agency don't usually have the space or the budget to keep complete, up-to-date libraries of city directories on hand. Many such libraries do exist throughout the United States, however, and these are listed in a 32-page booklet entitled Directory Libraries which has also been published by the Association of North American Directory Publishers. In the principal cities of the United States, for example, there are "Class A" libraries which contain not only local and state directories but also current directories for all other cities in the United States.

In other large cities and state capitals, the public or state libraries contain city directories for the particular state and contiguous areas.

The telephone street address directories (sometimes called "steet indexes" or "reverse directories") list telephone subscribers according to their street and building number under alphabetically arranged street name headings. Compiled from telephone company records, these directories are leased to business firms, investigative agencies, and other organizations. They are particularly important in areas for which no city directories exist. They can be used for numerous purposes, such as finding neighbors who might know the subject of an inquiry, and locating witnesses and relatives.

Credit Bureaus, Collection Agencies, and Banks

In today's world, credit touches about every phase of a person's life. The investigator is most often concerned with *private* rather than *public* credit information. The latter usually deals with federal, state, and local government financing, while the former is commonly divided into *investment credit*, *bank credit*, *commercial credit*, and *consumer credit*.

Investment credit usually concerns longer term obligations, such as real estate and corporate financing. Bank credit originates in the banking system, and commercial credit usually encompasses credit arrangements among business firms. Consumer credit is used by individuals when purchasing goods for personal or family use. Retail credit, which is the type of credit offered to consumers by retail and service businesses, is an important segment of consumer credit.

Consumer credit extended to an individual—and extensively recorded—might include automobile papers, other consumer goods papers, repair and modernization loans, personal loans, single payment loans, charge accounts, and service credit. The financial institutions involved in consumer credit include commercial banks, sales finance companies, credit unions, and personal finance companies. Retail outlets which extend personal credit include department stores, household appliance stores, and automobile dealers.

The greatest source of lead information for any investigator is the local member of the *Associated Credit Bureaus of America*. The check of local credit bureaus is a "must" for practically all investigators when trying to find out about a subject. Almost all persons use credit, and consequently the local credit bureau will have a record on almost anyone in town. In addition to the regular credit status information, these records provide considerable data on the subject's marital status, employment history, and previous addresses.

In certain cities and areas, supplementary credit bureaus exist which have as much information in their files as do the local member of the Associated Credit Bureau. They often have excellent reputations, so stores, attorneys, and associations turn to them when they need specific information on an individual or a company. An example of this type of business is Stone's Merchantile Agency in Washington, D.C.

For some reason, the average American often puts doctor, dentist, and hospital bills at the bottom of the list when bills are due. Thus, doctors, dentists, and hospitals have the highest percentage of unpaid bills. Careful records of persons who are late or negligent in paying such bills are often kept by bureaus or associations specially formed to serve medical agencies. For example, the Medical-Dental-Hospital Bureaus, headquartered at 510 North Dearborn Street in Chicago, was organized in 1938 as the National Association of Medical-Dental Bureaus. Today, there are member bureaus which offer special business and accounting services to physicians, dentists, hospitals, and clinics in practically all major cities and in many smaller communities throughout the country as well.

Radio and television commercials are always reminding us that millions of people every year borrow confidently from various finance companies. Investigators find finance company records very helpful. Since there are so many different finance companies around, however, it's sometimes difficult for the investigator to know which ones should be checked. The local loan exchange is usually a good starting place.

In all large cities, loan companies have joined together to form loan exchanges. These may have euphemistic names, but they're always referred to in the law enforcement field as "exchanges." Exchanges act as clearing-houses of loan information among their members. The exchange is a non-profit organization which never advertises, never has a social function, and never has a listing in the telephone directory.

Any publication dealing with credit emphasizes the importance of the three C's of credit: character, capacity, and capital. Banks analyze the three C's very carefully before extending credit, for example. To obtain satisfactory answers to the question of whether an applicant's C's are acceptable, the banker uses two methods: requiring the applicant to furnish information on forms, and conducting an oral interview with the applicant. The form and the information obtained during the interview are contained in the banks' file, as is any data received from investigation firms or from outside sources such as a computerized credit bureau check or a Dun and Bradstreet check. The bank officer who interviews the applicant may be able to supply additional information to the investigator about the applicant, such as his talents or deficiencies.

The American Bankers Association has taken the lead in preparing standard forms for use by member banks. Of primary interest to the investigator is *Form CC 2, Application for Personal Loan.* This form requires the applicant to furnish information on the purpose of the loan; his present and previous residences and employment; the place and city of his birth; marital status and dependents; other sources of income; debts; bank accounts; real estate holdings; life insurance; and judgments, garnishments, or suits against him. If there's a co-signer, information on his residence, employment, marital status, address, bank and income is also required.

Service Organizations

In addition to the many services and organizations which have already been recommended to the investigator—such as utility companies, street indexes and directories, and various credit organizations—the investigator will also find the following useful:

- title insurance companies;
- real estate organizations;
- civic, charitable, religious, and avocational organizations; and
- routine neighborhood service organizations.

Throughout the United States, the larger title insurance companies maintain title files, which they call title plants, which allow them to determine in a very short time whether clear title exists to a given piece of property. Many different filing systems are used, with the most common being a locality file and a general index supplemented by computerized information systems.

Title companies have abstracters at the various offices where instruments are filed, including the circuit court, county court, probate court, assessor's office, recorder of deeds, tax collector's office, and the U.S. District Court (if one sits in the area). Each day, abstracters copy all newly recorded information which may affect the titles to land in the area. In addition, a judgment index contains information on judgments which have been made against an individual, in addition to records of divorces, separate maintenance suits, annulments, defendants in foreign divorce cases, insanity judgments, bankruptcies, criminal actions, civil actions, federal tax liens, pending lawsuits (*lis pendens*), old age assistance claims, awards of Industrial Commissions, probate matters, powers of attorney, and corporate matters.

Many companies publish *real estate directories* covering items of information on all parcels of real property in a given area. The amount of information in such directories varies, from the mere listing of mortgagors and mortgagees put out by the Suffolk Public Record, East Moriches, Long Island, N.Y., to the extensive information published by the Charleston, West Virginia Retail Credit Association in its *Credit Bureau Weekly Bulletin.* This latter publication contains a listing of newcomers to the area, including their present address and former cities of residence, in addition to financing statements, notices of new corporations, marriage licenses, divorces proceedings initiated, divorces granted, divorces dismissed, annulments, proceedings in domestic relations, obituary notices, fiduciary proceedings, judgments, state tax liens, federal tax liens, permits to build and permits to repair, releases of deeds of trust and tax liens, suits, trust deeds on real estate, and bankruptcies.

Public Sources of Documented Information

An immense amount of information about people is found in the public domain, much of it in book form. Many fraternal and other associations publish membership directories which include at least some background data on each member. In addition, there are a number of biographical reference books (also known as "ego books") which are generally organized along geographic and occupational lines; for example, Who's Who in Atoms and Who's Who in Arkansas. Scores of these volumes and others like them are found in public libraries.

Americans are joiners to an incredible extent. Associations currently in existence number in the thousands. Sources for these can be found in the Encyclopedia of Associations. This large reference book comes with a base volume which is revised periodically; supplements are published at irregular intervals. This work is thoroughly indexed and broken down into eighteen categories of associations, as follows:

1. Trade, business, and commercial organizations.
2. Agricultural organizations and commodity exchanges.
3. Governmental, public administration, military, and legal organizations.
4. Scientific, engineering, and technical organizations.
5. Educational and cultural organizations.
6. Social welfare organizations.
7. Health and medical organizations.
8. Public affairs organizations.
9. Fraternal, foreign interest, nationality, and ethnic organizations.
10. Religious organizations.
11. Horticultural organizations.
12. Veterans, hereditary, and patriotic organizations.
13. Hobby and avocational organizations.
14. Athletic and sports organizations.
15. General organizations (not elsewhere classified).
16. Labor unions.

17. Chambers of commerce (international, bi-national, national, state, and local).

18. Greek-letter societies.

Each entry lists the full name of the association, along with its address, telephone number, and name of its chief executive officer. It also lists the number of members, various committees, and a list of the association's publications, which frequently includes a directory of members.

Investigators seem to be using published sources of information more and more, simply because the more traditional sources are becoming less and less available to them. Investigators shouldn't disregard these sources just because they deal with "respectable" citizens; criminals come from all social classes, and "white-collar crime" is on the increase. Information gathered from so-called "ego books" should be used with great caution, however, since it's usually obtained from the individuals listed and the result is often puffed-up.

People as Sources of Information

Much of the information an investigator collects during an inquiry won't be documented; instead, it will be verbally provided by witnesses, informants, victims, and other concerned citizens.

Witnesses and Victims

A witness is simply any person who possesses information which may be of assistance to the investigator who's looking into the circumstances of a specific crime. He may have observed an entire criminal act or only part of it, and, as a result, may be able to supply the investigator with background or peripheral information. A witness, in sort, can be anyone.

In most cases, the first witness an investigator interviews is the crime victim. The first investigator at the scene must act quickly in interviewing the victim since human memories tend to fail or change with time. The investigator should, of course, take into account the victim's physicial and emotional states.

In many cases, the victim is the only person who can identify the perpetrator. The skill of the investigator in obtaining pertinent facts in the beginning may make or break the case.

Any criminal investigation is somewhat like a jigsaw puzzle; one piece of information leads to another. The information itself provides direction. When leads don't prove fruitful, other witnesses must be sought. All kinds of people are out on the streets at different times of the day and night. Information may be obtained from mail carriers, cab drivers, meter readers, merchants, delivery persons, bus drivers, newspaper delivery persons, neighbors, and many others.

Informants

An informant is a person who has observed or heard something that he feels might be of value to the police. The investigator must be sure to find out as clearly as possible precisely why an informant wants to talk. (The courts may require this information at a later date.) The reasons might be very different, depending on the informant. He may simply have a sense of civic responsibility or duty, or, for personal reasons, might want to help "wipe out crime." He may turn state's evidence for consideration of leniency by the courts, to protect his own interests, or to divert the course of the investigation away from him and toward someone else. And, of course, some informants talk for money.

Generally speaking, there are three types of informants: the reliable informant, who has previously given truthful information to the investigator and can generally be trusted; the untested informant, whose reliability has not been proved; and the citizen informant, who speaks from personal knowledge about the crime and may have no interest in the matter at all except to assist the invesigator.

All police departments receive anonymous tips and information from a wide variety of individuals. If the case is important enough, each of these tips must be checked out.

Individual Police Officers

Last but not least, each officer is a valuable source of information for the criminal investigator. He can be of great assistance, since he usually has a pretty good idea of what's going on in a specific area or neighborhod, who knows whom, who can be trusted, who usually can be counted on to act as "window detectives," and so on. Simply taking time to talk to patrol officers can be very worthwhile for the investigator.

Summary

There are no hard and fast rules of information gathering; there are, however, some general guidelines which can prove useful. Some of these include:

1. Whatever you do, do it legally and ethically.
2. Follow the most promising leads first.
3. When starting from scratch, begin with your department's records and work out from that point.
4. Get APBs and other requests for information "in the works" as soon as possible.
5. Don't overlook obvious sources—such as the telephone book, postal service (for forwarding addresses), utility companies, and so on.

6. Be on the lookout for persons using false identification. If you think that a suspect may be guilty of this, conduct a careful check of the sources of his identification.

7. Don't discard or discount information, no matter how unimportant or trivial it may seem at first.

8. Make good use of your field notebook. Write down everything you think might be important to the course of an investigation—don't trust your memory.

9. Talk to people—all kinds of people. There's no substitute for legwork.

10. Be a good listener.

11. Know where to find information you need. It isn't enough to know that the facts are out there somewhere—you must know where they are and how to obtain them legally.

12. Always remember that you're dealing with human beings and facts which may affect their lives.

13. Regard all information as suspect; never accept any "fact" at face value. Always confirm each item of information independently. Records obtained from grammar schools, welfare departments, and mental health agencies should be viewed with even greater caution and suspicion.

The investigator will come across a great deal of information during the course of an average investigation. Some sources will be more reliable than others. Knowing where to find these sources—and how to use them properly—can be the key to any successful investigation.

Questions and Topics for Discussion

1. Discuss the role of the investigator in obtaining information from local, county, state, and federal government sources. Where's the best place to begin conducting an investigation? What are some of the factors which will determine what sources should be contacted?

2. Find out what published sources of information are available from your public library.

3. Why is the patrol officer an important source of information for the investigator?

4. If possible, arrange for a police investigator to visit your class and talk about how he goes about discovering information about a suspect. What sources does he use most frequently? What is he apt to find out from these sources?

5. Set up a debate in your class. One side should take this position: An investigator should obtain information in any way possible, regardless of constitutional limitations.

   The other side should take this position: The investigator should always abide by constitutional limitations when conducting investigations and gathering information. Participants in each side should do some careful research prior to the debate. The first side, for example, might want to find out how many cases are dismissed locally due to the fact that information has been obtained in a questionable manner. Participants might want to interview police officers and get their opinions on what might happen within the criminal justice system if some of these limitations were lifted.

   The second side should do some research into the various interpretations of the amendments which set forth the constitutional limitations. Participants should be prepared to quote from important Supreme Court cases. They also might want to interview local judges to get their opinions on the importance of these limitations.

5. Discuss the positive and negative aspects of using informants.

6. Some people say that the billions of dossieres kept on American citizens go against the principles of democracy. What's your opinion? Discuss the pros and cons of a country's keeping detailed records on its citizens.

7. Pretend that you're conducting an investigation on yourself. What local business are apt to keep files on you? What government agencies? Many people are concerned about the types of records which various organizations and agencies are keeping on them. Do some research into the Freedom of Information (FOI) act and find out what it could mean to those persons who have reason to believe that some records kept on them might be inaccurate or misleading.

Annotated Bibliography

Bouza, Anthony V., *Police Intelligence-The Operation of an Investigative Unit*, N. Y., AMS, 1976.

Bouman, R., *Sources of Information and Their Use-An Outline*, Salem, Oregon, Board On Police Standards and Training, 1968.

Buskkin, Arthur A. and Samuel I. Schaen, *Privacy Act of 1974 A Reference Manual*, Mc Lean, Va. Systems Redevelopment Corp., 1976

Carroll, John M. *Confidential Information Sources: Public and Private*, Los Angeles, Security World, 1975. A complete guide to the confidential personal information in public and private record systems, answering questions such as: Who is this person? How can he be identified? and What is his background?

Coon, Thomas F. "Intelligence Files," *Police*, 6:4 Mar.-Apr. 1962, pp 26-27.

Foster, R. K., *World Post Marks*, N. Y., Hippocrene, 1975.

Harney, Malachi L. and John C. Gross, *The Informer in Law Enforcement*, 2nd. Ed., Springfield, Ill. Charles C. Thomas, 1968.

Hewitt, William H. *Police Records Administration*, Rochester, N. Y., Lawyers Co-op, 1967.

Hosford, J. Sr., *Police Intelligence Operations*, North Miami, Fla., American Federation of Police, 1973.

International Telephone Directory 19th. Ed., N. Y., International Publications Service, 1975.

Liebers, Arther and Carl Vollmer, *The Investigators Handbook*, N. Y., ARCO, 1954.

Murphy, Harry J., *Where's What*, N. Y., Quadrangle, 1976. Excellent document prepared by CIA, for security investigators. Lists numerous sources of information.

Price, Carroll S., "Sources of Information," *Police*. 4:3, Jan-Feb., 1960, pp. 30-35, 4:4 Mar-Apr., 1960, pp. 47-51.

Regency *International Directory of Inquiry-Agents, Private Detectives, Dept. Collecting Agencies*, 10th. Ed., N. Y., International Publications Service, 1976.

Schultz, Donald O. and Norton Lorana, *Police Operational Intelligence*, Springfield, Ill., Charles C. Thomas, 1968.

Tannratn, A. M., *How To Locate Skips and Collect?*, Chicago; John A. Patton, 1948.

Van Diver, James V. "Acquisition and Disposition of Police Front Line Information," *Journal of Police Science and Administration*, 2:3 Sept. 1974, pp 288-296. Use of tactical intelligence and information by police organizations.

Whatmore, Geoffrey, New Information, The Organization of Press Cuttings in The Libraries of Newspapers and Broadcasting Services, London: ARCHON, 1965.

Zimmerman, M. A., M. E. O'Neill and D. F. King, *How to Implement Security and Privacy-Department of Justice Regulations, Title 28 and Beyond*, San Jose, Ca. THEOREM, 1976.

TEN

The Suspect

Chapter Objectives

After reading this chapter, the student should be able to:

☑ Give examples of different methods of suspect identification.

☑ Give some of the various interpretations and definitions of the word "suspect".

☑ Describe the details of suspect identification procedures.

☑ Explain the importance of determining a suspect's *modus operandi*.

☑ Give examples of ways in which information on a suspect can be gathered.

☑ List ways in which the police can encourage the public to participate in suspect identification.

☑ Explain ways in which the FBI distributes information on suspects.

☑ Detail the line-up and other pre-arraignment procedures and arrest procedures.

☑ Describe the importance of officer awareness during all stages of the investigation.

Identifying the Suspect:
The Investigator's Role

Developing evidence on a suspect or suspects involves sound police work on several different levels. Not only must the officer be extremely observant of physical characteristics, for example, but he must also know how to take meticulous notes on information provided by both witnesses and victims. There are many characteristics of a suspect that should be noted by the careful officer, in addition to those which most often become chief identifying factors during an investigation or in court.

The officer must know how to canvass the suspect's neighborhood, how to talk to the suspect's friends and associates, how to conduct a thorough field inquiry, and how to get cooperation from the public. In lineups and showups, he must know what to do—and what not to do—in order to establish fair identifications without running the risks of psychological suggestiveness and without bringing on a challenge from the suspect's attorney or the public defender's office.

There are a number of points which must be considered when making the final arrest as well. Many of these have been learned through experiences that have sometimes been fatal to police officers involved.

The police must be alert to possible similarities in the modi operandi of several crimes. They must learn how to listen carefully, even to passing remarks, and also must learn how to check out certain types of evidence at the scene of a crime that might seem odd or out of the ordinary. Some of these may appear to be insignificant or even trivial, but often they are the very facts which are needed to positively identify a suspect.

In short, then, the investigator must be fully involved in the total process of identifying the suspect or suspects. This process begins when the officer is first called to the scene and notices evidence there which might be used to connect a person or persons to the crime. It continues through interviews with witnesses and victims. It plays an important part in evidence processing. There is no step in the investigation which doesn't have something to
do with suspect identification, even if the connection may seem remote.

Suspect Identification
Procedures: Five Cases

Each case is different; no two are exactly alike, even when two crimes are committed in seemingly identical ways by the same person. How an investigator goes about determining the identity of a suspect will depend on the circumstances surrounding a crime, in addition to a number of related factors.

The following cases illustrate some processes which have proved successful in identifying suspects and closing cases. Each stresses the importance of constant awareness on the part of the investigating officers.

A Burglary

On responding to a call reporting a non-residence burglary, two patrol officers observed that an overhead outside light had been broken and that the glass in a rear door had been removed (after it had been cut with a glass cutter) and placed in the rear of a pickup truck. Once inside the establishment, the officers noticed that matches used to light the perpetrator's way had been scattered on the floor of the store. They then discovered that money had been the only object of the burglary, since nothing else had been removed, and that the burglars (two) had left via the front door.

With these facts to go on, the officers began to process the crime scene. Several latent prints were found on the glass, and these were properly processed and sent to the F.B.I. for identification. The officers were already aware that at least two burglars were operating in the general vicinity; one was known to them, and one was not.

After checking with the State Records Bureau, the officers were able to ascertain where one of the burglary suspects had last been arrested. A call to that department furnished them with the burglar's modus operandi, which was exactly like the one in this particular case. Now the officers had a real suspect. The F.B.I. checked the prints of the known suspect—the one who had been arrested for the previous burglary—against the ones taken from the glass at the most recent scene, and they matched. Both suspects were subsequently arrested and convicted.

An Infanticide

A new-born infant was murdered and left wrapped in a blanket inside of an apple box in a flower bed adjacent to a sidewalk. Two important facts were determined at the autopsy:

1. that the baby had been born, lived, and cried; and

2. that the umbilical cord had been cut in a crude manner, indicating that it had not been cut in a hospital but probably by the mother.

There were now two possible leads to the suspect:

1. the blanket; and
2. the crude cutting of the cord.

Local stores were checked in an attempt to find out where the blanket had been purchased. One store manager reported to the police that a woman had attempted to purchase such a blanket on the same day that the baby was found. The store manager was able to give the police the woman's name.

The officers then called the public library to see whether anyone had recently checked out books on natural childbirth. The same name that the store manager had given to the police appeared in the public library's records. At this point, the officers began the long, tedious task of checking the woman's employment records and the files of various physicians. Eventually, the woman was arrested. She was not convicted, however; instead, she was found to have been temporarily insane at the time of the murder.

A Stolen Safe

A drug store was burglarized and the safe "kidnapped." During the preliminary investigation of the premises, the officers found an empty beer can at the rear of the store. The particular brand was not too popular in the area—in fact, none of the local outlets sold it. The investigating officers went to the next city and found one place that did sell it. This establishment had recently sold a six-pack of this brand of beer to a person whom one of the officers had observed in the area of the burglarized store several hours earlier. The officers began to develop more detailed information on this suspect, who later was arrested and convicted. Through the assistance of a team of fish and game wardens, the police were able to recover the safe.

A Case of Fraud

Sometimes, an officer gets lucky—especially if he is a good listener. With excellent cooperation from the community, an officer can obtain information on a crime that hasn't even been reported. Suspects can usually be developed from that information. The case presented here concerned a telephone fraud involving a magazine subscription company.

A woman walked into a police station one day and inquired whether it was unlawful for a person to ask for and receive information over the telephone through a prearranged code without paying for the call. An officer at the station immediately became interested in what she was saying and asked her to elaborate.

The woman stated that her niece was selling magazine subscriptions for a company located two hundred miles away. Every business day, the niece's employer, known only as "Mr. Green," would telephone her person-to-person. The niece would answer the phone with one of two stock answers:

1. "No, she isn't here, but she should be back in ten minuntes," and
2. "No, she isn't here, she left five mintues ago."

The first answer meant that the niece was going to close ten orders later that day. The second meant that she already had closed five orders that day.

By using this prearranged scheme, and by calling person-to-person, "Mr. Green" was accomplishing two purposes:

1. he was avoiding having to pay the telephone company for long-distance calls; and

2. he was finding out precisely how much business each agent was doing.

Telephone company special agents were called in and, through a cooperative effort, the police were able to develop information on the suspect (whose name, of course, wasn't really "Mr. Green"). The suspect was finally arrested and convicted on several charges of "procuring communication services by fraud, by use of a code, prearranged scheme or some other similar strategem or device whereby said person, in effect, sends or receives information—a felony." (Formerly Oregon Revised Statute 164.125; since replaced by new Section.) This marked the first successful prosecution and conviction on this particular charge in the United States.

A Con Game

Many cases are closed in a matter of days or, at the most, a few weeks. The following case was an exception: it spanned a period of four years. The description is taken from page 30 of the June, 1961 issue of the *F.B.I. Law Enforcement Bulletin*.

Officer's Memory Results In Arrest of Wily Con Man

On September 30, 1959, through the cooperation of the FBI and several municipal police departments in the Pacific Northwest, a perpetrator of an unusual type of confidence game was brought to justice.

The case spanned a period of 4 years, during which the subject was particularly hard to track down because he was never seen by the victims, whom he bilked by long-distance telephone.

But for the bizarre coincidence that Philip G. Averill happened to be chief of police at Colville, Wash., where the fraud was perpetrated in 1955, then was chief at Tillamook, Oreg., when the same game cropped up in that city 4 years later, the elusive subject might not have been caught redhanded. Mr. Averill is now director of the Crime Prevention Division, Oregon State Department of Justice, Salem, Oregon.

On July 22, 1959, Chief Averill in Tillamook received a phone call from a restaurant operator in Richmond, Ind. The caller told of receiving a collect call from Tillamook from a man who identified himself as Joe Clark, driver of truck No. 447 of a large produce company. He stated his truck had broken down in Tillamook and that he could not locate his boss. Describing the Indiana man's restaurant in minute detail, Clark said he always ate there en route and would soon be coming back. He then asked the restaurant owner to wire him $51 so he could move his load of perishables out of Tillamook before they spoiled.

The restaurant operator informed the chief that he believed the transaction to be legitimate but was sending the money order in the officer's name with the request that he turn it over to Joe Clark if he checked out satisfactorily. Before the caller had finished his story, Chief Averill knew the driver would not "check out" because he had heard this song before. The tune was the same; only a few of the words were changed.

On August 27, 1955, a restaurant operation in Colville, Wash., had reported a similar case when Mr. Averill was chief of police there. He believed he had been "taken" by a man who had called him long distance 2 months previously. He said that on June 21, 1955, a man who identified himself as "Bill Harris" had called him from Lewistown, Mont., saying he was a truck driver who traveled extensively in eastern Washington and frequently ate in the restaurateur's establishment. He was carrying a load of perishables, he said, and needed money to buy two truck tires as he couldn't obtain any credit in Lewistown. He described himself as driver of truck No. 1447 of Northern Truck Lines (later ascertained to be nonexistent).

Readily believing the man to be a good customer, the restaurateur sent him a Western Union money order for $55. Two weeks later he had received a "cool-off letter" thanking him for the money and saying the recipient had been assigned another truck route and would not be in the Colville area for about 30 days, at which time he would be sure to come in and take care of the matter.

The fact that over 2 months elapsed before the restaurant operater became suspicious enough to bring it to the attention of the police considerably hampered investigation. After the truck company proved to be nonexistent, police in Lewistown, Mont., ascertained that the money order had been cashed in a local bar by an employee who had since left. There the trail cooled.

In Oregon 4 years later, thanks to the foresight of the Richmond, Ind., restaurant owner in seeking to have his money order relayed by the police (and the unlikely coincidence that the police chief in the Oregon city was the same who had been previously plagued by the Washington incident), the story had a different ending.

On receipt of the restaurateur's call, Chief Averill contacted the Tillamook, Oreg., Western Union office, only to find that the subject had left word for the money order to be relayed to him at Astoria, Oreg., some 80 miles up the coast. Chief Averill immediately called the FBI in Portland, Oreg., and informed a Special Agent of what had taken place, giving him a brief resume of the Colville, Wash., "Bill Harris" case.

On July 22, 1959, the same day he telephoned his most recent victim in Richmond, Ind., "Joe Clark" was arrested by an FBI Agent and a member of the Astoria Police Department, just as he entered the Western Union office in Astoria and asked for the money order under the name of Joe Clark.

On September 30, 1959, the prisoner, known as Joe Clark and by other aliases, entered a plea of guilty to interstate transportation of stolen property, fraud by wire, and was sentenced to the U. S. Penitentiary at McNeill Island, Wash., for a period of 6 months.

"Suspect": Definitions and Interpretations of the Word

The word "suspect" can be used either as a noun or as a verb ("to suspect"). Offhand, one would think that the meaning of the word is clear, but a review of various definitions shows that this is not the case.

For example, is "suspecting" the same as "believing?" Neither "suspect" nor "believe" are technical words in the legal sense, and this has led to many contradictory court opinions. Webster's Dictionary, intended as a compilation of words and their meanings in the ordinary, or *lay*, sense, is in some disagreement with Black's Law Dictionary on the ramifications inherent in the word. This is an example of how a term which seems perfectly clear to most people not involved in the legal profession can have vastly different legal interpretations. These, in turn, might lead the unwary police officer into complicated and possibly disastrous situations. Thus, when asking for a search warrant or when conducting some investigative procedure, the officer must be sure to act in accordance with his own district attorney's definition, which in turn will be based upon the law in that state. The following is an assortment of various definitions and interpretations of the word "suspect." The difficulties involved in defining and using the term—and in acting according to specific definitions—should be clear.

- *Webster's New World Dictionary*, 1968, page 1469, defines the term as follows:

  1. To believe [someone] to be guilty of something specified on little or no evidence.

  2. To believe to be bad, wrong, harmful, questionable, etc.; distrust.

  3. To imagine to be; think probable or likely; suppose, presume; surmise.

- *Black's Law Dictionary*, 1968, page 1615, defines the word as follows: "Suspect" with reference to probable cause as grounds for arrest without warrant is ordinarily used in place of the word "believe." U. S. v. Rembert, D. C. Tex. 284F. 996, 1001. But to "suspect and believe" that a person claiming to have been falsely imprisoned by a deputy sheriff, is a felon, is not the legal equivalent of belief on probable cause. Hill v. Wyrosdick, 216 Ala.235, 113 So. 49, 50.

- Among the many definitions contained in *Words and Phrases*, 1964, pages 570-571, are the following:

  - *Suspect*—Cross References; *Justly Suspected, Probably Suspected, Reasonably Suspected*.

  - "Suspect" with reference to probable cause as grounds for arrest without warrant is ordinarily used in place of the word "believe." U. S. v. Rembert, D. C. Tex., 284 F, 996 10001.

- "Suspect" is to have a slight or even vague idea concerning, but not necessarily involving, knowledge or belief or likelihood. Brown v. Broome County, 189 N.Y.S. 2nd 704, 708, 20 Misc. 2d 908.

- In the rule that a peace officer has a right to make an arrest if he has reasonable ground to believe that the accused has been guilty of felony, etc., "believe" is equivalent in meaning to the word "suspect," the latter word being generally used in stating the rule. Jackson v. Knowlton, 53 N.E. 134, 135, 173 Mass. 94.

- The use of the word "suspect," in a complaint for search warrant, that the complainant has cause to suspect and does suspect, etc., is not a sufficient compliance with the statute, requiring the complainant to make oath or affirmation that he believes the stolen goods are concealed in some house or place described in the complaint. "Suspicion" may be upon very slight grounds, and imports less degree of certainty than belief. Humer v. Tabor, 1 R.I. 464, 470.

- The word "suspected" in Gen. St. 190 § 4987, has its usual and ordinary signification. It does not necessarily involve knowledge or belief or likelihood; and if a person responsible for compliance with the statute entertains even a slight or vague idea of the existence of inflammable gases in an abandoned mine, no matter how it arose, whether on weak evidence or no evidence at all, his duty to take action is imperative under the statute. Cheek v. Missouri, K. & T. Ry. Co., 131P.617, 624, 89 Kan.247.

- The Uniform Arrest Act which permits a peace officer to stop any person whom the peace officer has "reasonable ground to suspect" has committed a crime is constitutional and is not void because it permits the police to stop any person whom the peace officer has "reasonable ground to suspect" has committed a crime, as distinguished from detaining on "reasonable ground to believe," since the words "suspect" and "believe" are equivalents in context of the statute. DeSalvatore v. State, 163 A.2d 244, 249, 2 Storey 550.

- "Suspect," as used in a complaint on oath stating that the complainant had reasonable cause to suspect, and did suspect, that certain property was concealed in a certain place, and praying for a warrant to search for the same, cannot be construed to have the same meaning as "believe" as used in Rev. St. c. 142 § 1, providing that when complaint shall be made an oath that personal property has been stolen or embezzled, or obtained by false tokens or pretenses, and that the complainant believes that it is concealed in any particular place, the magistrate, if he be satisfied that there is reasonable cause for such belief, shall issue a warrant to search for the property. "The words 'suspect' and 'believe' are not technical words, and have not by the approved use of the language the same meaning. Suspecting is not believing. That may be a ground for suspicion which will not induce belief." Commonwealth v. Certain Lottery Tickets, 59 Mass. 369, 371, 5 Cush. 369, 371.

- *Suspect and Believe*—In action against a deputy sheriff for false imprisonment, the defendant's plea that he arrested the plaintiff on reasonable suspicion for investigation to determine whether the plaintiff answered a description and photograph of a fugitive felon, and that he had reasonable grounds to "suspect and believe," that plaintiff was said felon, was held demurable; to "suspect and believe" not being the legal equivalent of belief on probable cause. Hill v. Wyrodsick, 113 So. 49, 50, 216 Ala. 235.

See also, *Focal Suspect, Inherently Suspect, Premises Under Suspect's Control.*

- As used in search warrants authorizing search of a building and all persons therein who shall be connected with or suspected of being connected with the operating or maintaining of gambling games, etc., "suspected" of being connected with gambling operations means that an officer may search a person found on premises covered by search warrant where he has reasonable grounds to believe that such a person is connected with the gambling operation. Samuel v. State, Fla., 222 So. 2d 3,4.

- *Suspect Classification*—With regard to tests to be used in determining whether statutory classification constitutes a denial of equal protection, "suspect classifications" are those based on race, alienage, national origin and sex. Anderson v. City of Detroit, 221 N.W.2d 168, 169, 54 Mich. App. 496.

- *Suspect Criteria*—Race and national origin may unequivocally be said to be "suspect criteria" within the rule that where suspect criteria are involved, legislative differentiation is constitutionally permissible only if it can pass the test of "rigid judicial scrutiny." Samuel v. University of Pittsburgh, D.C. Pa., 375 F.Supp. 1119, 1132.

- *Suspected Crime or Corruption*—Statute creating Special Inquiry Judge refers to special inquiry concerning suspected crime and corruption, and if the prosecutor has already charged the accused, he already has concluded that probable cause exists to charge the accused, and thus his inquiry is beyond "suspected crime or corruption" within meaning of statute. State v. Manning, 543 P.2d 632, 634, 86 Wash.2d 272.

- *Justly Suspected*—One resisting or fleeing from an officer attempting to arrest him without warrant may be lawfully killed by the officer only if he is a felon or justly suspected of felony; "probably suspected," and "justly suspected" being tantamount to "reasonable grounds" or "probable cause" which can exist only when the arresting officer has actual or historical knowledge that the accused has committed a crime. McKeon v. National Cas. Co., 270 S.W. 707, 712, 216 Mo. App. 507.

- "Reasonable and probable grounds of suspicion," warranting an arrest by an officer without a warrant where proper, is a reasonable belief in guilt of the person arrested. Johnson v. Reddy, Ohio App., 120 N.E.2d 459, 464.

- What constitutes "reasonable and probable ground of suspicion" that one arrested by police officer has committed an offense is incapable of exact definition, beyond saying that the officer must not act arbitrarily but must exercise his discretion in a legal matter, using all reasonable means to prevent mistakes. Russo v. Miller, 3 S.W.2d 266, 269, 221 Mo. App. 292.

- What constitutes "reasonable and probable ground of suspicion" that a person arrested by a police officer has committed an offense is incapable of exact definition, beyond saying that the officer must not act arbitrarily, but must exercise his discretion in a legal manner, using all reasonable means to prevent mistakes. State of Missouri ex rel., and to Use of Ward v. Fidelity & Depost Co. of Md., C.A.Mo., 179 F.2d 327, 332.*

- And, finally, the definition contained in *Corpus Juris Secundum*, Volume 83, 1933, pages 923-924 gives yet another perspective on the word:

Suspect: The term "suspect" which is not technical, is defined as meaning to imagine to exist; to have some, although insufficient, grounds for inferring; also to have a vague notion of the existence of, without adequate proof; mistrust; surmise. It has been distinguished from "believe."

The student who is interested in a historical definition of the word should see *Commonwealth of Mass. v. Certain Lottery Tickets*, 5 Cush. 369, 373, which was decided in 1851.

Identifying the Suspect

After it has been determined that a crime has been committed, the task which is faced by law-enforcement officers is that of establishing the identity of the person or persons responsible for it—in other words, of the suspect or suspects.

---

* Reprinted with permission from *Words and Phrases*, vol. 40A, 1964, Copyright © West Publishing Co., St. Paul, Minnesota.

While it may not be possible to obtain a complete physical description, even partial descriptions can be of value, especially when they can be compared with descriptions contained in other reports. Together, these descriptions may provide sufficient data to lead to the suspect's identity.

A complete description of a suspect should include the following information on that individual:

1. *Name, nickname,* and *aliases,* if known. If the suspect is a married woman, her maiden, or given, name should be included, as well as her married name.

2. *Address,* if known.

3. *Race*—white, yellow, black, etc.

4. *Sex*—sometimes, appearances can be deceiving.

5. *Age*—this may have to be estimated or approximated.

6. *Height*—this is often deceiving to the victim or witness. He should be asked to compare the suspect to someone he knows well.

7. *Weight*—this can also be deceiving to the victim or witness.

8. *Hair color and condition*—brown, black, red, blonde, grey, white, streaked, or salt and pepper; bald, receding, curled, or straight; if it's worn parted, the side of the head that the part is on should also be noted.

9. *Eye color and condition*—blue, brown, green, or hazel; bloodshot, squinted, or cross-eyed; type of glasses worn, if any.

10. *Complexion*—pale, red, sallow, tanned, or dark; the presence of acne or any distinguishing features of the complexion should be noted.

11. *Occupation,* if known, or if it can be gauged by the person's conversation, type of clothing, and manner of speech.

12. *Birthplace*—the country or part of the country in which a suspect was born can sometimes be determined by listening to his accent.

13. *Posture*—straight, bent over, military, or other.

14. If the suspect wears a *mustache or beard,* it should be noted and described according to its color and type.

15. *Nose*—flat; small, medium, or large; hooked, Roman, or aquiline.

16. *Forehead*—receding, medium, vertical, prominent, or bulging, etc. The height as well as the width of the forehead should be noted; other observations should include whether the suspect's forehead was wrinkled, either horizontally or vertically, and whether there were any indications that the suspect wears a permanent frown.

17. *Ears*—one of the most distinctive elements of the face, the ear, never changes. It has been said that it's almost impossible to find two identical ears. Now that men are wearing their hair longer, their ears are not as discernible as they used to be. If they are visible, however,

the officer should note their characteristics. For example, ears can have lobes or be without lobes. They can be round, rectangular, triangular, hairy, or cauliflowered; close to the head or protruding; and set low or normally, depending on their upper borders and where they fall in place along a vertical line at or below the level of the eyes.

18. *Lips*—thick, thin, protruding, or retracting over the teeth; bright, pale, or unusually colored.

19. *Mouth*—small, medium or large; turned up or turned down at the corners.

20. *Chin*—the slope can be receding, normal, jutting, or protruding; the chin itself can be small or pointed, large or square, dimpled, or double.

21. *Face*—the shape can be round, square, oval, long, or broad.

22. *Head*—round, egg-shaped, flat in back, flat on top, high in the crown, or bulging in the back.

23. *Shoulders*—broad, square, round, stooped; one shoulder may be lower than the other.

24. *Teeth*—clean, yellow decayed; braces false teeth or partials.

25. *Jewelry*—lodge rings, wedding rings of silver or gold, wide or thin band; wrist watches, silver or gold-colored, wide or thin band, metal or leather strap; religious emblems; union buttons.

26. *Clothing*—conservative dress, sport clothes, work clothes—all clothing from the head to the feet should be described in detail.

27. *Peculiarities*—wheezing, sneezing, coughing, or running nose; nervous twitches or limps; scars, marks, or tattoos.

Any other observations made about the suspect should also be recorded in detail. Did he smoke or chew tobacco? What was his vocabulary like? Did he sound well-educated or not? What was the condition of his health? Had he been drinking? Was he armed?

Determining a Suspect's Modus Operandi

Like all human beings, criminals are creatures of habit. If someone succeeds once in performing a specific criminal act in a certain way, he is apt to try it again using much the same approach. For example, if a man has found that it's easy to pass bad checks if he fills them in with odd amounts, claims that they're salary checks, and gets them cashed at busy times in busy places—for instance, around 5 p.m. at chain grocery stores—then he'll keep on doing it until he gets caught.

Think for a moment about the behavior patterns you yourself follow upon arising in the morning. Do you shower before you eat breakfast, or afterward? Do you dress before or after eating? Do you always sit at a certain place at the table? Which section of the morning paper do you turn to first?

Tomorrow morning, try changing your schedule, even if slightly. You'll probably get confused. Why? Because you're used to performing your morning routine in a certain, habitual way. Disturbing or changing this routine can cause problems for you.

After a person has done something once, the details of how and why it was done usually enter his memory. The next time he performs the same act, he will probably follow an almost identical sequence of steps as used the first time, and continue to do so again and again—depending on the success or failure of the act and the sensation of pleasure or pain, satisfaction or frustration which the person feels when doing it. If the person is committing a criminal act, and does it in much the same way over and over, he is said to have a modus operandi.

For example, a burglar may be successful if he enters the second story of a residence between the hours of 7:00 and 9:00 in the evening, when the family is having dinner downstairs or has gone out for dinner. He will continue using this modus operandi as long as it works.

During a series of burglaries committed in Massachusetts, a burglar seemed to have access to information as to where stakeouts were taking place. (It later was discovered that he was a friend of a high-ranking police official.) No one could ever catch him. This went on for a period of two or three weeks—during which large amounts of jewelry and silver were stolen from an exclusive section of a city. Finally, an alert police captain (who was not the high-ranking police official referred to above) decided to regroup his stakeout team, and the officers apprehended the suspect coming down a ladder leading from a window of a house he'd just burglarized.

Another series of thefts occurred only in church parsonages—and only while the clergyman was conducting services. Similarly, many burglars seem to prefer working apartment houses during weekdays when residents are at their jobs. Television sets, stereo equipment, jewelry, and cash are usually the objects of these crimes. One police chief in Oregon who was concerned about the rising number of apartment burglaries solved the problem by putting several detectives on high-powered bicycles and having them patrol the affected areas. The burglars were apprehended in a matter of days.

Of course, a burglar won't always use exactly the same tools, strike at the same time of day, and burglarize the same type of business, but he will use similar methods each time that will eventually lead to his identification and arrest if the investigating officers pay enough attention to the details of each crime scene.

Other factors besides habit will also affect a perpetrator's modus operandi. These include his physical capabilities, past training, and status as a fugitive, to name just a few; another determining factor might be the availability of a fence who will take stolen merchandise.

The investigator can use what he learns about a suspect's modus operandi to ascertain the facts of a crime and compile the final report. Each report is sent to the records bureau and indexed; when a number of similar reports have been submitted, patterns begin to take shape on the computer.

The ability to determine a suspect's modus operandi may not solve crimes, but it will help immeasurably in identifying the suspect. By paying attention to the modus operandi of a crime or series of crimes, then, the investigator can do the following:

- make a positive or nearly positive identification of a suspect;
- connect a series of crimes together, which will prove valuable during interrogations and when clearing related cases; and
- remind himself of what to look for at a crime scene and how to conduct the investigation.

In addition, modus operandi information will be valuable to police administrative officers when they're attempting to determine which areas of a particular jurisdiction needs increased police surveillance.

Seeking Additional Information on the Suspect

Canvassing a Neighborhood

Whether an investigator will decide to canvass a neighborhood will depend on the seriousness of the crime which has been committed, the strength of the department (in other words, the number of personnel and resources it has at its disposal), the investigator's own case load, and the amount of time he can spend on such a task. Once it's been determined that a neighborhood canvass could prove helpful, the investigator must be willing to not only devote a number of hours to it but also to exercise a great deal of patience and understanding. First and foremost, he will have to be a good listener. Often, a witness may be reluctant to furnish information about a crime or a suspect simply because he "doesn't want to get involved." A skillful and sympathetic investigator can elicit information from a person who may not at first want to reveal what he knows.

Ideally, a neighborhood should be canvassed on the same day as the crime was alleged to have been committed. If possible, the officer should visit several homes in the immediate area, especially those which are in close proximity to the crime scene or have a clear view of it.

Canvassing can be discouraging. If an officer does draw a blank while working a neighborhood, though, he shouldn't forget the fact that someone who doesn't know much about a crime may be able to direct him to someone else who does. A question such as, "Do you know of anybody else in the neighborhood who mentioned the crime to you or could have seen it?" may result in another investigative lead.

There are many people around the average neighborhood who should be checked out as possible sources of information. For example, a young person delivering newspapers could be most helpful, especially in describing the suspect's car. Garbage collectors can also be of considerable assistance, especially when the police are looking for stolen material or think that the suspect might have left some article of clothing in the area. Garbage collectors who have been notified by the police to look for a certain item may very well locate it; they can then inform to police as to which garbage can it came from, possibly providing still another investigative lead.

Employees of public utility companies can go from neighborhood to neighborhood without arousing suspicion. A telephone company employee sitting at the top of a telephone pole usually has an excellent view of the immediate area. Not only can he be a good witness to interview after a crime has been committed, but he may even witness the crime personally and notify his dispatcher immediately. The dispatcher will then usually turn around and communicate with the law-enforcement agency in the vicinity. Another group of people who have this ability to communicate events as they see them includes cab drivers. Since they're so often crime victims themselves, cab drivers are normally willing to cooperate with the police.

Once an officer has located a witness, he should keep two things in mind during the interview:

1. It's important to be honest with the witness. If he asks the officer what the chances are that he will have to testify in court, the officer should never deny that this could happen.

2. The officer shouldn't bring out his field notebook until after the witness has provided the information the officer is seeking. Once this information has been supplied, the officer should then take his notebook out and ask the witness if it's all right to take a few notes on what's just been said. It goes without saying that the officer should treat the witness with respect and consideration. The witness shouldn't be "leaned on"—after all, he isn't the suspect. Instead, he should be viewed as a helpful source.

Neighborhood grocers can also prove to be of great assistance during canvassing. A grocer might be able to tell the officer what brand of cigarettes the suspect smokes, what type of beer or wine he usually buys, and so on. This information can be passed on to the neighborhood garbage collectors, who just may find discarded packages or bottles that match the brands purchased by the suspect. And, if the grocer has been a recent victim—that is, if he has recently accepted a check from the suspect that bounced—he will probably be even more cooperative.

The officer should also check local bars—but discreetly. If it's a blue-collar bar, the officer should dress as a blue-collar worker. The officer shouldn't immediately look around every time a door is opened or every time someone walks past him—or an alert bartender or waiter will know right away that the officer isn't just an "average person."

Many officers make a common mistake when interviewing witnesses: they talk more than they listen. Whenever a witness is speaking, he is apt to provide vital information or evidence sooner or later. He should be allowed to talk as long as he wants—about anything he wants to discuss; the conversation will eventually get around to the subject of the crime.

Interviewing the Suspect's Friends and Associates

Friends and associates of the suspect are usually the most difficult people to get information from. There's no way to tell whether a suspect's friend or associate will go directly to the suspect after the officer has finished talking with him and jeopardize the investigation as a result. The officer who interviews this type of person should always be a good listener, ask as few questions as possible, and reveal only as much information about the case as is absolutely necessary.

There are several reasons why a suspect's associate might be willing to cooperate with the police. He may feel as if there might be something to gain from cooperating—be it self-preservation, revenge, or money. Friends, on the other hand, are apt to be less willing to talk; usually, they'll cooperate only if they feel that the suspect has committed a particularly horrible crime, or if they feel that the police are really trying to help their friend. For example, some friends of the suspect may think that it's all right to commit burglary, larceny, or forgery, but not to commit murder or rape. If the suspect is being sought for one of the more serious crimes, his friends may be more willing to participate in the interview.

Conducting Field Interviews

When and how an officer chooses to conduct a field interview will depend on departmental policies and procedures. In most circumstances, however, this technique is considered to be a valuable tool to use in obtaining information about a crime or a suspect.

Let's consider a situation where an alert young officer is patrolling his beat in approved manner. At 3:00 a.m., he notices a person driving an automobile around the area. For some reason, the officer's suspicions are aroused. Not enough probable cause exists for him to be able to make an arrest, but something tells him that things aren't exactly as they should be. He has two choices: he can either ignore the situation, or he can become interested and begin to carefully observe the person and the vehicle. Depending on circumstances and what his department recommends in cases like these, he will probably take the time to find out a bit about the situation. He may, for example, ask himself questions like the following:

• Does the vehicle "fit" the driver?

- Does the driver "fit" the vehicle?
- Is the driver dressed in a way that "fits" the neighborhood?
- Is the driver behaving in an odd manner?

A careful look at the automobile itself is also advisable:

- Does the rear end sag?
- Is it a two-door sedan or a station wagon?
- What condition do the springs and shocks appear to be in?

Sometimes, a sagging rear end on a car can mean that it's carrying more weight—possibly in stolen goods—than it normally does.

The officer should then take an even closer look at the driver:

- Is he behaving normally?
- Is he paying more attention to the officer than one would normally expect?

In one case, an officer noticed that a group of teenagers seemed to be very interested in the patrol car. The officer filled out a Field Interview card (F.I.) including a description of the teenagers and their car, carefully noting the presence of four brand-new tires. It was later found that the tires had been stolen; the F.I. card helped to solve this particular case.

When a department head insists that the officers in the department make frequent use of their F.I. cards, this can actually help to prevent crimes. Word will get around that the police are checking out individuals they either don't know or suspect for some reason or another, and persons intending to commit crimes will be more cautious and perhaps more reluctant to do so.

How should the officer approach a suspect on whom he wants to do an F.I.? First and foremost, very carefully. If the suspect is walking and the officer is driving a patrol car, the officer should get out of the patrol car and approach the suspect in a well-lighted area, keeping in mind his own safety as well as that of any bystanders. If the suspect is driving, the officer should stop the suspect's vehicle in a well-lighted area after providing the dispatcher with a description of the vehicle, including its license number, the number of occupants, the exact location where the car is being stopped, and the officer's opinion as to whether a backup unit is needed.

If the officer is alone, the suspect should be approached slowly and cautiously. If the suspect is in his car, the officer should first check the rear seat of the car, keeping the flashlight away from his own body so as not to serve as a lighted target. As the officer approaches the suspect, he should keep to the suspect's rear; this will mean that the suspect will have to turn around to answer the officer's questions and will be somewhat off guard.

The first words an officer says to a subject can be very important. It's recommended that the conversation begin something like this: "Good morning, sir, I stopped you because ... May I see your driver's license please?" This approach accomplishes two purposes: first, it informs the suspect as to why the officer has stopped him, and second, it gives the suspect some idea why the officer wants to see his driver's license (for example, "I stopped you because I noticed your left taillight was out . . ." or "I stopped you because you were exceeding the speed limit"). This information can sometimes help to put the suspect at ease. Once the officer has the suspect's driver's license in hand, he should make careful notes of the data it contains, mentally checking at the same time to see whether the suspect matches the description that appears on his license.

Naturally, not everyone stopped by the police will have recently committed a crime. Thus, it's important that these first few moments be carried out as professionally and smoothly as possible. There's no need for the officer to unduly embarrass the person who's been stopped—or for the officer to place himself in any unnecessary danger.

The Importance of Public Cooperation

Members of the general public—witnesses, victims, bystanders, and the like—must be willing to cooperate with and support the police in order for any investigation to be successful. This cooperation can't be bought, however; it must be earned. The police are out among the public a great deal—whether patrolling, responding to calls, or simply cruising areas or directing traffic. Regardless of their duties, though, they should be conscious of the need for good police/community relations. Many departments devote special units to this purpose or develop entire programs intended to improve the police image within the community. Media cooperation is, of course, an essential element in determining the success of such a program.

Many law enforcement officers will go out of their way to assist citizens in everyday matters. They may stop and assist motorists who appear to be having trouble on the highways. They may also work with children in setting up local school patrol efforts. Some departments sponsor Police Week displays and public awareness programs, along with neighborhood watch programs (such as "Operation ID") in which citizens are supplied with engraving tools to identify their valuable items. This makes them more difficult to fence after a robbery and may help in their retrieval.

Many citizens are reluctant to provide information to the police for a variety of reasons. They may personally believe that it's wrong to "tell tales;" they may simply not like the police; they may lack faith in law-enforcement agencies; they may fear reprisal from suspects. A good public relations program can help to at least partially alleviate some of these problems; it may take considerable time and effort to achieve this goal, however.

Police officers must be willing to admit that they need the public's help. One way in which this is accomplished is through the distribution of wanted posters. One of the most successful programs—and one which has resulted in a good deal of cooperation from the public—has been the FBI's Ten Most Wanted Persons campaign. Since this program was first introduced in 1950, many citizens have been willing to provide law enforcement officials with useful leads.

Wanted Notices

Posting wanted notices describing suspects and crimes has been a common practice in this country for over a hundred years. Allan Pinkerton, founder of the Pinkerton Detective Agency, began using wanted notice posters during the 1870's to inform the public about train robberies and other crimes. A typical wanted poster from this era is shown in Figure 10-1. (This poster has been taken from *Criminal Investigation Basic Perspectives*, Weston and Wells, 1974, p. 13.) This particular poster describes the kidnapped child in great detail, as well as providing excellent physical descriptions of the two suspects.

Wanted notices can be local, county-wide, statewide, regional, or national. The wanted person may be sought by a number of agencies; since it would be humanly impossible for every officer to remember every suspect clearly, this information is often stored in records or computers that provide descriptions to the investigating officer in a matter of seconds.

Occasionally, a reward is offered in connection with a wanted person. For example, the military distributes wanted notices describing those persons who have enlisted and then decided that the military life wasn't for them. Information about each such person is sent by the military to the law enforcement agencies located in the area where the person lived prior to enlisting, in addition to those areas in which his parents other relatives live, along with the city in which he enlisted. In cases where law enforcement agencies succeed in locating such persons, rewards may be payable to the individual officers involved or to the departments.

The best-known wanted notices are probably those which are put out by the FBI. They are grouped into four basic types. The first type, the 10 Most Wanted List, groups together what are considered to be the ten most dangerous criminals in the United States. It does not include persons wanted on drug charges. The second type is termed Identification Orders. Each Identification Order concerns only one of the members of the 10 Most Wanted List. It consists of an 8"x8" piece of paper on which is found the suspect's picture, fingerprints, descriptions, names, and aliases, along with the charges against him. It is stamped, coded, filed, and signed by the director of the FBI. Identification Orders are sent all over the country to agencies and locations on a mailing list. (Each Identification Order, by the way, costs about $25,000 to compile and send out; these are usually distrbuted nationwide only after the FBI has tapped all other possible leads.)

The third type of wanted notice is the Check Circular. This is a list containing the names and descriptions of those persons who are wanted for passing worthless checks; these people are usually considered to belong to groups, or "bad check rings."

Figure 10-1.

A Typical "Wanted" Poster of the 1870's *

$20,000 REWARD

Has been offered for the recovery of CHARLE BREWSTER ROSS, and for the arrest and conviction of his abductors. He was stolen from his parents in Germantown, Pa., on July 1st, 1874, by two unknown men.

DESCRIPTION OF THE CHILD.

The accompanying portrait (not shown) resembles the child, but is not a correct likeness. He is about four years old; his body and limbs are straight and well formed; he has a round, full face; small chin, with noticeable dimple; very regular and pretty dimpled hands; small, well-formed neck; full, broad forehead; bright dark-brown eyes, with considerable fullness over them; clear white skin; healthy complexion; light flaxen hair, of silky texture, easily curled in ringlets when it extends to the neck; hair darker at the roots,—slight cowlick on left side where parted; very light eyebrows. He talks plainly, but is retiring, and has a habit of putting his arm up to his eyes when approached by strangers. His skin may now be stained, and hair dyed,—or he may be dressed as a girl, with hair parted in the centre.

DESCRIPTION OF THE KIDNAPPERS.

No. 1 is about thirty-five years old; five feet nine inches high; medium build, weighing about one hundred and fifty pounds; rather full, round face, florid across the nose and cheek-bones, giving him the appearance of a hard drinker; he had sandy moustache, but was otherwise clean shaven; wore eye-glasses, and had an open-faced gold watch and gold vest-chain; also, green sleeve-buttons.

No. 2 is older, probably about forty years of age, and a little shorter and stouter than his companion; he wore chin whiskers about three inches long, of a reddish-sandy color; and had a pug-nose, or a nose in some way deformed. He wore gold bowed spectacles, and had two gold rings on one of his middle fingers, one plain and one set with red stone.

Both men wore brown straw hats, one high and one low-crowned; one wore a linen duster; and, it is thought, one had a duster of gray alpaca, or mohair.

Any person who shall discover or know of any child, which there is reason to believe may be the one abducted, will at once communicate with their Chief of Police or Sheriff, who has been furnished with means for the identification of the stolen child.

Otherwise, communications by letter or telegraph, if necessary, will be directed to either of the following officers of

PINKERTON'S NATIONAL DETECTIVE AGENCY,

Viz:

BENJ. FRANKLIN, Sup't, 45 S. Third St., Philadelphia, Pa.

R. A. PINKERTON, Sup't, 66 Exchange Place, New York.

F. WARNER, Sup't, 191 and 193 Fifth Avenue, Chicago, Ill.

GEO H. BANGS, Gen'l Sup't.

ALLEN PINKERTON.

PHILADELPHIA, September 1st, 1874.

(POST THIS UP IN A CONSPICUOUS PLACE.)

---

* Paul B. Weston and Kenneth M. Wells *Criminal Investigation:* Basic Perspectives, 2nd Edition, © 1974. Reprinted by permission of Prentice-Hall, Inc., Englewood Cliffs, New Jersey.

The fourth type of wanted notice is the National Bank Robbery Album. This is a list which includes photographs and descriptions of bank robbers, in addition to descriptions of each one's modus operandi and area of operation.

In addition to the four types of notices described above, the FBI utilizes one other: the Wanted Flyer. Wanted Flyers are full poster-size notices, similar to Identification Orders, that are sent to areas frequently traveled by the public. Often, citizens who see a Wanted Flyer (in the post office, for example) and think that they might know the person portrayed there will go to the police with this information.

Many law enforcement agencies keep an up-to-date bulletin board that lists wanted persons and serves the purpose of keeping both officers and the public notified of recent developments. In addition, each police department has on hand several examples of the various FBI notices.

The Line-Up

In a line-up, a group of people—some of whom may be suspects and some of whom may not be—stand in front of witnesses and/or victims so that these witnesses and/or victims can have the opportunity to identify a suspect in a crime. (In a show-up, on the other hand, only one person—the suspect—is brought before the victim or witness.)

There are many legal requirements by which officers must abide when conducting line-ups. These can best be illustrated by the case of *Foster v. California*. This case provides the most comprehensive overview of the requirements which apply to a legal line-up.

WALTER B. FOSTER, Petitioner,

v.

STATE OF CALIFORNIA

394 U.S. 440, 89 S. Ct. 1127, 22 L. Ed. 2d 402.

[No. 47]

Argued November 19, 1968. Decided April 1, 1969.

SUMMARY

In a prosecution for armed robbery in a California state court, it appeared from the testimony of the only eyewitness (1) that at the first police lineup one of the accused, who was close to 6 feel tall, stood out from the other two men in the lineup who were only 5 feet, 5 or 6 inches tall, by the contrast of his height and by the fact that he was wearing a leather jacket similar to that worn by the robber, (2) that when positive identification did not result from the lineup, the police permitted a one-to-one confrontation upon the witness's request to speak to the accused, the identification of the accused still remaining tentative thereafter, and (3) that definite identification of the accused occurred only after a second lineup consisting of five men was held a week or 10 days later, at which lineup the accused was the only person who had also appeared in the first lineup. The trial resulted in the conviction of the accused so identified, and the California Court of Appeal affirmed the conviction, the California Supreme Court denying review.

On certiorari, the Supreme Court of the United States reversed and remanded. In an opinion by Fortas, J., expressing the view of five members of the court, it was held that (1) although the rule that an accused must be given the opportunity to be represented by counsel at a lineup did not apply in the instant case, since the lineups in which that accusd appeared had occurred before June 12, 1967, the date of the United States Supreme Court decisions holding that an accused is entitled to aid of counsel at a lineup, nevertheless, the conduct of identification procedures, judged by the totality of the circumstances, might be so unnecessarily suggestive and conducive to irreparable mistaken identification as to be a denial of due process of law, (2) the police lineup procedure in the case at bar so undermined the reliability of the only eyewitness identification of the accused as to violate due process, the suggestive elements in such identification procedure making it all but inevitable that the witness would identify the accused whether or not he was in fact the man, and (3) the Supreme Court would decline to rule in the first instance upon whether the error was harmless, but would reverse the judgement of conviction and remand the case for further proceedings (Black, J., agreeing with the court on this point).

Black, J., dissented, expressing the view that although he agreed with the holding that the question of harmless error should not be passed on for the first time in the Supreme Court, the majority's opinon was ambiguous in failing to specify whether the eyewitness could testify at a new trial and in failing to indicate how the case should be handled on remand, and, more fundamentally, that the basic holding of the court was wrong, since (1) the majority's conclusion that evidence could be ruled constitutionally inadmissible whenever it resulted from identification procedures that the Supreme Court considered to be unnecessarily conducive to irreparable mistaken identification was contrary to the constitutional right to trial by a jury in criminal cases, the jury being the sole tribunal to weigh and determine facts, (2) the Constitution did not give the Supreme Court any general authority to require exclusion of all evidence that the court considered improperly obtained or insufficiently reliable, and (3) the "decency and fairness" due process test could not stand consistently with the written Constitution, the court having no power to make its own ideas of fairness, decency, and so forth, enforceable as though they were constitutional precepts.

White, J., with whom Harlan, and Stewart, JJ., concurred, was unwilling to disagree with the jury on the weight of the evidence, and would have affirmed the judgment.

Criminal Law — right to counsel — lineup — prospective operation of rule

1. The rule that because of the possibilty of unfairness to the accused in the way a lineup is conducted, a lineup is a critical stage in the prosecution, at which the accused must be given the opportunity to be represented by counsel, does not apply to a state criminal prosecution where the lineups in which the

defendant appeared occurred before June 12, 1967, the date of the United States Supreme Court decisions holding that an accused is entitled to aid of counsel at a lineup. (See annotation p. 909, infra)

Constitutional Law — due process — lineup confrontation

2. Judged by the totality of the circumstances, the conduct of identification procedures at a police lineup may be so unnecessarily suggestive and conducive to irreparable mistaken identification as to be a denial of due process of law. (See annotation p. 909, infra)

Constitutional Law; Trial — criminal prosecution — eyewitness identification — credibility

3. Although the reliability of properly admitted eyewitness identification, like the credibility of the other parts of the prosecution's case, is a matter for the jury, nevertheless in some cases the procedures leading to an eyewitness identification may be so defective as to make the identification constitutionally inadmissible as a matter of law.

Constitutional Law — due process — police lineup procedure

4. Unfair police lineup procedure so undermines the reliability of the only eyewitness identification of the accused in a state prosecution for armed robbery as to violate due process, where (1) in the first police lineup the accused, who was close to 6 feet in height, stood out from the other two men in the lineup who were only 5 feet, 5 or 6 inches tall, by the contrast of his height and by the fact that he was wearing a leather jacket similar to that worn by the robber, (2) when positive identification did not result from the lineup, the police permitted a one-to-one confrontation upon the witness' request to speak to the accused, the witness' identification of the accused still remaining tentative theratfer, and (3) a definite identification by the witness occurred only after a second lineup consisting of five men was held a week or 10 days later, at which lineup the accused was the only person who had also appeared in the first lineup, the suggestive elements in such identification procedure making it all but inevitable that the witness would identify the accused whether or not he was in fact the man. (See annotation p. 909, infra)

Appeal and Error — criminal case — remand for further proceedings

5. The Supreme Court of the United States—upon holding that a police lineup procedure relating to a state criminal prosecution was so unfair as to violate due process—will decline to rule in the first instance upon the question whether the error was harmless, but will reverse the judgment of conviction and remand the case for further proceedings.

OPINION OF THE COURT

Mr. Justice Fortas delivered the opinion of the Court.

Petitioner was charged by information with the armed robbery of a Western Union office in violation of California Penal Code § 211a. The day after the robbery one of the robbers, Clay, surrendered to the police and implicated Foster and Grice. Allegedly, Foster and Clay had entered the office while Grice waited in the car. Foster and Grice were tried together. Grice was acquitted. Foster was convicted. The California District Court of Appeal affirmed the conviction; the State Supreme Court denied review. We granted certiorari, limited to the question whether the conduct of the police lineup resulted in a violation of petitioner's constitutional rights. 390 U.S. 994, 88 S. Ct. 1201, 20 L. Ed. 2d 94 (1968).

Except for the robbers themselves, the only witness to the crime was Joseph David, the late-night manager of the Western Union office. After Foster had been arrested, David was called to the police station to view a lineup. There were three men in the lineup. One was petitioner. He is a tall man—close to six feet in height. The other two men were short—five feet, five or six inches. Petitioner wore a leather jacket which David said was similar to the one he had seen underneath the coveralls worn by the robber. After seeing this lineup, David could not positively identify petitioner as the robber. He "thought" he was the man, but he was not sure. David then asked to speak to petitioner, and petitioner was brought into an office and sat across from David at a table. Except for prosecuting officials there was no one else in the room. Even after this one-to-one confrontation David still was uncertain whether petitioner was one of the robbers: "truthfully—I was not sure," he testified at trial. A week or 10 days later, the police arranged for David to view a second lineup. There were five men in that lineup. Petitioner was the only person in the second lineup who had (394 U.S. 442) appeared in the first lineup. This time David was "convinced" petitioner was the man.

At trial, David testified to his identification of petitioner in the lineups, as summarized above. He also repeated his identification of petitioner in the courtroom. The only other evidence against petitioner which concerned the particular robbery with which he was charged was the testimony of the alleged accomplice Clay. (California law requires that an accomplice's testimony be corroborated. California Penal Code § 1111. There was also evidence that Foster had been convicted for a similar robbery committed six years before.)

(1,2) In United States v. Wade, 338 U.S. 218, 87 S. Ct. 1926, 18 L. Ed. 2d 1149 (1967), and Gilbert v. California, 388 U.S. 263, 87 S. Ct. 1951, 18 L. Ed. 2d 1178 (1967), this Court held that because of the possibility of unfairness to the accused in the way a lineup is conducted, a lineup is a "critical stage" in the prosecution, at which the accused must be given the opportunity to be represented by counsel. That holding does not, however, apply to petitioner's case, for the lineups in which he appeared occurred before June 12, 1967. Stovall v. Denno, 388 U.S. 293, 87 S. Ct. 1967, 18 L. Ed. 2d 1199 (1967). But in declaring the rule of Wade and Gilbert to be applicable only to lineups conducted after those cases were decided, we recognized that, judged by the "totality of the circumstances," the conduct of identification procedures may be "so unnecessarily suggestive and conducive to irreparable mistaken identification" as to be a denial of due process of law. Id., at 302, 18 L. Ed. 2d at 1202. See Simons v. United States, 390 U.S. 377, 383, 88 S. Ct. 967, 19 L. Ed. 2d 1247, 1252 (1968); cf. P. Wall, Eye-Witness Identification in Criminal Cases; J. Frank & B. Frank, Not Guilty; 3 J. Wigmore, Evidence § 786a (3d ed 1940); 4, id., § 1130.

(3) Judged by that standard, this case presents a compelling example of unfair lineup procedures. (The reliability of properly admitted eyewitness identification, like the credibility of the other parts of the prosecution's case is a matter for the jury. But it is the teaching of Wade, Gilbert, and Stovall, supra,

that in some cases the procedures leading to an eyewitness identification may be so defective as to make the identification constitutionally inadmissible as a matter of law.) In the (394 U.S. 443) first lineup arranged by the police, petitioner stood out from the other two men by the contrast of his height and by the fact that he was wearing a leather jacket similar to that worn by the robber. See United States v. Wade, supra, 388 U.S. at 233, 87 S. Ct. at 1935. When this did not lead to positive identification, the police permitted a one-to-one confrontation between partitioner and the witness. This Court pointed out in Stovall that "(t)he practice of showing suspects singly to persons for the purpose of identification, and not as part of a lineup, has been widely condemned." 388 U.S., at 302, 87 S. Ct., at 1972. Even after this the witness' identification of petitioner was tentative. So some days later another lineup was arranged. Petitioner was the only person in this lineup who had also participated in the first lineup. See Wall, supra, at 64. This finally produced a definite identification.

(4) The suggestive elements in this identification procedure made it all but inevitable that David would identify petitioner whether or not he was in fact "the man." In effect, the police repeatedly said to the witness, "This is the man." See Biggers v. Tennessee, 390 U.S. 404, 407, 88 S. Ct. 979, 980, 19 L. Ed. 2d 1267, 1269 (dissenting opinion). This procedure so undermined the reliability of the eyewitness identification as to violate due process.

In a decision handed down since the Supreme Court of California declined to consider the petitioner's case, it reversed a conviction because of the unfair makeup of a lineup. In that case, the California court said: "(W)e do no more than recognize . . . that unfairly constituted lineups have in the past too often brought about the conviction of the innocent." People v. Caruso, 68 Cal. 2d 183, 188, 65 Cal. Rptr. 336, 340, 436 P.2d 336, 340 (1968). In the present case the pretrial confrontations clearly were so arranged as to make the resulting identifications virtually inevitable. (304 U.S. 444)

(5) The respondent invites us to hold that any error was harmless under Chapman v. California, 386 U.S. 18, 87 S. Ct. 824, 17 L. Ed. 2d 705 (1967). We decline to rule upon this question in the first instance. Accordingly, the judgment is reversed and the case remanded for further proceedings not inconsistent with this opinion.

Reversed and remanded.

Mr. Justice White, with whom Mr. Justice Harlan, and Mr. Justice Stewart concur, being unwilling in this case to disagree with the jury on the weight of the evidence, would affirm the judgment.

Mr. Justice Black dissented with a lengthy opinion including numerous citations in support.

Other cases have also affected line-up practices and procedures. Earlier, for example, in 1967, *United States v. Wade* (388 U.S. 218, 87 S. Ct. 1926, 18 L. Ed. 2d 1149), the Supreme Court held that the right to counsel guaranteed by the Sixth Amendment applied to the states when conducting lineups. This is because courts often worry about the fact that line-ups can be partial and can influence eyewitnesses by the power of suggestion, which can overcome their ability to correctly identify the person who actually committed the crime. Another 1967 case, *Gilbert v. California* (388 U.S. 263, 87 S. Ct. 1951, 18 L. Ed. 2d 1178), is often cited in conjunction with the *Wade* case; lawyers generally refer to the *Wade-Gilbert rule* when questioning the legality of line-up procedures.

The main differences between the two cases (Wade and Foster) are factual—not legal. In essence, they compliment each other legally.

Factually, both involve robberies. Foster was an armed robbery of a Western Union Office. Wade was a robbery of a Federally insured bank.

In Foster, the defendant was arrested shortly after the robbery. There was one eye witness to the robbery. He was a manager for the Western Union Office. He went to the pretrial lineup at the police station. The lineup consisted of three men. Two were short (approximately 5'6") and one, the defendant, was tall (approximately 6'). The defendant was the only one in the lineup wearing a leather coat similar to what the robber wore. Witness could not positively identify the defendant. Right after the lineup the witness had a one on one talk with the defendant in a police office. Still the witness couldn't identify defandant. Ten days later, witness again went to police station for a second lineup. This time five men were in it. The defendant was one of the five and he was the only one present who participated in the first lineup. Everything, up to this point, was done without an attorney for Foster. The witness then identified the defendant as a participant in the armed robbery.

In Wade, eight months after the robbery the defendant, who had an attorney, was taken by an FBI agent to a courtroom for an identification lineup. The two witnesses, employees of the bank, to the robbery, were inside the courtroom. They observed the defendant alone with the agent. Shortly thereafter five to six other prisoners appeared in the hallway and joined the defendant and the FBI agent. The defendant and the other prisoners then entered the courtroom with strips of tape on their faces (similar to that of the robber). Each said "put the money in the bag." Both witnesses positively identified Wade as the robber.

Legally, Wade stands for the proposition that after the date of the decision (June 12, 1967) a suspect (defendant) is entitled to have an attorney present at any in-person identification lineup. Wade's basis for that holding is the 6th Amendment not 5th Amendment. Specifically, such a lineup is a critical stage in the proceedings and an attorney's presence is a safeguard to fairness of such proceeding. The court, in Wade, doesn't reverse the case but sends it back to the trial level with instructions to review the matter to see if the in-court identification was based upon observation of the suspect other than the lineup identification. Brennan wrote the Wade opinion.

Legally Foster is not based on Wade because the lineup of the defendant occurred more to the Wade decision. Consequently, the court held that the defendant was not entitled to have an attorney present during the lineup. The court did send the case back to the trial court, however, because the case, under the totality of the circumstances, presents a compelling example of unfair lineup procedure, the result being that it may constitute a denial of due process. The court instructed the trial court to review the case in that light with strong and obvious suggestions that they had either dismiss the case or grant Foster a new trial without reference to the lineup.

Summary – Differences

WADE

Factual

1. An arrest 8 months after court
2. 2 eyewitness
3. Lineup in courtroom
4. One lineup positive ID
5. Pre lineup suggestion (seeing defendant in hall alone with FBI man.)
6. No lineup suggestive or problems
7. Six in lineup
8. All spoke at lineup
9. No post lineup suggestion
10. No second lineup

Legal

As of date of holdup (June 12, 1967) a defendant is entitled under the 6th Amendment to have an attorney present for all pretrial identification lineups.

FOSTER

1. An arrest shortly after
2. One eyewitness
3. Lineup in police station
4. 2 Lineups (1st—unsure, 2nd—positive)
5. No pre lineup suggestion
6. Lineup suggestive—height, clothes, coat
7. 3 in 1st lineup
8. No speaking at lineup
9. Post lineup suggestion—victim, defendant, personal contact.
10. Second lineup—suggestive—defendant only one from 1st lineup.

Is not based on Wade because the lineup was pre-Wade (Before June 12, 1967) but held that this specific lineup violated defendants due process rights because it was an unfair lineup.

A Sample Line-Up Procedure

Line-up identification procedures, if improperly conducted, can cause problems for both the police and the prosecutor. The Clark County, Nevada procedure described here is intended to serve as an example of one which seems to work without too many difficulties.

Whenever law enforcement agencies in Clark County conduct a line-up for identification purposes, for example, a member of the District Attorney's office and a member of the Public Defender's office are always present. In this way, either attorney can make suggestions about the procedure and seek the agreement of the other. This helps to ensure that the line-up is held as fairly as possible. The following is a description of the criteria which apply to the Clark County procedure:

1. No line-up identification should be held without discussing the legal advisability of such lineup with the office of the District Attorney.

2. No line-up should be held without a member of the District Attorney's office being present.

3. No line-up should be held without a member of the Public Defender's office being present.

4. Insofar as possible, all persons in a line-up should be of the same general age, racial, and physical characteristics (including dress).

5. Should any body movement, gesture, or verbal statement be necessary, this should also be done uniformly and any such movement, gesture, or statement be done one time only by each person participating in the line-up and repeated only at the express request of the person attempting to make identification.

6. The customary line-up photograph should be taken and developed as soon as possible. A copy of such photograph should be made available immediately to the Public Defender's Office.

7. If more than one person is called to view a line-up, the persons should not be allowed, before the completion of all witnesses' attempted identification to discuss among themselves any facet of their view of the line-up or the result of their conclusions regarding the same.

8. All witnesses who are to view the line-up should be prevented from seeing the suspect in custody and in particular in handcuffs, or in any manner that would indicate to the witness the identity of the suspect in question.

9. All efforts should be made to prevent a witness from viewing any photographs of the suspect prior to giving the line-up.

10. All conversation between the police officer and prospective witnesses should be restricted to only indispensible direction. In all cases nothing should be said to the witness to suggest the suspect is standing in the particular line-up.

11. Should there be any more than one witness, only one witness at a time should be present in the room where the line-up is conducted.

12. There should be a minimum of persons present in the room where the line-up is conducted. A suggested group would include the law enforcement officer conducting the line-up, a representative of the District Attorney's office, a representative of the Public Defender's office, and an investigator of that office if requested by the Public Defender.

13. The line-up report prepared by the law enforcement agency conducting the line-up should be prepared in sufficient numbers so that a copy is made available at the line-up to the Public Defender.

14. Each witness, as he appears in the room where the line-up is being conducted, should be handed a form for use in the identification. Explanation for the use of the form is self-explanatory; a sample copy is attached hereto. This form should be signed by the witness, by a representative of the Public Defendant's office, and by the law enforcement officer conducting the line-up.

15. A copy of this Identification Form should be given to the Public Defender's office at the completion of the viewing of the line-up by each individual witness.

Witness' Line-Up Identification Form

To Witness:

The positions of the persons in the line-up will be numbered left to right, beginning with one (1) on your left.

1. If you have previously seen one or more of the persons in the line-up, place an "X" in the appropriate square corresponding to the number of the person in the lineup.

2. Then, sign your name and fill in the date and time.

3. When completed, hand this sheet to the officer.

1 2 3 4 5 6 7

_____   _____
Signature of Law Enforcement Officer   Signature of Witness

_____   _____
Signature of Public Defender or   Date and Time
Attorney for Suspect.

(From *Cases and Materials on the Administration of Criminal Justice*, 2nd edition, Sullivan et al., page 211.)

Pre-Arraignment Procedures

In 1975, the American Law Institute proposed "A Model Code of Pre-Arraignment Procedure" that offers many excellent suggestions for ensuring that any steps taken prior to arraignment of a suspect are conducted legally:

THE AMERICAN LAW INSTITUTE, A MODEL CODE OF PRE-ARRAIGNMENT PROCEDURE (PROPOSED OFFICE DRAFT, 1975)

Section 160.2. Conduct of Identification Procedures

(1) Personal Identifications: Line-ups, Confrontations, Unknown Suspects. The identification of a suspect by having a witness view the suspect shall be from an array of several persons, a reasonable number of whom are similar in dress and appearance to the person to be identified, except such lineup or other array is not required in any of the following circumstances:

(a) Confrontation promptly after commission of a crime. A law enforcement officer arranges a confrontation by a witness to a crime promptly following the commission of that crime, unless there is reason to believe that a line-up or other procedure is necessary to make the identification reliable.

(b) Suspect unknown or at large. The identity of the suspect is unknown, or the suspect is at large and his presence cannot practicably be secured pursuant to Article 170 (Article 170 provides for orders to appear for identification procedures of various kinds. For a similar provision, see proposed Rule 41.1 of the Federal Rules of Criminal Procedure, infra this chapter.) or otherwise.

(c) Consent of counsel. Counsel for the suspect consents to such other identification procedure as is carried out.

(2) Photographic Identifications. If the identification is to be made from photographs, drawings or other representations, the witness shall be presented with an array of representations of several persons. Such array shall so far as practicable include a reasonable number of persons similar to any person then suspected whose likeness is included in the array.

(3) Voice Identification. If a person is to be identified by having a witness hear that person's voice, whether in the speaker's presence, by recording, telephone or otherwise, such identifications shall be made from a selection of several voices, a reasonable number of which shall be similar to that of the person to be identified, and all of which shall be presented by sufficiently similar means to avoid any undue suggestion.

(4) Multiple Identification Procedures. A witness shall not be allowed, except as part of a judicial proceeding, to participate in more than one identification procedure involving viewing the same suspect or representation of that suspect unless

(a) a prior procedure was conducted at a time when the suspect was unknown or at large;

(b) the witness reasonably requests a subsequent procedure to resolve doubt;

(c) there are special circumstances such that there is reason to believe that a further procedure is necessary to produce a reliable identification; or

(d) counsel for the suspect requests a futher identification procedure.

(5) Avoidance of Suggestion. Any identification procedure pursuant to subsections (1) through (4) including any multiple identification procedure, shall be conducted to avoid so far as practicable any suggestion to a witness at or prior to the procedure that a particular person is the person suspected of involvement in the crime under investigation.

(6) Fingerprints, Blood Samples, Voice Prints and Other Technical Procedures. Identification procedures by fingerprints, voice prints, blood samples and other similar procedures shall be conducted by persons qualified by professional training to assure the accuracy of the procedure and to prevent injury to the subject of the procedure.

(7) Control of Identification Procedure. The regulations issued pursuant to Subsection 160.1(2) shall designate the law enforcement officer responsible for the conduct of any identification procedure pursuant to this Article and for assuring compliance with the provisions of the Code.

(a) Directions to suspects in custody or present pursuant to order to appear. Such officer may, in the case of a person in custody or present for an identification procedure by order of a court, direct the person to conduct himself in any manner reasonably related to the identification procedure including the making of gestures, wearing of masks or clothing, or speaking of words.

(b) Questioning of witnesses at identification. The officer shall determine what questions may be put to a witness.

(c) Suggestions of counsel. The officer shall take account of suggestions from counsel for the person to be identified.

(d) Maintenance of order. The officer shall maintain order at the identification procedure, and may exclude any person, including counsel for the person to be identified, if he obstructs the identification.

The Arrest

The arrest is considered by many to be the culmination of any investigation. Sometimes, an arrest can be made quickly—especially if the police officer happens to be in the right place at the right time. Then again, the investigation may take months or years before an arrest can be made. The officer should always keep in mind the statutes of limitations which relate to specific types of cases under investigation; these statutes vary from state to state.

In order to properly effect an arrest, the suspect must be identified as positively as possible. The first law-enforcement officer who arrives at the crime scene is a key person in this respect. He can literally harm the investigation by contaminating evidence, failing to obtain proper descriptions from the victim or witnesses, and otherwise behaving in an unprofessional manner. Thus, the scene must be processed carefully and properly, and all evidence that should be examined thoroughly should be turned over to the proper criminalistics laboratory.

Once information on the suspect has been gathered from examining the scene and talking with witnesses and victims, this information should be compared with information contained in the department's own records. If a search of local records doesn't produce results, then state records should be consulted, followed by national or federal agency records.

Once a suspect has been positively identified, a great deal of information has to be gathered about him. (See Chapter 9 for a more thorough discussion of this topic.) For example, local sources might include:

- Telephone books;
- City or county directories;
- Voter registration lists;
- Public libraries;
- Public and private utilities;
- Selective Service Boards;
- Credit reporting agencies;
- Welfare agencies;
- Hospitals, physicians, and dentists;
- Convenience stores (especially the type where credit can be obtained);
- Jail records;
- Newspapers and other mass media;
- Local department stores, especially charge accounts;
- Marriage, divorce, birth, and death records;
- Employers or past employers; and
- Post offices (for changes of address).

State sources might include:

- The Department of Motor Vehicles;
- The Department of Operators' Licenses;
- The Department of Fish and Game;
- The Department of Narcotics;
- The State Identification Bureau;
- State Libraries;
- The State Bureau of Vital Statistics; and
- State Unemployment Records.

National sources might include:

- The FBI and other national identification bureaus;
- Military records; and

• Social Security records.

Locating the Suspect

If the suspect has fled the area in which he is believed to have committed a crime, law enforcement officers should make an attempt to locate him in the same state so as to avoid extradition procedures. (Even though extradition between states is provided for by the Constitution, it can still be a complicated and lengthy process.) If officers believe that a suspect has indeed fled the state, and may have even gone to a particular city in that state, then they should send law enforcement agencies in that state a teletype containing the following information:

1. The name of the suspect and a physical description of him.

2. The identification number of the department submitting the information, in addition to any other state or national identification number.

3. Descriptions of any vehicles the suspect may be using.

4. Information on the court that issued the warrant, in addition to particulars on the charge and the bail.

5. And, most important, notification as to whether or not the prosecutor or district attorney will extradite the suspect if need be.

If the investigator doesn't know what state the suspect has gone to, then the local prosecutor or district attorney should contact the U.S. Attorney in the same jurisdiction and request that he or she file an UFAP (Unlawful Flight to Avoid Prosecution) report with the FBI. The FBI will then usually disseminate Identification Orders as well as wanted posters throughout the country, depending on the nature of the crime which was committed.

"Deadly Errors": Avoiding Unnecessary Dangers

All during an investigation, the officer is apt to meet people who are hostile to the police. This may, of course, include the suspect, but it may also include some victims, witnesses, associates and friends of the suspect, or people who just plain don't like the police. Thus, the officer may frequently be in some degree of personal danger. Many officers either aren't aware of this fact or don't take it seriously enough; they can make mistakes that are literally fatal. The danger factor is especially high when the officer is attempting to arrest the suspect.

Pierce R. Brooks has referred to these mistakes as the "Deadly Errors," and warns officers against making them. (Taken from *Officer Down, Code Three*, 1975, p. 6.) These errors are described as follows:

1. Failure to Maintain Proficiency and Care of Weapon, Vehicle, and Equipment. (If you have learned to shoot, will your gun fire when you pull the trigger? Will your car respond when you need it?)

2. Improper Search and Use of Handcuffs. (Many police fatalities here.)

3. Sleepy or Asleep. (How well can you react when you are?)

4. Relaxing Too Soon. (Usually at those "phony" silent alarm calls.)

5. Missing the Danger Signs. (Miss or don't recognize them; they can be fatal either way.)

6. Taking a Bad Position. (Write a citation or an FI card with your back turned to the subject. Or, while confronting the barricaded gunman, be casual or curious from your place of concealment rather than careful and cautious from a place of cover.)

7. Failure to Watch Their Hands. (Where else can the subject hold a gun, or a knife, or a club?)

8. Tombstone Courage. (Why wait for a backup?)

9. Preoccupation. (Worrying about personal problems while on duty may be the hard way to solve the problem.)

10. Apathy. (A deadly disease for the cynical veteran police officer.)*

It's a rare occasion when the success of an investigation is worth sacrificing a police officer's life. Thus, while care must be exercised that every phase of a criminal investigation is carried out professionally and thoroughly, the officer should always be aware of his own safety as well.

Summary

In this chapter, several case examples of "suspects" have been presented; how they came about and how they were developed to a successful conclusion. The reader should realize and take into consideration the fact that no two cases are alike and every officer must be able to adjust to many situations.

The law enforcement student should think about the meaning of two words: "suspect" and "believe." You will notice that not only have you been given the definition from a standard college dictionary, but we have also taken the definitions from many other sources. As you re-read the definitions, try to decide just how the law enforcement officer and also many of the appellate court judges react to the word and how they came up with their own interpretations.

Different ways of identifying a suspect from descriptions have been presented and learning them will help in a career in the field of law enforcement. Try describing your friends or associates and practice this technique whenever possible. There will always be one or two things in a description that will readily stand out in each person.

---

* Pierce R. Brooks, *Officer Down, Code Three*, 1975. Reprinted with permission of Motorola Teleprograms, Inc., Schiller Park, Illinois.

The sources of obtaining information on a suspect are unlimited. This chapter has outlined many of them, but, if you are innovative, you can double the size of the list. Don't forget the public library, which proved a successful resource in one of the cases described here. The public library is also a good source for obtaining handwriting exemplars. Locating a suspect, like an arrest, can be immediate or it can take months or years. This is all part of the profession. Be patient, innovative and discreet—and you should be able to locate the suspect.

Cooperation, good will, and trust from the public is probably one of the most important goals a law enforcement officer or agency can achieve. The slogan "To Protect and Serve" is now becoming a motto for many law enforcement agencies, as well as for crime prevention programs. Serving the community well is the best guarantee of community support and assistance.

Questions and Topics for Discussion

1. This chapter contained five examples of cases in which different suspect identification procedures were used. Find out about some other suspect identification procedures which are utilized by your local police department. If possible, invite an officer to speak to your class about cases he has worked on.

2. What are some of the various definitions and interpretations of the word "suspect?" How might the fact that so many different definitions exist affect the police officer?

3. Work in teams of three to conduct mock "suspect identifications." (Several different teams can work at the same time in different areas of the classroom.)

   One member of each team will be the "suspect." Another will be the "investigating officer." The third will serve as the "witness." The witness should leave the room during the first part of the identification procedure.

   While the witness is out of the room, the investigator will take a physical description of the suspect. (Remember—there are at least 27 different categories of information. Refer to the appropriate section of this chapter if necessary.) This description should be as complete as possible. After this part of the procedure has been completed, the suspect should leave the room and the witness should return. The investigator will then interview the witness to get his physical description of the suspect. It should be interesting to discover how observant—or how unobservant—you and your classmates are.

   When all identifications are complete, compare results.

4. Why is it so important to determine a suspect's modus operandi? How can this help to solve a case?

5. What are some of the problems involved in interviewing a suspect's friends and associates?

6. Find out what your local police department's policies and procedures are regarding field interviews.

7. Do some research into police public relations programs. Which have seemed to work, and why? (Don't confine your research to your own area.) After you've completed this part of the excercise and discussed your results with your class, concentrate on your own area. What evidence do you see that your local police are conscious of the importance of public support and cooperation?

8. If possible, obtain copies of some wanted posters or notices from your local police department. You might want to do some research in the library as to how wanted notices have changed over the years. How frequently are rewards offered today? And for what kinds of crimes? (Don't forget private individuals, who often post wanted notices and rewards of their own for kidnapped family members, for example.)

9. Discuss the legalities of the line-up and other pre-arraignment procedures. Research some other cases which have affected line-up procedures (for example, *Kirby v. Illinois*, 1972; *Stovall v. Denno*, 1967; both are Supreme Court cases).

10. Name and discuss as many aspects of the Clark County line-up criteria as you can.

11. Find out what extradition involves in your state, and hold a class discussion on your findings.

12. Discuss in detail the "deadly errors." Are there any others you can think of? You might want to ask a police officer his feelings on other errors officers can make that might prove dangerous or even fatal.

Annotated Bibliography

Black, Henry Campbell, *Black's Law Dictionary*, West Publishing Co., 1968, defines "suspect" in a different light and gives two Supreme Court decisions.

Brooks, Pierce R., *Officer Down, Code Three*, Motorola Teleprograms, Inc., 1975, is an excellent text written by Dr. Brooks who was formerly with the Los Angeles Police Department, then as a Chief of Police in Colorado and presently the Chief of Police in Eugene, Oregon, has described many police killings when attempting to arrest a suspect and who really puts his points across. On page 6 and 7 of the text he lists the ten deadly errors that every police officer in the world should be aware of.

Corpus Juris Secundum, Volume 83, 1933, p. 923-924, gives the student still another version of the word "suspect". American Lawbook Company.

Eldefonso, Edward; Coffey, Alan R.; Sullivan, James, *Police and The Criminal Law*, Goodyear Publishing Company. 1972. Chapter IX Interrogation and Confessions, outlines in great detail several U.S. Supreme Court decisions and an excellent paragraph on "Lineups" that appears on p. 184.

Estes, Ken, *Washington Crime Watch Newsletter*, Fall, 1976, Edmonds (Washington) Police Department Public Information Officer relates the successful program that the City of Edmonds sponsored with an excellent program.

F.B.I. Law Enforcement Bulletin, June, 1961. p. 30. Officers Memory Results in Arrest of Wily Con Man.

Miller, et. al. *Criminal Justice Administration and Related Process*, Foundation Press, 1971, has an excellent chapter on eyewitness identification and has reprinted The American Law Institute, a Model Code of Pre-Arraignment Procedure (Proposed Official Draft, 1975) by permission of the American Law Institute, as well as many other Supreme Decisions that would be of interest to the law-enforcement student. p. 721.

Nelson, John G. *Preliminary Investigation and Police Reporting, A Complete Guide to Police Written Communications*, Glencoe Press, 1970. Lesson 20, "Elements of Effective Police Reporting, p. 51 and 52. Even though this particular section is primarily for report writing, the "how" section relates to the Modus Operandi of the suspect.

Sullivan, *Cases and Materials on the Administration of Criminal Justice*, Foundation Press, 1969, is an excellent treatise on lineup for identification including Supreme Court case of United States v. Wade, 1967 388 U.S. 218, 87 S. Ct. 1926, 18, L. Ed. 2d 1149, as well as Gilbert v. California, Supreme Court of the United States, 1967. 388 U.S. 263, 87 S. Ct. 1951, 18 L. Ed. 2d. 1178, and the Procedure for Line-Up Identification currently used in Clark County, Nevada that is further described in this chapter, appearing on p. 211.

Webster's New World Dictionary, New World Publishing Company, 1968. p. 1469 gives the layman's terms for suspect as opposed to legal definitions.

Weston, Paul B., and Wells, Kenneth M. *Criminal Investigation Basic Perspectives*, Prentice Hall, Inc., 1974. This is an excellent text for the criminal investigator student, one which I used in a classroom setting for pre-service and in-service students. This is the text where the earliest reward poster or one of the earliest reward posters was displayed. p. 13.

Words and Phrases, Volume 40A, West Publishing Company, 1964, gives the student many definitions of the word "suspect" as have been handed down by Supreme and Appellate Courts.

ELEVEN

The Victim and the Witness: Sources of Information

Chapter Objectives

After reading this chapter, the student should be able to:

☑ Explain the concept of victimology.

☑ Describe the relationships which may exist between victim and suspect, victim and witness and witness and suspect; describe what implications these relationships have for the criminal investigator.

☑ Describe the role of the victim and witness in suspect identification.

☑ Explain the importance of victim assistance and describe various means of implementing it.

☑ Explain some of the ways hypnosis and chemicals are used to extract information from witnesses and victims which they may unconsciously possess.

The Crime Victim: A New Focus
for the Criminal Investigator

The primary emphasis in criminal investigation and in criminology has long been on the suspect. Criminal investigators have been concerned with identifying the offender, apprehending him, and establishing sufficient proof for conviction. Criminologists have traditionally concentrated on the offender, studying the possible biological, psychological, and sociological reasons for his behavior and exploring various treatment procedures. These concerns are still very real to investigators and criminologists today, and they are, of course, legitimate. In recent years, however, attention has begun to focus on the victim as well as the suspect:

> The issue of victimization poses special problems inasmuch as it refers to questions related to being a criminal's victim. Just as each criminal has his victim, each victim, Stephen Schaefer recognizes, has his criminal. Until recently, little attention has been given the relationship of the victim to the criminal. However, the growing body of new data points out that a large proportion of crimes in each category involve victims and offenders who are known to each other. But the question is even greater than this. Many contemporary states accept no responsibility for the criminal victim, even though the offender may have committed his crime against the person while on probation or parole under the legal supervision of the state. In such instances, the costs of being a victim are borne solely by the victim, his family and/or an insurance company. In place of this practice, Schaefer proposes a reassessment of the state's responsibility in the total crime situation.[1]

Emphasis has also shifted to the study of what makes certain victims vulnerable to certain crimes. Are specific "types" of people apt to be victimized more often than other "types?" If so, why? Stephen Schaefer, a well-known criminologist, also addresses this issue:

> Victim typologies, as they are presently known, try to classify the characteristics of victims, but actually they often typify social and psychological situations rather than the constant patterns of the personal makeup of the victims. The "easy" victim and the "difficult" victim appear according to the balance of forces in a given criminal drama. Nevertheless, although the First International Symposium on Victimology appears to be correct in stating that there are no "born" victims, there are indeed biological types of victims who, compared with temporary "situational" victims, seem to be continuously and excessively prone to becoming victims of crime. To be young, to be old, or to be mentally defective are not "situations" but biological qualities that indicate some degree of vulnerability to crime.[2]

This new trend toward greater study of the victim has been termed "victimology." Some see it as a branch of criminology, while others view it as an independent field of study. According to Schaefer,

> In recent years the growing interest in criminal-victim relationships has begun to challenge the "popularity" of the alarm and indignation against the criminal lawbreaker that has been coupled with a longstanding indifference to the victim of crime. The rapidly developing study of criminal-victim relationships has become called "victimology."[3]

According to this new field of study, victims can be classified according to the degree of their own involvement in the crime; for example,

1. The "completely innocent victim," such as children or those who suffer a crime while they are unconscious.

2. The "victim with minor guilt" and the "ignorant victim," such as the woman who provokes a miscarriage and as a result pays with her life.

3. The "voluntary victim" and the "victim as guilty as the offender," such as in certain cases of suicide and euthanasia.

4. The "victim more guilty than the offender," such as those who provoke or induce someone to commit a crime.

5. The "most guilty victim" and the "victim who is guilty alone," such as the aggressive victim who kills the attacker in self-defense.

6. The "simulating" or "imaginary victim," such as paranoids, hysterics, or senile persons.[4]

Victimology as a science is concerned with the significance of the victim's and witness's backgrounds. It recognizes the importance of dealing with their friends and associates. A relatively new focus has been on the issue of victim assistance, as well as on the use of hypnosis and drugs as inducements to recall.

No one can become an accomplished criminal investigator (or criminologist, for that matter) simply by reading about these issues. Learning about them, however, in combination with professional training and experience, should aid the investigator in understanding the importance of victimology as it relates to the criminal investigation and its efforts to solve crimes.

Exploring the Backgrounds of Victims and Witnesses

Since crimes are often linked to a variety of human emotions, motivations, reactions, and interpretations, an understanding of the persons involved in them—victims, witnesses, and suspects—as well as the types and degrees of their relationships is important to the success of any investigation.

The Victim

In many cases, no prior relationship exists between the suspect and the victim. This is particularly true in crimes against property, such as theft, burglary, joyriding, and so on. In other crimes, the victim and the suspect may have known each other as acquaintances, friends, neighbors, or even as spouses. Close relationships are not uncommon, then, in crimes against the person, such as assault, rape, or murder. In fact, it has been sarcastically said that if an individual wants to protect himself against the probability of becoming a victim of assault or murder, he should make sure to have neither friends nor family.

There are several reasons why knowledge of the relationship between the victim and the suspect could be useful to the police investigator. Three are most often cited; they are:

1. The relationship may influence the accuracy of the crime report in a number of ways.

2. It may serve as a lead in apprehending the suspect.

3. It may provide a motive or otherwise cast light on the total circumstances of the crime.

The second needs no lengthy explanation. Obviously, if the victim knows who committed the crime against him, identifying and apprehending the suspect should be much easier than if the victim has no idea of who the suspect might be. The first and third reasons deserve closer examination.

The Special Relationship and the Crime Report. Depending on any number of circumstances, a crime report may very well be a totally accurate account of the events of a crime as they occurred. Or, as is probably more than often the case, it may simply be an account of the events as the victim perceived them, even though the victim may have no intention whatsoever of deceiving or misleading the police. It's easy for the emotionally upset victim—whether angry, shocked, or grief-stricken—to exaggerate when reporting a crime to the police. Any blows actually struck seem to multiply in number. The small revolver becomes a cannon, or stolen items suddenly increase in value. The officer should be alert for these possibilities while simultaneously recognizing the necessity for tact and diplomacy.

Occasionally, a crime report is a complete fabrication. The "victim" may file such a report in an effort to get another person in trouble with the police. In one case, for example, a man reported a burglary in which the loss consisted of money and personal papers and photographs in which only his ex-wife could have been interested. A careful examination of the "crime scene" revealed that the window at the point of entry had been broken from the *inside*. Later interrogation of the supposed "victim" led to a confession in which he admitted having tried to get his ex-wife prosecuted.

The "victim" may also report offenses to influence other persons close to him. In one extreme case, a woman reported having been kidnapped and raped in a muddy field. The officers noted that her light-colored dressed was neither soiled nor wrinkled, and when no tire tracks were discovered in the area where the suspect's vehicle had supposedly been driven into the field, the woman finally admitted having invented the incident in an effort to "punish" her husband and cause him grief.

Insurance money can also be a factor. The reported crime may not have occurred at all. Or, while it may have really taken place, the loss may have been "padded" to provide some profit for the victim.

Crimes are also sometimes reported in an effort to cover up the "victim's" actual activities. One man who had failed to come home one night developed a dreadful kidnapping story which made his wife grateful that he was still alive. In another case, a young boy who had had an accident in a stolen vehicle told the police a long and detailed account of how he had been forced into the vehicle at gunpoint by a man who demanded that he drive the car. Careful interrogation brought out sufficient discrepancies in the boy's story to reveal the fact that he had in truth stolen the car on his own.

Cases like the ones just described make it clear that the police officer should be alert for any special relationship which might exist between the victim and suspect. He should also watch for any other circumstances which might influence the accuracy of the report. The officer must bear in mind, however, that the majority of crime reports filed are correct, at least to the best of the victims' knowledge.

While, as was previously discussed, the relationship between the victim and the suspect may be such that the victim is anxious to get the suspect in trouble with the law, the opposite may also be the case. The victim may report the crime only because the insurance company requires it, or because of family pressures, or because the victim wants the police to "counsel" the suspect for his own good. In any event, the victim may be either unwilling or reluctant to prosecute. If this is the case, it's important that the investigator be aware of it, for it usually determines how the case should be handled. Some police departments take only an "incident report" instead of a crime report if the victim doesn't wish to prosecute. While it's true that a crime is an offense against the state as well as the person, practical considerations dictate that scarce law enforcement resources not be devoted to those cases in which even the victim isn't anxious to prosecute. This is sometimes unfortunate in that it allows the habitual wife-beater, shoplifter, or bad check writer to carry on his activities, but the realities of the criminal justice system are such that priorities have to be established. No police agency should be in the business of "scaring" people or serving as a collection agency for merchants who want to be reimbursed for bad checks, for example. Limitations on time and personnel simply don't allow for these practices.

The Special Relationship and the Motive. The relationship between the victim and the suspect may also be important in that it can be linked to the motive, or the reason, for the crime:

Crimes may be divided into two classes from the standpoint of motive. Crimes such as robbery, rape, and burglary have "universal" motives which are of little value in furthering the investigation. Other crimes may have "particularized motives," for example, homicide, arson, and assault. In these crimes, when the motive is discovered, the relationship between victim and criminal may be deduced. The high clearance rate for homicide is based, at least in part, on this logic. Experience is helpful in ferreting out the particular motive for a crime. In some crimes a determination of who has benefited from its commission is suggestive as to motive; in others it is through adroit interviewing that the motive may be learned.[5]

In the vast majority of cases, the victim's personal background and activities are of no concern to the investigator. The reported theft, burglary, or robbery is just one of a great volume of cases assigned to the investigator who must proceed according to priorities based on the severity of the offense and the leads available. In some cases, however, the victim's personal, moral, professional, or criminal background may be of genuine interest to the police. Those factors may be evident in the biases which influence the perception of the offense and, by extension, the reporting of it. For example, the moral or religious orientation of the victim may color his view of liquor violations, obscenity, gambling, juvenile delinquency, or sexual behavior, as well as a variety of incidents often referred to as "crimes without victims."[6]

A victim's professional background may also play a role in a criminal offense. The burglary of a physician's vehicle, or the robbery of a pharmacist, may provide a clue to a drug-oriented offense. The industrialist's wealth may be the motive for blackmail, or the labor organizer's influence the reason behind a kidnapping or disappearance (note, for example, the Jimmy Hoffa case). In fact, individuals who are obvious representatives of the establishment (such as Wall Street brokers, oil corporation executives, key government officials, and so on) often find themselves today among those persons who, by virtue of their professions and connections, need to take extra precautions against being victimized.

If the victim has a criminal background, it may or may not be of significance in the investigation of an offense, depending on its type or nature. If a person convicted of writing bad checks ten years ago is the victim of a theft, burglary, or robbery, for example, there appears to be no reason why his record should be of any significance. If a person currently dealing narcotics is robbed, however, or a person running a house of prostitution is mugged, or someone with organized crime ties is blackmailed, the victim's criminal background may be of importance. This is because of the fact that an individual who is involved in illegal activity is particularly vulnerable to criminal activity. Other criminals generally—and often correctly—assumed that he will be reluctant to report a robbery, theft, burglary, or blackmail, even if he is the victim; this may put his own doings in the spotlight. Sometimes, even police officers take advantage of certain persons' unwillingness to report crimes against themselves. In one large Michigan city, for example, allegations of "dope pad" robberies by police led to the reassignment of some officers and the abolishment of specific police units.

A clear example of the relationship which may exist between a victim's own criminal activity and a crime which is perpetrated against him is found when a major narcotics dealer or a key member of organized crime is murdered or, in effect, "executed" by competitors. Although in cases like these, homicide investigators will go through the motions of investigating the offense, they will often do so without much enthusiasm. Some police officers feel that homicides of this nature don't represent a great loss to society and may even believe that the victims "had it coming." Under our legal system, attitudes like these aren't permissible since they allow the police, in essence, to decide who "deserves" to be murdered and who doesn't. On the other hand, in large cities where more murders take place than can be investigated efficiently, it may be understandable— though regrettable—that detectives have to establish work priorities which include the consideration of the identity of the victim.

A further judgment regarding the victim is often made by the district attorney or the prosecutor. This issue often focuses on how the victim will "look" to a jury. While the corpus delicti (or the elements of a crime) might clearly exist, the DA or the prosecutor may choose to concentrate instead on the more "practical" aspects of the trial. For example, will the jury believe the victim? Is the victim credible? Is the victim likeable? Is the victim socially and educationally able to impress a jury? Many people feel that these questions should have nothing to do with prosecution policies and decision; again, ideally, they shouldn't. If defendants are equal before the law, then victims should be also. Nevertheless, the practical issue facing the prosecutor is still one of whether or not he can win the case. Therefore, it can be assumed that a victim who won't be a good witness will weaken a case. If the victim has a criminal background, this can be an obvious detriment to a successful prosecution. Similarly, the victim's moral or social background may be such that the prosecutor is reluctant to bring the case before a jury. For instance, a person who is known to deal in stolen goods may find the prosecutor less than enthusiastic about bringing a case against someone who cheated him. Or, a known prostitute will probably experience greater difficulty in having a complaint issued for rape than will a middle-class housewife. Although these distinctions involve certain moral issues regarding equal access to justice which don't really belong in a courtroom, they must be taken into account anyway since they can influence the outcome of a trial.

The Witness

The outcome of a criminal case may often depend on the testimony of witnesses. Even when the suspect makes an admission or a confession, such a statement cannot be admitted into evidence before the corpus delicti has been established, and the proof needed to accomplish this usually originates with witnesses. For example, a suspect may confess to having committed a murder, and that confession will be virtually worthless unless the elements of the murder can be shown independently of that confession. Or, a driver who is involved in a traffic accident may admit to having consumed too much alcohol that evening. This admission cannot be used against him until it can be proved that he violated the law prohibiting driving under the influence; again, this proof must be established independently and must not be based on the admission.

Witnesses, then, are of great value in criminal investigations. One reason for this is because witnesses are often persons who, purely by chance or by accident, happen to be in a certain place at a certain time and have no particular allegiance to—or relationship with—either the victim or the suspect. (The term "witness" is usually applied to a person other than the victim, although in many cases the victim can serve as both a victim and a witness; i.e., both the target of the crime and an observer. This deserves some clarification. For example, a robbery victim will be present at the time during which the crime is committed, and thus will be both a victim and a witness. In most burglaries, on the other hand, the victim won't be present and thus won't be a witness to the offense. Even when a victim plays both roles, however, most police departments will refer to him as a victim only.)

Sometimes, the witness may have a definite relationship with the victim. This can, of course, be of importance to the police investigator. The relationship may be a very close one (such as marriage or friendship) or it may be a hostile one. In any case, the credibility of the witness may be an issue, since he may "color" his testimony according to personal allegiances or feelings. For instance, an assault may take place in a bar, and it will be necessary for the police to determine whether the witnesses are primarily friends of the suspect or of the victim. While the reporting officer may not be able to do much at the scene to resolve this issue, it nevertheless should be taken into account, since it will be important to the prosecution.

A witness may also have a particular type of relationship with the suspect; they may be spouses, close friends, neighbors, or enemies. Sometimes, such emotional ties are evident to the police officer conducting the preliminary investigation; at other times, they are revealed during the detectives' follow-up investigation. Occasionally, such partiality (whether pro or con) is discovered only in the course of a trial. The investigating officer is generally associated with the prosecution; nevertheless, he has a basic duty to ascertain the truth rather than merely to seek a conviction. Therefore, he should indicate in his report any pronounced partiality on the part of a witness. (Obviously, the best witness in any case will be the person who is unfamiliar with both the victim and the suspect and who has no personal stake in the matter.)

When more than one witness exists, they should be interviewed separately. Interviewing should be as private as possible. The presence of other potential witnesses encourages a "spill-over" effect during testimony.

The investigating officer must also question the witness's reliability. Several signs can indicate to the officer that the witness may not be as acceptable as one might wish:

(1) [a] hangdog appearance; (2) tendency to repeat questions; (3) talking in almost inaudible tones and acting as though he wishes the experience were over with; (4) unnatural emphasis; (5) defensive smile or nervous laugh; (6) unnecessarily minute accuracy; (7) repeated statement of desire to be truthful and frank, and uncalled-for swearing of truth.

Accurate appraisal of character is a difficult and elusive goal. It cannot be reached by reliance on inferences from the shape of the head or the contour of the physiogmony. But close observation of actual behavior, including posture, voice, eyes, and facial expression during the interview, yields clues which must not be ignored.[7]

And, of course the officer should never ask leading questions of a witness. For instance, a wrong question might be: "Was he a tall, thin male, white, wearing a red jacket and white slacks?" The same question, correctly phrased, would be: "Can you tell me his height, weight, and how he was dressed?" In other words, "questions should be phrased so that they contain no suggestion as to the most appropriate response."[8]

Officers should also avoid asking witnesses the same questions several times over. For example, an otherwise cooperative witness may well resent having to give the same account to first the patrol officer, then the patrol sergeant, and finally the detective. While some review by the police of a witness's account may be necessary, repetitious interviewing should not take place:

The manner in which preliminary investigations are handled can cause unnecessary inconvenience to witnesses, who generally prefer to tell their stories as few times as possible. The investigation that is handled from start to finish by one officer . . . is least inconvenient for the witness. If . . . the first officer on the scene prepares a report which is immediately available to the follow-up investigator, the citizen is likely to feel less frustration than if the first officer does a sloppy report or the follow-up officer begins asking questions without seeing that report.

An additional precaution which investigators should take for the protection of witnesses is the separation of the witness from the suspect. When this simple step is overlooked, the witness may be less cooperative and he may even be inclined to hide his identity from the suspect by falsifying his name or address.[9]

In summary, then, a witness may be a very important individual in a criminal investigation. The best witness is the one who knows neither the victim nor the suspect and thus may be reasonably considered to be totally impartial. If a witness is close to either the victim or the suspect, it isn't necessarily an indication that he will be unreliable, but this fact must still be taken into account. A witness who affiliates himself with other witnesses should be similarly viewed.

The personal background of a witness may influence his value to the prosecution. Regardless of how truthful a witness may or may not be, his bearing, appearance, profession, speech, background, directness, dress, and so on will serve either to increase or decrease his credibility before a jury. These factors are less critical in a court trial, where the judge is the one who decides both the law and the facts of a case (that is, the issue of guilt or innocence), because a judge is generally less subject to being influenced by impressions than a jury is.

If a witness has a criminal background, this can harm his credibility, especially if this background involved a felony conviction. The case is made even more difficult if the witness himself was involved in some manner in the offense being prosecuted. Sometimes, the prosecutor will grant immunity to one of the principals in the crime in return for his testimony. Such a witness can be of great value to the prosecution, for he will usually have exclusive knowledge of some of the details of a crime that other persons won't have had access to. However, the use of a witness like this can also backfire. For example, in one Orange County, California case, one person masterminded burglaries in which company checks were stolen. This person always had other individuals enter the company premises while he waited outside. And, when the stolen checks were passed, his accomplices were the ones who entered the various stores and markets while he simply provided the transportation. During his prosecution, the peripheral accomplices were granted special consideration in return for their testimony. Yet, because of their poor demeanor and dress (in addition to the fact that they were all heroin addicts with prior felony convictions), they presented such poor images as witnesses that the jury rejected all of their testimony and acquitted the main defendant.

The emotional states of witnesses and their powers of observation must also be taken into consideration. Most citizens are anxious to cooperate with the police. During a trial, when they suddenly find themselves at the center of attention, they may be especially eager to provide the police with useful information: sometimes, they may be *too* eager and end up exaggerating or stretching the facts to highlight their own roles as observers. Although this may simply be a part of human nature, it nevertheless must be questioned and examined. What could the witness have actually seen under the circumstances? What were the lighting conditions? How far away was the witness from the event? How much confusion was there at the time, and how could this have affected the witness's powers of observations? All of these questions—and more—must be asked in an attempt to determine what a witness really knows about a crime; even a witness who seems to be absolutely truthful (and means to be) may get carried away. The investigating officer shouldn't go out of his way to discredit a witness, of course, but should try to find out as much about what a witness really knows as possible to prevent surprises in the courtroom that may prove injurious to the prosecution.

In the vast majority of criminal cases reported to the police—such as the common theft, burglary, robbery, or check case—it isn't necessary to have a great deal of insight into the witness. In some cases, however—and certainly in all serious felonies—the character of the witness must be examined, and any special relationships he might have with the victim or the suspect must be discovered without delay. Once again, the main duty of the police officer is to establish the truth; how a witness feels about a victim or a suspect may very well affect his perception of the truth.

Investigating Leads and Identifying Suspects

Identifying the suspect in a crime ranges from being very easy to being nearly impossible. For example, a person might write a number of checks without having sufficient funds in his bank to cover them. The police may find that the suspect has given his real name when opening the account; that the address on the checks is correct; and that the suspect is arrested at home with little or no trouble. Or, a number of robberies may occur in which the suspect is of average height and weight, wears gloves and a ski mask, and disappears on foot without a vehicle being seen or heard. In the latter case, identifying the suspect can obviously be a task of great difficulty.

Crimes against the person are cleared more frequently than crimes against property. The clearance rate for murder is 80%; for aggravated assault, it's around 63%. Yet, the clearance rate for auto theft is only 15%; for larceny, 20%; and for burglary, 18%.[10] There may be several reasons why crimes against the person are investigated with greater success than crimes against property are. Seriousness, for example, may be one factor. In addition, there is usually a witness present during a crime against a person (even if the witness is also the victim) who can later describe the suspect.

Getting a Description

Obtaining a description of the suspect is obviously the first step in identifying him. The witness (or victim) can usually provide the best leads:

> The victim or eyewitness to a crime is often able to describe the criminal. The problem of transferring this information to other law enforcement personnel or to the public at large has been attempted in three ways: portrait parle, or a printed verbal description of the physical characteristics and clothing of the criminal; use of a police artist to capture the likeness; and use of a mechanical device to combine a limited choice of salient features—forehead, hairline, eyebrows, eyes, nose, mouth, chin, ears, and so on.[11]

When interviewing a witness or a victim, the investigating officer should be careful to take down as much information about the suspect as possible in the crime report, including his name, nickname, height, weight, hair color, eye color, and race; any unusual features; jewelry; tattoos; and clothing. If a vehicle was involved in the crime, and this information is available, the officer should also record the make, year, and color of the vehicle, in addition to its license number (or partial license number) and state of registration.

The suspect's appearance can be recorded in other ways besides the crime report alone. Most larger departments have police artists who, with the victim's or witness's guidance, can usually draw the suspect's face fairly accurately. An Identikit can also be used in creating such a likeness; it consists of a collecton of plastic slides, each of which shows a particular type or style or shape of some feature—such as hair, the nose, chin, ears, and so on. A trained officer can work with a witness to create an Identikit likeness of a suspect by placing several of the transparent slides on top of each other until the witness feels as if the portrait is reasonably accurate. Identikit slides are coded, and thus the information obtained from a collaboration between an officer and a witness can be transmitted by telephone or teletype from one agency to another.

The Modus Operandi

The suspect's modus operandi may also help in identifying him. Many criminal offenders are creatures of habit; once they experience success by using certain tactics or approaches, they're apt to repeat them. Thus, when an officer takes a crime report, he must also record information on the modus operandi, or M.O., of the crime. For example, "Suspect entered doctor's office by prying rear door at night time; took drugs only;" or, "Suspect entered bar by chopping hole in wall from adjoining business; took coins from pool tables;" or, "Suspect obtained bank deposit bag from restaurant by posing as a uniformed Brink's guard." The various types of M.O.'s are coded and entered in a state computer and can be retrieved for comparison purposes. A very unusual M.O. is of more value to the investigator than a common one, however. An M.O. such as, "Suspect entered home by prying screen in kitchen window; took TV set and small appliances" will probably have little value for comparison purposes. On the other hand, an M.O. like, "Suspect entered major supermarket by prying skylight, bypassd all alarm systems, and opened safe by torching" narrows the number of possible suspects. Thus, if an investigator is assigned a case with an unusual M.O., an inquiry directed to the state agency responsible for maintaining these records may provide information about similar offenses as well as suspects known to be responsible for such offenses. The investigator can then compare whatever physical evidence he has discovered (such as fingerprints) with the information on the suspects in question provided by the state.

Other Identifying Factors

Unusual features, jewelry, or tattoos may at times be of critical value. The Hollywood Division of the Los Angeles Police Department solved numerous rape cases when one patrolman noticed during a field interview that the subject was wearing a medallion similar to one described by several rape victims. The officer's alertness and the subsequent arrest of the person led to the solving of a number of Hollywood rapes. Similarly, an Orange County, California case involving a con man wearing a unique diver's watch led to his identification as a suspect.

The suspect's vehicle can be another important link to the offender. In ideal situations, a witness will observe the supect's vehicle, note its description (including, of course, the license number), and give this information to the police. Assuming that the suspect was driving his own vehicle at the time, such a lead could be invaluable. At other times, however, a stolen vehicle will be used by the suspect when committing a crime, and the lead will be less valuable. In such a case, the vehicle, when recovered, should be processed by a crime scene investigator, assuming that the offense justifies this effort. (For example, if the vehicle was used in a robbery, full crime scene investigation efforts ought to be applied; this may not be justified or necessary if the car was simply taken for joyriding.)

Even a partial license number can help to identify a suspect. It makes a real difference, though, whether a witness is able to indicate only the first letter in a suspect's vehicle's license number or state all but the last digit of the number. In the latter case, the investigator will easily be able to obtain information on the ten possible vehicles to ascertain which one matches the description given by the witness.

A quick radio broadcast after a crime has occurred can sometimes lead to the apprehension of the suspect by the reporting police agency or a nearby agency. The direction of travel may or may not be a clue to the suspect's destination. Most often, apprehending a suspect right after a crime has been committed may be a matter of outguessing him. As Thomas Adams, a one-time police academy instructor, once stated to a group of recruits: "Figure out what's the most logical path of the suspect's travel. Then proceed to some other location in your effort to catch him."

If a license number leads the investigator to a certain vehicle which is owned by someone who is probably not the suspect, an interview of that registered owner—whether an individual or a car rental agency—should produce further leads regarding the identity of the suspect. Car rental agencies tend to be very cooperative in such matters. An individual owner may be reluctant to provide information regarding the person who used the vehicle, however, and it may be necessary to discuss with that person what constitutes a principal in a crime or an accessory to a felony.

When several suspects are involved in the same crime, it sometimes becomes easier to identify them. One suspect may, for example, call another by name while the crime is in progress. Once one suspect has been identified, information can be obtained regarding that person's usual associates.

Once a suspect's name is ascertained, a record check should be run. Assuming that the offense was a felony, record checks should be run through the local agency, the state, and the FBI. The suspect's record will provide a great deal of information, such as his real name, aliases, date of birth, prior arrests, convictions, and sentences. When necessary, the investigator can further develop this information by obtaining crime and arrest reports for each case, jail or prison files, probation and parole reports, and so on. Each of these will provide additional information regarding the suspect's M.O., associates, demeanor, status in the criminal justice system, and a variety of miscellaneous information which may be of value.

Thus, one level of information can be developed into a second or even subsequent levels. This principle is used in major background investigations. The investigator contacts the references listed and then asks each reference to provide additional sources of information. When each of these new sources is contacted, the officer asks, "Whom do you know who might be able to provide information about this individual?" and the process is repeated with the next person. As each item of information is developed, it shouldn't be assumed to be complete, but rather should be used to uncover other leads.

For example, most adults in the United States drive motor vehicles. Running a record check on a suspect through the state motor vehicle division, the Secretary of State's Office, or the like can be most profitable. The investigator can first ask for the person's driving record and any information on vehicles owned by him; or, the officer may choose to inquire into the total ownership history of a specific vehicle. These inquiries will produce the suspect's driving record. The value of this record goes beyond the fact that it can tell the officer whether the suspect has ever been convicted of speeding, running a red light, or whatever. If the suspect has a prior record of driving offenses, the convictions can be traced back to particular courts which will have copies of the citations along with information on the dispositions. Thus, the officer can usually ascertain which vehicle the suspect was driving at the time of each citation. For example, is the vehicle the suspect's own, or a friend's? If the vehicle doesn't belong to the suspect, then what is the relationship between the suspect and the owner? Is the owner a possible co-suspect? Is the suspect living with the owner? Does the owner know the suspect's present where abouts? Was that particular vehicle described as being used during the crime under investigation for other crimes? Are some of the citations outstanding? If so, have the court dates been set? Is it possible that the suspect can be apprehended at a specific court on a certain date? These are but a few of the issues which can be raised—and sometimes answered—by an examination of a suspect's driving record.

In addition, a driver's license—at least in most states—provides the investigator with a physical description of the suspect, along with a photograph, a copy of his signature, and his date of birth. These items of information can be further developed as dictated by the circumstances of the crime.

Field Interrogation Cards

Field interrogation (F.I.) cards can be of assistance to the investigator when attempting to identify and apprehend a suspect. (While F.I. cards are commonly used in many jurisdictions, incidentally, they are virtually unknown in others.) An F.I. card is a form which is filled out whenever a police officer wishes to record his contact with a certain person during a certain event. For example, an officer may observe a suspicious person walking down an alley at midnight. Even though there may not be sufficient grounds to make an arrest, the officer may decide to stop that person, question him, and write up an F.I. card. Or, an officer may notice something unusual regarding a vehicle, such as a T.V. set in the back seat, and stop the driver for questioning. This will also be recorded on an F.I. card.

Each F.I. card lists certain basic information about an officer's contact with a subject, such as the subject's name, address, date of birth, and physical description; the car he was using; the names of his companions at the time; the date and time during which he was observed and interviewed; and a narrative description of the officer's observations. For example, "Observed subject walking southbound in the alley behind the 300 block of Green Steet at 12:03 a.m. Subject stated he was walking to his car from his girlfriend's house;" or, "Observed subject driving east on Westminister Avenue in vehicle with radiator leaking water. Subject stated she had been in reported traffic accident in Long Beach and was now driving home." F.I. cards allow detectives to compare the unusual events in their own jurisdictions with reported crimes in other areas, and this hopefully leads toward the solving of some crimes.

F.I. cards are legitimate police tools, yet the fact remains that very few crimes are solved because of them. The true value of the F.I. may lie in the fact that it may prevent crimes rather than solving them. It isn't known how many persons intent on committing a crime when they were "F.I.'d" decided not to proceed with it or to do it elsewhere.

Teletypes

Teletypes are of significant value in identifying suspects and solving criminal offenses. In serious crimes, such as most felonies and certain misdemeanors, the investigating agency sends out to other agencies a teletype describing the type of the offense and certain significant details. Teletypes are also sent out when cases are solved by arrest.

The value of this teletype communication network cannot be overestimated. It allows police agencies to cooperate in cases where they realize that similar crimes with similar M.O.'s have been committed. If a robbery suspect, for example, commits one successful bank robbery and then never repeats the offense, the suspect's chances of avoiding apprehension are fair. Most suspects, however, are arrested because they are able to commit more than one successful crime and continue their criminal careers until they're finally apprehended.

Teletypes can either describe a specific crime which has no known suspects, or it can describe a crime in which suspects are in custody. In either case, investigators having an interest in the various types of offenses should follow their daily teletype messages. Here, specialization can be of importance. A police department in which the investigators do not specialize makes the reading of hundreds of daily teletypes by each and every investigator a necessary part of the job. On the other hand, a police department which does have specialists can require these investigators to read only the teletypes which pertain to their areas of specialization.

Most police agencies find teletypes to be very valuable. Cases are generally cleared by falling into one of three categories:

1. *Arrest.* Suspect apprehended and charged.

2. *Exceptional.* Suspect identified, but circumstances beyond police control prevent them from taking the suspect into custody. (For example, a suspect is identified as having committed a petty theft. A check reveals that he is serving a 10 year to life sentence in the state prison. Or, a suspect in an armed robbery is identified and killed in a subsequent robbery.)

3. *Unfounded.* The offense never occurred at all, or the elements of the crime were lacking. (For example, a car reported stolen was actually repossessed, or a report of a theft actually involved the simple loss or misplacement of the property.)

The Importance of Setting Priorities

When, after a certain period of time, a case still remains unsolved, some police departments file it away or "inactivate" it. This isn't a true clearance in that the case hasn't yet been solved; the volume of criminal cases, however, does require that such a mechanism exist for removing some cases from the investigator's workload. A very basic consideration in criminal investigation is the fact that the sheer number of cases, combined with limitations on personnel and resources, means that not every case can be given the same amount of attention. In other words, priorities have to be established. Cases with leads take precedence over cases without leads. Serious cases (such as murder, rape, and armed robbery) take precedence over less serious cases (such as vandalism, petty theft, and trespassing). The number of criminal cases which reach the detective's desk makes it humanly impossible for him to investigate every one to its fullest extent. Given that fact, the setting of priorities is not only a defensible but a worthy administrative practice.

Victim and/or Witness
Identification of the Suspect

Once the investigator believes that he has identified the suspect, it's time to move to the next stage of the investigation: having the victim and/or witness identify the suspect personally. This can be accomplished in three different ways.

For example, in a street crime such as a mugging, if the police find a suspect in the vicinity of the crime soon after it occurs, they may show that suspect to the victim literally "on the street." An identification would decide whether or not the suspect should be released or arrested. This particular type of identification procedure could cause legal problems later on, but it's generally considered permissible as an emergency measure.

The suspect may also be identified through "mug shots," or a series of photographs of persons who have been booked into county jails or prisons. When mug shots are shown to victims or witnesses, however, care should be taken that a sufficient number of shots is made available (approximately half a dozen) and that all of the subjects are of similar ethnic origin. If the suspect is Mexican, for instance, showing a witness photographs of one Mexican and five Chinese is inappropriate. Other characteristics must also be taken into account. If the suspect is five feet tall, the showing of full-length mug shots of one short person and five tall individuals is not permissible.

Many police departments fail to keep a record of the mug shots they show. This can be a mistake. During a trial, a defense attorney might accuse the police of showing a victim or a witness a number of photographs which placed the suspect at a disadvantage. Therefore, the careful police investigator will not only ensure that the mug shots are generally similar in appearance, but he will also record which photographs are shown to which persons at which times. Some officers write follow-up reports in which they indicate the names of the persons whose pictures were shown. This procedure isn't the best, since certain individuals may be photographed at various times and a number of pictures of the same person may thus be available, any of which may be shown. A safer method involves taking the mug shots which are shown at any given time to a witness or a victim and then recording this procedure by making photocopies of the pictures themselves for the record. This procedure not only preserves the pictures, but also any identifying features, such as the prisoner's name, the date and year during which the picture was taken, and the jurisdiction in which it was taken. It enables either the prosecution or the defense to duplicate the actual mug shots shown should the need ever arise.

In order to ascertain whether a victim or a witness can identify a suspect in person, investigators also conduct line-ups. A line-up may be conducted in a room especially designed for such a purpose; if a special room is not available, an appropriate assembly room can be used. During a line-up, the suspect and approximately half a dozen other persons of similar appearance stand against a wall. They may be directed to turn sideways or to speak certain words which the suspect used during the crime. Ideally, the persons in the line-up should not be able to see or hear the witness. If a witness recognizes one of the persons in the line-up as the suspect, he should indicate so to the officer who has been assigned to be with the witnesses during the line-up.

The fairness of the line-up can be a legally critical matter. Therefore, some police departments standardize the line-up procedure, including all instructions spoken to the witnesses.[12] In addition, a defendant who is placed in a line-up has the right to have an attorney present. The attorney cannot prevent the line-up or interfere with it; he must simply observe it and do whatever is necessary to ensure that it is conducted fairly and impartially. (See Chapter Ten pp. 295 - 303.)

An investigator who is seeking a suspect is not limited to any of the methods described here, of course. He should only be limited by his imagination and restrictions dictated by law.

Identifying Stolen Property

Not all stolen property is identifiable. For example, how many people whose car batteries were stolen could even recognize them later, much less positively identify them? Other types of property can, of course, be identified because of their unique characteristics. Scratches or other marks on an item are often familiar to its owner and can be helpful during identification. The following case will help to illustrate this fact.

A patrol officer stopped a pick-up truck late one night for a traffic violation. When he observed torching equipment and a money sack in the bed of the truck and the driver couldn't account for the presence of those items, the driver and his passenger were both arrested on suspicion of burglary. An area teletype describing the arrest was sent out. Los Angeles County Sheriff's Department safe burglary investigators noted the teletype and felt that the suspects could be responsible for the safe burglary of a lumber yard that had occurred during the night in question. The officers had the owner view the money bag, which contained a sum of money identical to that which had been in the safe. Also in the sack was a plastic container of postage stamps. The owner could later testify that the stamp container belonged to him because of a pattern of small cracks and unique markings. Both suspects entered guilty pleas.

Items of property which best lend themselves to positive identification include those which have been marked with serial numbers, such as guns, televisions, typewriters, certain small appliances, cameras, and so on. Ideally, people should note the serial numbers on all their possessions and keep these numbers on record. A special identification problem exists with guns, however. A manufacturer may assign the same serial number to a two-inch revolver and a four-inch revolver, thereby making it possible for some confusion between the two to exist. This is particularly true if the four-inch revolver is ever sawed off to become a two-inch model.

A police program called "Operation Identification" has been helpful to citizens and police officers alike. It involves etching a number—each person is assigned a different one—into items of property; this makes them not only identifiable but traceable. Unfortunately, the system has not been coordinated on a nationwide basis or even on a statewide basis. This has resulted in some persons using their driver's license numbers and others using their social security numbers. A driver's license number doesn't indicate the state where the license was issued; nevertheless, it's the better of the two numbers to use for this purpose since it is traceable by the police. Social security numbers, on the other hand, are not traceable since the police don't have ready access to them.

When identifiable property is reported stolen and a crime report is compiled, the police should enter information on the property into the state computer system. If the property is observed by another officer at a later date, a check will reveal that it is stolen, thereby permitting recovery and, hopefully, arrest. Such information on stolen property should also be entered into the federal computer system known as the NCIC (National Crime Information Center).

Pawn shops bear particular watching by investigators assigned to theft and burglarly details. Most items of property are easily sold at pawn shops, which are required to fill out "pawn slips," or records of their daily transactions. These slips are open to police inspection. In some states, pawn shops are also required to mail copies of their pawn slips to the police departments in the cities where the sellers of the items reside. Unfortunately, if a theft occurs in some other city, the police generally have no system for sharing that information.

In major cases, police departments send circulars to pawn shops asking them to look out for certain items. Pawn shops tend to be cooperative in their dealings with the police.

Some offenders earn their incomes from running "fencing operations;" that is, they buy stolen property and later resell it. When such operations come to the attention of police, it's often wise to keep their locations under surveillance for a while before acting upon this information, thereby not only gaining additional knowledge of the fencing operation itself but also learning who frequents the place and how often. If sufficient time and personnel are available for large-scale surveillance, a "net," or group, of offenders may be discovered.

Bicycle thefts present a particular problem because of the great volume of such thefts. A city can minimize this problem by establishing a bicycle licensing program whereby each bike bears a sticker license and also has a corresponding number stamped into its frame. This number is kept on file by the police for reference should the bicycle be reported stolen.

Interviewing Friends and Associates of the Victim, Witness, and/or Suspect

A large percentage of offenses are committed by persons known to their victims, as opposed to stranger-to-stranger crimes. It's estimated that at least one third of all personal crimes of violence involve a confrontation between persons acquainted with one another, and it's determined from this figure that 25% of the rapes, 14% of the robberies, and 40% of the assaults reported to the police are not stranger-to stranger incidents.[13] Therefore, the investigator often deals with persons who have been victimized by their friends and associates and perhaps even close relatives. A District of Columbia Witness Survey points out that the closer the relationship between the victim and the defendant, the greater are the implications that the victim as a witness will be regarded as a non-cooperator.[14] The study further offers this rationale:

> When the witness knows the defendant, the former may develop a forgive-and-forget or a fear-of-reprisal attitude, and therefore not testify. Also, prosecutors have been observed to reject cases when there is a nonstranger witness-defendant relationship in anticipation of noncooperation even though lack of cooperation was not observed in these cases.[15]

The task of interviewing victims and/or witnesses in cases in which the accused is known to the subject presents a real challenge to the investigator. The interviewer must display much patience in these matters in order to elicit pertinent and essential information. The psychological fear factor, which causes the victim to feel that others will regard him as a "stool pigeon" if he discloses inormation about a crime to an authority figure, is a trait which is firmly ingrained in our society and is most difficult to overcome. Often, the only way to break through this barrier is by appealing to the victim's or witness's pride or sense of civic duty or responsibility.

Conversely, witnesses and victims may purposefully provide misleading or incorrect information about accused friends or associates in an attempt to harm or "get even" with accused wrongdoers. It's therefore imperative that the interviewing investigator swiftly ascertain the relationship between the victim and the accused; in addition, the investigator must always be cognizant of the possibility that misleading information, whether pro or con, may be given because of that relationship.

One investigative technique which is often utilized is that of interviewing other friends or associates of victims in an effort to determine prejudices or biases, especially if there are conflicting elements in the various accounts of the incident. One effective interviewing method is to confront victims and witnesses with contradictory information (in a non-interrogative manner, of course) and to ask polite but pointed questions about the nature of their relationships with accused persons and how such associations might influence their testimonies. The non-verbal reactions of subjects to questions of these types might reveal a great deal to the investigator about how much they can be trusted to tell the truth.

In homicides or other cases in which the victim is deceased or otherwise unable to communicate, the search for witnesses or other providers of information will usually begin with the victim's immediate family members, relatives, and close associates. If a suspect is unknown and little evidence exists that the offense was committed by a stranger, relatives, friends, and associates of the victim are usually able to steer the investigator toward possible suspects. Thus, composite interviews provide the investigator with a better chance of identifying suspects than a few scattered interviews are able to do.

When victims are hysterical, extremely frightened, or otherwise unable or unwilling to provide needed information to the police, their friends and associates can be called upon to calm them or offer advice. These friends and associates, who will not have been directly involved in the offense, will usually be more rational about the situation, and their participation in the interviewing process can be reassuring to the disoriented victim.

In a middle-class, law-abiding community, the cooperation of a suspect's friends and associates can usually be expected. The mere fact that the police are looking for a person is normally enough to ensure full and, at times, even enthusiastic cooperation from the public. However, the investigator may find that a suspect's friend may wish to cooperate but is hesitant because of a loyalty conflict. In cases where circumstances permit a promise of confidentiality or anonymity is usually enough to motivate the person to provide information about the suspect and his whereabouts. In addition, appealing to the friend's civic duty might prove successful; i.e., an approach like, "If this crime had happened to you, wouldn't you want someone to help the police to solve it?" may move the friend to cooperate.

Once a suspect has been identified, the police may contact his friends in an attempt to locate him. In an effort to ascertain who those friends and associates might be, several methods can be employed. Individuals close to the suspect might volunteer such information. A check of the suspect's local records (arrests, traffic accidents, miscellaneous reports) may mention companions. F.I. cards may show that he was contacted at certain times in the company of specific individuals, and was seen driving or riding in certain cars. Further, a check with his employer may reveal certain close connections among other employees. (In this regard, the police will usually experience excellent cooperation from security personnel or investigators in companies such as the telephone company, the gas company, the electric company, and certain major industrial firms and defense companies.) Regular police intelligence files can, of course, add much to this effort to determine the status of a suspect and the active and potential roles of his associates.

Victim Assistance

Many persons believe that a crime hasn't been solved simply because a suspect has been arrested and convicted. The effects of a criminal act on a victim can be lifelong; thus, recent emphasis has fallen on aiding the victim as well as locating and identifying the suspect.

There are many forms of assistance which police investigators routinely provide to victims. Most of these involve referring the victim to other appropriate agencies or units within the police department for problem resolution. For example, the police may convince a burglary victim to avail himself of the services of the department's crime prevention unit by having a full survey of the premises conducted, making needed corrections, and hopefully preventing future burglaries. Other types of problem assistance might include referral of a victim to a rape/sexual assault care center or to public or private agencies specifically designated to assist with monetary, legal, medical, or personal problems.

The need for proper referral of victims was made evident in a recent study conducted in New York City, where about 80% of the 234 victims interviewed admitted that they were not aware of the various governmental sources of assistance open to them. Further, over 85% of the surveyed victims stated that they would avail themselves of a centralized "Crime Victims Service Center" if such an organization existed.[16]

Within recent years, government agencies have shown renewed interest in awarding compensation to crime victims, particularly those who were subject to violent crimes involving personal injuries. Compensation for property loss due to theft or vandalism still lies, in the main, with private insurance claims or through civil court action.

A study of victim compensation programs in several state and foreign countries was recently conducted. During this study, it was found that nearly thirty jurisdictions had adopted criminal injury compensation programs.[17] Programs like these are usually established through legislation and administered by appointed boards. Applications are made by victims who have been injured, and decisions on awards are made based upon established criteria and standards (which differ from jurisdiction to jurisdiction). Therefore, it's essential that investigative personnel be familiar with local laws and procedures for making application for compensation, not only so that they can more properly advise victims, but also so that they can prepare their own crime reports more clearly and accurately with respect to that victim. Information contained in such reports may later be required by victim compensation boards when making deliberations on claims.

Because a rather high percentage of criminal injuries are victim-invited, victim-induced, or victim-precipitated, inquiry into the events leading up to an incident is extremely important. A clear difference exists between an altercation in a bar between persons who know each other and an assault in which an unsuspecting citizen is severely beaten by an unknown mugger who was lurking in the bushes. Victim compensation boards must analyze each case on its own merits, and the investigative information and reports form the basis for much of this decision-making, which usually occurs many months after the incident.

The concept of restitution by the offender to the victim, which has its roots in ancient Mosaic Law, is being viewed in contemporary times by many court and correctional officials as a very effective rehabilitative tool. Correctional restitution, with money or services coming from the offender's own resources, is felt to enhance the offender's contribution to the reformative and corrective goals of criminal law while at the same time compensating the victim, relieving the state of some of the burden of responsibility, and permitting the offender to pay his debt to society and the victim.[18]

The average citizen who becomes a victim has little knowledge of or experience with the criminal justice system and its processes. Thus, it's incumbent upon police personnel to be aware of current policies and practices of the local courts, probation departments, and correctional institutions concerning restitution programs and to transmit this information to appropriate victims. One common method by which police assist victims amounts to nothing more than maintaining a good working relationship with prosecution and corrections personnel, providing factual information about the offense to the victim, and perhaps even acting as a "broker" to bring the victim in contact with the appropriate person or agency who might be interested in suggesting an offender restitution plan to the court.

As Albert Morris points out, "The key to prevention is increased citizen awareness."[19] When a citizen becomes a victim of a criminal offense, it might be said that his "interest is captivated," and at that point he may be assumed to be receptive to advice about how to prevent recurring victimization. The citizen-victim might also develop anti-criminal justice attitudes if it's felt that his treatment by the authorities is nothing more than routine. Some progressive police departments have instituted a regular procedure by means of which investigators follow up personal contacts with victims, even if there's been little progress made toward case closure, to reassure the victim that neither he nor the incident has been forgotten. Such a procedure is meaningless, however, unless the follow-up contact information is truthful, case progress is explained, and a genuine concern is displayed by the officer. Of course, follow-up contact with victims might also provide additional information which recalcitrant victims had originally shielded, or helpful information which had simply been forgotten during initial contacts.

Hypnosis and Chemicals
as Investigative Tools

There are occasions when victims and/or witnesses sincerely want to provide information about offenses or suspects but simply can't remember. Frequently, victims will "block" from their memories unpleasant incidents, particularly if the offense was especially painful or embarrassing. Likewise, potential witnesses who may have been at the scene of a crime may have difficulty recalling specific details because of the passage of time or deficiencies in their own powers of observation. (A traditional role-playing exercise is used in many law schools during which a person rushes into the classroom, "shoots" the professor, and promptly dashes out the door. Students are then asked to describe the "assassin," and the responses tend to prove the point that people aren't really very observant during unexpected or dramatic incidents.)

It has been determined that a subconscious treasure-house of information may exist in the minds of victims and witnesses alike. This may include information which is not readily evident in the conscious memory patterns. The eye has often been described as being like the lens of a movie camera, transmitting images onto a never-ending "belt" which is fed into our "memory banks" for possible later retrieval. To gain access to a person's suppressed "memory bank," it's necessary to have the proper "access code" or "key." Some of the "keys" which have been used to secure repressed memories include the practice of hypnosis and chemical methods. These techniques must only be practiced on willing victims and witnesses and by professionally qualified people, however; in most cases, the investigator should secure a signed waiver from each subject ahead of time.

One factor which must be taken into consideration when an investigator is contemplating the use of hypnosis or truth-serum drugs is the very real probability that any information obtained while the subject is under induced unconsciousness will not be admissible in a court of law. The reliability of information obtained while a subject is in a hypnotic trance or under the influence of drugs is often open to question. Thus, the real value of such methods lies not with the evidence collecting they will enable, but with the possibility that they might be used to develop further investigative leads.

Truth serum drugs (such as sodium pentathol, sodium amytal, scopolamine, and the like) should be administered only by a physician; he should be physically present during all stages of the interview process and the recovery period. In addition, the setting should be that of a hospital or a well-equipped clinic should emergency medical complications develop.

Essentially, the rationale behind the use of truth serums is to reduce the subject's inhibitions. However,

> Some people are able to withhold information despite the administration of a "truth-serum." It is not unusual for material to come out with the third or fourth narcosis which the subject was able to bottle up very successfully the first and second times.[20]

One reason why hypnosis as a technique to elicit information has generally lacked credibility in the courts is because of the unknown factor of autosuggestion. Self-induced opinions by victims and witness often become part and parcel of their unconscious responses and thus may lack validity. One interesting recent case involved two Michigan nurses who were brought to trial on charges of homicide by poisoning. They had allegedly injected fatal doses of a muscle relaxant drug into the intravenous medication tubes of several patients at the Veteran's Administration Hospital at Ann Arbor.[21] One elderly patient did not die from the drug, and he was placed under hypnosis in an effort to determine any subconscious recollections of the incident which he might have. The famed hypnosis specialist, Dr. Martin Orne, was able to effectively argue before the court that although the patient did in fact identify one of the nurses as having been in his room just before he became unconscious, this declaration might have been influenced by the suggestions of the interrogators (in this case, FBI agents) and was probably based largely upon his own unconscious beliefs about the controversial case (which had received a great deal of publicity, and undoubtedly was a constant topic of conversation and speculation at the hospital where the deaths occurred—and where the patient-witness was in residence). As is the case with the use of chemical agents to probe the memories of victims and witnesses, a reputable physician or psychiatrist who specializes in hypnosis should always be employed to induce the hypnotic state and to be physically present during all stages of the process.

Summary

Police have traditionally focused on the suspect in criminal cases. In recent years, however, a greater interest in the victim has developed. We are now concerned with victim typology, the significance of the victim's background and the special relationships which often exist between the victim and the suspect prior to the crime.

Victimology—the study of victims and issues related to victims—has emerged as a specialty within criminology. While there has been no effort to minimize the importance of the role of the suspect in a criminal case, it has been recognized that it is also important to understand the roles of victims and witnesses in criminal cases.

Family, friendship, business or other personal ties frequently exist between the victim and the suspect prior to the crime. This is true more often in crimes against persons than in crimes against property. Such relationships are of interest not only to the theorist or the academician but also to the criminal investigator since these relationships can have a bearing on the accuracy of the crime report, may explain the motive for the crime, or may provide leads toward identifying the suspect. This may aid the police in understanding why crime reports may be totally correct, may represent what the victim perceived (whether accurate or not), may be exaggerated, or may be completely fabricated.

If the victim has a criminal or otherwise questionable background, this fact may sometimes serve to shed light on the total circumstances of the reported offense. In fact, the type of person a victim is, can be a factor in the jury's reactions to the case.

A victim is sometimes also a witness. This is particularly true in such crimes against the person as assault, robbery or rape. However, the victim is not often a witness to such crimes against property as theft, malicious mischief, or burglary. Just as a victim has a personal interest in the account of the crime, so does a witness other than the victim sometimes make statements which are influenced by his special relationship to the victim or the suspect. The best witness is a person who is not acquainted with either the victim or the suspect and who has no special loyalties to the parties in the case.

The investigator must learn to employ proper interviewing techniques. Whenever possible, all persons from whom the officer will obtain statements must be separated so that one can not overhear any of the others. This is important to insure the integrity of the statements. The officer should also ask questions in such a way that the witness (or the suspect or victim) can respond by giving his own reply. The investigator should, in other words, avoid asking the questions in such a way that the witness is lead into giving the answer the officer expects. The police should also, as far as possible, avoid subjecting a witness to repeated interviews. Whenever possible, arrangements should be made to allow the person to give only one full account of the events. No witness enjoys giving the same statement first to the patrol officer, then the sergeant, followed by interviews by a team of detectives.

Promising immunity from prosecution to a suspect or a witness should be done only after the officer carefully weighs all the advantages and disadvantages, only within policies of the police agency and the prosecutor, and only when the officer is certain that his promise will be honored.

In evaluating statements obtained from citizens, the officer should take into account their special interests or loyalties, their emotional state, and their ability to actually having seen or heard what they claim to have perceived.

Identifying a suspect in a criminal case is at times very easy, at other times nearly impossible. Suspects are identified and cases cleared more frequently in crimes against persons than in crimes against property. The officer should always attempt to obtain a physical description of the suspect as well as any other information which may aid in his identification and apprehension. Vehicle descriptions can be a valuable aid. The Identikit is used successfully by many police agencies to create a composite picture of the suspect. The suspect's modus operandi (the M.O.) can assist the police in determining the identity of the suspect, particularly if the M.O. is a unique one which only a limited number of suspects would utilize. The suspect's unusual features, tattoos, jewelry, etc. should be carefully noted.

Once the investigator has located or believes he has identified a suspect, the next step is to have the victim and/or witness provide an identification. This identification could be one of three types: (1) an "on the street" showing of the suspect to the victim and/or witness; (2) an identification through mug shots, or (3) a line up. In all three types, the investigator should be aware of and follow the legal standards that are required to insure reliability and accuracy of the identification.

Not all stolen property lends itself to ready identification by victim or police. Items with serial numbers are the easiest to keep on record and to identify. Other property has been made identifiable through "Operation Identification" in which the police will mark citizens' property with a special number, often the owner's driver's license number.

More and more states have now created agencies and programs designed to provide various forms of assistance to victims of crime, including financial assistance in serious, violent crimes. Since the public is generally not aware of the availability of such assistance, local police agencies can render a public service by referring victims to the proper governmental departments.

In cases where cooperative victims or witnesses are unable to remember certain events related to a crime, hypnosis and drugs have been used to assist the person in recollection. Such practices are contemplated only in rare cases of particularly serious offenses, and should be undertaken only by a physician with appropriate specialized training.

Questions and Topics for Discussion

1. Discuss some of the reasons why it is important for the investigator to focus on the victim as well as the suspect. How can this help the investigative process? How can the victim benefit?

2. Name and discuss the three major ways in which the victim's relationship to the suspect can affect the investigation.

3. If possible, invite a local police investigator to speak to your class about the importance of these "special relationships."

4. Why is it important that witnesses be interviewed separately and privately? And why should the investigator avoid asking "leading" questions?

5. Discuss the effects that you think these two different cases might have on the criminal justice system, and how you feel each might be handled:

   A. A man who has a prior conviction for "dealing" narcotics comes home from work one day and finds that his apartment has been burglarized. He reports this burglary to the police, and mentions that the suspect might very well be another "dealer."

   B. A woman who is a known prostitute is raped. She admits that her assailant was a former "client."

   Make sure to take into consideration the various aspects of each case. Do you think that either would be considered a "priority" case by the police or the prosecutor? Why or why not? You might want to set up a debate with your class centering on these two cases with discussion of the pros and cons of each. Should a victim's former record make any difference? Why or why not?

6. If possible, obtain an Identikit from your local police department and find out how it's used.

7. Name the three ways in which criminal cases are cleared. Discuss the different aspects of each way.

8. Why should the investigator be willing to set priorities? What are your feelings on this matter?

9. What are some requirements that the investigator should keep in mind when showing a series of "mug shots" to a witness or a victim?

10. Discuss the psychological fear factor and how it might influence the outcome of an investigation.

11. What forms of victim assistance are available in your area? Do some research on the programs which have been set up—if any—and report to the class on your findings.

12. Do some research in your local law library to find out about cases in which hypnosis or chemical methods have been used with witnesses or victims. Report your findings to the class.

Footnotes and References

1. Richard D. Knudten, *Crime in a Complex Society* (Homewood, Ill.: The Dorsey Press, 1970), pp. 79-80.

2. Stephen Schaefer, *Introduction to Criminology* (Reston, Va.: Reston Publishing Co., 1976), p. 156.

3. *Ibid.*, p. 143.

4. *Ibid.*, p. 156.

5. Carroll R. Hormachea, *Sourcebooks in Criminalistics* (Reston, Va.: Reston Publishing Co., 1974), p. 23.

6. Edwin M. Schur, *Crimes Without Victims* (Englewood Cliffs: Prentice-Hall, 1965).

7. Walter Van Dyke Bingham and Bruce Victor Moore, *How To Interview* (New York: Harper and Row, 1959), p. 196.

8. Raymond L. Gordon, *Interviewing: Strategy, Techniques, and Tactics* (Homewood, Ill.: The Dorsey Press, 1969), p. 214.

9. Peter B. Bloch and Donald R. Weidman, *Managing Criminal Investigations* (Washington, D.C.: U.S. Government Printing Office, 1975), p. 16.

10. Clarence M. Kelley, *Crime in the United States* (Washington, D.C.: U.S. Government Printing Office, 1975), p. 43.

11. Carroll R. Hormachea, 1974, p. 20.

12. Bloch and Weidman, 1975, p. 103.

13. National Crime Panel, *Crime Victimization in the United States* (Washington, D.C.: U.S. Government Printing Office, 1975), pp. 2-3.

14. Frank J. Cannavale, Jr. and William D. Falcon, *Improving Witness Cooperation* (Washington, D.C.: U.S. Government Printing Office, 1976), p. 6.

15. *Ibid.*

16. *Ibid.*, p. 30.

17. James Brooks, "How Well Are Criminal Injury Compensation Programs Performing?" *Crime and Delinquency*, Vol. 21, No. 1 (January 1975), pp. 50-56.

18. Stephen Schaefer, "The Proper Role of a Victim-Compensation System," *Crime and Delinquency*, Vol. 21, No. 1, (January 1975), pp. 45-49.

19. Albert Morris, "What About the Victims of Crime?" *Correctional Research*, No. 16 (November 1966). pp. 1-15.

20. Samuel R. Gerber and Oliver Schroeder, Jr., eds., *Criminal Investigation and Interrogation* (Cincinnati: W.H. Anderson Co., 1972), p. 333.

21. *The Detroit News*, January 28, 1977, page 5B.

Annotated Bibliography

Bloch, Peter B. and Weidman, Donald R. *Managing Criminal Investigations.* Washington, D.C.: U.S. Government Printing Office, 1975. Developing goals in investigation, criminal investigation management issues, decision making, and case studies of the investigative units of various police agencies.

Gordon, Raymond L. *Interviewing: Strategy, Techniques and Tactics.* Homewood, Ill.: The Dorsey Press, 1969. Perspectives, strategy, techniques, tactics and skills in interviewing. A broad approach to interviewing, not limited to criminal.

Knudten, Richard D. *Crime in a Complex Society.* Homewood, Ill. 1970. A very comprehensive criminology text dealing with criminological theories, crime data and trends, agencies of criminal justice. Includes a section on victimology.

O'Hara, Charles E. *Fundamentals of Criminal Investigation.* Springfield: Charles C. Thomas, 1973. A comprehensive text on criminal invetigation including steps and methods in investigation, specific offenses, court testimony, and criminalistics.

Schaefer, Stephen. *Introduction to Criminology.* Reston, Va.: Reston Publishing Co., 1976. A basic criminology text dealing with the more important theories, data, and criminal justice processes. Includes a section on victim relationships.

TWELVE

The Quality
of Investigations:
A Matter of Management

Chapter Objectives

After reading this chapter, the student should be able to:

☑ Explain the major factors which contribute to the maintenance of quality investigations.

☑ Outline the various organizational structures which are utilized in implementing the investigative process.

☑ Explain the importance of the preliminary and initial investigative processes in the successful termination of a case.

☑ Give case screening models for the ejection of cases which do not contain solvability factors.

☑ List the pros and cons of one-person and two-person investigative assignments.

☑ Give criteria for the selection of investigators and outline a program for training investigators.

☑ Outline a case management system for investigations.

☑ Identify an approach for quality control in the management of continuing investigations.

☑ Describe several suggestions for improving police-prosecutor relationships.

☑ Give criteria for evaluating the effectiveness of investigations.

Investigation and
the Need for Improvement

The criminal investigation process is a high-cost police function with low productivity. In 1966, the President's Commission on Law Enforcement and the Administration of Justice emphasized the problem when it noted that only about 25% of all crimes reported to the police were cleared, and "...if the suspect is neither known to the victim nor arrested at the scene of the crime the chances of ever arresting him are very slim."[1] The problem looks even worse when one realizes that the probability of arrest is only about 35%.

More than a decade later, the situation has not improved. In fact, there has been a substantial *increase* in the crime rate, particularly concerning crimes of violence and serious property offenses. That there has been no substantial improvement in the rate and quality of apprehensions and convictions suggests that it may be time to modify the investigative process. Improved management procedures are necessary if the quality of investigations is going to get better; it certainly cannot be allowed to get worse, and it's questionable as to whether maintaining the status quo is desirable.

The Importance of
Management to the Investigative Function

Management of criminal investigations involves two distinct but interrelated functions. The first has to do with the way a department is organized to perform the investigative function and to manage the personnel and units responsible for the function. The second deals with case management, which relates to the processes involved in the movement of cases investigated, beginning with the initial complaint or officer-initiated action and proceeding through the various stages until a case is closed, cleared, or no further action is deemed feasible. Management must also extend to include police involvement in court actions. The way in which a department is organized to perform and manage investigations is directly affected by the relationships between the uniformed patrol officers, detectives, and juvenile officers, in addition to the responsibilities of the records and criminalistics units and the management support units (such as personnel and planning). It also involves the responsibilities of departmental managers in policy-making and issuing directives necessary to the investigative function. Case management specifically has to do with the technical aspects of the investigative process and the impact upon the people who are involved. Or, in other words, case management has to do with the maintenance of control over what happens to each case from its inception until no further action can be taken. This involves careful review of reported actions during every phase of an investigation, in addition to ongoing evaluations of the steps which have been taken. This evaluation encompasses both the police investigators' actions as they relate to the impact upon the victim, the offender, and the witnesses, and the actions of the prosecutors and others who may be affected.

Clearly, the most effective way to ensure quality investigations is to have capable and well-qualified investigators and support personnel available during all aspects of the investigative process. The frequently held belief that detectives are the only members of a police department who investigate cases and who are qualified to do so is wrong. The more qualified field officers are, and the more involved they get in the investigative process, the better the chances are that cases will have successful conclusions. It's equally important, however, that other qualified personnel be on hand to process records, maintain evidence, control property, and keep track of crime laboratory processing of evidence to ensure that no weak links develop in the total process. Thus, the selection and training of new employees for all phases of police operations should be designed in such a way that only the best qualified personnel are admitted into the department.

Quality in-service training and planned investigative experiences are also essential to prepare officers to become thoroughly qualified investigators. Such training and experiences are necessary for non-officer personnel as well, since they are the ones who most often search the records, type the reports, and process and/or take custody of the evidence, and in some departments even monitor and audit the cases in order to maintain quality control.

The timeliness of investigations also has a great deal to do with their outcome. There is increasing evidence that the initial information given to the first officer responding to a criminal complaint and the investigative efforts which take place within the first few hours, either by the responding officer or by an investigator, are of overwhelming importance to the solving of a case.[2] If information which uniquely identifies the perpetrator is not available and presented at the time a crime is reported, the perpetrator, for the most part will not be subsequently identified.[3]

If the perpetrator is not initially identified, but information concerning his license number, physical description, and movements is known, or if he has stolen easily traceable property, then immediate investigative efforts may still pay off.

When no early solution to a case exists, follow-up efforts may be called for, but a careful determination must be made that such efforts will be productive. Considerable evidence shows that relatively few cases are solved by follow-up work, and that these are solved largely by the application of routine procedures. Thus, a department should establish a careful screening method by which only those cases which have a reasonable chance of being solved are designated for follow-up. At the same time, this screening method should provide for careful supervision of investigators and cases.

Departmental Organization: An Overview

There is no one best way to organize a department in order to maximize the effectiveness of the investigative process. However, there is increasing evidence that the more quickly evidence is received from a complainant and action is taken upon that information, the more likely it is that a successful solution to the case will be reached. This requires the full participation of uniformed field officers followed by immediate support from investigators. Follow-up investigative activity, if deemed necessary, may be assigned to the uniformed patrol officers, to investigators who will work closely with those officers, or to detectives who are based in a special criminal investigation division. Certain types of investigations, such as those which involve fraud, arson, vice, and narcotics, will usually be the exclusive responsibility of specialized units in the criminal investigation division.

If the patrol unit is given primary responsibility for both initial and follow-up investigations, the uniformed field officer will end up performing the majority of criminal investigative duties. Detectives can aid and assist the uniformed field officers by doing those tasks which the field officers cannot reasonably be expected to perform during their normal tours of duty, such as checking pawnshops, locating suspects, making modus operandi comparisons, and doing some records checks. Detectives should keep the field officers informed of their actions by providing them with copies of reports; in turn, detectives should receive copies of field officers' reports. Detectives will also do follow-up work on cases referred to them by policy decisions, such as major burglaries, certain robberies, homicides, and complicated rape cases. Likewise, detectives should usually have exclusive responsibility for cases such as arson, fraud, vice, and narcotics. Detectives may also be assigned to coordinating those cases which involve more than one field officer.

When the patrol officer has the primary responsibility for conducting an investigation, supervision of the investigative process becomes a duty of the field sergeants. They are called upon to continually evaluate the tasks performed by the field officers and also to evaluate the quality of case preparations. The sergeants may be assisted in performance of these supervisory functions by a report review clerk in the records unit or a review officer in the criminal investigation division. The sergeants must also maintain a balance between field officers' investigative efforts and the performance of other field responsibilities. The balanced workload is at least partially dependent upon periodic *beat surveys* which adjust beat boundaries to ensure reasonably equal workload responsibilities.

The normal case workload for field officers with full investigative responsibility requires that an officer respond to about three calls for service during each tour of duty and carry approximately seven to ten cases requiring follow-up work at any given time. This necessitates proper planning and scheduling; supervision is a key, of course, since all officers don't have the same capabilities.

Departments which have adopted a team policing model generally have assigned increased responsibility to the uniformed patrol officer for making initial investigations, but have generally retained follow-up responsibility for the criminal investigation division. However, a few departments have assigned generalist investigators to teams for the purpose of enhancing initial investigations. Other departments have reorganized their criminal investigation divisions in order to have a team of generalist investigators available to support each patrol team for the purpose of follow-up investigation of all cases except the more complex ones, which are referred to specialty details.

The team policing model emphasizes increased involvement of the uniformed field officers in the inititial investigative processes and generally provides for reasonably immediate involvement of generalist investigators as needed. Specialist investigators' efforts are limited to the more complex cases. The criminal investigation division assumes responsibility for monitoring cases, coordinating departmental efforts, analyzing crime patterns, tracking major offenders, and performing specializaed investigative functions.

The patrol command officer and/or team leaders may assign a sergeant or senior investigator as a staff person to serve as a liaison between teams and the central detective unit to facilitate the investigative processes between the two major departmental units, patrol and investigation. This person may also be assigned to review cases periodically for the purpose of suggesting improvements in the investigative process, particularly in the field operations.

The supervision of detective personnel operating from centralized units is at best a difficult task. In its publication, *Prescriptive Package: Managing Criminal Investigations,* the National Institute of Law Enforcement and Criminal Justice provides some insights into how several departments have approached the supervision of investigative personnel. Excerpts from that publication follow.

    1. *The detective mystique.* The nature of detective work sometimes makes it hard for a manager to find out what specific tasks have been done. Nevertheless, most departments contacted felt strongly that permitting the detective to give

ambiguous answers about his work was an abdication of management responsibility.

At a series of conferences held by the Police Foundation, the prevailing view among managers of detectives was that adequate supervision requires overcoming the "detective mystique," the attitude that detectives are uniquely talented individuals, superior to all other officers. It causes detectives to treat other police employees as inferiors and leads them to resent any attempt to monitor and direct their activities. This mystique is the cloak of mystery into which a detective sometimes withdraws when trying to account for his activities—as when a pleasant two-hour stint at a bar is described as "cultivating informants."

A variety of supervisory techniques can be used to pierce the detective mystique and provide constructive, supportive direction to detectives. For example, in Washington, D. C., detectives no longer have individual desks; squads share a table and maintain common files. Detectives are dispatched just like patrol personnel and may be reassigned to new tasks through the radio dispatcher.

In Fremont [California] and New York City, detectives are required to keep updated files on each case so that any detective may take over the case and any supervisor may easily determine its status. In the team experiment in Rochester, [New York], an individual detective may be assigned to a case but the files on that case are the team's files, and any officer may be placed on a particular aspect of the case. Detectives in DeKalb County [Georgia] are encouraged to help each other: performance evaluations are based on overall contribution to the department's activities as well as on performance on assigned cases.

The only city in the study which receives formal feedback from the prosecutor about individual performance is Washington, D. C., where reports of police errors are sent to an individual's commander. This report is the subject of a conference between the officer and his supervisor. The frequency of these reports is tabulated by unit.

Competent personnel need not be subject to detailed scrutiny of their every move. The more skilled and highly motivated the investigator, the less necessary and more wasteful such scrutiny would be. The core of an accountability system is that the supervisor be aware of the size and difficulty of the workload of each investigator and his success in responding to that challenge.

2. *Investigation in a team approach.* In Rochester and New York City, patrol commanders are responsible for the performance of detectives assigned to their commands. In Rochester, a lieutenant commands a team of about 45 sworn personnel, including about six detectives. In New York City, a captain or deputy inspector commands a precinct with 250 or 380 sworn personnel, including up to 25 or 30 detectives.

In Rochester's teams, the patrol and investigative personnel attend the same roll-call meeting, at which time they exchange information. Then the detectives may get together for a further exchange of information and a division of tasks on that tour. The patrol sergeant responsible for the shift often will attend both meetings; although he may be less likely to attend the detectives' meeting if the detective sergeant responsible for detective personnel is working that particular shift. One official reviews all preliminary reports and coordinates all investigations. It is obvious to the outside observer, even on brief exposure, that there is a spirit of cooperation between the patrol and detective personnel in these teams.

In New York City, the precinct investigative unit reviews the preliminary investigation reports filed by patrol personnel and develops a fair level of awareness of the capabilities of each officer. A single official—in one case, a detective lieutenant—reviews all cases in the precinct and coordinates all investigations. This somewhat closer level of association among detectives and patrol officers seems somewhat better than an entirely specialized and centralized system.

In Cincinnati, which has experimented with the assignment of investigative specialists to both teams and police districts, no final decision has been made as to which approach works better. Preliminary evidence indicates district-wide assignment has an advantage in processing follow-up cases but the team method produces a somewhat better record for the overall police operation (including patrol).[4]

The *Managing Criminal Investigations Manual*, prepared by the University Research Corporation for the Institute of Law Enforcement and Criminal Justice of the LEAA, presents the three common types of organizations found in police departments. Excerpts from that publication follow.

Agencies throughout the nation have different organizational structures for criminal investigation, with substantially different characteristics. Basically, however, there are three common types:

- Detective Specialist/Centralized Model

- Detective Specialist/Centralized and Decentralized Model

- Detective Specialist/Centralized and Detective Generalist/ Decentralized and Patrol Division (Team Policing) Model.

In addition, a few departments in the nation have a "generalist" model in which the primary responsibility for the investigation of crimes rests with the patrol officer. In these agencies, detectives, if there are any, function essentially as consultants and advisors to the uniformed officer.

The police agency in Fremont, California, employs such a model. The responsibility for investigation of crime is assigned as follows:

The investigation of crime is considered to be an essential police function for which each officer in the department is responsible ... To a great extent, the investigation section serves the field officers. Much of the investigative load is handled by patrol officers. An investigator is called to assist a patrol officer on a case only if a Patrol Section supervisor or Operations Officer determines the need for one according to the following criteria:

- Special knowledge or expertise of the investigator that would materially enhance the investigation.

- If a suspect is known but not in custody, and there is need for an immediate follow-up and apprehension.

- The nature of the investigation precludes sector officers from completing it, due to unusual constraints, e.g., investigation out of the city, need to respond to other calls for service, etc.

- A suspect is known and in custody and is providing information that would be valuable in clearing other serious offenses.

- Other unusual situations as approved by Operations Officers, the Investigative Commander, Division Commander, or Chief or Police.[5]

This model is generally most useful in smaller cities where the size of the agency and the crime problems do not warrant investments in specialized units.

[Figure 12-1] shows the most prevalent organizational arrangement for investigating reported crimes. In this model, responsibility for investigating crime is assigned to the specialized Criminal Investigative Division. Members of the Patrol Division play a perfunctory and minimal role of collecting basic information when they respond to the scene of a crime.

While there are a number of advantages to having a specialized detective division, there are an equal number of disadvantages. Both sides of the issue can be briefly outlined as follows

Advantages

- Definite, fixed investigative responsibility

- Enhanced development of higher skill levels

- Facilitation of training in latest investigative technologies

- Development of higher morals and pride in accomplishment

- Stronger sense of identification with goal and investigative performance levels

- Development of public interest and support

- More time for uniformed officers to patrol their areas.

Disadvantages

- Internal communication of information is stymied and ineffective

- Negative impact on the morale of the uniformed officer

- Timely response and, thus, the effectiveness of investigation suffers

- Increase in administrative and clerical work loads

- Negative impact on public relations because of time delays in the investigation. [Task Force Findings, Multnomah County, Oregon Sheriff's Office.]

While this listing can be expanded upon in support of either position, it is sufficient to make the point that the plusses and minuses should be weighed and considered.

Figure 12-1.

**Typical Organizational Structure
Detective Specialist/Centralized Model**

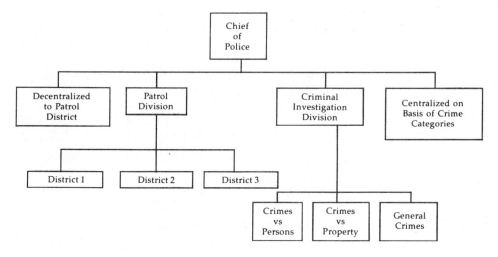

Since the ultimate measure of effectiveness is whether the organization is producing the desired results and outcomes, the assessment of current levels of performance must be directed toward evaluating that end. Whatever the outcome of the final determination, there is a need to critically challenge the worth of the existing arrangement in each police agency. Even if the determination is that the existing organization is efficient, effective, and productive, the police administrator will at least feel more comfortable as a result of the reaffirmation of prior judgments. On the other hand, he may find that there are better ways to maximize the results of the criminal investigation effort.

In many agencies, where that hard critical assessment has been made, changes have, in fact, been made and experimentation with different organizational models has begun. [See Figure 12-2.] In these agencies, at least, there was dissatisfaction with performance and productivity levels in the criminal investigation system.

One variation of the traditional model features a decentralization of some investigators to the district or precinct level. Essentially, however, this model retains the same basic characteristics of the purely centralized model, that is, the assignment of investigative responsibility remains in the Criminal Investigation Division, there is a distinct organizational reporting relationship to the chief, specialized crime units by category remain at the centralized level, and the uniformed officer's role is both perfunctory and minimal.

Figure 12-2.

Typical Organizational Structure:
Detective Specialist/Centralized and Decentralized Model

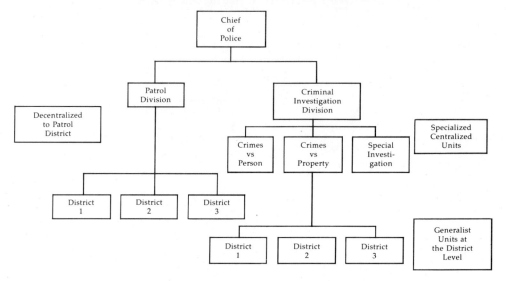

The placement of some portion of the criminal investigators at the decentralized level (or "street" level) appears to be designed to accomplish several benefits. They are:

- Assigning the investigators closer to the community they serve

- Fostering a better communication with patrol officers

- Making possible a more timely response to reported crimes

- Facilitating the cultivation of sources of information

- Increasing the generalist's knowedge about generalist criminals in the particular community.

Still another modification to the traditional organization is the Team Policing Model. [See Figure 12-3.]

This model features a specialized centralized detective unit with the decentralized generalist investigator assigned to the Patrol Division Commander. In this arrangement [the] uniformed officer and investigator work together in a "team" which is assigned to a particular community or segment of the jurisdiction to be policed. In essence, this represents a partial return to the generalist model mentioned earlier.

The operations of the "team" policing unit has been found to promote, among other benefits, a good relationship between uniformed and investigative officers, a more rapid response by the investigator to the scene of a crime and the development of community identification with "its" police.

Figure 12-3.

**Typical Organizational Structure:
Detective Specialist/Centralized Detective Generalist
Decentralized and Patrol Division (Team Policing Model)**

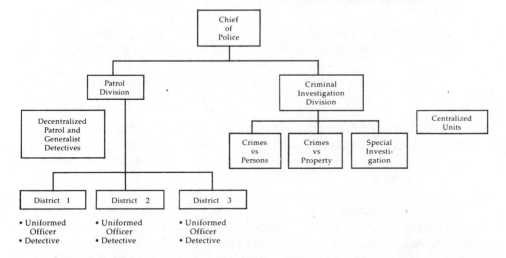

Many departments throughout the country have adopted this model or have begun experimenting with a team policing concept. One of those agencies is in Rochester, New York.

In early 1971, the Rochester Police Department began experimenting with a Coordinated Team Patrol (CTP) to determine whether improved activities in investigation and apprehension could be affected. Over the period of the experiment, evaluations and adjustments were made. The results of assigning teams of patrol officers and investigators to work together in fixed geographical areas (sectors) were as follows:

- Teams made arrests in a higher percentages of burglary, robbery and larceny cases than did nonteam personnel in other sectors.

- Teams cleared a higher percentage of burglaries, robberies and larcenies than did nonteam personnel.

- Teams made on-scene arrests in robbery and larceny cases more often. However, there was no apparent difference in burglary cases.

- Teams on-scene arrests for burglary, larceny and robbery were less likely to result in prosecutions than those made by nonteam personnel.

- No significant differences were found in the quantity of information contained in the preliminary investigation reports of team and nonteam personnel.

- Burglary and robbery arrests resulting from follow-up investigations were made in a larger percentage of cases by team personnel than by nonteam personnel.

- Prosecutions resulting from follow-up investigations did not vary between team and nonteam cases.

- Both team and nonteam personnel felt that the CTP method was more effective in dealing with crime.

- Both team and nonteam personnel felt that the CTP model helped to improve the relationship between patrol and detective personnel.

- Team patrol officers reported a much higher level of cooperation with team investigators than with nonteam investigators.

While these results may not necessarily be typical, the outcomes produced by the criminal investigation process were improved upon in that city by altering the organizational structure and changing the allocation mix of investigative resources.

In 1975 the Multnomah County Sheriff's Office in Oregon undertook the "difficult process" of self-analysis which included a critical review of the way in which crimes were being investigated by that agency. There was not only dissatisfaction with the performance results obtained by the traditional organizational approach, but also a growing concern that the potential of the better educated personnel in the agency was not being fully maximized. Job satisfaction and enrichment for the uniformed officer were real concerns.

Their self-analysis led to substantial organizational changes which emphasize the generalist investigator approach. An interesting and informative overview of the self-analysis process was detailed in a concise publication entitled *The Generalist Investigator: A New Role for the Patrol Officer Under Neighborhood Team Policing.*[6]

Multnomah County's analysis is representative of many signs that a growing number of police agencies are challenging the effectiveness of their current approach to criminal investigations. While there may not be a single best way to improve the process, the encouraging factor is that agencies are actively seeking the best ways for their agencies to conduct investigations.

In summary, almost all police administrators believe there is a need for establishing a specialized investigative capability. However, there is a growing concern about how large that commitment should be. The value of returning investigators to perform more generalist duties and assigning some percentage to a decentralized model are being increasingly considered and, then, adopted.

It would apear that the current trend points toward a decentralized component which relates more directly, and promptly, to the local communities in the jurisdiction served.[7]

Special Considerations for Police Management

The Question of Specialization

As has been indicated, the trend is toward the generalist investigator approach for investigations with a simultaneous reduction in the number of specialists. This appears to have come about due to a recognition that, for the bulk of crimes investigated, criminals themselves have not "specialized." In addition, most crimes reported to the police require only routine investigative efforts most effectively undertaken during the initial period of investigation rather than in the development of new leads. And, finally, there is an increasing number of young, well-educated personnel choosing law enforcement careers who are capable of understanding and dealing with a wide variety of cases. However, there will always be the need for some specialization in the larger departments and, to a lesser degree, in smaller departments as well.

The principal reasons for specialization are as follows:

- There are several classes of crimes which do not lend themselves to investigation by generalists. These include such offenses as fraud, narcotics, vice, arson, confidence games, child beating, and organized crime.

- Major crimes such as safe burglaries, fine art thefts, some homicides, some robberies, valuable gem burglaries, some rapes, and kidnappings often are of a complex nature requiring special skills and experiences which the average generalist investigator simply doesn't have.

- The volume of cases in a particular crime class may be such that specialized investigators will become more proficient in working on a specific type of offense within the class; i.e., burglaries may be divided into residential and commercial, with separate units being responsible for each.

- Crime analysis by use of computers to "interrogate" data banks requires a staff of computer operator specialists who do not need to be peace officers. They may be supervised by a peace officer, however, and the data used for analytical purposes can be developed by both peace officers and computer operator personnel. In addition, non-peace officer analysts may screen cases for follow-up work by use of a case scaling checklist methodology instead of depending on each investigator to analyze all cases for which follow-up work may be effective.[8]

The more common practice is to have three major organizational units within a criminal investigation division, based upon specialization for crimes against persons, crimes against property, and special investigations. Specialty details may be organized within each unit. The larger the department, the more specialization there is to be found.

Within a crimes against property unit, for example, principal sub-units or details will usually be based on classes of offenses including burglary, larceny or theft, auto theft, and checks. Sub-units may be organized under burglary to include residential, commercial, and safe-cracking details. Under larceny or theft, fine art theft, shoplifting, petty theft, and grand larceny details may be formed. A breakdown in an auto theft unit may include an auto theft ring detail.

The crimes against persons unit may include homicide, sex offenses, and robbery details. Further sub-units may formed, such as a bank robbery detail, a rape detail, and a sex offenses against children detail.

The special investigations unit usually includes sub-units specializing in narcotics and vice investigations, intelligence, and organized crime.

There are some classes of crimes which peculiarly affect juveniles, and these are usually assigned to the departmental juvenile unit. These include offenses related to family relations cases, such as child beating, unfit homes, and lost children. School vandalism cases may also be assigned to the juvenile unit, along with bicycle thefts in some jurisdictions.

One-Person Assignments vs. Two-Person Teams

Controversy continues over whether a department should have one-person assignments for detective operations or two-person teams. The general rationale for two-person teams revolves around the corroboration of facts and data gathered, the protection of the detectives from false allegations from victims or suspects as to their demeanor during investigations, and their personal safety in making arrests or conducting touchy investigations. The renowned author, educator, and police administrator, O.W. Wilson, has been for the past four decades the principal proponent for the one-person assignment. He first makes a strong case for the one-person patrol car operation, saying that it results in officers giving their full attention to their police duties, which reduces officer delinquencies and makes for greater officer safety because two officers together tend to visit more, are more often tempted to violate rules and neglect routine duties. Also, an officer patrolling alone is often safer than a team of officers. One-person patrol is also more efficient than two-person because the number of patrol units in the field is thereby doubled and a city an be divided into twice as many patrol areas. In addition, the frequency of patrol is increased, as is the number of back-up patrol units which will be available to assist an officer. Wilson asserts that all of these same reasons apply with equal force to one-person detective operations. He further states that most investigations may be conducted more effectively by one person, and that the economy of a one-person assignment over a two-person one is apparent.[9]

However strong the case may be for one-person assignments, there will always be dangerous investigations and arrests where assistance from another detective or a patrol officer will be needed. Also, situations often arise in which an investigator may need technical assistance from another detective, an identification technician, or a criminalist.

Investigating Juvenile Crimes

The primary investigators assigned to follow-up duties should usually investigate to conclusion all crimes in the classes of offenses assigned to them, even though juveniles may be involved in some cases as either victims or perpetrators. The reasons for this are as follows:

- The offender's age is seldom known prior to arrest and cannot be determined until an investigation is undertaken.

- To assume a perpetrator's age before the identity is known often results in controversy and friction, as the follow-up investigator may initiate a reclassification of an offense as juvenile in order to avoid work or the embarrassment of a low percentage clearance rate.

- Divided responsibility is undesirable; thus, cases in one class should be assigned to one division or unit.

- There are cases which peculiarly involve juveniles; thus, some classes of cases may be assigned to a juvenile unit for follow-up investigations. Such classes include school vandalism, child beating, and missing children cases, which may be logically assigned to the juvenile unit.

- The detective division has as its primary purpose the investigation and clearance by arrest of assigned classes of cases, and its members are usually best qualified to investigate them.

- Accountability for case investigations and clearances is achieved when there is clear-cut assignment of responsibility to one division or unit of specified classes of cases. Individual investigators can be evaluated on the basis of their accomplishments when there is no division of responsibility.[10]

The juvenile unit should have exclusive responsibility for the disposition of juvenile offenders, and juvenile investigators should participate in interrogations. This requires juvenile investigators to make social background investigations in sufficient depth to ascertain facts and personal information about the juveniles in order to make proper dispositions. Departmental policy might also require that a juvenile investigator participate in the interrogation of all juvenile offenders, since there is often a very different psychological relationship between investigators and juveniles.[11]

Strike/Task Forces

Investigative strike/task forces are specialized units consisting of investigative personnel assigned to concentrate their efforts on selected offenses. They can be relatively productive, particularly against burglaries and fencing offenses. They have a significant potential for increasing arrest rates for targeted offenses, but efforts must be concentrated and carefully circumscribed to prevent them from diverting their efforts to other activities.

A strike/task force is a unique police operation which requires personnel who are both motivated and innovative. To gain in their use becomes illusory, however, when the mere quantity of arrests is emphasized, for then their efforts tend to be diverted to arrests that are not the results of their own unique capabilities.

Use of strike/task force units must be based upon careful procedural and legal planning to protect the involved officers and to ensure that the offenders they identify may be successfully prosecuted. In addition, the unit's activities must be closely monitored by senior officers to minimize over-aggressiveness which may infringe upon individual privacy.

Strike/task forces should be limited in their operations, and when the objectives for which they have been organized have been achieved, they should be disbanded. This will reduce the possibility of their diverting their efforts and perpetuating the performance of tasks which are normally the responsibilities of other ongoing units.[12]

Selecting Investigators

In most departments, investigators occupy a unique position and have unique job titles, often with civil service status. Job titles include senior officer, agent, investigator, and detective, the latter being the most common. Some few departments, usually in the San Francisco Bay Area, use the title of inspector instead of detective. The Rand survey indicated that, in the average department, 14.5% of all peace officer personnel are designated as investigators.[13]

The Rand survey also found that the officers selected for investigators usually have spent from three to five years on patrol assignment. In departments which have no civil service positions defined according to specific criteria, the more aggressive patrol officers are usually selected for investigative assignments, presumably because they make a larger number of arrests than other officers do and have the "appropriate" type of initiative and insight to make good investigators. Even when established civil service criteria exist, the more aggressive officers tend to be selected for investigative positions.

For the most part, the selection of investigators is based upon a subjective evaluation of whatever criteria are used, since little is really known about what makes a good investigator. Investigators have traditionally been rather silent about of their activities, creating a mystique about them which has not been subjected to objective study and research. What is known about the selection processes revolves around personal and professional attributes which are believed to reflect the needs of the job. The attributes most commonly evaluated include the *cognitive*, the *psychomotor*, and the *affective*.

The cognitive attributes have to do with perception, judgment, and memory. In addition to having the unusual endowments associated with these cognitive abilities, the "ideal" investigator is also assumed to be more vigorous than others and to have an exceptional fund of psychic and physical energy. Thus, the officer who demonstrates in his activities as a patrol field officer the ability to solve cases, to make arrests resulting in prosecutions, and to testify effectively in court—and who appears to be continually aware of and "on top of" what's going on the field—is the one who is most likely to be selected as an investigator. In addition, the officer who demonstrates considerable vigor and energy and who appears to be able to pursue leads in investigations based on intuition and psychic insights will also be favored.

The psychomotor attributes have to do with the relationships of muscular activity to mental processes; in other words, the coordination of thoughts and actions. It's generally believed that the better coordinated a person is in mind and body, the more capable he will be of carrying out the tasks of an investigator particularly under stress or during lengthy investigations when it might not be possible to get very much sleep.

Affective attributes have to do with feelings and emotions. Many investigations are undertaken in stress situations involving interactions with victims, offenders, or witnesses who may be hurt or emotionally upset. This requires the investigator to remain calm and collected in order to be objective in gathering facts, data, and evidence; it also often requires the investigator to calm the upset individuals and aid them in returning to reasonable, normal behavior. In addition, the investigator is often confronted with gruesome crime scenes, such as homicides involving decomposed bodies; these can be quite upsetting. Thus, the officer who has demonstrated emotional stability and the ability to remain calm under trying circumstances is favored during the selection process.

Whether formalized by written and oral examinations or set up in a noncompetitive way, the selection process will usually take into consideration an officer's knowledge of criminal law, investigative procedures, the corpus delicti of specific types of crimes, in addition to an awareness of and respect for departmental policies and procedures. Lack of a reasonable amount of demonstrated knowledge in any one of these areas may disqualify an officer from consideration for an investigator position. However, demonstrated knowledge in these areas, which may be tested, is in and of itself an insufficient basis for the selection.

Training Investigators

Training for new investigators is relatively limited and is usually conducted on-the-job. Recruit training programs include some investigative training to help officers in their patrol work, but there are few special classes for officers who have been recently assigned to investigative positions. Only a small number of departments offer continuing training for officers in investigative assignments. Thus, most officers assigned to investigative positions learn by doing and by working with other experienced investigators. However, this doesn't mean that formal training for investigators isn't needed, isn't available, and can't be developed.

A few larger departments have developed courses for newly appointed investigators. Such courses include a variety of subjects and focus on investigative techniques which are applicable to specific classes of crimes. An increasing number of departments are introducing annual and semi-annual in-service courses which emphasize investigative techniques for all first-line personnel. In addition, State Commissions on Peace Officer Standards and Training are prescribing periodic in-service training courses for all first-line personnel.

The FBI offers a variety of courses on investigative techniques to individual departments or to several agencies on a zone-school basis. These courses may be general in nature, or they may be highly technical, depending on the clientele.

Specialized training for juvenile officers, narcotics and vice investigators, intelligence investigators, and other specialists is available from a number of sources. For example, the Delinquency Control Institute at the University of Southern California in Los Angeles has, since 1946, provided training for juvenile officers. The Drug Enforcement Administration of the U.S. Department of Justice has developed special courses for narcotics investigators. In addition, a number of private and public institutions have instituted training courses for polygraph operators.

In the final analysis, each department must determine its own training requirements for its own investigators. Departmental personnel can then either develop their own courses or select from the many which are available throughout the United States.

Effective Case Management

Quality case preparations result from effective management of the processes involved in the movement of case investigations from the initial complaint or officer-initiated action through the various stages until a case is closed, cleared, or no further action is feasible. This includes, of course, police involvement in court actions. This section presents in brief a management system for case preparations which maximizes investigative efforts for all cases.

All criminal cases should be as thoroughly investigated as evidence and circumstances permit from a practical standpoint. Thus, cases for which only limited or no evidence is available at the initial stage do not merit further action. Cases in which sufficient evidence and leads are available during the initial investigation should be pursued to a successful conclusion, including arrest and prosecution, or to whatever stage at which it's determined that further action will be neither feasible nor productive.

Case Screening

Case screening is a mechanism that will facilitate making a decision concerning the continuation of an investigation. It is based upon the existence of solvability factors determined during the initial investigation or developed during follow-up. Solvability factors are those elements of information which relate to a crime and have in the past proved to be important in determining the likelihood of solving that type of crime. The purpose of case screening is to determine at the earliest possible stage in the investigative process whether it's desirable to continue to devote investigative resources to the process.[14]

Development of a system for case management which utilizes a decision-making model for the screening of cases enhances the investigative process in a number of ways. Such a system includes but is not limited to the following:

1. Screening cases during the preliminary investigation leads to:

   • Prompt action to effect apprehension of the offender;

   • Prompt on-scene investigation which enhances successful closure of a case during follow-up investigation; and

   • Prompt ejection from the investigative process of unpromising cases.

2. Screening of cases during the follow-up investigation provides for ejection of unpromising cases after a specified period (approximately ten days, except in extreme circumstances).

3. Cases subjected to intensive follow-up beyond steps 1 and 2 above may be subjected to intensive periodic review and ejected when it is apparent that no useful purpose can be served by continuing the investigation except in extreme circumstances.

The idea of case screening is not a new one, but formalization of the process is now considered essential for effective management of criminal investigations. This formalization takes the decision-making authority for the investigation of reported crimes out of the hands of individual officers, principally detectives, and places it in the hands of management, where it belongs. The decisions relative to the continuation of investigations are made based upon established policies and procedures rather than the experience and intuition of the individual officer. The system can also reduce the amount of time invested in cases, reduce the number of cases referred to detectives, and improve the quality of preliminary investigations by patrol officers because their efforts in the investigative process are given more recognition.[15]

In the *Managing Criminal Investigations Manual,* two major approaches to case screening criteria are presented. Excerpts follow.

Development of a Case Screening Model. There are two major approaches to case screening criteria.

The first approach involves the development of a listing of unweighted criteria for the screening of cases, and the second establishes a listing of weighted criteria. Both of these methods work best when a task force, representative of personnel who will eventually utilize the case screening criteria and who have a real input into the design of the program, is created to establish the criteria. The task force should include managers as well as investigative line personnel. The acceptance of another agency's system without internal review by the staff who will be expected to carry it out is likely to lead to strong resistance within the organization and may lead to the development of a system which is not responsive to the needs of the particular agency.

Unweighted Case Screening Approach. Inherent in the "unweighted screening" approach are two basic methods for establishing the criteria. They can be established by a unilateral determination by a police executive or by the task force of experienced investigative personnel without the benefit of an in-depth statistical analysis of how cases have been solved in the past.

The Rochester Unweighted Case Screening Approach.—In Rochester, New York, a departmental task force designed and field-tested a case screening system using experimental solvability factors. After considerable testing, the department became convinced that the most productive initial investigation by the uniformed officer involved a search for solvability factors and a decision as to whether early closure was appropriate.

Consequently, patrol officers were reoriented from viewing the initial investigation as an exercise in miscellaneous data collection to viewing it as an integral part of the investigative process. A review of the patrol officer's decision is conducted by a supervisor before the decision on closure is finalized.

In order to respond to special and community demands for a follow-through investigation, the supervisor who reviews the early closure recommendation is accorded some flexibility to continue an investigation, even if the solvability factors suggest that it should be closed.

The new form developed by Rochester asked the field officer to answer the following solvability questions:

1. Was there a witness to the crime?

2. Can a suspect be named?

3. Can a suspect be located?

4. Can a suspect be described?

5. Can a suspect be identified?

6. Can the suspect vehicle be identified?

7. Is the stolen property traceable?

8. Is there a significant M.O. present?

9. Is there significant physical evidence present?

10. Has an evidence technician been called? Is the evidence technician's report positive?

11. Is there a significant reason to believe that the crime may be solved with a reasonable amount of investigative effort?

12. Was there a definite limited opportunity for anyone except the suspect to commit the crime?

The Case Analysis Approach.—Other departments throughout the country have developed similar programs to use solvability factors in determining the outcome of initial investigations. They have derived case screening rules, in part, from an analysis of cases which have been successfully solved. In effect, the agencies have learned from their successes and failures.

These agencies have also established representative task forces consisting of patrol and detective personnel to evaluate the results of successful case investigations to design a case screening plan which incorporates those informative items which have led to successful case outcomes.

To select cases with the highest probability of solution, the factors which most often lead to a successful investigation are isolated so that they may be incorporated into the screening procedure. A named suspect has proven to be the strongest solvability factor.

To determine whether a case should be continued as an active investigation, the answers to the following questions are often critical:

1. Can complainant or witness identify the offender?

2. Is the offender known to the complainant or witness?

3. Does the complainant or witness know where the offender is located?

4. Is there physical evidence at the scene which would aid in the solution of the case (fingerprints, other physical evidence)?

5. Is the complainant or witness willing to view photographs to aid in identifying the offender?

6. Can the complainant or witness provide a meaningful description of the offender (home address, auto driven, scars or other distinctive features)?

7. If the offender is apprehended, is the complainant willing to press the complaint in court?

In order to evaluate whether the case should be further investigated, the initial investigation should provide information concerning the following so that supervisory review is more meaningful and on target.

1. Estimate of the reaction of the community to the crime, based on the opinion of the reporting officer.

2. Does the crime involve a sensitive or unusual place or person (church, temple, school; child, cripple or mental defective, etc.)?

3. Is there a pattern of such crimes in the area which point to a single individual or gang operating in the area?

4. Does the number of similar type crimes in area raise questions concerning the department's image as to performance and efficiency?

The process should require that cases identified as not solvable because insufficient success criteria exist, be closed as soon as possible.

Weighted Case-Screening Approach—The weighted case-screening methodologies vary from the nonstatistically derived system of Multnomah County, Oregon, to the statistically derived system of Oakland, California.

Multnomah County, Oregon. The department's team-policing task force attempted to list types of cases in their order of priority.[16] This step was believed to be a critical part of the department's "despecialization program." The system that resulted is viewed as flexible enough for field officers to be able to establish case priorities after conducting preliminary investigations. In this approach to establishing investigative priorities, officers consider the seriousness of the crime, the amount of readily available information about suspects, the availability of Agency resources, and community attitudes. The officers consider four major aspects of the crime and rate its priority numerically. [See figure 12-4.]

Oakland, California. In 1975, the Stanford Research Institute (SRI) developed a case follow-up decision model for the Oakland Police Department (OPD). This *"Felony Investigation Decision Model"* study by B. Greenberg, et al., grew out of a 1973 SRI study in Alameda County, California, "Enhancement of the Investigative Function." In the first study, the authors developed a checklist of activities to guide patrol officers and detectives in the investigation of burglary cases. A case follow-up decision model was statistically derived through an examination of past cases. A set of weighted variables emerged that predicted case outcome with a high degree of certainty. [Figure 12-5] shows the burglary case disposition decision rule which was developed.[17]

The 1975 study, also conducted in Oakland, California, resulted in the development of a robbery decision model that could be used to identify cases that had sufficient probability of clearance to warrant follow-up investigation. The SRI research team sought to minimize the police investigator's intuitive judgment on case handling by statistically analyzing factors that have significantly contributed in the past to case clearance. The study results suggested that "unless offender identification was made by the responding officer, case solution at the detective level was minimal." [Figure 12-6] shows the dominate case-solution factors related to the victim's knowledge of the offender.[18]

Figure 12-4.

Priority Rating Factors
in Multnomah County

A. **Gravity of Offense**
   a. Felony = 4 points
   b. Misdemeanor = 3 points
   c. Victimless crime = 2 points
   d. Violations/status offense = 1 point

B. **Probability of Solution**
   Whether there are:
   a. Suspects
   b. Witnesses
   c. Physical evidence
   d. Undeveloped leads

   (Score one point for each factor present.)

C. **Urgency for Action**
   a. Danger to others = 4 points
   b. Immediate action required = 3 points
   c. Impact on victim = 2 points
   d. Pattern/frequency of crime = 1 point

D. **Supervisory Judgment**
   a. Department policy
   b. Totality of circumstances
   c. Investigator's caseload

   (Total possible: 4 points.)

Scoring and Application of Priority System:

Priority	Points	Report Investigative Process Within:
A	16-22	1-5 days
B	10-16	15 days
C	4-10	30 days
D	Less than 4	Suspended (form letter to victim)

An analysis of the two decision models shows that there is a similarity between variables and their relative weights in contributing to case clearance. In both models, a witness or victim provides the most useful information leading to case clearance. One difference which should be noted

Figure 12-5.
Burglary Case Disposition
Decision Rule

Information Element	Weighting Factor
Estimated time lapse between crime and the initial investigation:	
Less than 1 hour	5
1 to 12 hours	1
12 to 24 hours	0.3
More than 24 hours	0
Witness's report of offense	7
On-view report of offense	1
Usable fingerprints	7
Suspect information developed— description or name	9
Vehicle description	0.1
Other	0

TOTAL SCORE:

INSTRUCTIONS

(1) Circle the weighting factor for each information element that is present in the incident report.

(2) Add the circled factors.

(3) If the sum is less than or equal to 10, suspend the case; otherwise, follow up the case.

between the two models is the dominance of vehicle information in the robbery decision model as the next-most-important information element.

It appears clear, regardless of the method used, that there are certain critical pieces of information needed if a case is to be solved through investigative activities. The practical experience of police agencies and efforts by researchers suggest that the following items of information appear to be vital to successful conclusion of an investigation:

1. Witness to the crime
2. Suspect named
   Suspect known
4. Suspect described
5. Suspect identified
6. Suspect previously seen
7. Vehicle identified
8. Traceable property

9. Significant MO

10. Limited opportunity for anyone other than the suspect to have committed the crime

11. Significant evidence

12. Lapse of time between crime and initial investigation less than one hour

Figure 12-6.
Robbery Investigation Decision Model

Information Element	Weighting Factor
Suspect named	10*
Suspect known	10*
Suspect previously seen	10*
Evidence technician used	10
Places suspect frequented named	10*
Physical evidence	
Each item matched	6.1
Vehicle registration	
Query information available	1.5
Vehicle stolen	3.0
Useful information returned	4.5
Vehicle registered to suspect	6.0
Offender movement description	
On foot	0
Vehicle (not car)	0.6
Car	1.2
Car color given	1.8
Car description given	2.4
Car license given	3.0
Weapon used	1.6

INSTRUCTIONS

(1) Circle the weighting factor for each information element that is present in the incident report.

(2) Add the circled factors.

(3) If the sum is less than 10, suspend the case; otherwise, follow up the case.

(4) Weighting factors do not accumulate; i.e., if both the auto license and color are given, the total is 3.0, not 4.8.

---

*These values as calculated actually exceed the threshold of 10. The values provided here are conceptually simpler and make no difference in the classification of groups.

The Application of a Case-Screening System. In summary, the components of a case-screening system are:

a. Accurate and complete collection of crime information by the patrol officer.

b. An on-scene determination of the sufficiency of crime information collected.

c. Permitting the patrol officer to make decisions concerning follow-up investigation.

d. Review of that decision by a supervisor.

Putting these componenets into effect will require an agency to:

a. Redefine the mission of the major divisions.

b. Redefine roles for patrol officers, supervisors, investigators, and managers in the case screening process.

c. Develop and use crime collection forms that incorporate early closure information; and

d. Provide training in the use of the new system to all affected personnel.

The incorporation of case-screening creates the need to develop a monitoring or management information system which will provide to police administrators sufficient feedback on the system's effectiveness.[19]

Managing Continuing Investigations for Quality Control

A principal responsibility of a department's criminal investigation division is the continuation or follow-up after the preliminary or initial investigation of reported crimes has been completed by the uniformed field officers and investigators assigned to the patrol division. The number and categories of crimes referred will depend upon departmental policies governing the case screening process. A model management system is presented in the *Managing Criminal Investigations Manual;* excerpts from that source follow.

Police administrators have increasingly recognized the necessity for establishing a management system for the continuing investigation process. In 1973, the National Advisory Commission on Criminal Justice Standards and Goals recommended that:

"Every policy agency should establish quality control procedures to insure that every reported crime receives the investigation it warrants. These procedures should include:

a. A follow-up report of each open investigation every 10 days and command approval of every continuance of an investigation past 30 days;

b. Constant inspection and review of individual team and unit criminal investigation reports and investigator activity summaries; and

c. Individual team and unit performance measures based at least on arrests and dispositions, crimes cleared, property recovered and caseload.[20]

While it may not be clear how much improvement can be achieved by establishing a management system in the investigation process, it seems reasonable to assume that some improvement is likely in comparision with the non-managed process. And even if there is little or no improvement, the manager will at least be able to make intelligent decisions about resource allocations and alternative courses of action.

In establishing the management system for continuing investigations, the overall goal should be to increase the number of case investigations of serious crimes that are cleared by prosecutable arrests of criminals responsible.

Objectives of a managed investigation process could include:

• Assigning case investigations more effectively

• Improving on the quality of case investigation and preparation

• Monitoring the progress of case investigation and making decisions about continuation.

• Evaluating results on the basis of investigative outcomes.

The supervisor of the investigative unit, as is the case for all managers, should be held accountable for achieving stated goals and objectives through the effort of his team. The supervisor must:

• Organize the unit

• Establish work schedules and deploy resources

• Determine effective and economical assignment policies

• Organize workloads

• Assign cases on an equitable and skills basis

• Make decisions about "exceptional" investments of time to certain cases

• Coordinate and direct the unit's investigative efforts

• Develop required records to facilitate direction, monitoring, and evaluation of efforts

• Supervise personnel on a continuous basis

• Evaluate performance

• Train and develop investigators

• Promote a rapport with internal and external units that affect the ability of the unit to meet its goal.

Other management activities may also be called for. However, the above listing should be a good starting point.

In organizing the unit, the supervisor must make decisions about hours of operation, deployment of investigative personnel based on workload needs, and whether investigators will work alone, in pairs, or as part of a team.

Many agencies place stress on the economic advantages of having investigators work alone and reject the "luxury" of a team approach. However, the mix of resource use is limited only by the imagination of the supervisor or the requirements of a fixed policy that mandates a particular assignment pattern.

One of the most important decisions to be made is the assignment of a referred case. Not only must the manager consider current caseloads, but he must also assess who has the skills required to bring the case to a successful conclusion. If the case is of low-level priority or the investigative abilities and skills of each member are reasonably equal, this assessment need not involve more than a quick judgment. On the other hand, if the case is very serious or will require special skills or expertise, a reasoned judgment must be made as to who is best qualified to conduct the investigation. If putting the right investigator on the case requires a re-shuffling of workloads, the manager must take this decision.

Such a judgment obviously assumes that the supervisor knows the investigative backgrounds, strengths, and weaknesses of all of his personnel. In units with many investigators, it may be necessary to develop a skills profile of each investigator for the supervisor's reference.

Case assignment records should be maintained by both the supervisor and the investigator to provide adequate and timely information concerning case assignments and ensure proper review of investigative process. Such records would indicate the date the case was assigned, the category of crime, a list of review decision dates, and closure or continuation information...

The supervisor should also maintain a record of the distribution throughout the unit of case assignments. Assignment of unequal caseloads, unless done deliberately for good reasons, can be self-defeating for efficient and effective performance ... Clearly, the supervisor should also be knowledgeable about the activities undertaken by criminal investigators....

One recent research study found that investigators' time in several different agencies was generally spent as follows:

1. 45 per cent on non-case work
   Administrative assignments
   Speeches
   Travel
   Surveillance of specific locations
   Etc.

2. 55 percent on case work, broken down as follows:
   40 percent (22 percent of the total) investigating crimes that are never solved

12 percent (7 percent of the total) investigation crimes that are solved 48 percent (26 percent of the total) on cleared cases after arrest.[21]

While these percentages may not reflect the breakdowns in every agency, they at least furnish some idea of how investigators' efforts are currently allocated.

If every investigator were required to prepare a Daily Activity Plan/Results Report, supervisors would have a way of monitoring their activities and of eliminating duplication of effort by investigative teams. It would be possible to use one investigator to do the work of two or three who are all in the same locale to do the same thing . . . .

Another vy important responsibility of the supervisor in monitoring case investigations is to review progress on a regular basis with each of the investigators so that decisions can be made as to whether various investigations should be continued. The investigator should be required to make a recommendation. If his recommendation is to continue, the investigator should be required to show why he believes the case can be solved.

The supervisor must be accountable for the decision reached. If the case is an exceptional one, the supervisor alone bears the responsibility or the decision to continue the investigation. (At some point, the commissioner must be told that his daughter's stolen bicycle case will not be solved!) In all other cases, the supervisor must make a "hard-nosed" assessment based on the principle of diminishing returns. He must recognize the inadvisability of investing considerable additional effort to go from say 85 to 90 on the "likelihood" scale when the chances of success are still uncertain. He must decide that the investigation is to be discontinued when further effort would be neither economical nor productive. The time for making this decision will depend on the seriousness of the crime, the information available, and the political factors, if any.

This type of decision-making review of the status of an investigation can only be done when the investigator is required to analyze the information in the case, prepare an investigative plan, and maintain a case folder that is current and complete. While such a procedure is not generally followed at present in most departments a policy decision can change the situation virtually overnight.

Upon receipt of the preliminary investigation report, the investigator should carefully analyze the amount and quality of information supplied. An experienced investigator will look for the key, solvability, as well as for the emotional factors in the case . . . . It should be clear that a well-constructed preliminary investigation form . . . will provide the bulk of the information needed and will substantially reduce the amount of time needed to conduct a case analysis.

Once the analysis has been made and a decision reached that the case should be investigated further, the investigator should develop an investigative plan. After the approaches, strategies, and work format have been outlined, the plan should be discussed with the supervisor. There should be agreement as to the decision to continue, the appropriateness of the plan, and the first review date to further decide on continuation. . . .

A folder for each case should be established, containing complete and current records of the status of the case:

- An index sheet to record inclusions
- A copy of the initial investigation report completed by the uniformed officer
- A copy of the case analysis
- An investigative plan
- An investigator's checklist. . .
- A list of review dates on case progress
- Supplementary investigative reports
- Photos
- Lab reports.

Each case folder becomes the property of the investigator and the supervisor. The supervisor, not the investigator, should control access to the information. Other investigators seeking information on the case, or access to the folder, should seek approval from the supervisor. This rule not only maintains the integrity of the information but facilitates the supervisor's task of coordinating the unit's entire investigative effort.

Another critical responsibility of the supervisor is to measure the efficiency and effectiveness of the unit's, as well as the individual's, performance. While not perfect, the current measuring stick is generally the number of cases cleared by arrest.

To evaluate the results of activities and determine performance levels, it will be necessary to develop several summary information report forms. Most departments already have such forms. The following forms should be adequate, provided they are kept relatively simple in format:

- *Investigator's Monthly Workload Report*. . .
  Provides basic information on cases assigned, dispositions of cases, and arrest information. Also requires a separate accounting for exceptional clearances. . .

- *Unit Monthly Workload Report*
  Provides the same basic information, for the entire unit, as the previous report. . .

- *Monthly Arrest/Clearance Performance—Individual Investigators*
  Provides information on individual performance for each member of the unit. . .

- *Unit Arrest Performance—Prosecutor Acceptances*
  Provides information on prosecutor acceptances of arrests. Similar information for each investigator could be revealing of individual performances. . . .

These report forms provide basic information on the performance of the individual investigator, the overall performance of the unit, and the relative performance of each investigator as well as an indication of the quality of the investigative effort as viewed by the prosecutor.

Many other reports could be developed to measure performance. Many factors impact upon the performance of the individual investigator as well as the unit, and the manager must carefully consider all these factors before arriving at a decision concerning the effectiveness of an individual investigator.

As far as can be determined, few police agencies have instituted a formal system to manage the continued investigation process. The Troy, N.Y., Police Department established a system to deal with this function several years ago. While the department is a relatively small one (12 Investigators), some of its methods could profitably be used by substantially larger departments. . .

Continuing to do business as usual, with the investigator making his own management decisions, will only perpetuate the very dismal record of cases cleared by arrest. Indeed, the police administrator may well acknowledge that the present investigative process is really an exercise in wishful thinking.

While it is not a certainty that substantive improvements in investigative performance will occur once management assumes control of the investigative process, it is reasonable to assume that improvements are likely. Managers would be able to make more responsible decisions about allocation of resources and alternative courses of action to deal with the continually escalating crime problem.[22]

Police-Prosecutor Relationships

How police manage and prepare cases for prosecution is influenced in many ways by prosecutors themselves. The prosecutor determines which cases will be prosecuted, the offense charge for which an arrested person will be prosecuted, whether plea bargaining will be allowed, and the general conduct of the prosecution. The policies and general practices of prosecutions' offices, along with the practices of individual prosecutors, determine in many respects how the police define their enforcement policies and prepare cases. Thus, the police must be attuned to the policies and practices of prosecutors; however, the shared responsibility for the preparation and presentation of cases for prosecution must be recognized. This calls for the establishment of mutual trust, respect, and professional involvement.[23]

There can be no question that the police are responsible for conducting thorough and complete investigations of all cases; for preparing comprehensive reports; for gathering, processing and making available all of evidence they discover; and for assembling witnesses. Each case for which the police plan a prosecution should be thoroughly prepared, whether or not a prosecution follows. However, questions do arise when prosecutors refuse to prosecute certain types of cases, tend to reduce offense charges, and make plea bargain dispositions which are inconsistent with police expectations. When this sort of thing happens, there is a real need for the two agencies to get together to determine where things are going wrong and what changes need to be made. Formalization of sound working relationships is most desirable since:

- the prosecutor's caseload depends on police arrest policies and practices; and

- the police department's arrest performance and effectiveness substantially depends on the prosecutor's screening policy and priorities.[24]

The *Managing Criminal Investigations Manual* sets forth a realistic program for improving police-prosecutor relationships. Excerpts follow.

Benefits of an Improved Relationship. A comprehensive improvement in their relationship holds many potential benefits for both the police and prosecutor. For example, a formal system for obtaining feedback can help a police manager spot trouble within the organization on the matter of investigative performance and evaluate the relative effectiveness of units. It also can help the police manager identify training needs, evaluate managerial effectiveness, and identify areas where corruption may exist. Importantly, a good relationship will help officers and investigators improve their case preparation. Similarly, police feedback to the prosecutor can provide important suggestions concerning operating policies, procedures, and practices.

Most of the elements of new approaches to managing criminal investigations are concerned with internal police agency operations. In any effort to improve the management of criminal investigations, however, consideration must be given to the element of the police/prosecutor relationship since this relationship provides the necessary external linkage between the police and the next stage of the criminal justice process—prosecution. The inputs generated by a meaningful police/prosecutor relationship will facilitate the assessment of internal police policies and procedures which affect the impact of the initial investigation, case screening, follow-up, case management, monitoring, and reorganization.

1. **Feedback and Case Disposition Analysis Systems**

One of the most important questions to ask in the development of a case disposition feedback system is: "What does a chief or manager need to know in order to improve the investigative effort?" The police administration needs to know:

- The disposition of cases.

- Why a case was rejected for prosecution, or
- Why a case submitted by the prosecutor resulted in a dismissal.

The American Bar Association, like the National Advisory Commission on Criminal Justice Standards and Goals, has underscored the importance of a case disposition feedback system. The development of such a system is a needed and appropriate project which will encourage the police and prosecutor to work together toward improving the outcome of the judicial process.

The need to establish such a system was addressed in 1973 by the National Advisory Commission on Criminal Justice Standards and Goals. The Commission recommended these actions:

Every police agency immediately should develop policies and procedures to follow up on the disposition of criminal cases initiated by the agency. This should be done in cooperation with local courts and prosecuting agencies.

1. Every police agency, in cooperation with local courts and prosecuting agencies, should provide for the administrative followup of selected criminal cases. Policies and procedure should be developed:

a. To identify criminal cases which, because of extenuating circumstances or the defendants' criminal histories, require special attention by the prosecuting agency; and

b. To require a police representative to attend personally all open judicial proceedings related to these cases, and to maintain close personal liaison with assigned prosecutors.

2. Every police agency should review administratively all major criminal cases in which prosecuting agencies decline to prosecute or later cause to be dismissed. That review:

a. Should result in a referral of each such case to the concerned officer's commanding officer for administrative action to correct any police deficiencies which may have weakened the case; or

b. Should result in a referral of each case to the prosecuting agency for that agency action to correct any deficiencies for which it may have been responsible.

3. Every police agency should encourage courts and prosecuting agencies routinely to evaluate investigations, case preparation, and the courtroom demeanor and testimony of police officers and to inform the police agency of those evaluations. [National Advisory Commission on Criminal Justice Standards and Goals, *Police*, U.S. Government Printing Office, Washington, D.C., 1973, p. 86.]

It is significant that the commission suggested thorough review and evaluation of pertinent information in order to effectively manage the outcome.

Other questions to be asked concerning feedback systems are:

- What does the police manager have to know to effectively manage?
- Who has to know?
- What do they do with the information they receive?
- When is the process subjected to evaluation and, then, rethinking?

For example, The Chief of Police may want only major case summaries and broad comparative data. On the other hand, the Chief of Detectives and Chief of Patrol will want to have much more detail. In short, as the information descends through the departmental layers its form will change. Another factor to consider is how often various managers need information. . . .

The data needed may be the number of cases in various crime categories that are:

    a.   Presented for prosecutorial screening.

    b.   Rejected by prosecutor (with reasons).

    c.   Accepted for prosecution.

    d.   Returned for investigation.

Throughout the agency, this information will be needed in different forms. The Chief of Detectives may want this information in a form that will allow him to identify it by investigative unit or section. Within the detective division, commanders of units will have slightly different needs for information. A unit commander may require data keyed to individual investigators to identify performance. In addition, this management information system may need to be designed to provide feedback to the manager on individual detective caseload, status of case, and age of cases. . . .

The results of an information needs analysis will facilitate the development of feedback forms and procedures. Serious efforts must be made to resist developing unneeded forms and data. It is all too common for managers to figuratively drown in data generated for data's sake particularly when a computer is available.

The tendency to create and use unnecessary forms and data is a very real and counterproductive threat which must be guarded against. On the other hand, a method should be developed to provide a current status check monitoring on each case under investigation.

The informational needs of police managers may be met by collecting data from two primary forms, a *case feedback form* and a *case load report*. The data may be compiled by detective bureau clerical personnel or any other unit within the agency. In Dallas, this is done by the Legal Liaison Division. It must be summarized for managers. Data from the caseload reports should be transferred to a master form and routed to the chief of detectives who will summarize the data for the chief. A listing of all data summaries from case feedback forms should follow a similar route.

A simple summary with a line graph to show trends over time should be sufficient to inform most police chief executives, and the plotting of a line graph under the supervision of the chief of detectives should enable the chief to be thoroughly familiar with what it represents.

2. Improving the Quality of Investigations: Identifying the Prosecutor's Needs for Information.

The police must investigate professionally, carefully gather all the available evidence, evaluate the facts at their disposal, make arrests where warranted, and present the evidence upon which charging is justified.

The prosecutor must then evaluate the evidence, and accept or reject the case on the basis of the facts presented to him. If he chooses to accept the case for prosecution, he must then prepare the case for trial and formally charge the defendant in the manner prescribed by the court that has primary jurisdiction over the offense and the geographical area in which the crime was committed. When the case is called for trial, the prosecutor must then present the case and prove beyond a reasonable doubt that a crime did in fact take place and that the defendant committed it.

Through the experience gained in court, the prosecutor is in the best position to delineate the elements of information that he must be able to present to substantiate charges in court, and, consequently, which should be presented to him as evidence at the screening conference. Frequently, almost all of the information can be collected during the initial investigation and the booking process.

The Rand Institute, in its study of the effectiveness of criminal investigations, developed a data form on the basis of discussions with prosecutors, detectives, and police supervisors. The form contained informational elements judged to be needed to effectively prosecute robbery cases. Rand also has indicated that the form can be modified to apply to other crimes. It also has potential utility for investigator training, as a checklist in conducting an investigation, as a performance measure for investigator supervisors, and as an aid to the prosecutor's office in making decisions on complaint filing. [Greenwood et al., 1975, Vol III, p. 105.]

An analysis of the Rand data indicated that virtually all the information that the prosecutor needs can be effectively gathered during the initial investigation. Jointly developed forms which also serve as investigational guidelines may thus be seen as time- and cost-effective, and can play a large part in increasing the ratio between cases accepted for prosecution and cases presented for screening. . . . *Each agency must determine the informational needs of its own prosecutor if any appreciable improvement is to occur.*

Identifying Mutal Priorities of Police and Prosecutors

Major developmental effort should be devoted to setting forth joint investigatory and prosecutorial priorities. Since all offenses committed cannot be investigated by police, there is a need for each law enforcement agency to establish priorities of enforcement based on the chief's judgment of the best interests of the community. The failure of managers to set enforcement priorities result in the determination being made by each officer at the street level. Therefore, the police executive should establish priorities to guide his agency in day-to-day general operations.

Enforcement priorities usually are set to address major community concerns or areas of potential difficulty anticipated by the chief. Emphasis may also be placed on those crimes which generate other crimes, such as those related to narcotics and organized drug distribution systems or high-stakes gambling operations. The need to get large amounts of money quickly leads to a whole series of serious crimes: robbery, burglary, street muggings, fraud, murder for hire, loan sharking, and many others.

A clear understanding of the priorities set by the police will help the prosecutor's office gear-up for more effective prosecution of these crimes, particularly if the prosecutor also sees them as priority items. Mutual priorities are preferred in order to increase the combined impact of the police/prosecutor relationship. But, at least an understanding of the priorities of both prosecutors and police should be seen as a necessity. A prosecutor's commitment to the priority of prosecution of recidivists has well understood implications, and the knowledge of that priority by police officers will affect the style of their investigation and the speed at which an arrested recidivist will be presented for charging.

Mutual priorities should be seen as preferable because of the progress that can be made by both police and prosecutors toward achieving their goals. Interactive goal orientation will tend to bind the two elements into a more professional, cohesive, and unified organization in the interests of justice in the community. Agreeing on and clearly stating mutual priorities also will aid in the development of more effective approaches to dealing with crime.

Assignment of Liaison Responsibility

Increased activity to strengthen the liaison between police and prosecutors has stemmed from the concept of the police legal advisor. While the police legal advisor chiefly provided legal advice and guidance to police, legal liaison units have been established primarily to provide a working link between the police and the prosecutor's office. The advisor acts as a facilitator of problems arising between the agencies by serving as a legal advisor for police, a point of contact for the prosecutor, and an advocate for both agencies. Other benefits derived from the use of police legal advisors have included more adequate preparation of case statistics and identification of training needs through the information gathered by the advisor. ... [the] Dallas Police Legal Liaison project is an outstanding example of the use of the police legal advisor.

Toward An Integrated Program

The record-keeping function of a legal liaison unit should not be minimized. The unit is a perfect place for the compilation and clarification of data from case feedback forms that is so important to the interactive relationship between the police and prosecutor. Here, data can be quantified, problems identified, and solutions developed.

The following procedure may be used to operationalize the unit's activities. An investigator or officer wishing to file charges may contact the liaison unit before going to the prosecutor's office. The liaison unit will advise him on the completeness of the case work-up and make suggestions to improve it. If requested, a liaison unit member may accompany the arresting officer to the prosecutor's office for case screening to assist in the filing. After screening, one copy of all case feedback forms will be directed to the unit for analysis and data input. Monthly reports will be generated by the unit for the chief of detectives and the prosecutor detailing the activity during that month, the quarterly totals, and yearly figures....

Many police agencies throughout the nation have improved upon their investigative outcomes, measured in terms of an increased ratio of prosecutions to number of the arrests made for serious crimes, by developing a working relationship with the prosecutor which, as a beginning point, promotes the following interrelationships:

- A formal feedback system on case dispositions to keep police management informed re: investigative activities.

- A formal police/prosecutor liaison unit or person who develops a fuller exchange process between the two elements of the criminal justice process.
- A greater degree of involvement on the part of the prosecutor in the development of adequate standards of case investigation and preparation.

The benefits to be derived from a well developed formal relationship with the prosecutor's office are substantial and worth the development effort required by the police agency.[25]

A Model Monitoring System

A monitoring system is essentially a Management Information System which provides police administrators and managers with timely and pertinent data relating to the effectiveness of the several components of the total investigative system. It is aimed at evaluating a broad range of indicators which are critical for effective police agency management. One of the principal uses of the system is to maintain quality control over investigations.

The *Managing Criminal Investigations Manual* set forth the essential elements of a monitoring system. Excerpts are provided below.

A Monitoring System: The Components

A monitoring system is a management information system which provides police administrators with the statistical data on investigative performance that they can use to make judgments about performance. It is an essential tool for police administrators to use in evaluating both system effectiveness and detective and patrol performance. To fully understand how monitoring systems operate, the police administrator should be familiar with the following terms:

1. *Investigative Outcomes:* The investigative product or result produced at the end of an investigation. Outcomes must be stated in quantifiable terms, such as number of arrests, case closures, case clearances, prosecutions, and convictions.

2. *Investigative Activities:* The specific activities undertaken by criminal investigators and patrol officers. Examples include interrogations, crime scene searches, interviews, and surveillances. These activities must be stated in quantifiable terms.

3. *Productivity:* The number of investigative outcomes or activities per person hour or person day (such as number of clearances per case assigned for each investigator per day). The greater the ratio of outcome per period of time worked, the higher the productivity of the unit or the individual investigator.

The monitoring system provides the police administrator with a means to interrelate these concepts into a management information system. Much of the data collected can also be used as a resource for case collation, which is the comparison of information from one case with that from another to identify similarities and patterns. But the primary objective of the monitoring system is to provide the police administrator with continuous feedback on the investigative process.

Monitoring systems have five major components: data collection, data analysis, reporting mechanisms, data validation, and evaluation. Each component must be carefully designed, tested, revised, and perfected if the monitoring system is to be useful to the administrator.

Data Collection—Obviously, a system which analyzes data requires the accumulation of high quality data on every relevant aspect of the investigative process. The availability of data will vary from one police agency to another. Some police departments have well structured report forms upon which investigating officers record large amounts of information about crimes and the investigative actions taken. In many departments, officers are well trained and supervised, thereby leading to thorough completion of these reports. But even comprehensive reporting will not provide all the data required for successful operation of a monitoring system, for the system also requires the input of information about case activites throughout the entire investigative process.

Before data can be collected, the types of data needed must be identified. This is best accomplished by determining who system users will be, what outcomes they expect, and what evaluative criteria—or standards—will be applied. The items of information upon which these judgments can be based then must be determined.

The data collection component is also concerned with the point at which data is inserted into the monitoring system. Even if information is available, the police agency must identify when and by whom data is to be entered into the system. For example, should the data from the initial investigation be entered into the system by records clerks in the data processing unit or should this function performed by personnel in the centralized investigative unit? Developing the data collection component of the monitoring system includes identifying where the data is to be collected as well as what data is required.

Data Analysis—Once data is collected, it must be analyzed to provide the required comparisons needed to make judgments about performance.

The method of analyzing data depends strictly on the tools available. Smaller agencies may have to process information by hand and by individual analysis; larger departments will require mechanical or computer processing. In either case, developing of data analysis methods is a difficult, specialized function which requires professional assistance. The type of analysis to be done will depend upon the system outputs desired. It is important that the analysis undertaken directly relate to output needs. There is often a tendency for police administrators to yield to data processing professionals when there is an apparent conflict between data analysis capabilities and administrative requirements of the system. It is important that administrators recognize that the data analysis function—whether manual or mechanical—is a tool for their use. Police administrators must clearly identify the expected outputs from the system; [they can then] rely on technical specialists to analyze the data and put it in the format they require.

The types of data available through analysis is broad. A few examples are:

- Number of offenses investigated by patrol units.
- Number of cases closed by on-scene arrest by the patrol unit.

- Number of cases (and percent) assigned for follow-up investigation and number cleared by unit, individual, time spent, etc.
- Duration of follow-up investigations.
- Number of cases reclassified by specialized investigative elements and by patrol personnel (generally supervisors).

Numerous other analyses can be made. They should be identified as previously described, according to the performance evaluation criteria the department decides to apply to each aspect of the criminal investigation function.

Reporting—The department should develop reporting formats which will make it as easy as possible for people receiving the reports to read, understand, and use them. So, if there is to be a monthly report on investigations/clearances, for example, it should be formatted the same way each month. The reports should be as simple and straightforward as possible. They should tell the story, rather than requiring system users to draw inferences. That is, they should not consist of columns of numbers which require each reader to make his own interpretations; instead, they should be organized so that the interpretation of the data will be obvious and clear.

At the same time, the reports should include supporting data—the statistics on which conclusions are based. Managers should not have to rely solely on the judgment of the analysts. In addition, the reports should present data, insofar as possible, in a variety of ways, most importantly in both numerical and percentage form....

Data Validation—This is a quality control requirement to insure accuracy in data being presented in the reports produced by the system. Since input into the system occurs from various units, and the analysis mechanism may be fairly complex, there is a substantial chance that data inaccuracies may occur. A procedure to check this accuracy is necessary.

The best check is the random comparison of automated records with those maintained in the police agency's patrol units. This will require the selection, on a monthly basis, of one patrol unit as the object of study. Patrol records of offenses should be compared with the automated records. It will be common to find some inconsistencies, but large differences should not exist. When inconsistencies occur, the department must determine the cause and move to implement corrective action that will eliminate the problem.

Responsibility for data validation should be placed with either the department's inspection or planning units. By placing responsibility apart from units involved in data collection or analysis, objectivity of the validation will be enhanced.

Evaluation Criteria—All the data collected will be valueless unless it can be used within the context of what is expected, what is considered good performance, and what constitutes satisfactory investigative outcomes. Those standards are based on what is important to the administration of the department, such as high rates of clearance per total case load. The department administrator should decide what is important based on local needs and local concerns, and should base judgments on those matters determined to be important.

In a department in a city which has been the target of a large number of street robberies, for example, satisfactory performance might consist of quick arrival by detectives and uniformed officers, long interviews, a great deal of reassurance of victims and the generation of large amount of information. In another department, where the administrator is prosecution-conscious, good performance might consist of careful preparation of evidence for trial, and the criterion might be prosecutable cases per arrest. The criteria should be customized, changing to respond to local conditions and concerns; but they should be widely understood in the department so that investigative performance can be measured against them.

Who Uses the System

As suggested earlier, there is only one criterion for designing a data system—the needs of its users. If the data produced are what these users need to make decisions and if the data are presented to them in usable form, the system is a good one. If, on the other hand, it produces information they cannot use or understand or which is in a format which is difficult to use, the system will not work. This is why it is so important that the precise needs of the users be fully understood before the system is designed. Obviously, it must fulfill the administrator's needs since he is the principal system user.

Based upon the data generated by a monitoring system, a police administrator can make decisions about personnel allocations (choosing between patrol and investigators, for example), personnel evaluations (on which departmental rewards and assignments might be based), case status (to emphasize investigation of certain crimes rather than others), effectiveness of various kinds of procedures, and analysis of investigative outcomes.

A second potential user is the chief of detectives, who must make decisions about the day-to-day administration of centralized investigative units. For example, he must decide whether those cases referred to the detective specialist are worth pursuing. To do so, he should have information about case status, caseload, and related factors important to his decision-making. He also should have information about the performance of individuals and units under his command and should be in a position to advise them, direct them, and discipline them, if appropriate.

A third potential user is the patrol commander, whose subordinates are responsible for initial and follow-up investigations, for identification of witnesses on the scene, for interrogations at the time of the crime, and for a variety of other investigative functions which in many agencies actually determine the referral of cases to the specialized centralized detectives. Like the chief of detectives, the patrol commander needs information about the effectiveness of his subordinates, including the volume of cases closed by arrest, early case closure status, case clearance data, and the number of cases which are prosecutable.

Finally, the system can serve the needs of individual investigators by giving them frequent reports on the status of their cases, comparisons of their output and performance with that of other officers, and a means of interpreting that information so that they can improve their own performance voluntarily rather than as a result of coercion.[26]

The Importance
of Coordination and Cooperation

Coordination and cooperation are essential in order for any department or agency to function smoothly. These two qualities are most likely to be achieved when a department institutes well-defined policies and procedures which clearly delineate the responsibilities of uniformed officers and investigators and define the relationships which should exist between the two divisions. With respect to police-prosecutor relationships, a professional approach based on mutual respect is fundamental. This should be supplemented by a clear understanding of each others' operational policies and procedures.

In order for coordination and cooperation to be fully realized, it's necessary to break down the mystique which generally surrounds the detective function. This is gradually happening as more and more departments place greater emphasis upon a generalist approach to the investigative processes and call upon the services of the uniformed field officers more frequently. In addition, generalist investigators are replacing the traditional specialist detectives in the follow-up investigation of all cases except those classified as major or complex and those which require specialized investigative talents and abilities. As these changes are taking place, it is becoming increasingly apparent that the patrol and detective roles can no longer be viewed as separate and distinct. Instead, personnel in both units need to work closely together in their efforts to control crime by arrests, clearance, and closure of cases.

As departments modify their organizational structures to increase the involvement of the patrol division in the investigative process, it usually follows that the number of personnel in the patrol division increases while the number of personnel in the investigation division decreases. As a result, the criminal investigation division becomes more dependent upon the patrol division to complete the preliminary or initial investigative stages of those cases which are referred to them for follow-up. In addition, the patrol division becomes more involved in investigative efforts associated with stake-outs, strike/task forces, and arrests, supplementing the efforts of detective personnel. This is facilitated by increased communication between the two divisions and heightened training efforts. Some departments now have a special liaison officer in patrol to coordinate the efforts of that division with those of the criminal investigation division. Managers of some criminal investigation divisions are forcing closer liaison of their personnel with patrol by increasing the numbers of contacts that detectives must make with patrol officers in order to do their jobs. One training technique involves assigning all patrol officers to one- or two-week orientation periods in the criminal investigation division.

Formalized feedback of the disposition or outcome of cases from the prosecutor to the police department—and particularly to the involved officers—can facilitate coordination and cooperation between those two agencies. Likewise, feedback from the criminal investigation division to the patrol division is important.

Measuring the Results of Criminal Investigations

Each year, the FBI gathers and publishes data on serious crimes which include the estimated number of offenses committed and their clearance rates. These data are collected from police agencies throughout the United States and provide a gross measurement of the effectiveness of the police agencies. In 1974, for example, some 10.1 million serious crimes were reported, with a 21% clearance rate. In the same year, the United States Census Bureau, in a survey for the Law Enforcement Assistance Administration, reported that there had actually been 39.6 million serious crimes committed. This means that a more accurate clearance rate for 1974 would have been 5.2%, and that of some 40 million serious offenses, only 2 million were cleared. In other words, about 38 million of the 40 million serious crimes committed were unaffected by the workings of the criminal justice system. [27]

The purpose of presenting these observations and statistics here is to dramatize the monumental task which confronts every police investigator and administrator in the United States. Perhaps it is not within the realm of possibility for the police to significantly improve on the clearance rate of reported crimes; instead, the solution to the problem may rest more with other social and governmental institutions. However, the challenge is there for the police. Perhaps, in some small way, each individual investigator and patrol officer may contribute to the improvement of the clearance rate and, by extension, to the control of crime.

Basically, each department should be concerned with how well it is currently doing in its efforts to control crime as compared with its past efforts. The major tangible evidence of effectiveness revolves around the number of reported crimes and the outcomes of the investigations of each. Questions like the following can be asked in order to find answers to these problems:

- Have the suspects been identified?
- Have they been arrested?
- Have they been prosecuted?
- How many cases have been cleared by suspects identified, by suspects arrested, and by suspects prosecuted?
- How much property has been recovered? How much has been returned to the rightful owners?
- How many arrested and charged persons have actually been convicted?

- How many cases have been filed without being closed with a suspect being identified or arrested?

- Have persons generally been convicted of the offenses for which they were charged, or for lesser offenses?

- Are the victims satisfied with police efforts?

Answers to these and other questions translate into measures of a department's effectiveness. The relative weight of each measure depends on the importance a department places on it, since no universal standards have been developed and adopted for their evaluation.

Each department should also be concerned with its officer productivity. With respect to criminal investigations, questions like the ones listed above may be asked to determine how many offenses were investigated by each officer, how many cases were cleared by arrest, how many were cleared by identification of suspects and by prosecution, how much property was recovered, and so on. When the questions were answered they would translate into measures of each officer's investigative effectiveness. Again, the relative weight of each measure depends upon the importance a department places upon it.

The Rand study of the criminal investigation process found that differences in investigative training, staffing, workload, and procedures appear to have no appreciable effect on crime, arrest, or clearance rates. The study also found that the method by which investigators were organized (for example, team policing, specialists vs. generalists, patrol officer-investigators) cannot be related to variations in crime arrests and clearance rates.[28] However, the study reflects data gathered prior to 1975, when departments began to conscientiously introduce organizational and operational changes designed to improve the investigative process. Preliminary data shows that introduction of case screening techniques, team policing organizations, changes in police-prosecutor relationships, introduction of case monitoring systems, and changes in the managing of continuing investigations have improved arrest and clearance rates and reduced crime in some jurisdictions. For example, Rochester, New York reports that its team policing approach (which associates investigators with uniformed field officers in the initial investigative and early follow-up processes) substantially improved arrests and case clearances over the traditional organizational approach.[29] The Santa Monica, California Police Department in 1977 reduced the number of follow-up investigators needed for burglary investigations from four to two after introducing an effective case-screening system; increased arrests and case clearances also resulted. The Santa Ana, California Police Department showed a substantial reduction in all crimes in 1976 after introducing its Community Oriented Policing program, a form a team policing.

The final evaluation of project involving several departments in the managing of criminal investigations, which is being sponsored and financially supported by the Institute of Law Enforcement and the Administration of Justice of the U. S. Department of Justice, will not be completed until sometime in 1978, but preliminary findings indicate that substantial results for improvement in investigative efforts may be achieved by modification of a department's organization and operations.

Summary

This chapter has presented a comprehensive management approach by which a reasonably high quality of criminal investigations may be assured. Emphasis is on the role and functions of an agency's managers and supervisors as a necessary replacement for each investigator doing his own "thing." However, important suggestions are made as to how the investigators may better manage their own case loads.

The chapter focuses upon how any agency may improve its management of criminal investigations by close attention to organization. Several organizational structures have been presented dealing with the varied roles and functions of specialized investigators (detectives) vis-a-vis investigators assigned to the patrol field operations and the uniformed patrol officers.

Case management is dealt with from the standpoint of determining the amount of investigative effort which should probably be devoted to each case. Several methods have been described by which cases are screened for the purpose of deciding which cases have the best chances for solution based upon solvability factors. Cases which obviously may not be solved may be ejected from the investigative process, thus freeing investigators for great concentration upon cases which are likely to be solved.

There is a trend away from a large number of detectives who specialize, toward generalist investigators who work closely with the uniformed officers and who are often assigned to the patrol division. The pro's and con's of one-person assignments vs. two-person teams for investigations have been presented with the merits of a mixed approach included. Use of specialized investigators for juvenile crimes has been discussed and the merits of an organization for strike/task forces to deal with specific crimes is covered.

Although there is no validated system for the selection and training of investigators, various methods and approaches have been suggested. The importance of improving police-prosecutor relationships with suggestions as to how it may be accomplished to enhance the successful conclusion of an increased number of cases has been presented. An innovative approach to achieving quality control over investigations has been developed based upon improved cooperation between the police and prosecutors. A model for monitoring investigations has been proposed.

There are no precise criteria for measuring investigations. Several approaches have been presented to assist agencies in reasonably evaluating successes and failures. Cases cleared by arrests still remains one of the better measurement criteria. Managers should beware of over reliance on the Uniform Crime Reports presented by the Federal Bureau of Investigation in its annual report on *Crime in the United States.*

Questions and Topics for Discussion

1. What are the two distinct but interrelated functions involved in managing criminal invtigations? How are they interrelated?

2. How does the placing of greater investigative responsibility upon the uniformed field officer affect the organization of a department? What changes take place in the criminal investigation division as a result?

3. Describe the three common types of police organizational structures for criminal investigation. What are the key features of each?

4. What are the principal reasons given for specialization of the investigative function?

5. What are the advantages and disadvantages of one-person assignments?

6. How can the "image" of a patrol officer influence his selection as an investigator?

7. Work with your class to develop a model training program for investigators.

8. What is case management? What are the key features of case management which lead to quality case preparation?

9. What are the two major approaches to case screening criteria? How does case screening affect the investigative process?

10. How does good management of continuing investigations lead to quality control?

11. How do good police-prosecutor relationships affect the police investigative process?

Footnotes and References

1. Peter B. Bloch and James Bell, *Managing Investigations: The Rochester System,* (The Urban Institute and the Police Foundation, Washington, D. C., 1976), p. iv.

2. Bernard Greenberg, et al., *Felony Investigation Decision Model - An Analysis of Investigative Elements of Information* (Stanford Research Institute, Menlo Park, California, 1975), p. 21.

3. Peter W. Greenwood, Joan Petersilia, et al., *The Criminal Investigation Process,* Vols. I and III, (Rand Corporation, Santa Monica, California, 1975), p. vii.

4. Peter B. Bloch and Donald R. Weidman, *Managing Criminal Investigations: Prescriptive Package*, (National Institute of Law Enforcement and Criminal Justice, Law Enforcement Assistance Administration, U. S. Department of Justice, U. S. Government Printing Office, Washington, D. C., 1975), p. 27.

5. *Ibid.*, p. 31.

6. R. Kauffman, "The Generalist Investigator: A New Role for the Patrol Officer Under Neighborhood Policing," An article from Donald F. Cawley, *et al., Managing Criminal Investigations Manual*, (University Research Corporation, A manual prepared and published for the Office of Technology Transfer, National Institute of Law Enforcement and Criminal Justice, Law Enforcement Assistance Administration, United States Department of Justice, Washington, D. C., 1976), p. MM275.

7. Cawley, *et al.*, 1976, pp. 260-274.

8. Greenberg, *et al.*, p. 44.

9. O. W. Wilson and Roy C. McLaren, *Police Administration, 3rd Edition*, (McGraw Hill, New York, NY, 1972), pp. 339 and 378.

10. *Ibid.*, p. 379.

11. John P. Kenney and Dan G. Pursuit, *Police Work With Juveniles and the Administration of Juvenile Justice, 5th Edition*, (Charles C. Thomas, Springfield, Illinois, 1975), p. 153.

12. Greenwood and Petersilia, 1975, p. 22.

13. *Ibid.*, p. 11.

14. Crawley, *et al.*, 1976, p. MM53.

15. *Ibid.*, p. MM54.

16. Lee P. Brown, "Team Policing: Management of Criminal Investigations", (Police Chief, International Association of Chiefs of Police, Gaithersburg, Virginia, September 1976), pp. 65-67.

17. Bernard Greenberg, *et al., Enhancement of the Investigative Function, Vol., IV*, (Prepared by the Stanford-Research Institute, Menlo Park, California and reproduced and distributed by the National Technical Information Service, U. S. Department of Commerce, Washington, D. C., 1973), p. ii.

18. *Ibid.*, p. xxv.

19. Cawley, *et al.*, 1976, pp. MM 57-66.

20. National Advisory Commission on Criminal Justice Standards and Goals, *Police*, (U. S. Government Printing Office, Washington, D. C., 1973), p. 233.

21. Greenwood, Petersilia, *et al.*, 1975, p. 16.

22. Cawley, *et al.*, 1976, pp. MM99-108.

23. Bloch and Weidman, 1975, p. 14.

24. Cawley, *et al.*, 1976, MM169.

25. *Ibid.*, pp. MM169-187.

26. *Ibid.*, pp. 237-248.

27. A. C. Germann, "Law Enforcement: A Look at the Future", *Police Chief*, (November, 1976), p. 3.

28. Greenwood and Petersilia, 1975, p. vi.

29. Bloch and Bell, 1976.

Annotated Bibliography

Bloch, Peter B. & Donald R. Weidman, *Managing Criminal Investigation: Prescriptive Package*, U. S. Government Printing Office, Washington, D. C., 1975. This publication presents a comprehensive overview of the key issues involved in the management of criminal investigations. It presents case studies of six major police agencies' approaches to the managing criminal investigations.

Cawley, Donald F., et. al., *Managing Criminal Investigations Manual*, University Research Corp., Washington, D. C., 1976. The manual provides much "how to" for managing criminal investigations with supporting documents gathered from numerous police agencies. It is the basic training document used by the University Research Corporation in providing training to police agencies throughout the United States under a grant from the U. S. Department of Justice.

Greenberg, Bernard, et. al., *Felony Investigation Decision Model—An Analysis of Investigative Elements of Information*, Stanford Research Institute, Menlo Park, Calif. 1975. This publication makes a major contribution to the development of case screening systems. Based on research in the Oakland, California Police Department it presents decision models for four felony classes—robbery, assault with deadly weapon, car theft and rape.

Greenwood, Peter W., et. al., *The Criminal Investigation Process*, Volumes I through IV, Rand Corp., Santa Monica, Calif. 1975. These reports reflect the most comprehensive research of the police investigative process ever undertaken. They provide a number of recommendations and suggestions for improvement, some of which have been controversial.

Kenney, John P., *Police Administration*, Thomas, Springfield, Ill., 3rd Rev. Printing, 1975. This book combines theory with practice in addressing the investigative process. It reports early research on the subject and presents a workload methodology for determining investigator personnel. Its organizational models include the latest in team policing.

National Advisory Commission on Criminal Justice Standards and Goals, *Police*, U. S. Government Printing Office 1973. In a sense, this publication is a manual dealing with all facets of police administration and operations. It contains many helpful suggestions for the management and operations of the investigative process.

Wilson, O. W., & Roy C. McClaren, *Police Administration*, 3rd Ed., McGraw-Hill, N.Y. 1972. A comprehensive book dealing with the administration and operation of the police function in a detailed manner! It presents in depth organizational and operational concepts most germaine to the investigative process.

THIRTEEN

The Investigator and the Case in Court

Chapter Objectives

After reading this chapter, the student should be able to:

☑ Outline the relationship between crime investigation and crime prosecution.

☑ Explain the various degrees of proof required at each step of the prosecution.

☑ Write a short essay identifying the role of the defense counsel in an adversary system of justice.

☑ Explain the importance of following constitutionally acceptable practices during investigations.

☑ List alternate disposition procedures which may be used prior to trial.

☑ Describe the necessity of a good relationship between the investigator and the prosecutor.

☑ Explain the importance of thorough preparation for all pre-trial proceedings.

☑ Identify appropriate methods for preparing testimony for trial.

☑ List the key phases of a criminal trial.

The Investigator: Playing a
Key Role in the Criminal Justice Process

Popular folklore depicts the trial as the climax of the criminal investigation. The prosecutor is frequently shown as being the person who organizes the investigation, manages it, and gets personally involved in every aspect of each case. Reality bears little similarity to this image, however. The prosecutor's office is often understaffed and frequently not even consulted until an arrest has been made and it's time to file charges. Plea bargaining, along with other means of disposing of cases, has drastically reduced the number of cases that go to trial; some jurisdictions report that as few as 6% of those persons charged with crimes are actually tried.[1]

These conditions make two requirements of the criminal investigator. First, he must be familiar with court decisions and be knowledgeable about and willing to comply with rules concerning arrests, searches and seizures, confessions, and other aspects of the investigative process. Second, he must be prepared for every stage of the court proceedings; establishing a record during the initial stages may be the only chance he will have to show the strength of the case.

The investigator functions as the primary liaison between the police and the prosecutor; only a very few prosecutors have their own investigative resources. The police officer in charge of an investigation should be able to present complete information about its progress and any problems that may arise to the prosecutor as needed. Frequently, the prosecutor will be carrying such a large case load that his personal involvement in a specific case—or even the opportunity to review an investigation thoroughly—won't be possible. This means that the investigator and the prosecutor must have a good working relationship and that each must be able to understand and appreciate the responsibilities of the other. Policies should be established that clearly describe the roles of each to prevent unnecessary confusion or duplication of tasks. Policies and procedures vary from jurisdiction to jurisdiction, and even among individual departments if a prosecutor's office is very large; thus, it should never be taken for granted that one prosecutor will operate in the same way as another. Determining the extent of these differences is another responsibility that the investigator must be willing to assume.

The Decision to Prosecute

The investigator normally has the responsibility for presenting the case to the prosecutor so that the prosecutor can file formal charges against the suspect. Prior to meeting with the prosecutor, of course, the investigator should carefully review the case at hand in case there have been any new or recent developments. For example, since thorough investigation often develops information which wasn't available when the case was first brought to the attention of the police, the investigator should review each possible charge that may be brought against the defendant. This includes itemizing the elements of each original charge to determine whether sufficient evidence has been found to substantiate it. Sometimes, it may be more realistic to charge a defendant with a lesser offense instead of a more serious one simply because enough evidence may not exist to justify the serious charge. The prosecutor has a great deal of discretion when filing charges, so all possible charges should be presented to him for consideration and evaluation.[2]

To help in reviewing the possible charges in a case, and as an aid in later stages of the court proceedings, it is beneficial for the investigator to prepare an *outline* of the case. This outline should include the following:

- a narrative statement of the facts;
- a statement of the charges;
- an analysis of each charge, element by element;
- a list of witnesses and what each may be expected to testify;
- notes that may be of aid in cross-examining witnesses;
- signed statements from witnesses, if possible; and
- a description of each item of evidence to be presented, along with a notation of its current location.

This outline should be updated whenever necessary to indicate witnesses' changes of addresss, discoveries of new evidence, losses of evidence, and so on. Keeping this outline current from the beginning of the court proceedings can prevent many problems which may result from simple memory lapses.

The investigator must also be familiar with the basic requirements of the local courts. He must first determine which court will try the case. Minor offenses are usually covered by municipal ordinances and must be tried by a different officer—for example, the city attorney—than those offenses which are prosecuted under state laws. Venue requirements must also be checked to determine which court will hear the case within the state. And, of course, the investigator should attempt to comply with the local prosecutor's wishes regarding the format of the reports submitted. Due to the close nature of the relationship between the police and the prosecutor, unnecessary strains should not be allowed to develop due to petty grievances.

The prosecutor reviews the case and decides what charges are to be filed. It is his responsibility to go over the facts and ascertain whether a prima facie case exists—in other words, that a crime has been committed and the accused was involved in it. In addition, the prosecutor will consider whether any legal problems exist that might affect the case, such as the expiration of the statute of limitations, or some violation of the suspect's constitutional rights, or any thing else that may result in important evidence being declared inadmissible. A list of reasons for *not* filing a complaint might include the following:

- Departmental policy

- No Corpus Delecti
  No Specific intent
  No criminal act

- No Connecting Evidence
  Statement problems
  Witness problems
  Physical evidence problems

- Insufficient evidence
  Facts weak
  Evidence not available
  Incomplete investigation
  Witnesses not available
  Evidence inadmissible
    Illegal detention
    "Fruit of poisoned tree"
    Search warrant problems
    Search and seizure
    Warrant of arrest
    Miranda warnings problem

- Lack of jurisdiction

- Statute of limitations

- Offense misdemeanor or felony

Prosecutorial Discretion

In addition to performing the basic duties involved in analyzing the evidence presented by the police, the prosecutor exercises a great deal of discretion in making a final decision. Many reasons are given for the exercise and existence of this discretion. The most frequently mentioned include:

- legislative "overcriminalization," resulting in too many criminal laws;

- limitations on available resources due to crowded court calendars and limited numbers of prosecutors; and

- the need to individualize justice to coincide with the personal culpability of each defendant.[3]

Items specifically related to the discretionary decision *not* to prosecute might include:

- the victim has expressed the desire that the offender not be prosecuted;
- the costs of prosecution would be excessive in view of the nature of the injury to the public;
- undue harm would result to the defendant and his family if he were prosecuted;
- non-prosecution of this particular crime would be likely to aid in solving others (using the suspect as an informant); and
- the problem may be best settled by civil recourse.

The amount of discretion available to the prosecutor has been widely criticized, and many recommendations have been made for either reducing it or forcing the prosecutor to state on each case record the rationale behind his final decision. In any event, the investigator must be aware of the existence of prosecutorial discretion and would be well advised to anticipate the considerations that might to be involved in the decision-making process.

The Rejection of a Case by the Prosecutor

Departmental policies vary as to the procedures which are taken if the prosecutor rejects the charges or the investigator decides not to seek charges. Frequently, the prosecutor will complete a rejection form that states the reasons why charges were not filed. If such a form is completed, a copy should be kept in the case file. One important fact should be noted if the charges are rejected. The Fifth Amendment protection against double jeopardy does not attach until the trial stages of the prosecution. If the rejection can be turned around due to further investigation before the statute of limitations has run, prosecution may still take place at a later time.

Arraignment

After the prosecutor decides which charges are to be filed, the suspect is brought before a magistrate and officially informed of the charges against him. This official notification is called an arraignment. Statutory limitations determine how much time may pass between arrest and arraignment. These are typically worded, for example, as "without unreasonable delay," or specified by a number of hours, such as "within 48 hours, excluding Sundays and holidays." The investigator must be familiar with the time limits that apply within his jurisdiction, since failure to comply may result in a case being dismissed or important evidence obtained during the delay being declared inadmissible.

During the arraignment, it is common for the court to advise the defendant of the right to counsel, to appoint counsel for the indigent defendant, and to set bail if none has previously been set. The defendant may also be allowed to enter a plea to misdemeanors at this time. Since the charging process for felonies is not complete until a preliminary hearing is held, pleas are not normally accepted at the arraignment. Dates for future court appearances are also set at this time. Since the arraignment does not require the presentation of evidence, it is not usually necessary for the investigator to be present.

Plea Bargaining

The practice of allowing the defendant to negotiate with the prosecutor for a lighter sentence has become recognized as a standard procedure in the criminal courts. Plea bargaining may occur for a number of reasons. For example, the defendant may plead guilty to a lesser offense, or it may be recommended that he be awarded a lighter sentence due to his cooperation in not requiring the court to spend its time and resources on a full trial. Some jurisdictions formally recognize plea-bargaining as a legitimate (or at least prevalent) procedure, while others allow it to take place without official comment. At least one major jurisdiction has established a policy of filing only the charges it is prepared to go to trial on and not negotiating with the defendant at all. How long such negotiations take in other jurisdictions, and how much bargaining is done during them, varies a great deal, depending on local custom and the preferences and practices of the defense and prosecuting attorneys.

Plea bargaining as a practice has been severely criticized. Prosecution-oriented writers have claimed that the practice results in undue leniency and is a mockery of justice. The opposing view is that too many defense attorneys find plea bargaining an expedient way to dispose of their cases, and end up exerting undue pressures upon their clients to accept whatever the prosecutor will offer and waive their right to a trial on the merits. The U. S. Supreme Court has reviewed the practice and decided that the presence of counsel for the defendant is sufficient protection of his constitutional rights.[4]

The actual practice of plea bargaining usually results in one of the following three basic situations:

- the defendant pleads guilty to a lesser offense;
- the defendant pleads guilty as charged based upon a promise of a lighter sentence; or
- the defendant pleads guilty as charged to one offense and other charges against him are dropped.

The logic behind plea bargaining is more complex than this breakdown may make it seem, however. Overcrowding in the criminal courts has been blamed for fostering plea bargaining. It's clear that court calenders would be in impossible shape if all cases went to trial. Many people believe that the prosecutor is especially prone to indulge in generous plea bargaining when the number of cases awaiting trial exceed the available court resources. Statutory limits on the length of time a defendant can be forced to await trial also place burdens on the prosecutor's office.

On the other hand, several authorities have suggested that prosecutors are more willing to accept guilty pleas to lesser offenses when the judge consistently gives sentences that the prosecutor feels are much too lenient. A similar tendency has been noted when the prosecutor feels that the cases before him represent an unjust imposition of archaic or unrealistic criminal statutes.

A more readily apparent cause of plea bargaining is the prosecutor's attempt to obtain a guilty plea when he fears that the evidence available may not be sufficient to convince a jury of the defendant's guilt beyond a reasonable doubt.

In some instances, the negotiations between the prosecutor and defense attorney begin even before charges are filed; this practice is termed charge bargaining. More frequently, though, the bargaining process occurs somewhat later on in the process but before trial begins. Occasionally, it may take place during the trial itself but before the verdict has been returned. During these negotiations, the prosecutor may consider a vast array of factors in addition to the charges which have been brought against the defendant. The strength of the case is the obvious bargaining point, but the defendant's prior record and any aggravated circumstances of the crime may also prove influential. Policies of the prosecutor's superiors, the courts, and the state or local correctional departments will also affect the prosecutor's decision. Some reports indicate that a few lawyers are so willing to bargain that the final result is not very different from the sentence that would have been imposed had the lawyer not been involved in the case at all. Famous lawyers, on the other hand, indicate that they are rarely able to drive an acceptable bargain because prosecutors feel that winning a case against them is a great distinction.[5]

Plea bargaining practices like prosecutorial discretion, are largely hidden from public view. It is rare that the investigator will be called in or even notified that the process is taking place. Thus, it's important that the report given to the prosecutor by the investigator include as much relevant information as possible.

The Preliminary Hearing

Depending on the level and seriousness of the offense, a preliminary hearing may be held following the arraignment to further assess the case and determine whether sufficient evidence exists to warrant a trial. It's common for state criminal codes to require preliminary hearings for felonies but not for misdemeanors, for example. In addition, it's sometimes possible for the defendant to waive the hearing. During the preliminary hearing, witnesses are called and testimony and physical evidence are used to establish the elements of a crime, or corpus delecti. Normally, a preliminary hearing is attended by a magistrate; this review of the case by an objective party is considered important, as the prosecutor is frequently viewed as "working for the police."

The preliminary hearing is usually the first public confrontation for the prosecutor and the defense attorney. Each represents a necessary part of our adversary system of justice. The adversary process is based on the idea that the best method of obtaining the truth is to have two distinct and conflicting interests advocated with vigor by skilled, partisan attorneys representing each side. (This concept may offend the investigator who has spent many hours on the case in a sincere effort to determine the truth, but it nevertheless serves as a foundation for our criminal justice system.)

Insight into the functions of prosecutors and defense attorneys can be gained from the American Bar Association's *Code of Professional Responsibility*.[6] This Code and its canons govern the conduct of lawyers and specifies two distinct roles for prosecution and defense in criminal cases. The prosecutor's role is described in the Code as follows:

A) A public prosecutor or other government lawyer shall not institute or cause to be instituted criminal charges when he knows or it is obvious that the charges are not supported by probable cause.

B) A public prosecutor or other government lawyer in a criminal litigation shall make timely disclosure to counsel for the defendant, or to the defendant if he has no counsel, of the existence of evidence, known to the prosecutor or other government lawyer, that tends to negate the guilt of the accused, mitigate the degree of the offense, or reduce the punishment.

Canon 5 adds:

The primary duty of a lawyer engaged in public prosecution is not to convict, but to see that justice is done. The suppression of facts or the secreting of witnesses capable of establishing the innocence of the accused is highly reprehensible.

The duties of the defense lawyer are noticeably different, however:

It is the right of the lawyer to undertake the defense of a person accused of crime, regardless of his personal opinion as to the guilt of the accused; otherwise innocent persons, victims only of suspicious circumstances, might be denied proper defense. Having undertaken such defense, the lawyer is bound, by all fair and honorable means, to present every defense that the law of the land permits, to the end that no person may be deprived of life or liberty, but by due process of law.

Canon 15 adds:

It is improper for a lawyer to assert in argument his personal belief in his client's innocence or in the justice of his cause.

The lawyer owes "entire devotion to the interest of the client, warm zeal in the maintenance and defense of his rights and the exertion of his utmost learning and ability," to the end that nothing may be taken or be withheld from him, save by the rules of law, legally applied. No fear of judicial disfavor or public unpopularity should restrain him from the full discharge of his duty. In the judicial forum the client is entitled to the benefit of any and every remedy and defense that is authorized by the law of the land, and he may expect his lawyer to assert every such remedy or defense. But it is steadfastly to be borne in mind that the great trust of the lawyer is to be performed within and not without the bounds of the law. The office of attorney does not permit, much less does it demand of him for any client, violation of law or any manner of fraud or chicane. He must obey his own conscience and not that of his client.

In addition to the responsibilities set forth in the Canons of Ethics, it should be recalled that the right to counsel is mandated by the U. S. Constitution.

Establishing the Prime Facie Case

During the preliminary hearing, it is necessary for the prosecution to present sufficient evidence to establish a prima facie case against the defendant. This must be done through the testimony of witnesses and the presentation of physical evidence. The investigator should review the charges with the prosecutor and determine all necessary items of evidence that will be needed to establish each element of the charges. The outline that was made when the case was initially presented to the prosecutor will be helpful in identifying and subpoenaing needed witnesses. Since only a prima facie case must be presented, it will not be necessary to call all of the witnesses if their testimony merely duplicates that given by other witnesses.

Subpoenas. The investigator should make sure that subpoenas are served in a timely manner. It is advisable to interview the witnesses prior to the hearing and explain the proceedings to them. The courtroom will be awesome and forbidding to many witnesses; the thought of being on the witness stand can be frightening. Because witnesses are generally unfamiliar with court proceedings, they may feel personally threatened and insulted when objections are made to their testimony or the defense attorney challenges their truthfulness during cross-examination.

Witnesses. Even though some witnesses will volunteer to appear at the hearing, they should still be subpoenaed. Last-minute changes of heart and other excuses are easier to handle if the subpoena power of the court has been extended to require the attendance of the witness.

Reviewing Notes and Reports Ahead of Time

Since a period of time will inevitably elapse between the commission of a crime and the preliminary hearing concerning it, it is wise for the investigator or prosecutor to have all persons who will be called upon to testify review their recollections of the incident ahead of time. This practice helps to ensure that witnesses will be more comfortable about testifying and will be prepared to offer their testimony without hesitation or confusion. There is nothing deceitful about rereading notes made at or near the time of an incident if this is done only to refresh one's memory; common sense indicates that a report written a brief time after an incident will be much more accurate than one which is drawn from a person's memory some weeks later.

If a witness decides to review notes or reports prior to taking the stand, and the defense counsel asks him or her if this was done, the witness should always admit to it instead of attempting to deny it. The questions that follow will probably be asked in an attempt to determine precisely which documents were consulted during this review; again, the sources of these documents and the ways in which they were compiled should be fully disclosed. Refusal to admit that reports were reviewed can lead to embarrassing consequences.

The Function of the Preliminary Hearing

The function of the preliminary hearing is to allow an objective magistrate to assess the evidence presented and determine whether sufficient credible evidence exists to establish probable cause to hold the defendant for prosecution. In practice, the preliminary hearing has other functions as well. It enables the prosecutor to assess the strength of the witnesses and to evaluate the probability of obtaining a conviction. Similarly, defense attorneys use the hearing to evaluate their cases. The defense has the right to cross-examine witnesses and require that physical evidence be proved to be genuine and as near to its original condition as possible. The record established at the preliminary hearing usually becomes the basis for plea bargaining. For this reason, it is important to take the preliminary hearing seriously even though it may not have all of the formalities of a trial.

In some jurisdictions, the defendant may ask that the transcript of the preliminary hearing be presented to a judge in lieu of a formal trial. In this situation, the judge reads the transcript and pronounces judgment based on what the transcript contains. In jurisdications where this procedure is used, the investigator should take particular care in preparing for the preliminary hearing.

Standards of Proof and Dismissal

Failure to meet the required standard of proof at the preliminary hearing results in a dismissal. This dismissal is considered as occurring before jeopardy attaches, which means that the case may be refiled if additional evidence can be found before the statute of limitations has run. Dismissals are common when witnesses become unavailable.

If the evidence presented during this hearing establishes that a misdemeanor has been committed instead of a felony, the magistrate may be able to amend the complaint accordingly.

The Role of the Investigator During the Preliminary Hearing

The role that the investigator will play during the preliminary hearing will vary from case to case and from jurisdiction to jurisdiction. Frequently, he will be seated at the same table as the prosecutor and may confer with the prosecutor during the hearing as the witnesses testify. Sometimes, the investigator may be called to testify in order to provide evidence that connects the defendant with the crime. The prosecutor's caseload will normally make it unlikely that he or she will have had the time to become as familiar with the case as the investigator. The investigator should expect this and not treat it as a sign of incompetence or neglect on the part of the prosecutor. Often, a single prosecutor will have to attend numerous preliminary hearings during the same day; thus, it's impossible for the prosecutor to be as involved in each case as the investigator who is able to spend many hours of hard work in developing it. The investigator should be prepared to give the prosecutor information when needed; in addition, the investigator should know the backgrounds of witnesses who are likely to be vulnerable to cross-examination.

The Defendant's Right to Counsel

The defendant has a constitutional right to counsel at the preliminary hearing. This includes the right to have counsel appointed if he is indigent, or too poor to pay for an attorney. Defense counsel is allowed to play an active role in the preliminary hearing; this means that he may cross-examine all witnesses and present witnesses and physical evidence of his own. The evidence that the defense presents will be based upon tactical considerations. Defense counsel may view the hearing as a chance to discover the prosecutor's case without having to reveal his own case. Many defense attorneys view the practice of presenting witnesses at the hearing as advisable only if there is a strong chance that the charges may be dismissed. Even those defense attorneys who choose to present witnesses will rarely call the defendant to the stand to testify.

The Grand Jury Indictment

Indictment by a grand jury is a constitutional right for defendants in federal criminal cases who have been charged with infamous crimes. This right has not been extended to the states, however, some states require grand jury indictments for all or some crimes, while others make their use optional. Normally, indictment by a grand jury replaces the preliminary hearing, but some states require both.

The grand jury is an investigative body and as such may initiate a criminal investigation on its own. Or a completed investigation may be presented to the grand jury by the prosecutor. The grand jury has many advantages and privileges; for example, it can compel testimony and insist that certain documents relating to a case be produced. At the same time, the grand jury has the right to maintain secrecy concerning its own proceedings. In addition, the grand jury must authorize the release of its own transcripts before they can be made public.

A witness before the grand jury ordinarily is not entitled to have counsel present but may invoke the Fifth Amendment right against self-incrimination. The defendant has no right to be present or testify before the grand jury, but he or she may be subpoenaed. The grand jury is frequently used, even when not required by state law, for complex cases that would involve an undue amount of time if they were presented at preliminary hearings. It is also used to hear cases that [might cause undue injury to the defendants if they were presented at a public hearing.] The grand jury also gives the prosecutor the chance to present the case to a group of lay persons for evaluation before formal charges are made. The high volume of criminal cases normally handled by the prosecutor makes the use of the grand jury for all cases extremely impractical, however.

The Process of Discovery

Discovery is a process whereby each side in a case is entitled to view information contained in the files of the other side. It is extensively used in civil cases and includes the right to examine the opposing party under oath, the right to insist that certain documents be produced, and even the right to require the opposing party to submit to medical examination if his physical condition is an issue in the case. The right to discover is more frequently employed in civil cases than in criminal cases; for some reason, it has been slow to develop for criminal cases.

In the past, the prosecution has traditionally held the upper hand in criminal discovery, as it has had the right to use a grand jury to call witnesses and compel testimony prior to formally seeking prosecution. Grand jury proceedings have been confidential in nature, and even the defendant hasn't had the right to obtain a copy of the proceedings prior to trial.

The defendant's right to discovery has developed slowly and sporadically and varies a great deal from state to state. The federal courts are very restrictive in this matter. (California is perhaps the most liberal state in criminal discovery.) Discovery procedures are now based on a combination of two ideas: that "surprise" during a trial is not the best method of determining the truth, and that due process requires that evidence favorable to the defendant not be intentionally suppressed by the prosecution. The more traditional view—that the defense should specify the content of the items they desire to examine in the motion requesting them—is generally considered to be unfair. Since it's unlikely that the defense will know what evidence the prosecution has, it will probably not be able to obtain copies of extremely damaging evidence. Items that some jurisdictions have made available to the defense now include the following:

- copies of statements and confessions made by the defendant;
- results of chemical analyses of blood and other items of evidence;
- results of ballistics and other laboratory tests performed;
- photographs of places and persons important to the case;
- autopsy reports;
- copies of statements made by witnesses;
- the identities of informers; and
- lists of witnesses whom the prosecution intends to call during trial.[7]

While motions for discovery will normally be handled by the prosecution, the investigator should still be familiar with what items are currently considered "discoverable" in his state. Investigative files should be kept in an orderly fashion so that documents can be produced upon demand. Failure to produce items so ordered by the court may result in a dismissal of the case if prejudice results from not having received the items. For these reasons, items subject to discovery must be preserved as carefully as any other items of evidence. In the absence of the investigator, someone else must be able to locate them quickly and on demand.

The Fifth Amendment privilege against self-incrimination has been used to prevent many discovery procedures from being utilized by the prosecution. It has also been held, however, that requiring the defense to indicate certain affirmative defenses and their intention to use an alibi as a defense is not a violation of the U. S. Constitution.[8] Exact requirement vary from jurisdiction to jurisdiction.

Pre-Trial Motions

The timing of defense motions to challenge court proceedings will vary. State laws may allow certain items—such as the admissibility of evidence discovered without a search warrant—to be determined before the trial and provide for an immediate right to appeal. When no specific requirement exists that such matters must be settled before the trial, the defense counsel may use his discretion to determine which alternate procedure will be most effective. Some states may only allow such matters to be determined during the trial; many of these pre-trial motions will be handled by the prosecutor without notification of the investigator. Other states will require hearings at which the investigator and other witnesses may be called.

Motions to dismiss based on insufficiency of the complaint normally must be made prior to the preliminary hearing. The challenge is usually based on the investigator's failure to establish probable cause for detaining the defendant. Challenges may also be levelled at the legality of the arrest itself or of the affidavits used to support the arrest warrants.

Following the preliminary hearing, motions may be made challenging the sufficiency of the evidence presented at that hearing. Other challenges to the preliminary hearing may concern the failure to give the defendant a timely hearing, or procedural errors which occurred during the hearing. Defects in the document filed at the conclusion of the preliminary hearing, usually called an information, may also be challenged. These errors may include the failure to list all the elements of a crime, vagueness, and the failure to negate exemptions allowed by the state.

The defense may also attack the constitutionality of a statute. Each such challenge must be considered by the court; examples include:

- a challenge to an improperly enacted statute;
- a challenge to a statute that infringes upon constitutionally guaranteed rights;
- a challenge against ex post facto laws and bills of attainer; and
- a challenge against vagueness in statutory language.

Such challenges are frequently reserved until after the trial.

The court itself may be challenged for lack of jurisdiction. This term encompasses those offenses which have been committed outside the court's jurisdiction, or those which are required by statute to be tried by a different level of the court. A change of venue motion acknowledges the court's jurisdiction but requests that the court transfer the case to another court. This is frequently requested on the grounds of prejudicial pre-trial publicity and the inability to obtain an unbiased jury. The granting of this motion is discretionary with the court.

A variety of other grounds may be alleged, including:

- denial of the right to a speedy trial;
- failure to prosecute within statutory time limits;
- statutory immunity that covers the defendant; and
- double jeopardy.

The judge may be challenged if he has previously been a member of the law firm that represents the defendant, or was a prosecutor on the case prior to appointment to the bench. Occasionally, a judge will be challenged on the grounds of bias due to other activities, his relationship to a potential witness, or public statements he has made concerning the case.

The Investigator
and Motions to Suppress Evidence

The motions that are most likely to require the presence of the investigator or other police personnel at the hearing are those which are made to suppress evidence. The more frequent grounds for this type of motion are violations of U. S. Constitutional guarantees as set forth in the Fourth, Fifth and Sixth Amendments; violations of state constitutional guarantees; and violations of state statutes. An adverse ruling on any of these motions can harm the prosecution's case and impede its progress; again, the investigator must know and abide by proper police procedures.

Evidence seized pursuant to a valid search or arrest warrant is presumed valid. This places the burden of showing that the evidence was unlawfully obtained upon the defendant. A warrantless search is per se unreasonable, and the prosecution has the burden of establishing that the search falls within one of the exceptions to the requirements for using a warrant. The primary exceptions to the requirement for a search warrant are:

- a consent search;

- a search incident to a valid arrest;

- a stop and frisk;

- emergency or exigent circumstances;

- abandonment of property; or

- an instance in which the item was in plain view.

To challenge the search, the defendant must establish standing. The minimum requirement for establishing standing are set forth in *Brown v. U. S.*, a case heard in 1973 during which the Supreme Court held that the defendant must either have had a proprietary or possessive interest in the premises, or must have been on the premises when the search was conducted. Where a necessary element of the charge is the possession of the item seized (possession of heroin, for example), admission of possession is not required to object to the search. Any admission of possession made at the hearing on this type of charge on the motion to suppress the evidence is not admissible at trial. Some states have more liberal rules, called vicarious exclusionary rules, that allow the defendant standing to object to any unlawful search.

In preparing for a hearing on a motion to suppress evidence, the investigator should locate all persons who were involved in the search or in the procuring of the confession. Each person should go over his notes on the occurrence and refresh his memory of the event in question. Since a motion such as this is usually an isolated event during the entire investigation, care should be taken to call only the persons who have knowledge of the specific event in question.

The Question of Sanity

The prosecution of the defendant may not proceed if the defendant is not considered legally sane. There are two areas of the trial process during which the question of sanity may arise. First, the defendant must be judged sane at each critical phase of the proceedings, including arraignment, trial, and sentencing. In the standard test used to determine sanity for these purposes, the defendant is questioned about whether he is capable of understanding the nature of the proceedings against him and assisting in the preparation of a defense. If the defendant is not found to be sane at some point he will be committed as necessary and the proceedings will be postponed until such time as sanity is regained. This is not a defense which applies to the crime, nor is it concerned with the mental state of the defendant at the time when the crime was committed. Since the question of sanity is raised for this purpose at each critical phase of the proceedings, a hearing to determine competency to stand trial may occur at any time during the pretrial period, at the commencement of the trial, or even during the trial.

The second instance during which the issue of sanity is raised is as a defense to the commission of the crime. Pleading procedures for the insanity defense vary from state to state. The defendant frequently must plead "not guilty by reason of insanity" before the trial, and during the hearing of his case testimony will be presented on the issue of the defendant's sanity at the time of the commission of the crime. Other jurisdictions will hold a trial on guilt first, and, if the defendant is convicted, then hold a trial on the sole issue of his sanity at the time when the crime was committed.

Since the two procedures focus on different time periods, it is clearly possible to have a "not guilty by reason by insanity" defense without a sanity hearing, or to have a defendant claim current insanity without alleging insanity at the time of the crime. Sanity is an issue in all cases, but it is frequently raised by the defense only when the crime charged carries a lengthy sentence or is a capital offense. If a defendant is judged insane, he will usually be committed to an institution for an indeterminate period of time. Authorities at the institution must declare that the defendant has returned to sanity before he can be released. The insanity defense seems to be gaining in popularity, but it isn't always the best one to use, at least as far as the defendant is concerned. A person who has been judged as possibly criminally insane is considered dangerous to society. Authorities at the institution may be reluctant to release him, and the chances are good that the defendant will be incarcerated for a much longer time than he would have been had he been convicted for a minor offense instead. The alternative may be a short prison sentence or even a fine; in such cases, the defense will frequently waive the options of pleading insanity or seeking to delay the trial due to the defendant's lack of mental capacity to stand trial.

While the insanity plea is an option of the defense, the motion to discontinue proceedings due to the defendant's incompetency to stand trial may be made by the prosecution, the defense, or even the judge. Convictions have been overturned in cases in which the defendant's erratic behavior during the trial clearly indicated that he lacked the ability to understand the proceedings; often, in these instances, the judge relied on pre-trial determination of sanity instead of having the defendant re-examined.[9]

While the majority of testimony taken at a sanity hearing will be that of professionals in the mental health and medical fields, the testimony of lay witnesses who have had an opportunity to witness the behavior of the defendant may also be requested. If the investigator is called to such a hearing, he should clearly describe those actions of the defendant that he has personally witnessed. The investigator is not considered competent to diagnose mental illness and must leave opinions on the mental capacity of the defendant to the experts in that field.

Final Pre-Trial Preparation

Just before the actual trial date, that investigator should thoroughly review the case in preparation for testifying. The outline prepared earlier should be reviewed and notes should be made of all witnesses that may be called and all items of evidence that will have to be produced at the trial. These preparations are similar to those which were made for the preliminary hearing, of course. At that stage, it was only necessary to produce sufficient testimony and physical evidence to sustain a prima facie case. If one witness could positively establish a point, it was not considered necessary to call additional witnesses. At the final trial itself, however, the prosecution will have the burden of establishing each element of the crime beyond a reasonable doubt. This is a very high standard, and all available witnesses who can give testimony on a point should be called. Sheer numbers of witnesses will not win a case, however, and care should be taken to make sure that a witness will be able to provide testimony that will be useful to the prosecution. Witnesses that have no recollection of the event, were not able to observe anything at the time of the event, or have no other evidence to present are detrimental to the case since they take up a great deal of time and tend to distract the jury.

Two rules of evidence determine how a person may be allowed to refresh his memory in preparation for a trial. These rules are usually referred to as past recollection recorded and present memory refreshed. For example, a witness may use anything at all to help refresh his memory of an event related to the case at hand. Once he has done this, however, the witness must testify from memory, not from the item he used in an effort to recall the events. This refreshing may be done either before or during the trial. The defense may request—and will frequently be allowed—to see the item the witness used to refresh his memory and may cross-examine the witness in order to establish that his memory actually *was* refreshed and that he was not merely quoting the content of a document. The defense may also be allowed to introduce this item or document into evidence. If something is used to refresh a witness's memory, then, it should be readily admitted and produced should the defense ask for it. It is only logical to assume that information recorded at the time of the crime will be more accurate than that which is drawn from a person's memory long after the crime occurred.

Past recollection recorded permits the introduction of written items made at or near the time of the occurrence and is based on an exception to the hearsay rule. A prerequisite for introduction is the fact that reviewing the document does not refresh one's memory, but rather serves to "replace" it. Once it has been established that the witness has *no* present recollection of the event, a foundation must be laid for the admission of the writing that was made at or near the time of the occurrence by the witness or at his direction. It is not required that the writing be in any special form. The witness must testify that the writing was true at the time when it was made. This appears to contradict the idea that the witness cannot recall the facts were and is thus forced to seek written reinforcement; this isn't the case, however. The witness must simply state that it is his habit to record such items accurately or, perhaps, that he would not have signed the statement after reading it if he knew it to be inaccurate. It will be necessary to authenticate the document in the same manner as any other writing, of course. In addition, this procedure must be distinguished from that of refreshing present recollection. In past recollection recorded, the witness does not testify to any of the events; instead, he simply attests to having made an accurate recording of the event when they occurred. No cross-examination on the witness's memory of the event is allowed; only the making of the writing may be challenged. If past recollection recorded is to be used, it will be necessary to have the witness present to testify to the making of the writing even though he can add nothing by present testimony. If, on the other hand, it is claimed that the witness' memory is refreshed by reviewing the writing, then the witness will testify from his memory and will be cross-examined regarding the event itself. The document will be made available to the defense counsel. If at this time the witness can only testify to the exact content of the document, his credibility will be weak.

Physical Evidence

All items of physical evidence that are to be admitted must be proved to be in the same condition as they were at the time of the crime. If changes or alterations have occurred—such as those caused by laboratory tests—these must be strictly accounted for. The normal procedure for doing this is to establish the chain of custody of each item of evidence and prepare a list of all witnesses that may be necessary to substantiate the chain. It is also common to tag evidence in advance. Although this saves time during the trial, extreme caution should be used to follow the format used by the court and to avoid altering the evidence in the process of tagging it.

Subpoenas

Prior to the trial, the prosecutor will issue subpoenas for witnesses. The investigator should prepare the list of witnesses for the prosecutor and present it to him. The subpoena power for criminal cases usually allows the subpoenaing of witnesses from further distances within the state than is allowed in civil cases. If it is shown by affidavit or testimony before a judge that a material witness resides outside the state, proceedings to ensure his presence (including taking the person into custody, if necessary) can be obtained in most states through the *Uniform Act to Secure the Attendance of Witnesses from Without the State in Criminal Cases.* The investigator will be responsible for making sure that all witnesses are served. It is even necessary to subpoena "friendly" witnesses to maintain the power of the court to call them should they have a last-minute change of heart. A subpoena can also compel the presence of a witness who is forgetful of the court date or claims to be unable to attend at the time specified. If the trial is to be lengthy, or it is anticipated that it may not get started on time, it may be possible to place witnesses on "standby" and notify them shortly before they will need to be in court rather than require their daily attendance at the trial. If a witness is unavailable, this fact should be brought to the prosecutors' attention long enough prior to the trial to allow him to alter his trial strategy. He may be able to obtain a continuance if the witness will be available at a later time. Or, there may be other witnesses who can supply the same information, or it may be possible to use other sources (such as transcripts of prior testimonies) to introduce the testimony of that particular witness. If the witness is crucial to the case and no alternate method of obtaining the information is available, it may be necessary to dismiss the case. A dismissal at this point may be made without prejudice and the case may be refiled when the necessary testimony becomes available provided that the statute of limitations has not yet run. Waiting until after the beginning of the trial to request a dismissal will result in jeopardy attaching, and reprosecution will not be allowed.

In reviewing the list of witnesses prior to issuing subpoenas, the prosecutor will consider any stipulations that have been entered upon the record. When making a stipulation, the prosecutor and defense attorney are willing to admit certain facts and thus save trial time. This procedure is not as common in criminal cases as it is in civil cases. No testimony is required to prove an item which has been stipulated. For example, the right to confront witnesses belongs to the defendant; only the defendant, through his attorney, can enter stipulations that will result in a loss of the right to cross-examine a witness who is testifying against him.

The Trial

If the case has not been dismissed or settled by the entry of a guilty plea, the trial will be the culmination of the investigator's efforts. Trials are very time-consuming and must be prepared for with great care; once a trial starts, the defendant can successfully plead double jeopardy to subsequent prosecutions unless the prosecution can show manifest necessity.[10] This showing is difficult to make.

The Role of the Judge

The judge plays the role of impartial referee during the trial proceedings. He rules on the admissibility of testimony and evidence and instructs the jury to disregard information that he has decided should be striken from the record. He has the duty to ensure fundamental fairness during the trial. This gives him the right to make some motions on his own initiative. The judge may also question witnesses. The judge must not appear to take sides during the trial and, although he may cross-examine witnesses, it is considered misconduct to do so in a manner that leads the jury to believe that the judge personally doesn't believe the witness. (Jurors may also be permitted to question the witness; usually, the juror will write out the question and the judge will ask it of the witness.)

The judge is also responsible for instructing the jury at the end of the trial. In this instruction, the judge informs the jury of what the law applying to the case is, i.e. what the prosecution must prove and what burdens of proof each party bears.

The Right to Counsel

The defendant has a right to counsel during the trial if there is any possibility of imprisonment.[11] This right includes the right to effective assistance of counsel. The date of appointment of the defense counsel is not as important as the quality of the defense presented. When counsel's performance is so inadequate as to "reduce the trial to a farce" or be a "a mockery of justice," the conviction obtained at trial will be reversed.[12] Some courts use an even higher standard of competence than this.

The defendant also has the right to make an intelligent waiver of counsel.[13] When the defendant wishes to represent himself at a trial, it is the judge's duty to ascertain whether the defendant understands the seriousness of the proceedings. Forcing the defendant to choose between being represented by an unacceptable counsel and representing himself will not result in an effective waiver. When in doubt, the judge may appoint counsel to assist the defendant in representing himself.

Effective assistance of counsel can only be obtained if the defendant is able to work with the attorney in the preparation of the defense. For this reason, the defendant may be able to petition the court for a substitution of attorneys. Effective assistance may also be denied if the attorney represents two or more defendants in one case and the evidence needed to defend one defendant would jeopardize another. A common solution to this is to appoint separate counsel for each defendant. It may also be solved by granting separate trials to the defendants.

The Right to Trial By Jury and the Selection of the Jury

The right to jury trial applies to all offenses with a possible penalty of six months or more imprisonment.[14] This constitutional right, like most others, may be waived if this waiver is undertaken intelligently. When the defendant chooses to exercise his right to a jury trial, he is entitled to a trial by an impartial jury. This implies that the jury must be selected fairly, and that individual jurors may be screened to eliminate those who are prejudiced. The selection process may not systematically exclude persons on the bases of race or sex.[15] While selecting the actual jury for the trial, both the defense and the prosecution will be allowed to ask (or to have the judge say) prospective jurors questions to determine whether they are biased. This questioning is called voir dire. Obvious reasons for disqualification of a juror would include:

- some relationship to the victim or defendant;

- the admission of preconceived notions regarding the defendant's guilt or innocence;

- some relationship to the attorneys; or

- racial bias against the defendant.

Depending on the facts of the case, other factors may also be important in establishing prejudice. Persons disqualified for possible bias are considered to be challenged for cause. Each side is permitted a statutory number of additional challenges, called peremptory challenges, which may be used at will. The U.S. Supreme Court has upheld the right of the prosecutor in one case to use peremptory challenges to exclude members of one race from the jury.[16] The court did comment at this time that it might have ruled in the opposite manner if it had been shown that it was the practice of the prosecution to systematically exclude one race from all juries. In addition to the rights of counsel to exclude jurors, potential jurors may themselves seek to be relieved of their obligation to serve on grounds of hardship or some other grounds specified by statute. While grounds of hardship are most commonly used when the trial threatens to be extremely lengthy, they are also invoked by persons on daily wages who are not reimbursed by their employer for time off work due to jury duty. Concern has been expressed over this practice, since it effectively excludes lower-income persons from jury service.

The size of the jury is subject to local variation. Juries of fewer than twelve persons have been challenged on constitutional grounds, but the U.S. Supreme Court has found that the apparent "requirement" of twelve jurors was a historical accident and not a constitutional guarantee. For example, juries of six have been upheld.[17] The concept of a unanimous verdict has met with a similar reception from the Court; it has held that verdicts of 10 to 2 or 11 to 1, when permitted by state law, serve the purpose of "having the judgment of his peers interposed between himself and the officers of the State who prosecute and judge him,"[18] every bit as well as a unanimous verdict can.

Once the jury has been selected (along with alternates, if a long trial is anticipated), each member is sworn in by the judge. At this point, jeopardy attaches. An acquittal or any misconduct by the prosecution that causes a mistrial will bar reprosecution of the defendant on the same offense. An example of misconduct that can cause a mistrial is one in which persons representing either the defense or the prosecution communicate with members of the jury in some other way than through official court personnel. Care should be taken to avoid what might appear to be attempts to communicate or even hold discussions in the presence of members of the jury while the court is not in session.

The Right to a Public Trial and the Right to be Present

The defendant has the right to a public trial. This may be waived by the defendant. Certain parts of the trial, based on local procedures, may proceed after bystanders have been removed from the courtroom. While clearing the courtroom is more common during preliminary hearings, some courts may cautiously do so during trials. One of the most common situations in which a courtroom is clear is when a child molestation case is being heard and the child victim is testifying. The defendant remains in the courtroom, however. The court has the right, separate from the right of the defendant, to maintain the decorum of the court and may exclude unruly bystanders.

Normally, either side in a case may request that witnesses be excluded from the courtroom prior to their testimony. This is termed asking for the rule on witnesses. It is based on the idea that it's easier to test the memory and accuracy of the witness if he has not had the chance to hear the testimony of other witnesses and possibly attempt to make his own testimony coincide with what he has heard. This order is made at the discretion of the court; the witness should take it as a routine practice and not feel that his personal integrity is being challenged.

A criminal trial is not normally held in absentia; in other words, the defendant has the right to be present during proceedings. The defendant may waive his right, however. If the defendant conducts himself in such a disruptive manner that the court cannot function, the appropriate procedure is to remove the defendant from the courtroom rather than stop the trial. It is also possible, especially when numerous co-defendants are being tried together, for the defendant to be excused from attending court upon his own motion.

Opening Statements

Once the jury is seated, each side has the right to make opening statements, with the prosecution going first. The basic purpose of the opening statements is to provide a "roadmap" for the jury to follow as each witness is presented and to help the jury to understand what the case is about. The opening statement may *not* be used as evidence to convict, however. The defense is entitled to make its opening statement to the jury immediately following that of the prosecution. Many courts allow the defense to elect to reserve their opening statement until after the prosecution has presented its evidence and the defense is ready to present theirs.

The Prosecution's Case in Chief

Following the opening statements, the prosecution will present its case in chief. During this presentation, the prosecution must present evidence on every element of each crime charged unless the defense has stipulated to an item. In the case of a stipulation, the prior agreement will be brought to the attention of the court and jury. Failure to cover all of the elements will result in a directed verdict of acquittal. The defense frequently makes such a motion as a routine matter at the end of the prosecution's presentation. In ruling on this motion, the judge will attempt to consider whether a reasonable juror could find for the prosecution beyond a reasonable doubt based on the evidence presented. This involves a weighing of credibility of witnesses as well as of the substance of the testimony. The prosecution is given the benefit of all rational inferences in making this decision. Such motions are allowed, even though they invade the province of the jury because only a ruling in the defendant's favor will prevent the defendant from presenting his case to the jury. A ruling for the defense ends the case immediately with a verdict of not guilty. As with any acquittal, the case cannot be retried. A ruling against the defense merely continues the trial in its normal manner. The prosecution in a criminal case has no similar motion for a verdict of guilty.

The prosecutor will determine the order in which the witnesses will be called and what information he will seek to have introduced. Since the investigator is usually more familiar with the witnesses than the prosecutor is, the investigator should follow the questioning closely and be prepared to suggest various lines of questioning. The method in which this assistance is provided will depend upon the rapport the investigators have developed with the individual prosecuting attorneys. In no case should the investigator detract from the decorum of the courtroom by attempting to interrupt. Officers and witnesses should be instructed prior to the trial to answer all questions as simply and directly as possible while testifying and not to volunteer information. The attorney has a plan in mind when he selects the order in which he will ask questions, and this plan should be respected and not interfered with.

Following the questioning by the prosecutor, the defense will be allowed to cross-examine. The extent of the cross-examination is within the discretion of the defense attorney and will depend upon his trial strategy. The scope of the cross-examination is frequently restricted to items the witness testifed about during direct examination and to matters which may impeach the witness, such as personal bias against the defendant, prior inconsistent statements, or the inability to have actually observed incidents testified about. During cross-examination, the defense will attempt to convince the jury that the witness is either not certain about the matter he has testified about, that he is untruthful, or that he has personal motives for testifying against the defendant. When prior inconsistent statements are shown, the purpose is to demonstrate that the witness is now claiming something different and therefore is either lying or uncertain. Which of a witness's statements is correct is not an issue. Personal biases—such as those resulting from family relationships, hatred of the defendant, or being paid to testify—also tend to discredit a witness's testimony. Prior felony convictions are usually admissible to cast doubt on the witness's truthfulness. Showing that a person is nearsighted tends to discredit eyewitness accounts. Similar attempts are made to show that a witness was incapable of hearing reported conversations. A lenghty time lapse between an event and the making of a report is used to cast doubt on the accuracy of the report, since the recollection of the incident may have diminished with time. In addition, testimony concerning a witness's reputation in the community may be judged admissible to show that a person lacks credibility.

Defense manuals often recommend that the defense attorney approach the investigator in a kindly manner and allow the investigator to tell the jury that he is both a qualified investigator and an expert on proper police procedures. Naturally, departures from proper procedures, such as the late filing of reports, blanks in reports, the failure to list all elements of the crime in the first report, or mishandling of evidence will make the investigator look negligent and greatly diminish the value of his testimony.[19] While the investigator must establish his proficiency in order to convince the jury of the soundness of the charges brought, he should not allow the defense attorney to play on his vanity or portray himself as being above all human error. It should also be noted that the officer should not be afraid to testify "I don't remember." The jury will understand that, over time, minute details are likely to slip one's mind. This also leaves the investigator with the opportunity to answer the question later if the answer is recalled.

Following the cross-examination, the prosecution has a limited right to *re-direct* examination. This is used to clarify matters brought up on cross-examination. It may be used to "rehabilitate" a witness by showing some logical reasons for prior inconsistent statement he may have made. It is *not* supposed to be used to present new evidence, however. The traditional rule still followed by many courts is that the side calling a witness *vouches for the witness*. This means that if the witness testifies in an unexpected manner the attorney may not show that the witness is untruthful. More recent trends have allowed the witness to be challenged by the party calling the witness if it is shown that the testimony is surprising or damaging. If this view is followed, the attorney will be allowed to ask questions to show the prior favorable testimony or possibly to show that the witness is currently lying.

The Defense's Case in Chief

After the prosecution has called all of its witnesses and introduced its evidence, the defense may produce its own witnesses and evidence. Since the prosecution has the burden of proof, the defense does not have to introduce any evidence. If witnesses are called, the defense attorney will examine them and the prosecution will then have the right to cross-examine. The defense will also be allowed to re-direct examination where appropriate. Since the defendant has a Fifth Amendment right to refuse to incriminate himself, he may refuse to take the witness stand. The prosecution cannot compel him to testify. If the defendant does *not* testify, the prosecution may not mention the fact as an inference of guilt when summing up the case to the jury. The defense will weigh many factors when deciding whether or not to place the defendant on the witness stand. These include:

- the desirability of having the defendant "come clean" before the jury;
- whether the same testimony can be made by another witness;
- whether the defendant has testimony that is legally or factually supportive of his defense; or
- the evidence the prosecution has that will impeach the defendant.[20]

This decision is crucial because the defendant who takes the witness stand can be compelled to answer cross-examination questions concerning all matter in his testimony. It is also important because the rules of impeachment allow the prosecution to introduce evidence to show the defendant's prior felony record and prior statements that might not be admissible as part of the prosecution's case in chief. The defense attorney may strenuously urge the defendant to remain silent, but the defendant is the one who makes the final decision. Occasionally, the defendant will take the stand and testify to facts that are far more damaging than any evidence the prosecution was able to produce. Since the convicted defendant may appeal on the grounds that his failure to testify was coerced by the defense attorney and was prejudicial to him at the trial, some judges will have the defendant take the stand without the jury being present and testify for the record that he voluntarily invoked the Fifth Amendment right to remain silent.

The defense may present as many witnesses as it desires. These may be alibi witnesses, witnesses to the crime (who testify to different facts than the prosecution witnesses), or expert witnesses. If the defendant is pleading not guilty by reason of insanity, for example, the defense will present expert witnesses on the issue of sanity. The defense may also seek to introduce character witnesses. The general rule is that the prosecution may not attack the character of the defendant except by establishing the crime charged, but the defendant may place his character in issue if he desires.[21] Putting the defendant's character in issue is an attempt to convince the jury that the defendant is a good person and therefore probably not guilty of the crime. Normally, the defense must limit its character evidence to the traits in question. If the offense charged is theft, honesty would be a relevant trait of character, but peacefulness would not. The traditional rules of evidence have only allowed testimony concerning a person's reputation in the community to prove his character traits. The witness must be able to testify that he knows of the defendant, is acquainted with the community where the defendant is known, and is familiar with what people of that community think of the defendant. The witness's own opinion of the defendant's character is not admissible unless the particular jurisdiction has expanded the traditional rule.

After the defense raises the issue of character, the prosecution may cross-examine the character witness or present its own evidence. The method of presentation is also restricted by many traditional rules. Since many courts do not require the defense to disclose its case in advance, the investigator is vital in aiding the prosecution in discrediting character witnesses. First, the investigator should make a list of potential rebuttal character witnesses in case the defense should use this tactic. The prosecutor should be consulted regarding subpoenaing these witnesses since it is impossible to ascertain in advance whether they will be needed. Second, once a character witness is called, the investigator should carefully note any items that may be used to impeach the witness. If it is widely known in the community that the defendant has a certain trait and the witness testifies contrary to this, the witness may be impeached by showing that he does not in fact have knowledge of the defendant's reputation. If the witness's own truthfulness is questionable, this may also be shown to impeach him.

In a criminal case, the court has the right to call a witness on its own motion. The prosecution or defense may request that the court exercise this power when neither side wants to vouch for the witness, or when it is felt that the witness is hostile and the only effective way to obtain meaningful testimony from him is by cross-examination. If the court feels that some important aspect of the case has been left untouched by both sides, or that justice requires additional information that can only be supplied by a witness that has not been called, it will call the witness. Once the witness has been called both sides have the right to cross-examine and impeach him.

At the close of the defense's case, the prosecution may be allowed to call additional witnesses in rebuttal of the facts developed by the defense. The scope of this right is restricted to *new* matter, and it is rarely allowed to be used simply because the prosecution has forgotten to call a witness or ask an important question. This is followed by a defense rebuttal, in which the evidence presented by the prosecution during its rebuttal may in turn be rebutted.

Final Arguments

Final arguments by each side conclude the presentation. The final argument frequently combines a summary of the evidence, presented in the light most favorable to the side doing the summation, and an appeal to the jury for a favorable verdict. This statement, like the opening argument, is *not* evidence. The prosecution speaks first; some states also allow the prosecution to rebut the defense's closing argument as well.

Jury Instructions

By the time a case is reaching a close, each side will have selected jury instructions that it wishes to have used. A jury instruction is a statement of the law that the jury is supposed to apply to the facts. All relevant points of law must be covered by the jury instructions. Frequently, each side will select some of the same jury instructions along with others that are conflicting or opposing. The judge must decide which ones will be given to the jury. This decision is a very important one and is frequently a basis for appeal. Some instructions are fairly standard, such as those concerning the burden of proof and the evaluation of the credibility of witnesses. Standard jury instructions are usually available in the law library; they frequently incorporate language from appellate court decisions. If the case is unusual, the attorney may have to compose the jury instructions. If both sides have failed to request instructions on a vital point, it will be up to the court to provide an appropriate jury instruction.

After the closing arguments, the judge will *charge* the jury. Most jurisdictions provide for the judge to summarize the evidence before the jury is sent to deliberate. Some allow the judge to comment on the evidence. The judge's comments are restricted, however, in that he can only state the facts that are up to the jury to decide. He may *not* appear to be biased. The judge will also read aloud the instructions to the jury at this time. In some states, the jury receives a written copy of the jury instructions to use as they discuss the case.

Jury Deliberations

Once the jury members retire to the jury room for deliberations, they are carefully watched to avoid outside interferences. It is the general rule to sequester juries in criminal cases during deliberations even though they may not have been sequestered during trial. This means that they are fed, housed, and kept under court supervision at all times. All deliberations are conducted in the jury room. During meal breaks and nightly housing, jurors are instructed not to discuss the case. Local rules govern what items jurors may take to the jury room with them. Exhibits from the trial may occasionally be taken to the jury room, but the rule is far from uniform. The jury may request further instructions from the court or ask that testimony be read to them from the transcript that was taken during the trial. If the jury is unable to reach a verdict after a considerable length of time, the judge may call them in and instruct them to try harder. The amount of pressure that the judge is allowed to exert varies considerably from state to state. The "dynamite charge" that exerts great pressure on the jury to reach a verdict is increasingly looked upon with disfavor.[22] If the judge determines that the jury is unable to reach a verdict, a mistrial or "hung jury" will be declared. The defense may object to this in an attempt to establish grounds to assert double jeopardy if the charges are retried.

Sentencing

Although the court is normally empowered to impose sentence immediately after a guilty verdict has been returned and recorded, the trend today is to have a probation and sentencing report prepared to assist the judge in making this decision. The report is usually prepared by a probation officer, who acts as an officer of the court. In preparing the report this officer reviews court records, along with the records of any prison, military service, employment, school, or hospital that might be available. He may interview the defendant and his family, neighbors, and clergy.

The workload of the probation officer assigned to the case may not allow him to prepare as thorough a report as might be desired, however. Various channels of information may be available to help facilitate this task. Sometimes it's possible for a source of information to personnally discuss the case with the officer. At other times, formal communication via correspondence is required. Some jurisdictions allow the prosecution to submit independent sentencing reports directly to the court. The investigator should be familiar with the procedures appropriate to his state, as he frequently has access to pertinent facts that should be considered in the sentencing decision. The factors that are considered in imposing a sentence are vastly different than those which determine the admissibility of evidence during the trial. The report will attempt to evaluate the defendant and determine if he is amenable to rehabilitation. His entire personal background will be considered, as well as his environment and surroundings. If special circumstances are noted (of aggravation or mitigation, for example), the investigator should make them known to the court or the probation officer prior to the actual sentencing.

The investigator will probably not be required to be present at the sentencing. If he is, he will note what is called the right of allocution. This is a right normally afforded the defendant to address the court personally prior to the imposition of sentence. The court asks each defendant for any comments that he might have, and the defendant's answer is not governed by the rules of evidence. He may plead for leniency in any manner that he desires; no impeachment is allowed at this time.

Post-Conviction Motions

Once the trial is over, there are a number of motions that the defense may make. These are normally heard by the judge without calling witnesses, so the investigator doesn't usually have to be present. If the motions succeed, however, the investigator may find himself faced with having to prepare for a complete retrial of the case. If the defense wins an appeal on grounds other than those which concern the sufficiency of the evidence, the prosecution has the right to retry the case. In this instance, the defendant waives double jeopardy. Grounds for appeal include the following:

- a motion to set aside the judgment based on the insufficiency of the evidence;
- a motion for a new trial based on prejudicial errors comitted during the original trial; and
- a motion for a new trial

Grounds which normally succeed in the request for a new trial include:

- a verdict against the preponderance of the evidence;
- errors committed during pre-trial proceedings;
- errors committed during the trial itself; and
- newly discovered evidence.

Newly discovered evidence usually must be shown to have been discovered after the trial. Generally, it must be either evidence of false testimony by prosecution witnesses or some fact that the defense discovered after the trial that so materially changes the evidence that the jury verdict would probably have been different had they known about it. The defense must show due diligence before the trial in efforts to discover evidence. This motion may never succeed if the evidence was intentionally not presented during the trial. While the defendant is entitled to his "day in court," the law considers that there is a point at which things should be settled and left alone. In order to refute the motion for a new trial on new evidence, then, the investigator may be responsible for determining the validity of the claim that the new evidence is material and that it was previously unknown.

Prior to destroying any files or personal notes on the case, the investigator should verify that the time for appeal has passed and no appeal is pending.

A Final Note on the Investigator's Role During the Judicial Process

Sometimes it's difficult, but the investigator must keep his sense of perspective all during the trial process. It may seem as if the American system of justice is weighted in favor of the accused; the investigator's task is a demanding one, and even well-handled investigations may not always result in convictions. Each investigator, then, must strive to uphold the highest personal standards and not allow disillusionment and bitterness to interfere.

Summary

The investigator normally has the responsibility of following a case through court. This means repeated contacts with the prosecutor's office. Because of this, it is important that investigators familarize themselves with the procedures of the local prosecutor's office and understand what function the investigator plays in the case after a suspect is arrested. A good rapport between investigator and prosecutor is invaluable and efforts should be made to maintain one.

To obtain the original complaint the investigator will have to present the case to the prosecutor. The entire file should be reviewed for the purpose of deciding what formal charges will be sought. The charges for which the suspect was arrested are not binding at this stage. Each possible crime should be reviewed and evidence to support the elements of the crime determined. Information obtained after the arrest may show that elements of the crime are not provable or that evidence now is available to prove crimes not thought to be present at time of arrest. While it is useless to seek a complaint if elements of the crime are missing, it is not conversely true that a complaint will be sought if all the elements can be proven. Both police and prosecutor are vested with a great deal of discretion. One method of exercising this discretion is by not filing complaints for all crimes committed. It may be helpful to keep this in mind when preparing to present the case to the prosecutor. If experience has shown that the local prosecutor normally does not file complaints in certain circumstances, it may be very useful to have sound arguments prepared when seeking a complaint in such cases in order to convince the prosecutor that this is an appropriate case to deviate from the rule.

As soon as it is apparent which charges are to be filed, the investigator should make an outline of all information available on those charges. The case is still fresh in mind at this point and the task will be much easier and the result more accurate than if it were done several months later when the case comes to trial. The outline should include names and addresses of all witnesses and description and location of all items of physical evidence. Summaries of all statements and confessions involved in the case should be included. From time to time this outline should be reviewed and updated if addresses have changed, new evidence has been discovered or evidence has been ruled inadmissible or become lost.

A preliminary hearing will be held for felonies. While this is not a full adversary trial, it is necessary to establish a prima facie case against the defendant or the case will be dismissed. Since it is not necessary to prove the case beyond a reasonable doubt, it may not be necessary to have all witnesses testify at the hearing. In selecting which witnesses to call, the investigator should remember that evidence must be presented to show each element of every crime charged and to tie the defendant to each crime. Witnesses should be subpoenaed. If the judge finds that a prima facie showing has been made, the case will be bound over for trial and the prosecutor will file an information. If the case is presented to a grand jury and it is found that sufficient evidence was presented, an indictment will be filed. If a sufficient case has not been shown the case will be dismissed. When additional evidence is available that was not presented, such as a witness who did not testify, the case may be refiled by the prosecutor or represented to the grand jury.

It is not uncommon for the investigator to totally lose contact with the case after the information or indictment has been filed. Most commonly this is due to plea bargaining. The prosecutor will meet with the defense attorney and an agreement reached whereby the defendant pleads guilty to some crime or crimes and the prosecutor agrees to give the defendant some consideration. The prosecutor may drop some charges, accept pleas to lesser included offenses, drop alleged enhancements (such as prior offenses or use of a firearm during the crime), or agree to ask the judge to impose a lenient sentence. If such an agreement is reached, the case will be settled without trial. The investigator is rarely involved in these negotiations. However, it cannot be assumed that a case has been closed in this manner simply due to lack of contact with the case over a long period of time. Prior to closing the file, the investigator should check to verify that all court proceedings have been completed.

Another set of procedures that frequently occur before trial are suppression motions and motions to dismiss. The suppression motion is brought by the defense attorney and seeks to have evidence ruled inadmissible. Most commonly this involves allegations of illegal search and seizure or illegally obtained confessions. The hearing on the motion may be based solely on the transcript of testimony given at the preliminary hearing or witnesses may be called. The only witnesses necessary for this type of motion are those who actually saw or participated in the allegedly illegal conduct. The defense usually selects the witnesses to be called. Thus, the investigator may not be called if not personally involved in the incident in question. The motion to dismiss may come alone or be combined with the suppression motion. If any evidence has been ruled inadmissible, the defense will seek to show that there is no longer sufficient admissible evidence to support the charge or charges. If the evidence suppressed was crucial to the case, the motion to dismiss will be granted. The motion to dismiss is also used for technical defects in the information of indictment and to challenge the sufficiency of evidence given at preliminary hearing or before the grand jury. A motion to dismiss may be granted for any one or all charged crimes. If the motion to dismiss is granted due to technicality, or due to insufficient admissible evidence and there is additional evidence not introduced at the preliminary hearing or to the grand jury, the prosecutor is permitted to refile the case.

When the trial date nears, the investigator will need to make a final review of the case and determine which witnesses will be needed. Subpoenas should be secured and served on each witness. It should also be ascertained that each witness can recall the events in question. The location of each item of physical evidence should be verified. If it is discovered that evidence has disappeared or a crucial witness has forgotten important facts, the prosecutor should be notified as soon as possible in order to allow time to reassess the case. The investigator should review the file in order to refresh recollection of the case in preparation for testifying. Background information on potential witnesses, both prosecution and defense, should be reviewed in order to provide the prosecutor with information to impeach or rehabilitate a witness.

At trial the prosecutor may ask the investigator to sit at the counsel table. If this is allowed, the investigator should pay close attention to the examination of each witness and provide the prosecutor with necessary information in a non-disruptive manner. When called to the witness stand the investigator should directly answer those questions put without interjecting unnecessary or unresponsive material. Caution should be used to avoid mention of facts previously ruled inadmissible. On cross-examination questions should be answered directly without displaying hositility toward the defendant or defense attorney. If a question asks for information that cannot be recalled at the moment, this should be forthrightly admitted. Investigators should be cautious in answering questions by the defense attorney which permit them to depict themselves as conducting a perfect investigation. This is a device frequently used to make minor errors that occurred appear to indicate that a poor investigation was conducted.

Following a jury verdict of guilty, the prosecutor may be permitted to submit a memorandum in support of either a harsh or lenient sentence. If this is permitted and the prosecutor indicates that such a memorandum will be filed in the case, the investigator may be called upon to submit appropriate information. Since the verdict has been returned at this point, evidence not otherwise admissible is accepted at this stage to show that defendant's background and behavior indicate that a certain type of sentence is most likely to serve society's interests. It is a good idea to check with the prosecutor to determine what is sought prior to conducting further investigation into the case.

Due to a variety of post-trial motions and appeals that are available to a convicted person, the file must be retained for a considerable time after trial. The investigator is rarely involved in the handling of these procedures. If the result of the motions and appeal is a reversal or setting aside of the guilty verdict, the case will be returned and a new trial may result. At this time the investigator again becomes an active participant in the case. The exact length of time files should be retained to allow all such procedures to be completed should be determined by consulting with the local prosecutor.

Questions and Topics for Discussion

1. Obtain copies of crime reports from your local police station, if possible. Then review them to determine?

   a) What information is needed to obtain a complaint;

   b) What kinds of witnesses and physical evidence are necessary for preliminary hearing; and

   c) What kinds of witnesses and physical evidence are necessary for a trial.

2. Attend a felony trial. Afterward, discuss with your class:

   a) the amount of time that was involved;

   b) the witnesses who were called;

   c) the strength of the case presented; and

   d) whether the investigation and trial preparations served to have been thorough.

3. Should the prosecutor have discretion in determing what charges are filed against a defendant?

4. Should plea bargaining be allowed?

5. Should the judge consider factors other than the evidence presented at a trial when imposing a sentence? If so, name some of these factors.

6. Is a preliminary hearing a necessary step in affording the defendant a fair trial, or is it a waste of time?

7. Is our method of selecting jurors an appropriate method of ensuring a fair trial?

8. Role-play courtroom demeanor and testimony in your class. Appoint class members to act as the prosecutor and defense attorney. Have them examine a member of the class who has been assigned the investigator's role. Then have them cross-examine the investigator. If desired, assign other class members to act as witnesses.

Footnotes and References

1. Albert W. Alschuler, "The Defense Attorney's Role in Plea Bargaining " *The Yale Law Journal*, 84:6 (May 1975), page 1207.

2. "Prosecutorial Discretion in the Initiation of Criminal Complaints," an unsigned comment in the *Southern California Law Review*, Vol. 42 (1969), pp. 531-532.

3. Wayne R. LaFave, "The Prosecutor's Discretion in the United States," *The American Journal of Comparative Law*, Vol. 18 (1970), pp. 533-535.

4. *Brady v. United States*, 397 U.S. 742, 90 S.Ct. 1463, 25 L.Ed.2d 747 (1970); *McMann v. Richardson*, 397 U.S. 759, 90 S.Ct. 1441, 25 L.Ed.2d 763 (1970).

5. Albert W. Alschuler, "The Defense Attorney's Role in Plea Bargaining," *The Yale Law Journal*, 84:6 (May 1975), page 1187.

6. American Bar Association, *Code of Professional Responsibility* (Chicago: American Bar Association, 1970), Rule DR 7-103, Canons 5 and 15.

7. Robert L. Fletcher, "Pretrial Discovery in State Criminal Cases," *Stanford Law Review*, Vol. 12 (March 1960), pages 297-308.

8. Robert L. Fletcher, *ibid.*, page 315.

9. *Pate v. Robinson*, 383 U.S. 375, 86 S.Ct. 836, 15 L.Ed.2d 815 (1966).

10. *Wade v. Hunter*, 336 U.S. 684, 69 S.Ct. 834, 93 L.Ed. 974 (1949).

11. *Argersinger v. Hamlin*, 407 U.S. 25, 92 S.Ct. 206, 32 L.Ed.2d 530 (1972).

12. *Powell v. Alabama*, 287 U.S. 45, 53 S.Ct. 55, 77 L.Ed. 158 (1932).

13. *Faretta v. California*, 422 U.S. 806, 95 S.Ct. 2525, 45 L.Ed.2d 562 (1975).

14. *Baldwin v. New York*, 399 U.S. 66, 90 S.Ct. 1886, 26 L.Ed.2d 437 (1970) conformed to 297 N.Y. 731, 314 N.Y.S.2d 539, 262 N.E.2d 678.

15. *Peters v. Kiff*, 407 U.S. 493, 92 S.Ct. 2163, 33 L.Ed.2d 83 (1972).

16. *Swain v. Alabama*, 380 U.S. 202, 85 S.Ct. 824, 13 L.Ed.2d 759 (1965).

17. *Williams v. Florida*, 399 U.S. 78, 90 S.Ct. 1893, 26 L.Ed.2d 446 (1970).

18. *Apodaca v. Oregon*, 406 U.S. 404, 92 S.Ct. 1628, 32 L.Ed.2d 184 (1972).

19. Anthony G. Amsterdam, *Trial Manual for the Defense of Criminal Cases* (Philadelphia: American Law Institute, 1974), page I-371.

20. Anthony G. Amsterdam, *ibid.*, page I-386.

21. Charles T. McCormick, *Handbook of the Law of Evidence*, 2nd edition; Edward R. Cleary, editor (St. Paul: West Publishing Co., 1972), page 454.

22. *Huffman v. U.S.*, 297 F.2d 754 (5th Cir. 1962) certiorari denied 370 U.S. 955, 82 S.Ct. 1605, 8 L.Ed.2d 820.

Annotated Bibliography

Alschuler, Albert W., "The Defense Attorney's Role in Plea Bargaining," *The Yale Law Journal*, Vol. 84, Number 6, May 1975, pp. 1179-1314. The results of a law professor's one year study of plea bargaining are presented giving the results of interviews with defense attorneys, public defenders, appointed attorneys, and defendants who represented themselves.

Armstrong, Anthony G., *Trial Manual for the Defense of Criminal Cases*, Philadelphia: American Law Institute, 1974. An extremely detailed analysis of each aspect of a criminal trial is presented from the viewpoint of the defense attorney. The approach is useful in anticipating the opposition.

Goldstein, Abraham S., "The State and the Accused: Balance of Advantage in Criminal Procedure," *The Yale Law Journal*, Vol. 69, 1960, pp. 1149-1199. Discussion of various changing factors that effect the criminal trial and how advances in some areas have been hindered by the lack of progress in others: Proof beyond reasonable doubt, pretrial screening, disclosure and discovery.

Graham, Fred P., *The Due Process Revolution*, New York: Hayden Book Company, 1970. Decisions of the Warren Court that effect law enforcement and criminal trials are reviewed in light of surrounding circumstances and the personnel of the Court.

Heymann, Phillip B. and William H. Kenety, *The Murder Trial of Wilbur Jackson*, St. Paul: West Publishing Co., 1975. An edited transcript of an actual trial and copies of exhibits used at trial are used along with a limited amount of narrative to illustrate trial proceedings.

Miller, Frank W. and Robert O. Dawson, George E. Dix, Raymond I. Parnas, *The Mental Health Process*, Mineola, N.Y.: The Foundation Press, Inc., 1971. Selected cases and journal articles are used to discuss competency to stand trial, hospitalization after a verdict of not guilty by reason of insanity, and civil committment procedures.

—————————————————, *The Correctional Process*, Mineola, N.Y.: The Foundation Press, Inc., 1971. Selected cases and journal articles are used to discuss factors considered in sentencing and legal restrictions during imprisonment and parole.

Southern California Law Review, "Prosecutorial Discretion in the Initiation of Criminal Complaints, (Unsigned Comment), Vol. 42, 1969, pp. 519-545. Prosecutorial discretion is reviewed in light of traditional concepts and the process currently used to obtain criminal complaints.

Traynor, Roger J., "Ground Lost and Found in Criminal Discovery," *New York University Law Review*, Vol. 39, April 1964, pp. 228-250. Criminal discovery procedures are compared for the most restrictive jurisdictions and the more liberal states.

Uviller, H. Richard, *The Processes of Criminal Justice: Adjudication*, St. Paul: West Publishing Co., 1975. Case decisions and codes are used to discuss the trial process, right to counsel, right to speedy trial and trial by jury and the roles of defendant, prosecutor and judge.

Appendix
Most Frequently Used
Forms and Formats

Arrest Report Form

OFFENSE REPORT ☑	DEPARTMENT OF PUBLIC SAFETY	1. DR. No. 84-112
INCIDENT REPORT ○		

2. DATE & TIME REPORTED 3/8/77 2100 hrs.	3. TYPE OF OFFENSE/INCIDENT Possession of marijuana for sale	4. STATUTE NO. 1002	5. COUNTY Burns	6. ROUTED TO Det. Bur.

7. DATE & TIME OCCURRED 3/8/77 2100 hrs.	8. LOCATION OF OCCURRENCE Interstate 22 MP 46.8 DNA	9. NAME OF BUSINESS	10. LICENSE DNA	11. LIC. NO. DNA

VICTIM

12. NAME STATE	13. ADDRESS	14. OCCUPATION

15. BUSINESS ADDRESS	16. SEX	17. RACE/NATIONALITY	18. PLACE OF BIRTH	19. D.O.B.	20. HT.	21. WT.	22. HAIR	23. EYES

24. OTHER	25. SOCIAL SECURITY NO.	26. HOME PHONE	27. BUSINESS PHONE

VEHICLE

28. SUSPECT ☒ VICTIM ○	29. COLOR 30. YEAR blk/ blu 1969	31. MAKE Ford	32. BODY STYLE 4 dr.	33. LIC. NO. PRB 467	34. STATE AZ	35. OTHER I.D. VIN 998364748

36. NEXT OF KIN	37. ADDRESS	38. PHONE	39. RELATIONSHIP

40. PERSON WHO REPORTED OFFENSE TO D.P.S. On view	41. ADDRESS	42. HOME PHONE	43. BUSINESS PHONE

SUSPECT

44. NAME Robert John JONES	45. ADDRESS 1868 E. 7th St. Burns, AZ.	46. OCCUPATION Lab. Tech.

47. BUSINESS ADDRESS Unemployed.	48. SEX M	49. RACE/NATIONALITY W	50. PLACE OF BIRTH Welch, WV	51. D.O.B. 5/8/48	52. HT. 5'11	53. WT. 166	54. HAIR blond	55. EYES blue

56. OTHER light complexion	57. ALIAS, MARKS, SCARS, TATTOOS, ETC. 6 in. scar on rt forearm outer	58. SOCIAL SECURITY NUMBER 488-81-5688

59. LOCATION OF ARREST I 22 MP 46.8	60. DATE & TIME OF ARREST 3/8/77 2100 hrs.	61. LOCATION BOOKED OR REFERRED Burns SO#186	62. CITATION NUMBER(S) 2460394

LIST ALL OTHER SUSPECTS/WITNESSES

ADDITIONAL CHARGES
Transportation of marijuana 1002.07
Possession of marijuana 1002.05

EVIDENCE
Items 1 through 200 200 (hundred) kilos of marijuana

WITNESS LIST:
James R. (only) Leon, MW (Mexico) 29 yrs. DOB: 2-4-45, Transit

Ofc. J. Roan #168, DPS, Burns
Ofc. E. Smith #552, DPS, Burns

SUBPOENA LIST
Criminalist DPS Crime Lab, Anytown, AZ.

Ofc. J. Roan, # 168, DPS, Burns (Transported suspect's veh. to DPS Burns)
Ofc. E. Smith, #552, DPS, Burns (Arresting Officer)

63. THE FOLLOWING WARNINGS WERE GIVEN TO THE ARRESTED PERSON: 1. YOU HAVE THE RIGHT TO REMAIN SILENT. 2. ANY STATEMENT YOU MAKE CAN AND WILL BE USED AGAINST YOU IN A COURT OF LAW. 3. YOU HAVE THE RIGHT TO CONSULT WITH AN ATTORNEY AND HAVE HIM PRESENT PRIOR TO AND DURING QUESTIONING. 4. IF YOU CANNOT AFFORD AN ATTORNEY, ONE WILL BE APPOINTED FOR YOU PRIOR TO ANY FURTHER QUESTIONING, IF YOU SO DESIRE.	SUBJECT INFORMED OF THE OFFENSE (S) FOR WHICH ARRESTED. YES☒ NO☐ SUBJECT ADVISED OF HIS RIGHTS. . . . . YES☒ NO☐ SUBJECT INDICATED HE UNDERSTOOD. . . . . YES☒ NO☐ SUBJECT WAIVED HIS RIGHTS. . . . . YES☐ NO☐ JUVENILE ADVISED THAT HE MAY BE REMANDED TO ADULT COURT. . . . . YES☐ NO☐ PARENTAL APPROVAL OBTAINED FOR QUESTIONING OF JUVE- NILE BY ARRESTING OFFICER? . . . . YES☐ NO☐ PARENT OR JUVENILE P.O. CONTACTED (HOUR) SUBJECT ADVISED OF RIGHTS (HOUR) 2100 hrs

64. PENDING ○ CLOSED BY ARREST ☒ CLOSED, OTHER ○	65. OFFICER(S) E. Smith, #552	I.D.	DISTRICT 3.	66. REVIEWED BY:
				67. DATE & TIME TYPED 3/10/77 0800
				68. CLERK NO. 01

DPS FORM W Rev 7/7

Arrest Report Form (Continued)

DEPARTMENT OF PUBLIC SAFETY   SUPPLEMENTARY REPORT

1. DATE	2. TYPE OF OFFENSE	3. DR No.
3/8/77	Possession of Marijuana	84-112

4. DATE OCCURRED	5. LOCATION OF OCCURRENCE	6. ROUTE TO:
3/8/77	I-22 MP 46.3	

7. FAULT OR VICTIM	8. ADDRESS	
Robert John JONES	1868 E. 7th, Burns, AZ	

SYNOPSIS

On 3/8/77 at 2100 hrs. at MP 46.3 on I-22 Robert John JONES was found to be in possession of marijuana for sale, transportation of marijuana, and possession of marijuana.

On 3/8/77 at 2055 hrs., I was parked in the median at MP 45.6 on I-10. I observed a veh. eastbound which was traveling at a slower speed than the rest of the traffic. I began following the veh. and observed that it apparently had two occupants. I clocked the veh. and found that it was doing 50MPH in a 55MPH posted zone. I stopped the veh., a blk/blu 1969 Ford, 4 dr, bearing AZ license PRB 467 at MP 46.3.

I approached the veh. and was met at the left rear fender by the driver, Robert John JONES. Mr. Jones was asked for his driver's license and veh. reg. I also advised Mr. Jones that he had not committed any traffic violation, but was stopping him to see if he was fatigued. The pass. remained in the veh. seated at the right front.

While examining Mr. Jones' CA driver's license, C12345, I detected a faint odor of marijuana. I asked Mr. Jones to step to the right side of the veh. out of the roadway. Mr. Jones did as directed. As we arrived at the right side of the veh., Mr. Jones gave me the AZ title to the veh. The title showed that the Veh. was registered in Mr. Jones name.

I questioned Mr. Jones and said, "Why is your vehicle sitting so low in the rear?" Mr. Jones replied, "The veh. probably has bad schocks." He volunteered: "I am driving from Burns to Kansas City to look for a job." As I was talking to Jones, I again smelled an odor of marijuana while standing at the right rear of the veh.

I asked Mr. Jones if he would open the trunk of the car. Mr. Jones asked me, "Do I have to open the trunk?" I replied, "No." I then asked Mr. Jones, "Who are you driving for and how much stuff do you have? " Mr. Jones replied, "I won't lie to you, I have a little, you know how it is, I need the money."

I asked Mr. Jones for the keys to the trunk, which he removed from his right front pocket and handed to me, saying nothing. I placed the key in the lock and opened the trunk. As the trunk lid opened, I observed that the trunk was full of green wrapped bricks. Based upon my training and observations in the past and the odor of marijuana, I opened one of the bricks and observed a green leafy substance, which appeared to me to be marijuana.

I then advised Mr. Jones of his Miranda rights, at 2100 hours, and that he was under arrest for possession of marijuana for sale, transporting marijuana, and possession of marijuana. I handcuffed Mr. Jones and placed him in my patrol

9. PENDING ☐	10. OFF CER(S)	I.D.	DISTRICT	11. REVIEWED BY:		
CLOSED BY ARREST ☒	E. Smith	#552	3			
UNFOUNDED ☐				12. DATE & TIME TYPED	13. CLERK NO	
EXCEPTIONALLY CLEARED ☐				3/10/77 0840	01	
PREVIOUSLY CLEARED ☐				14. DR No.		

Arrest Report Form (Continued)

DEPARTMENT OF PUBLIC SAFETY   SUPPLEMENTARY REPORT (cont)

DATE	TYPE OF OFFENSE	DR NO.
3/8/77	Possession of Marijuana	84-112

DATE OCCURRED	LOCATION OF OCCURRENCE	ROUTE TO:
3/8/77	I-22 MP 46.3	

SUSPECT OR VICTIM	ADDRESS
Robert John JONES	1868 E. 7th, Burns, AZ

vehicle.

During the entire conversation with Mr. Jones, the passenger remained in the right front seat of the veh. After securing Mr. Jones, I approached the veh. and opened the pass. door. I asked the pass. to step out onto the roadway. I then asked the subject for some type of identification, which he could not produce. The subject then told me in broken English that he had just crossed the Mex. border several hours ago and that the driver of the veh. had picked him up as he was hitchhiking along I 22. The subject identified himself as James R. (only) LEON whose home was in San Rafael, Mex. The illegal alien was placed under arrest and handcuffed and placed in officer's vehicle.

I requested assistance from another unit to transport Jones' veh. to the DPS office in Burns, and Ofc. J. Roan, #168, arrived at approx. 2130 hrs. and took possession of the suspect's veh. and transported it to the DPS office in Burns.

At 2140 hrs. as I was driving to the Burns office, Mr. Jones voluntarily said: "I was going to receive $1,800 to drive the car from Burns to Kansas City." And   Mr. Jones said: "I think that one kilo of that stuff is worth about $260 in Kansas City." I asked Mr. Jones who had hired him to transport the marijuana to Knasas City. Mr. Jones refused any info. as to the other parties involved. He said he was afraid for his family if he said anything about who had hired him.

Mr. Jones was transported to the Burns SO for booking. The suspect veh. was secured at the DPS compound in Burns for storage and processing at a later time. See supplement by Ofc. J. Roan.

The evidence was secured at the DPS office at Burns and will be transported to the Crime Lab on 3/8/77 by reporting officer.

Leon was turned over to border patrol authorities.

STATUS	OFFICER(S)		DISTRICT	REVIEWED BY:		
PENDING ☐	E. Smith	#552	3			
CLOSED BY ARREST ☒						
UNFOUNDED ☐				DATE & TIME TYPED	CLERK NO.	
EXCEPTIONALLY CLEARED ☐				3/10/77 0840	01	
PREVIOUSLY CLEARED ☐				DR No.		

Accident Report Form

1	Accident Report	**DATE** YEAR MONTH DAY HOUR 7 7 0 4 1 7 0 5 3 5	AGENCY USE	**REPORT NUMBER** 77-03888

INJURY SEVERITY CLASSIFICATION
1 NO INJURY
2 POSSIBLE INJURY
3 NON-INCAPACITATING EVIDENT
4 INCAPACITATING
5 FATAL
6 UNKNOWN

NCIC NO.   OFFICER'S ID NO.   DAY OF WK

0 8 9 9 0 0 3 2 1 7   TOTAL NO. OF SHEETS 3

2 TOTAL UNITS 1 TOTAL INJURIES 1 TOTAL FATALITIES 0 ESTIMATED TOTAL DAMAGE X OVER MINIMUM / UNDER MINIMUM / FATAL / HIT/RUN / GOVT. PROP. DISTRICT OR GRID NO. 0 8 0 7

3 LOCATION ON NAME OF STREET OR HIGHWAY Interstate 10 N/B   X INSIDE / OUTSIDE CITY Anytown COUNTY Zuma

INTERSECTING STREET, ROAD /M.P. OR R.P.   AT / FROM 55.7   NORTH EAST / SOUTH WEST / PLUS MINUS DISTANCE MILES FEET

4 TRAFFIC UNIT NO.

STATE AZ CLASS 2 LICENSE OR SOCIAL SECURITY NUMBER L 679817 X DRIVER / PEDESTRIAN / PEDALCYCLIST NAME David Allen JONES SEX M INJ 3

RESTRICTIONS A DATE OF BIRTH 1-9-27 ADDRESS 340 West Mary Drive, Deep Gorge, AZ. CITY STATE

PLATE NUMBER SJS 562 STATE AZ YEAR 77 X SAME AS DRIVER OWNER'S NAME ADDRESS CITY STATE

COLOR White YEAR 70 MAKE Opel BODY STYLE 2 door sedan CAMPER VIN 15220657 DR'S EST SPEED

REMOVED TO Walker Buick, Anytown REMOVED BY Bills Towing ORDERS OF S-321 POSTED SPEED LIMIT 55 OFC EST SPEED 50 OFC EST REAS 30

TRAILER (OTHER UNIT) PLATE NO. n/a STATE YEAR DESCRIPTION OF TRAILER OR OTHER UNIT

STATE CLASS LICENSE OR SOCIAL SECURITY NO. DRIVER / PEDESTRIAN / PEDALCYCLIST NAME SEX INJ

RESTRICTIONS DATE OF BIRTH ADDRESS CITY STATE

PLATE NUMBER STATE YEAR SAME AS DRIVER OWNER'S NAME ADDRESS CITY STATE

COLOR YEAR MAKE BODY STYLE CAMPER VIN DR'S EST SPEED

REMOVED TO REMOVED BY ORDERS OF POSTED SPEED LIMIT OFC EST SPEED OFC EST REAS

TRAILER (OTHER UNIT) PLATE NO. STATE YEAR DESCRIPTION OF TRAILER OR OTHER UNIT

5 PASSENGERS

SEATING POSITION DIAGRAM 07 04 01 08 03 02 09 06 03

13 NOT IN PASSENGER COMPART
11 MOTORCYCLE, BUS
12 OTHER
13 UNKNOWN
14 PEDALCYCLE

INJURED TAKEN TO/BY

UNIT	SEAT POS	NAME	ADDRESS	CITY	STATE	AGE	SEX	INJ

6 OTHER PROPERTY DAMAGE (DESCRIBE)

OWNER'S NAME ADDRESS CITY STATE TELEPHONE NUMBER

7 WITNESSES

NAME ADDRESS CITY STATE TELEPHONE NUMBER AGE

8 ARRESTS

NAME A.R.S. NO. OR CITY CODE CITATION/ARREST NUMBER(S)

9 PHOTOS TAKEN / YES X NO PHOTOGRAPHER'S NAME, ID NUMBER, AND AGENCY INVEST AT SCENE X YES / NO DATE INVEST 4-17-77 TIME INVEST 0700

OFFICER'S SIGNATURE AND ID NUMBER E. Smith #35 AGENCY Uniform Dist. 7 DATE COMPLETED 4-18-77

Accident Report Form (Continued)

11 - INDICATE NORTH	12 - SKIDDING OCCURED	INDICATE WHICH VEHICLES SKIDDED BY NUMBER
	☐ YES ☐ NO	

13 - ACCIDENT MEASUREMENTS

15 - CLASSIFICATION BY TYPE

YES NO
☒ ☐ RAN OFF ROADWAY PRIOR TO FIRST HARMFUL EVENT

COLLISION BETWEEN A MOTOR VEHICLE IN TRANSPORT AND
1 ☐ PEDESTRIAN
2 ☐ MOTOR VEHICLE
3 ☐ RAILWAY TRAIN
4 ☐ PEDALCYCLIST
5 ☐ ANIMAL
6 ☐ FIXED OBJECT
7 ☐ OTHER OBJECT

NONCOLLISION INVOLVING A MOTOR VEHICLE IN TRANSPORT
8 ☐ OVERTURNING
9 ☒ OTHER NONCOLLISION

14 - DESCRIBE WHAT HAPPENED See Attached Supplements

5 - LIGHT CONDITION
CHECK ONLY ONE
1 ☐ DAYLIGHT
2 ☒ DAWN OR DUSK
3 ☐ DARKNESS

YES NO
1 ☒ STREET LIGHT
2 ☐ STREET LIGHT FUNCTIONING

7 - WEATHER CONDITIONS
CHECK ONLY ONE
1 ☒ CLEAR
2 ☐ RAINING
3 ☐ CLOUDY
4 ☐ SNOWING
5 ☐ STRONG WIND
6 ☐ DUST
7 ☐ FOG

8 - ROAD SURFACE TYPE
CHECK ONLY ONE
1 ☒ ASPHALT
2 ☐ CONCRETE
3 ☐ GRAVEL
4 ☐ DIRT
5 ☐ OTHER

19 - TYPE OF LOCATION
CHECK ONLY ONE
1 ☐ INTERSECTION
2 ☐ JUNCTION AREA
3 ☒ NON-JUNCTION AREA
4 ☐ DRIVEWAY ACCESS
5 ☐ ALLEY ACCESS

20 - INTERSECTION RELATED
☐ YES ☒ NO

21 - SPECIAL LOCATION
CHECK ONLY ONE
1 ☐ SCHOOL CROSSING
2 ☐ PEDESTRIAN CROSSWALK (STRIPED)
3 ☐ PEDESTRIAN CROSSWALK (NO STRIPING)
4 ☒ BRIDGE
5 ☐ TUNNEL
6 ☐ RR CROSSING
7 ☐ ALLEY
8 ☐ BIKE PATH
9 ☐ 2-WAY LEFT TURN LANE

22 - UNUSUAL ROAD CONDITION
CHECK ONLY ONE
1 ☐ UNDER CONSTRUCTION, TRAFFIC ALLOWED
2 ☐ UNDER CONSTRUCTION, NO TRAFFIC ALLOWED
3 ☐ UNDER REPAIRS
4 ☐ HOLES, RUTS, BUMPS
5 ☐ OBSTRUCTION - PROTECTED
6 ☐ OBSTRUCTION - UNPROTECTED
7 ☐ OBSTRUCTION - UNLIGHTED AT NIGHT
8 ☐ DEFECTIVE SHOULDERS
9 ☐ CHANGING ROAD WIDTH
10 ☐ FLOODED
11 ☐ TEMPORARY LANE CLOSURE

23 - TRAFFIC CONTROL DEVICES
LEGEND A - DEVICE PRESENT
B - DAMAGED OR NON-FUNCTIONAL PRIOR TO ACCIDENT

CHECK ANY THAT APPLY
A B
1 ☐ ☐ STOP AND GO SIGNAL
2 ☐ ☐ YIELD SIGN
3 ☐ ☐ STOP SIGN
4 ☒ ☐ WARNING SIGN
5 ☐ ☐ RAILROAD SIGNAL
6 ☐ ☐ FLASHING SIGNAL
7 ☐ ☐ FLAGMAN OR OFFICER

24 - NON-INTERSECTION ROAD CHARACTER
CHECK ONLY ONE
1 ☐ 2-WAY STRIPED CENTERLINE
2 ☐ 2-WAY, NO STRIPE
3 ☐ 2-WAY, PAINTED MEDIAN
4 ☐ 2-WAY, RAISED MEDIAN
5 ☐ 2-WAY, BARRIER MEDIAN
6 ☒ 2-WAY, DEPRESSED MEDIAN
7 ☒ 2-WAY, EXTENDED MEDIAN
8 ☐ 1-WAY STREET

25 - ROAD GRADE
CHECK ONLY ONE
1 ☒ LEVEL
2 ☐ DOWNGRADE
3 ☐ UPGRADE
4 ☐ HILLCREST
5 ☐ DIP

26 - UNUSUAL ROAD SURFACE CONDITION
CHECK ONLY ONE
1 ☐ WET
2 ☐ LOOSE SAND, DIRT OR GRAVEL
3 ☒ ICY
4 ☐ FRESH OIL
5 ☐ OTHER
6 ☐ UNKNOWN

27 - PHYSICAL CONDITION
TWO CHOICES PER PERSON MAY BE SELECTED
1 ☒ NO APPARENT DEFECTS
2 ☐ HAD BEEN DRINKING
3 ☐ APPEARED TO BE UNDER INFLUENCE OF DRUGS
4 ☐ ILL - ABILITY INFLUENCED
5 ☐ SLEEPY - FATIGUED
6 ☐ OTHER BODILY DEFECTS, INFIRMITIES
7 ☐ UNKNOWN

28 - VIOLATIONS / BEHAVIOR
TWO CHOICES PER PERSON MAY BE SELECTED
1 2
1 ☐☐ NO IMPROPER DRIVING
2 ☒☐ SPEED TOO FAST FOR CONDITIONS
3 ☐☐ EXCEEDED LAWFUL SPEED
4 ☐☐ FAILED TO YIELD RIGHT-OF-WAY
5 ☐☐ FOLLOWED TOO CLOSELY
6 ☐☐ RAN STOP SIGN
7 ☐☐ DISREGARDED TRAFFIC SIGNAL
8 ☐☐ MADE IMPROPER TURN
9 ☐☐ DROVE IN OPPOSING TRAFFIC LANE
10 ☐☐ KNOWINGLY OPERATED WITH FAULTY OR MISSING EQUIPMENT
11 ☐☐ REQUIRED MOTORCYCLE SAFETY EQUIPMENT NOT USED
12 ☐☐ PASSED IN NO PASSING ZONE
13 ☐☐ UNSAFE LANE CHANGE
14 ☐☐ OTHER UNSAFE PASSING
15 ☐☐ INATTENTION
16 ☐☐ DID NOT USE CROSSWALK
17 ☐☐ WALKED ON WRONG SIDE OF ROAD
18 ☒☐ OTHER
19 ☐☐ UNKNOWN

29 - VEHICLE CONDITION
TWO CHOICES PER VEHICLE MAY BE SELECTED
1 2
1 ☒☐ NO APPARENT DEFECTS
2 ☐☐ DEFECTIVE BRAKES
3 ☐☐ DEFECTIVE STEERING
4 ☐☐ DEFECTIVE HEADLIGHTS
5 ☐☐ DEFECTIVE TAIL LIGHTS
6 ☐☐ DEFECTIVE TURN-SIGNAL
7 ☐☐ PUNCTURE OR BLOWOUT
8 ☐☐ ONE OR MORE SMOOTH TIRES
9 ☐☐ FIRE
10 ☐☐ DEFECTIVE WINDSHIELD WIPER
11 ☐☐ DEFECTIVE EXHAUST SYSTEM
12 ☐☐ OTHER DEFECTS
13 ☐☐ NO TRAILER BRAKES
14 ☐☐ UNKNOWN

30 - TRAFFIC UNIT ACTION
CHECK ONE PER UNIT
1 2
1 ☒☐ GOING STRAIGHT AHEAD
2 ☐☐ SLOWING IN TRAFFICWAY
3 ☐☐ STOPPED IN TRAFFICWAY
4 ☐☐ MAKING LEFT TURN
5 ☐☐ MAKING RIGHT TURN
6 ☐☐ MAKING U TURN
7 ☐☐ ENTERING ALLEY OR DRIVEWAY
8 ☐☐ LEAVING ALLEY OR DRIVEWAY
9 ☐☐ OVERTAKING/PASSING
10 ☐☐ CHANGING LANES
11 ☐☐ BACKING
12 ☐☐ AVOIDING VEHICLE, OBJECT, PEDESTRIAN
13 ☐☐ ENTERING PARKING POSITION
14 ☐☐ LEAVING PARKING POSITION
15 ☐☐ PROPERLY PARKED
16 ☐☐ IMPROPERLY PARKED
17 ☐☐ DRIVERLESS MOVING VEHICLE
18 ☐☐ CROSSING ROAD
19 ☐☐ WALKING WITH TRAFFIC
20 ☐☐ WALKING AGAINST TRAFFIC
21 ☐☐ STANDING
22 ☐☐ LYING
23 ☐☐ GETTING ON OR OFF VEHICLE
24 ☐☐ WORKING ON OR PUSHING VEHICLE
25 ☐☐ WORKING ON ROAD
26 ☐☐ OTHER
27 ☐☐ UNKNOWN

31 - VISION OBSCUREMENT
CHECK ONE PER UNIT
1 2
1 ☒☐ NOT OBSCURED
2 ☐☐ BY PARKED STOPPED VEHICLE
3 ☐☐ BY MOVING VEHICLE
4 ☐☐ BY BUILDING
5 ☐☐ BY EMBANKMENT
6 ☐☐ BY SIGNBOARD
7 ☐☐ BY HILLCREST
8 ☐☐ BY LOAD ON VEHICLE
9 ☐☐ BY TREES, BUSHES
10 ☐☐ BY HEADLIGHT
11 ☐☐ BY SUN GLARE
12 ☐☐ BECAUSE OF BAD WEATHER
13 ☐☐ OTHER
14 ☐☐ RAIN, SNOW, FOG ON WINDSHIELD
15 ☐☐ WINDSHIELD OBSCURED - OTHER
16 ☐☐ UNKNOWN

Accident Report Form (Continued)

Supplement	ACCIDENT DESCRIPTION (Narrative)	#1

SYNOPSIS

Veh #1 was northbound on Interstate 10. In traversing the El Camino Road overpass, the vehicle went out of control due to the cement surface being frosted over from a sudden and unexpected freeze at sunrise.

NARRATIVE

The driver of Veh #1 voluntarily identified himself five minutes after my arrival on the accident scene when he drove back to the scene in another vehicle. The driver (David Allen JONES) voluntarily stated the following:

"I was going to Anytown, north. The car started to slide on the bridge at 50 MPH. I then rolled off the highway to where you see the car now."

Investigation disclosed the following facts and information:

Veh #1 had departed from Deep Gorge and was enroute to Anytown to open his place of business for the day. At the El Camino Rd. overpass the driver lost control of the veh. on the overpass cement surface which was iced over by a frost created just prior to and during the change in temp. at sunrise. The driver had traversed the bridge and the last portion of the bridge the veh. went into a broadside slide to the right, with the left side of the veh. facing a northerly direction of travel. Upon the veh. sliding onto the emergency shoulder, it commenced a rolling tupe action from the change in the veh. center of gravity and vaulted. This action carried it a distance of (points "n to Q") 28 ft. where it touched the soft dirt area on the down slopped bank to the right side of the emergency shoulder of the northbound traffic lanes. The veh. struck the dirt and continued to be bounced into the area and did not touch ground for a distance (points "S to V") 29 ft. where it caused the veh. to complete its rolling action and turning movt. Veh. at final rest was on its wheels, facing a northerly direction.

The driver stated he did not know the bridge overpasses were frosted over. Yet the last overpass prior to the El Camino Road overpass was also frosted over and the cdriver had to cross it to get to Anytown. I physically checked checked that overpass in attempting to locate this accident when dispatched to the scene. It still had frost on it. This should have indicated to the driver that other overpasses would be possibly frosted over too. The normal

prudent driver would have prepared himself for this and adjusted his speed slower than the posted 55 MPH at which the driver attempted to traverse the El Camino Road overpass on the morning of the accident.

I feel from my personal investigation that the driver had failed to adjust veh. spped for the highway and weather conditions and thus violated 7762 of the traffic code. The fastest and safest speed at which I could traverse the frosted overpasses on the morning of the accident was 30 MPH, thus the reasonable and prudent speed was 30 MPH.

Veh. #1 driver sustained minor injuries to his legs and shoulders. Abrasions, contusions were sustained and he stated he would seek his own medical help. It should be noted that the Dept. of Trans. was sanding overpasses iced over on I. 20 E, from MP 270 to the co. line and attmpting to sand all overpasses on I.10. Due to the sudden change in temp. and conditions, they were unable to reach all areas at once. This accident was a result of an act of nature which cannot be controlled by man and the failure by the driver to apply proper precautions which a normal driver would have done once he was aware of road and weather conditions. Veh. #1 was inventoried and removed by Bills Towing Svc. Stored at Walker Buick, Anytown at the owner/driver's request.

INVESTIGATOR'S SIGNATURE

Sgt. E. SMITH #35   8 April 1977. CLOSED.

DATE

Accident Report Form (Continued)

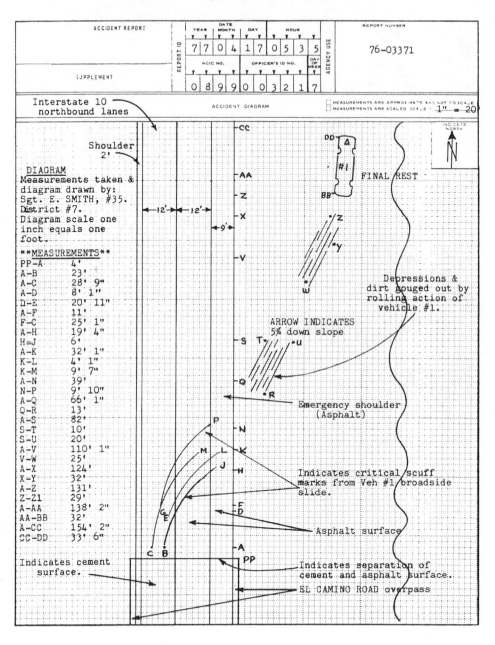

Interstate 10 northbound lanes

DIAGRAM
Measurements taken & diagram drawn by:
Sgt. E. SMITH, #35.
District #7.
Diagram scale one inch equals one foot.

MEASUREMENTS
PP-A	4'
A-B	23'
A-C	28' 9"
A-D	8' 1"
D-E	20' 11"
A-F	11'
F-C	25' 1"
A-H	19' 4"
H-J	6'
A-K	32' 1"
K-L	4' 1"
K-M	9' 7"
A-N	39'
N-P	9' 10"
A-Q	66' 1"
Q-R	13'
A-S	82'
S-T	10'
S-U	20'
A-V	110' 1"
V-W	25'
A-X	124'
X-Y	32'
A-Z	131'
Z-Z1	29'
A-AA	138' 2"
AA-BB	32'
A-CC	154' 2"
CC-DD	33' 6"

Indicates cement surface.

ACCIDENT REPORT

REPORT ID
DATE
YEAR 7 7 MONTH 0 4 DAY 1 7 HOUR 0 5 3 5
NCIC NO. 0 8 9 9 OFFICER'S ID NO. 0 0 3 2 1 DAY OF WEEK 7

SUPPLEMENT

AGENCY USE

REPORT NUMBER
76-03371

ACCIDENT DIAGRAM

☐ MEASUREMENTS ARE APPROXIMATE AND NOT TO SCALE
☐ MEASUREMENTS ARE SCALED SCALE: 1" = 20

Shoulder 2'

FINAL REST

Depressions & dirt gouged out by rolling action of vehicle #1.

ARROW INDICATES 5% down slope

Emergency shoulder (Asphalt)

Indicates critical scuff marks from Veh #1 broadside slide.

Asphalt surface

Indicates separation of cement and asphalt surface.

EL CAMINO ROAD overpass

Incident Report Form

DEPARTMENT OF PUBLIC SAFETY
INTEROFFICE MEMORANDUM

DATE: 20 August 1977

TO: Col. Mayhall, Superintendent
ATTN: Lt. R. Grubb
FROM: Sgt. E. Smith #35

SUBJECT: Citizen Complaint

Number: 86-87178

Complainant: Jerry Anderson JONES
Address: 3423 E. Nelson Road, Anytown, AZ.
Date of Complaint: 11 August 1977
Time: 1800-1830 hours
Location: U.S. 72 and Apple Rd., MP 231

1. The complainant alleged in a telephone conversation with Lt.
   Grubb on 11 August 1977 that he had been stopped by an unknown
   Department of Public Safety officer driving a yellow Buick
   patrol unit at Apple and U.S. 72. JONES alleged that he and
   his wife were treated in an abusive manner, for an alleged
   driving violation.

2. After seven attempts to make contact with the complainant
   I was finally able to contact him on the evening of 20 August
   1977 at 2025 hours and advised him that I was conducting an
   investigation into the alleged complaint which he had made via
   telephone to the Department of Public Safety, District Office,
   on 11 August 1977. JONES stated at this time in a sarcastic
   tone, "It's my word against his (the officer's) and I am the
   dummy. I have no witnesses, so let's drop it here." When I
   attempted to continue the investigation the complainant became
   very adamant and insisted that the complaint be dropped. I
   thanked him for his time and terminated the investigation.

3. Investigation disclosed that the complainant was stopped for
   a minor traffic violation (a slight weaving movement) on U.S.
   72 in front of the Man Motel, 3/4 of a mile south of the
   Apple area while he was southbound. Ptlm. VARGAS, #150,
   observed a slight odor of an alcoholic beverage on the complainants' breath and requested that he perform some physical
   objective tests. The tests were performed satisfactorily.
   Further investigation disclosed that the complainant and his

Incident Report Form (Continued)

Page Two - Citizen Complaint   20 August 1977

    wife were returning from a weekend camping trip in the
mountains and that the complainant was fatigued due to no
vehicle refrigeration, extreme hot weather and lack of
proper sleep. The complainant was allowed to continue
upon satisfactory completion of the tests and field interview by the officer.

4.   I recommend that this complaint be marked as "Unfounded"
    since the complainant refused to pursue the matter upon
    personal contact.

                                    Respectfully submitted,

                                   _____

                                   E. Smith, #35
                                   Sergeant
                                   Western Sector

Index

F

G

H

I

West's

Criminal Justice Series

WEST PUBLISHING COMPANY

St. Paul, Minnesota 55102

January, 1979

CONSTITUTIONAL LAW

Cases and Comments on Constitutional Law 2nd Edition by James L. Maddex, Professor of Criminal Justice, Georgia State University, 486 pages, 1979.

CORRECTIONS

Corrections—Organization and Administration by Henry Burns, Jr., Professor of Criminal Justice, University of Missouri-St. Louis, 578 pages, 1975.

Legal Rights of the Convicted by Hazel B. Kerper, Late Professor of Sociology and Criminal Law, Sam Houston State University and Janeen Kerper, Attorney, San Diego, Calif., 677 pages, 1974.

Selected Readings on Corrections in the Community, 2nd Edition by George G. Killinger, Member, Board of Pardons and Paroles, Texas and Paul F. Cromwell, Jr., Director of Juvenile Services, Tarrant County, Texas, 357 pages, 1978.

Readings on Penology—The Evolution of Corrections in America 2nd Edition by George G. Killinger, Paul F. Cromwell, Jr., and Jerry M. Wood, about 350 pages, 1979.

Selected Readings on Introduction to Corrections by George G. Killinger and Paul F. Cromwell, Jr., 417 pages, 1978.

Selected Readings on Issues in Corrections and Administration by George G. Killinger, Paul F. Cromwell, Jr. and Bonnie J. Cromwell, San Antonio College, 644 pages, 1976.

Probation and Parole in the Criminal Justice System by George G. Killinger, Hazel B. Kerper and Paul F. Cromwell, Jr., 374 pages, 1976.

Introduction to Probation and Parole 2nd Edition by Alexander B. Smith, Professor of Sociology, John Jay College of Criminal Justice and Louis Berlin, Formerly Chief of Training Branch, New York City Dept. of Probation, 270 pages, 1979.

CRIMINAL JUSTICE SYSTEM

Introduction to the Criminal Justice System 2nd Edition by Hazel B. Kerper as revised by Jerold H. Israel, 520 pages, 1979.

Introduction to Criminal Justice by Joseph J. Senna and Larry J. Siegel, both Professors of Criminal Justice, Northeastern University, 540 pages, 1978.

Study Guide to accompany Senna and Siegel's Introduction to Criminal Justice by Roy R. Roberg, Professor of Criminal Justice, University of Nebraska-Lincoln, 187 pages, 1978.

Introduction to Law Enforcement and Criminal Justice by Henry M. Wrobleski and Karen M. Hess, both Professors at Normandale Community College, Bloomington, Minnesota, 525 pages, 1979.

CRIMINAL LAW

Cases and Materials on Basic Criminal Law by George E. Dix, Professor of Law, University of Texas and M. Michael Sharlot, Professor of Law, University of Texas, 649 pages, 1974.

Readings on Concepts of Criminal Law by Robert W. Ferguson, Administration of Justice Dept. Director, Saddleback College, 560 pages, 1975.

Principles, Cases and Readings on Criminal Law by Thomas J. Gardner, Professor of Criminal Justice, Milwaukee Area Technical College and Victor Manian, Milwaukee County Judge, 782 pages, 1975.

Principles of Criminal Law by Wayne R. LaFave, Professor of Law, University of Illinois, about 600 pages, 1978.

CRIMINAL PROCEDURE

Teaching Materials on Criminal Procedure by Jerry L. Dowling, Professor of Criminal Justice, Sam Houston State University, 544 pages, 1976.

Criminal Procedure for the Law Enforcement Officer 2nd Edition by John N. Ferdico, Assistant Attorney General, State of Maine, 409 pages, 1979.

Cases, Materials and Text on the Elements of Criminal Due Process by Phillip E. Johnson, Professor of Law, University of California, Berkeley, 324 pages, 1975.

Cases, Comments and Questions on Basic Criminal Procedure, 4th Edition by Yale Kamisar, Professor of Law, University of Michigan, Wayne R. LaFave, Professor of Law, University of Illinois and Jerold H. Israel, Professor of Law, University of Michigan, 790 pages, 1974. Supplement Annually.

EVIDENCE

Criminal Evidence by Thomas J. Gardner, Professor of Criminal Justice, Milwaukee Area Technical College, 694 pages, 1978.

Criminal Evidence by Edward J. Imwinkelried, Professor of Law, University of San Diego; Paul C. Giannelli, Professor of Law, Case Western Reserve University; Francis A. Gilligan, Lieutenant Colonel, Judge Advocate General's Corp; Fredric I. Lederer, Major, Judge Advocate General's School, U.S. Army, 425 pages, 1979.

Law of Evidence for Police, 2nd Edition by Irving J. Klein, Professor of Law and Police Science, John Jay College of Criminal Justice, 632 pages, 1978.

Criminal Investigation and Presentation of Evidence by Arnold Markle, The State's Attorney, New Haven County, Connecticut, 344 pages, 1976.

INTRODUCTION TO LAW ENFORCEMENT

The American Police—Text and Readings by Harry W. More, Jr., Professor of Administration of Justice, California State University of San Jose, 278 pages, 1976.

Police Tactics in Hazardous Situations by the San Diego, California Police Department, 228 pages, 1976.

Law Enforcement Handbook for Police by Louis B. Schwartz, Professor of Law, University of Pennsylvania and Stephen R. Goldstein, Professor of Law, University of Pennsylvania, 333 pages, 1970.

Police Operations—Tactical Approaches to Crimes in Progess by Inspector Andrew Sutor, Philadelphia, Pennsylvania Police Department, 329 pages, 1976.

Introduction to Law Enforcement and Criminal Justice by Henry Wrobleski and Karen M. Hess, both Professors at Normandale Community College, Bloomington, Minnesota, 525 pages, 1979.

JUVENILE JUSTICE

Text and Selected Readings on Introduction to Juvenile Delinquency by Paul F. Cromwell, Jr., George G. Killinger, Rosemary C. Sarri, Professor, School of Social Work, The University of Michigan and H. N. Solomon, Professor of Criminal Justice, Nova University, 502 pages, 1978.

Juvenile Justice Philosophy: Readings, Cases and Comments, Second Edition, by Frederic L. Faust, Professor of Criminology, Florida State University and Paul J. Brantingham, Department of Criminology, Simon Fraser University, 467 pages, 1979.

Introduction to the Juvenile Justice System by Thomas A. Johnson, Professor of Criminal Justice, Washington State University, 492 pages, 1975.

Cases and Comments on Juvenile Law by Joseph J. Senna, Professor of Criminal Justice, Northeastern University and Larry J. Siegel, Professor of Criminal Justice, Northeastern University, 543 pages, 1976.

MANAGEMENT AND SUPERVISION

Selected Readings on Managing the Police Organization by Larry K. Gaines and Truett A. Ricks, both Professors of Criminal Justice, Eastern Kentucky University, 527 pages, 1978.

Criminal Justice Management: Text and Readings, by Harry W. More, Jr., 377 pages, 1977.

Effective Police Administration: A Behavioral Approach, 2nd Edition by Harry W. More, Jr., Professor, San Jose State University, about 350 pages, 1979.

Police Management and Organizational Behavior: A Contingency Approach by Roy R. Roberg, Professor of Criminal Justice, University of Nebraska at Omaha, 350 pages, 1979.

Police Administration and Management by Sam S. Souryal, Professor of Criminal Justice, Sam Houston State University, 462 pages, 1977.

Law Enforcement Supervision—A Case Study Approach by Robert C. Wadman, Rio Hondo Community College, Monroe J. Paxman, Brigham Young University and Marion T. Bentley, Utah State University, 224 pages, 1975.

POLICE—COMMUNITY RELATIONS

Readings on Police—Community Relations, 2nd Edition by Paul F. Cromwell, Jr., and George Keefer, Professor of Criminal Justice, Southwest Texas State University, 506 pages, 1978.

PSYCHOLOGY

Interpersonal Psychology for Law Enforcement and Corrections by L. Craig Parker, Jr., Criminal Justice Dept. Director, University of New Haven and Robert D. Meier, Professor of Criminal Justice, University of New Haven, 290 pages, 1975.

VICE CONTROL

The Nature of Vice Control in the Administration of Justice by Robert W. Ferguson, 509 pages, 1974.

Cases, Text and Materials on Drug Abuse Law by Gerald F. Uelman, Professor of Law, Loyola University, Los Angeles and Victor G. Haddox, Professor of Criminology, California State University at Long Beach and Clinical Professor of Psychiatry, Law and Behavioral Sciences, University of Southern California School of Medicine, 564 pages, 1974.